The Protestant Work Ethic

By the same author:

Social Situations (with Michael Argyle and Jean Graham).

The Psychology of Social Situations (edited with Michael Argyle).

The Economic Mind (with Alan Lewis).

Social Behaviour in Context (edited).

Culture Shock (with Stephen Bochner).

Personality Psychology in Europe (edited with Alois Angleitner and Guus van Heck).

Lay Theories: Everyday Understanding of Problems in the Social Sciences.

The Anatomy of Adolescence (with Barrie Gunter).

The Protestant Work Ethic
The Psychology of Work-Related Beliefs and Behaviours

Adrian Furnham

Reader in Psychology
London University

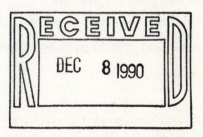

Routledge
London and New York

Dedication

For my mother
Lorna Audrey Furnham

who always took work too seriously

First published 1990
by Routledge
11 New Fetter Lane, London EC4P 4EE

Simultaneously published in the USA and Canada
by Routledge
a division of Routledge, Chapman and Hall, Inc.
29 West 35th Street, New York, NY 10001

© 1990 Adrian Furnham

Laserset from the publisher's word-processor disks by
NWL Editorial Services, Langport, Somerset, England

Printed in Great Britain by
Richard Clay Ltd, Bungay, Suffolk

British Library Cataloguing in Publication Data
Furnham, Adrian, 1953 –
  The Protestant work ethic: the psychology of work-related beliefs and
  behaviours.
  1. Work. Attitudes of Society
  I. Title
  306'.36

Library of Congress Cataloging in Publication Data
  Furnham, Adrian.
  The Protestant work ethic: the psychology of work-related beliefs and
  behaviours / Adrian Furnham.
  p.   cm.
  Bibliography: p.
  Includes index.
  1. Protestant work ethic–Psychological aspects.   I. Title.
  HD4905.F87   1990   89–33213
  306.3'613–dc20   CIP

ISBN 0–415–01704–1 (hbk)   ISBN 0–415–01705–X (pbk)

Contents

Foreword

Dr J. Greenberg

It was in 1972, during my second year as a doctoral student, when I met James Garrett in Detroit. I was aware of one of his research investigations on the Protestant work ethic, and so I was pleased that my adviser, Gerald Leventhal, invited me to his house to meet Jim. (Besides, a hungry graduate student could hardly pass up an opportunity for a free meal and a chance to ingratiate himself with his mentor. Such opportunities don't come along often.) It seems Jim was passing through town, giving me this special occasion to meet someone whose work I had just read. Although I still enjoy the process of attaching faces and personalities to the more colourless abstractions of their words on paper, this was to be an especially auspicious occasion. It was the first time I really got to talk to someone in whose research I had an abiding interest. More importantly, it was the first time anyone actually listened and talked back.

Jim was clearly flattered that a graduate student was aware of his then relatively obscure research on the Protestant work ethic. Seems he, along with his mentor from Ohio State, Herbert Mirels, had recently published an article reporting a scale to measure people's beliefs in the work ethic. Hearing what wonderful predictions Mirels and Garrett were able to make about human behaviour given this 19-item scale just fascinated me. Just ask a few questions, and those who answer differently also behave differently. With a terrible naïveté of a second-year doctoral student, 'This was psychology', I thought to myself. Sharing my enthusiasm for this work with Garrett was one of those acts of unbridled unprofessional enthusiasm that made, I'm afraid, terrible dinner conversation. 'How did you ever think of . . .?' 'Why did you . . . ?' I wanted to know, and Garrett wanted to answer, giving little thought to the indifferent reactions of our hosts and spouses. Surely, we must have thought they were just as interested in this 'shop talk' as we were, but were too shy to involve themselves. In hindsight, what other rationalization could we have conjured up for our rudeness?

I was impressed with Garrett's research, and he was impressed with my being impressed. To this day I cannot say whose feelings ran deeper. But, speaking for myself, I can say that this chance to share ideas about this topic was an important socializing experience for me. And, it's one I recall fondly whenever I now also find myself excited about another's research. The excitement of learning and exploring ideas in true scholarly fashion over a few glasses of wine reminds me so much of a mating ritual. You learn about the other, and you respond with joy, anger, or indifference. The more you agree, the more you invite further exploration. 'Isn't it just wonderful', the social scientists coo in their pillow talk, 'how the scale shows construct validity?' The joy of scholarly discourse can be quite exhilarating. And, like one's first love, I find it hard to forget my first 'scholarly mating session'.

Indeed, it was a mating session, for it spawned offspring – albeit in the form of ideas. Having ideas as a graduate student can be dangerous, as I recall. But with reckless abandon, I pursued them. On my own, I secured the needed resources – the subject pool, some empty rooms called a laboratory, and an ample supply of mimeographed questionnaires – and began doing my own research. All of this research dealt with the Protestant work ethic – the children of my conversation that night with Jim Garrett. Some people respond to failure by rising to the occasion, while others take the failure message as a sign to give up. The former, I reasoned, must be the ones who endorse the Protestant work ethic, while the latter were those who rejected it. Months of laboratory work, and reams of computer read-outs later I found I was correct.

Proudly, years later I presented these findings at the meeting of the American Psychological Association, where I had only a few years earlier heard Garrett present his research. Although most of the audience members were indifferent, opting to take in the sights of Chicago rather than endure my litany of interactions (reported to the last decimal place), there was one distinguished member of the audience who asked questions about the research with surprising background familiarity. Impressed and surprised, I did my best to answer, but made a point of wanting to meet this gentleman later on. Beating me to the introductions, Herb Mirels presented himself to me. No wonder he knew about the research – he was, after all, Garrett's former mentor, and the co-developer of the Mirels–Garrett Protestant ethic scale I had used in my research.

Several more studies later using the Mirels–Garrett scale, I had passed from graduate student to young professor turning on his own students with this work. I began carrying the banner of the Protestant work ethic in my own experimental research, citing Mirels and Garrett (who had since moved on to other things) more than they did themselves. Coming up with ideas was easy to do, for the concept has a great deal of appeal to any student of psychology or business. After all, who doesn't realize that there are individual differences in people's work-related values? Some people work hard and some do not. We have all probably spent some time making judgement of others' work ethic endorsement. It is somewhat ironic, come to think of it, that my first brush with making systematic contributions to my chosen field – that is, practising the work ethic – dealt with the topic of the work ethic itself.

At this point I must ask the reader's forgiveness for my overly indulgent reminiscences, but it is these memories that come to my mind whenever the topic of the Protestant work ethic comes up. I suppose there can be no more central topic to the field of occupational psychology than this. We, as individuals, operate within a cultural milieu that makes work more or less important to us – and which constantly reminds us of it. Whenever we work, or play, our central life values infiltrate our actions, inextricably colouring our behaviours. Even when we dream, I suppose, we are not immune from reminders about the role of work values. Clearly, the values we place on work represent as much a part of who we are as individuals, as polarization on these central life values once was responsible for distinguishing between political and religious groups throughout history (as this book details quite well).

Given this ubiquitous status of the Protestant work ethic as an individual difference variable (of interest to psychologists), a set of cultural values (of interest to sociologists), and a moderator between job attitudes and performance (of interest to management researchers and consultants), there can be little doubt that the topic is indeed worthy and deserving of the scholarly treatment it receives in this book. As the snake oil salesman of the old American west would say, 'My friends, this is something you cannot do without'. While this phrase usually connotes hucksterism, it applies here quite well.

Not only does the present work skilfully synthesize the myriad of interdisciplinary scholarly studies on the topic, but it goes beyond this. It provides us with insight into more basic psychological processes such as:

- The relationship between attitudes and behaviour.
- The connection between job satisfaction and job performance.
- The role of work as a central life value.

To its credit, the present work also addresses such controversial topics as:

- The role of the work ethic in economic development.
- The importance of work values on non-work activities.
- The morality of attempting to manipulate work values.

As a result, the present volume represents an effort that should be of interest to all social scientists (professional and amateur alike).

One of the most exciting things about Professor Furnham's book is that it promises to stimulate more professional arguments than it will put to rest. When directed at any social scientist, that is the ultimate compliment. The very importance of the topic to all of us promises to make this volume just that lively. As such, I am confident that reading Professor Furnham's words in this volume will be at least as stimulating to most readers as my own initial contacts with one of the earliest researchers in this field. It will, no doubt, serve the same purpose – namely, stimulating the reader into thinking about the importance of the Protestant work ethic in many life activities. The high level of scholarship and maturity within this work clearly promises to take more students of the world of work much further much faster than my casual conversation. There is a lot of professional exhilaration contained in these pages. I know you will enjoy your journey through them, thinking of it not as a test of your own work ethic, but as an intellectually enriching experience.

Jerald Greenberg, Ph.D.
Faculty of Management and Human Resources
The Ohio State University
Columbus, Ohio
USA

Preface

As an undergraduate I read history, theology, and psychology, though I spent a protracted, but highly enjoyable, graduate career reading psychology exclusively. I have degrees in developmental, cross-cultural, and social psychology but have never lost interest in both history and theology. Perhaps the Protestant Work Ethic (PWE) is one of the few concepts that bridges the above three disciplines and hence accounts for my attention to, and interest in, it.

A second explanation for my interest may be the often made observation that psychologists, who stress empirical objectivity and theoretical disinterest, frequently study problems of great personal concern, that is, they study their own problems, behaviour patterns, or belief systems. Thus psychologists abnormally attached to their mothers study Oedipal problems; those who find it difficult communicating study social skills; those who are victims of discrimination study prejudice. But it is not all compensatory. Those who are manifestly successful at, or attached to, some activity such as sport or music may be attracted to research on those topics, partly to explain the processes underlying this ability. I enjoy academic work; it is my hobby and passion, and hence I spend a lot of time at it. There appears to me, nothing quite so enjoyable as going to bed feeling that one has done a good day's work; of having achieved something worthwhile. I may be, in some areas, then, a good example of a latter-day Puritan, at least in my dedication to work.

Psychology as a discipline tends to be ahistorical in two senses. With the exception of the life history of certain, frequently famous, individuals like Luther or Freud, psychological research is almost never consciously concerned with the historical antecedents to, or determinants of, psychological processes which are examined *in vacuo,* out of any temporal, social-economic, or political context which may well shape those processes. Social and clinical psychologists, as well as psycho- and socio-linguists, have frequently made this point, but these warnings have seldom been heeded and the vast majority of psychological research pays no attention to the possibility that social, historical, or economic factors may influence psychological processes.

Secondly, psychological research may occasionally document the *Welt-*

anschauung of particular groups, but tends to be ignorant of the fashions and fads that dictate research interests in their own discipline. In times of wealth psychologists have been interested in poverty, but in times of high unemployment that topic comes under the psychological microscope. Other topics and processes, like conformity behaviour or altruism, show periodic peaks and troughs of research interest that appear to follow no pattern. Psychological research in the PWE, too, has been influenced by fashion though there are no doubt sociological factors determining these patterns.

The PWE is one of the very few concepts or theories that spans nearly all of the social sciences, though it is clearly more central to some (sociologists) than others (political scientists). Anthropologists, economists, historians, theologians, sociologists, and a very few psychologists have, in the eighty or so years since it was first proposed, argued over various aspects of the thesis. Moreover, the thesis, albeit simplified and even distorted, is frequently discussed by journalists, commentators, and lay people at least insofar as they lament the decline of the work ethic or 'explain' economic success or failure by recourse to it. The sort of questions that have been posed are numerous and far ranging:

● Is Weber's socio-theological and historico-economic thesis correct in its entirety, in some but not all of its parts, or not at all? If the historical thesis is basically correct is it still true that PWE beliefs lead to capitalistic enterprise?
● Can one apply the Weberian hypothesis to non-Christian societies like current-day South East Asia?
● To what extent can one trace the PWE in popular literature such as Bunyan's *Pilgrim's Progress* or Smiles' *Self Help*?
● Could one see the 'Do-it-Yourself' or 'Ecological self-sufficiency' as a latter-day version of the PWE?
● Is the PWE in decline in post-industrial western democracies but in the ascendance in the former Asian and African colonies?
● Is the PWE exclusively found among the middle class or is it also found among the working class?
● To what extent are PWE beliefs responsible for the distinction between the deserving and the undeserving poor?
● How does one measure PWE beliefs?

These and many other issues have fuelled the debate on the PWE. As a discipline, psychology came late to the PWE. Ideas from Weber's work can be found in the, by now, fairly extensive literature on Achievement Motivation but the term never really appeared in the abstracts until the late 1960s and early 1970s. Psychologists have been less concerned with whether Weber's thesis was tenable than with devising valid and reliable measures of the PWE which they recognized to be a fairly commonly held system. There has been, however, more interest in measuring general work attitudes, beliefs, and behaviours which may be partly related to the PWE.

Whether or not the PWE exists today is for most psychologists an empirical question. It can be debated whether psychological measures of the PWE actually tap the concept proposed by Weber, that is, whether the self-report measures are valid. But while psychologists have not contributed much to the Weberian controversy they have investigated concepts and processes integral to the PWE. These include locus of control beliefs; beliefs in the just world; the Type-A behaviour pattern; psychological conservatism; postponement of gratification; and need for achievement. In this sense psychology has been doing salient PWE research for some time, but until now it has not been 'brought together' under this rubric.

This book may disappoint historians, sociologists, or theologians who had hoped for a detailed analysis of Weber's thesis from the perspective of their discipline. I am not qualified to perform such a task, which, in any event, has already been executed a number of times. This book covers *psychological* perspectives on the work ethic, with all the advantages and limitations that such an approach may imply. I do not seek to ignore, downplay, or dismiss the perspectives of these disciplines. Rather, I seek to supplement them by a social-psychological perspective, which, in my opinion, has been missing.

Furthermore, the scope of this book extends beyond the confines of Weber's thesis. I have subtitled the book: *The psychology of work-related beliefs and behaviours* because it covers a number of topics in industrial, organizational, personality, and social psychology. Just as the work ethic is truly a multi *inter*-disciplinary topic I am treating it from a multi *intra*-disciplinary point of view.

I have a few people to thank for stimulating my interest in the PWE and supporting research. For the past seven years or so I have shared an early morning cup of tea with Peter Kelvin at University College. In the course of these enjoyable and enlightening conversations we have frequently touched on the PWE. Although we hold different opinions as to the origin or even the existence of the PWE, he has continued to stimulate my interest in the topic. Jerry Greenberg and I share empirical interests in the PWE and I have appreciated his papers as well as occasional letters and conversations. My old friend Christopher Forsyth at Cambridge and I have consistently lamented British inefficiency and how our restricted Calvinistic childhoods somehow imbued us with the energies and intolerances that result from holding the ethic.

Being attracted to self-sufficiency I have not applied for a research grant to carry out research. However, I have been the recipient of a few awards from the Tregaskis Bequest, the Nuffield Foundation, and the Professor Dame Lillian Pension Scholarship to collect data which have gone into the book. I would like to express my gratitude to Lee Drew who typed, and at times edited, my drafts with efficiency and good humour.

Adrian Furnham
Bloomsbury

Acknowledgements

We would like to thank the following for permission to reprint previously published material: Academic Press, New York, for (1) Fig. 2.2, p. 41 from 'A Theory of Psychological Antecedents', in *The Psychology of Conservatism*, by G. Wilson (ed.), (2) Table 2.6, p. 41 from *Type A Behaviour Pattern* by V. Price, (3) Fig 2.1, p. 35 from *Achievement Motivation in Perspective* by H. Heckhausen, *et al.*; American Management Association, New York, for Fig. 1.3, p. 18 and Tables 4.5, 4.6, 4.7, 4.8, 4.9, 4.10, and 5.1, pp. 123, 124, 125, 126, and 143 from *The Work Ethic* by D.J. Cherrington; American Psychological Association, for material from The Journal of Abnormal Psychology, 64, 136–42, by R. de Charnis, and G. Moeller; The British Psychological Society, for Tables 6.1 and 6.2, pp. 180 and 181, from the Journal of Occupational Psychology, 55, 277–85 by A. Furnham; Doubleday, New York, for Table 4.3, p. 120 from 'The Religious Factor . . . ' by G. Lenski; Doubleday, Canada, for Table 2.9, p. 60 from *Mind Over Money* by N. Forman; Gower Publishing Group, for (1) Tables 4.11 and 4.12, p. 128 and p. 129 from British Social Attitudes, The 1986 Report, by J. Jowell, S. Witherspoon, and L. Brook (eds),, and (2) material from *Future Work* by J. Robertson; C. Hampden-Turner, for Tables 1.2 and 1.3 from *Maps of the Mind*; Macmillan, for (1) Tables 4.13 and 4.14, pp. 130 and 131 from *Values and Social Changes In Britain* by M. Abrams, D. Gerard, and N. Timms (eds), and (2) material from *Contrasting Values In Western Europe* by S. Harding, D. Philips, and M. Fogarty; John Wiley and sons Ltd, for material from European Journal of Personality, 1, p. 101 by A. Furnham; Oxford University Press, for material from *Work, Unemployment and Mental Health* by P. Wan; Pergamon Press, for Table 2.5, p. 46 from 'Personality and Individual Differences' by A. Furnham; International Thomson Publishing Services, for material from The British Journal of Sociology, 26, 52–65 by M. Rotenberg; Yale University Press, for Table 4.2, p. 118 from the World Handbook of Political and Social Indicators by B.M. Russet, *et al.*

Every effort has been made to obtain permission to reproduce copyright material throughout this book. If any proper acknowledgement has not been made the copyright holder should contact the publisher.

Chapter one

The origin of the concept

Baptised in the icy waters of Calvinist theology, the business of life, once regarded as perilous to the soul, acquired a new sanctity. Labour is not merely an economic means; it is a spiritual end.

R.H. Tawney

Seest thou a man diligent in his business. He shall stand before kings.

Proverbs XXII, 29

Later puritanism was a tonic which braced its energies and fortified its already vigorous temper.

R.H. Tawney

He who neither worketh for himself, nor for others, will not receive the reward of God.

The Prophet Mohammed

Introduction

The Protestant Ethic and the Spirit of Capitalism was published, in German, over eighty years ago by Max Weber as a two-part article in the 1904/5 issue of the journal *Archiv für Sozialwissenschaft und Sozialpolitik*. Some fifteen years later it was revised and published as a single volume with rebuttals to criticism of the earlier work. It was the revised edition which was first translated into English by Talcott Parsons in 1930.

The work reflects the multi-disciplinary scholarly interests of Weber who had a broad knowledge of religion, political economy, the law, and most other social sciences. His disregard for traditional disciplinary boundaries gave the work considerable breadth and explanatory power which could, of course, be criticized at many different levels and from different perspectives. It is perhaps for this reason that the work remains a source of interest and debate to so many disciplines today: primarily sociology, theology, and economic history. Indeed, the thesis has survived as one of the best known and controversial works in all the social sciences.

Weber's writings are extensive and he is remembered in different intellectual contexts for many different contributions (Giddens, 1972). Clearly a polymath, he attempted to synthesize diverse approaches to the study of human behaviour. He was, of course, highly influenced by the academic debates of his time such as the hermeneutic tradition and Marxist theories. Indeed, both Marx and Weber were interested in explaining the origin and future of western capitalism – the *Zeitgeist* of their times.

For Weber the central problem was explaining the fact that people pursue wealth and material gain (the achievement of profit) *for its own sake*, not because of necessity. That is, the aim of obtaining, accumulating, and storing money/capital is an end in itself, not a means to an end. Weber located the answer to this problem in Puritan asceticism and the concept of calling for the individual to fulfil his or her duty in this (rather than the other) world. Weber maintained that Puritans felt obliged to be regarded as chosen by God to perform good works. Success in a calling (occupational rewards) thus became to be seen as a sign of being the elect. Puritans thus sought to achieve salvation through economic activity.

Weber understood capitalism as a mass phenomenon: a culturally prescribed way of living, a moral doctrine to advance individuals' material interests. Secondly, capitalism went against the traditionalist sense of effort and value of work because it replaced the idea of self-sufficiency with accumulation. He explained the origin of capitalism by arguing that the acquisitive motive was transformed from personal eccentricity into a moral order which destroyed reliance on traditional forms of economic satisfaction and replaced it with the rational calculus of returns coming from the investment of given amounts of capital and labour.

It should be pointed out that Weber is not naive enough to attribute the entire rise of Western capitalism entirely to Puritanism. He mentions several other important factors that facilitated its emergence in the West, such as urbanization; the development of co-operatives and guilds; a codified and developed legal system, a bureaucratic nation state; book keeping systems, etc. Furthermore, he was aware that religious (spiritual) and economic (material) factors interacted to produce the spirit of capitalism.

The thesis of this work is worth examining in some detail, if only to fully understand the various components of the ethic as described. A summary of *The Protestant Ethic* is given in the Appendix. It is hoped that this will give some feeling for the range, tenor, and nature of Weber's arguments.

The Protestant Ethic is a polemic and proselytizing work directed against vulgar Marxist ideas of economic determinism and the relentless laws of history. It is, therefore, not surprising that his work has provoked such controversies from political scientists, economic historians, and Protestant theologians. The criticisms may be seen as primary and secondary; original and contemporary; those resulting from misunderstanding and those resulting from profound disagreement. But various attempts have been made to classify or codify the major objections to Weber's thesis (Sprinzak, 1972). Giddens (1972) has listed five major criticisms of the work:

1. Weber's understanding of Protestant theology and lay beliefs, particularly Calvinism, Lutheranism, and American Puritanism, was erroneous.
2. Similarly, he misunderstood Catholic doctrine particularly as it differed from Protestantism on economic detail.
3. The data Weber used to support his thesis were limited to mainly Anglo-Saxon material while other European (German, Dutch, Swiss) data fail to support his hypothesis.
4. Weber's distinction between modern and earlier forms of capitalism was unwarranted because the 'spirit of modern' capitalism was apparent in earlier periods.
5. The supposed causal correlation between Puritanism and modern capitalism is unfounded and indeed it may be argued that Puritan ideology and practices were themselves merely epiphenomena of previously established economic changes.

The Weberian PWE hypothesis has received a number of reactions that can be classified thus:

- *Negative.* As an explanation for the rise of capitalism it is descriptively inaccurate, explanatorily tautologous, and scientifically meaningless. Calvin was not the parent of capitalism. Marx might have 'inverted' Hegel but Weber was wrong to do so to the Marxists' ideas about the origin of capitalism.
- *Neutral.* Weber's hypothesis, like the proverbial curate's egg, is good in parts but cannot alone account for the origin or maintenance of capitalism in Western Europe. As an explanatory factor the PWE is necessary but not sufficient.
- *Positive.* To identify the PWE as a crucial factor in the origin of capitalism was a remarkable piece of scholarship. Though recognizing the importance of the PWE does not exclude the possibility that other economic, sociological, or psychological factors were operating.

The debate has been long, scholarly, and at times acrimonious. A very useful collection of papers may be found in Green (1965), which contains some of the most thoughtful reflections on Weber's actual work.

It is quite beyond the scope of this to review and integrate the plethora of comments, criticisms, and analyses of the PWE hypothesis (Razzell, 1977). Not only is this an enormous scholarly task but many others have already attempted it. For instance, Nelson (1973) has attempted to put Weber's work in historical context *and* comment on his critics. He criticizes Weber's critics for too narrow an interpretation, not understanding Weber's purpose, or of seeing how specific errors in interpretation did not invalidate the whole thesis.

One of the most famous critics of Weber was Tawney (1963) who pointed out that Calvinism and Puritanism were influenced from the very beginning by the urban, merchant, and craftsman background of their teachers. Followers of Calvin adapted his teachings to their needs and aspirations, for instance by weaker corporate themes and strengthening individualistic themes. But Tawney did believe Weber was correct in stressing the Puritan doctrine of calling and the condemnation of self-indulgence as important factors in creating new values highly conducive to economic progress.

Others have attempted to catalogue the various objections made to the original Weberian hypothesis. Green (1973) has very helpfully tabulated some of these more important criticisms (see Table 1.1).

However, one should not assume that the PWE debate is over, academically unfashionable, or itself only of historic interest. A range of academic

Table 1.1 Protestantism and capitalism

Author	Summary of ideas
Werner Sombart (economist)	In 1902 developed the concept of 'the spirit of capitalism' and concluded that capitalism had originated long before Protestantism. He believed that the primary source of the spirit of capitalism lay in the attitudes and economic practices associated with Judaism (Sombart, 1967).
R. Stephen Warner (sociologist)	By presenting systematic evidence for the importance of religion in the development of capitalism, Weber extended Marx's ideas about the role of the class struggle in that development. Weber correctly understood that human behaviour is complex, and we should not misunderstand him as claiming Protestantism to be the sole source of capitalism (Warner, 1970).
H.M. Robertson (economic historian)	Capitalism results from the material conditions of civilization – not from a religious impulse. French Catholic preachers emphasized industrious and frugal living no less than Puritan ministers did (Robertson, 1933).
R.H. Tawney (economic historian)	Although Protestantism was an important factor in the rise of capitalism, the whole Protestant movement was responsible and not just Calvinism and Puritanism. Also, general political, social, and economic conditions during the sixteenth and seventeenth centuries must be taken into account (Tawney, 1963).
Kurt Samuelson (economic historian and newspaper editor)	Weber's approach does not explain the industrialization of Catholic Belgium. It is not the saving of small amounts of money that produces capitalism but rather vast risks, luck, and enormous capital gains on unexploited natural assets. Weber pays too much attention to theory and too little to facts (Samuelson, 1957).
H. Stuart Hughes (historian)	Weber's approach is subtle and wide-ranging. It combines 'imaginative boldness' with careful scholarship and documentation; it is an important contribution to knowledge. We should understand Weber's work as an assertion of the importance of Protestantism as *one* factor – but not the only one – in the development of Capitalism (Hughes, 1958).

Source: Green, 1973.

disciplines still manifest consistent interest in the PWE. For instance, tremendous debate remains as to the validity of the historic analysis of the PWE. It had been assumed that Calvinist Scotland was a nice counter example which invalidated the PWE hypothesis. However, Marshall (1982) claimed that the argument was false because previous authors either misunderstood Weber, or used inappropriate evidence to test his argument and provided his own evidence to 'vindicate' Weber. However, he is taken to task by Dickson and McLachlan (1983) who claim that Marshall does not have the evidence (about motivational states and the spirit of capitalism) to support his thesis. Much of the argument pertains to the validity of inference and causal connections which is, of course, a serious problem for all historical research.

There have been some scholarly *historical* treatments of the PWE, such as that of Rodgers (1978) who examined it in industrial America between the years 1850 and 1920. It cannot be easy to do such an analysis as the PWE is about work beliefs and the necessary representative documents do not always exist. Illiterate people whose PWE beliefs may be crucially important may be neglected, while a small minority of scholars who published their work may be grossly over-represented. Similarly it may be very unwise to infer work beliefs from records of particular behaviour.

Among the many interesting historical insights, Rodgers (1978) brings in a demonstration of the secularization of the PWE over this period and also feminist versions of the PWE. He consistently stresses the power and longevity of the moral imperatives in the American PWE. The PWE was the gospel of the bourgeoisie who preached it from all the 'institutional fortresses' of the middle class. Work rhetoric clearly served useful political ends.

Two points are consistently made which can be found in other historical writing: the supporters of the PWE were a small minority and secondly, the PWE had within it the seeds of its own destruction.

The work ethic helped impel the restless personal energies of the Northern manufacturers, blessed their enterprises with a sense of mission, and gave them a transcendent sanction. It helped anaesthetize employers to the eleven- and twelve-hour days they imposed on their workers and the pace at which the factories drove them. The work ethic provided the language of calculation, system and diligence into which the efficiency engineers poured their new and stricter meanings, turning the new plants into matchless hives of industriousness. But if the factories were creatures of middle-class work ideals, they devoured those ideals as well. In disturbing ways, the transformation of labour undercut virtually all the mid-nineteenth-century assumptions about the moral pre-eminence of work.

Industrialization upset the certainty that hard work would bring economic success. Whatever the life chances of a farmer or shop hand had been in the early years of the century, it became troublingly clear that the semi-skilled labourer, caught in the anonymity of a late-nineteenth-century textile factory or steel mill, was trapped in his circumstances – that no amount of sheer hard work would open the way to self-employment or wealth. Still more rudely, the factory system overturned the equation of work and art. Amid the subdivided and monotonous tasks, the speed, and the discipline of a box factory or an automobile plant, where was the room for mind or for the impress of individual creativity? Even the success of the industrial transformation unsettled ideas and values. As the factories poured forth an ever-larger volume of goods into the homes of the middle class, the ascetic legacies of the Protestant ethic slowly and steadily eroded, giving way to a noisy gospel of play and, at the fringes of middle-class thought, to a cultivation of a life free of effort itself. As industrialization shook the idea of the permanence of scarcity, as the measure of economic health turned from how much a society produced to how equitably and conscientiously it consumed, it became harder and harder to insist that compulsive activity, work and usefulness were the highest goals of life.

The moralists did not perceive these troubling questions all at once. When they did there were always the ancient maxims to fall back on. Work, they continued to insist, was what man was made to do – the foundation of happiness, the condition of existence since the days of Adam's husbandry in the garden. But industrialization could not be stopped from wedging into the preserve of ethics. And as the economy was transformed a deeply rooted set of presumptions cracked and shifted.

(Rodgers, 1978, pp. 28–9)

Randall G. Stokes (1975) took a somewhat different approach to the Weberian thesis. He showed that those beliefs comprising the PWE do not inevitably lead people to engage in behaviour that results in economic development. Calvinism did not produce the same results it had in Europe when it was transplanted by Dutch and French Huguenot settlers to South Africa. Although Afrikaner Calvinism was theologically identical to European Calvinism, it had a conservative rather than innovative economic impact. Stokes suggested that the South African Calvinists came to regard themselves as a Chosen People by virtue of their identification with the ancient Israelites and their long series of confrontations with the indigenous Black population. This led them to conceive of the Elect in collective rather than individual terms. As such they did not suffer the same kind or degree of anxiety about salvation that plagued the Europeans and motivated them to seek this worldly success as a mark of other worldly salvation. Further, the Afrikaners defined themselves as a sacred society, and accordingly, they came to uphold traditional ways with a passion while viewing innovations with suspicion. Thus, the same religion can have quite different consequences in differing social contexts.

Theologians too have been deeply interested in the PWE. To argue that Weber saw Calvinism as the parent of capitalism is mistaken. As Tawney (1963) has pointed out, Calvinism was the 'tonic which traced its energies and fortified its already vigorous temper'. In other words the capitalist spirit pre-dated the Calvinist era but the latter harnessed it.

Theologians have devoted a great deal of ink to this problem as Hudson (1961) pointed out. Some have argued that Catholicism was not opposed to capitalism and others that Calvinism has no clear pro-capitalist philosophy. Many are of the opinion that instead of fostering, shaping, strengthening, or reinforcing the spirit of capitalism, Calvinism was itself being altered and transformed by the development of the factors that it sought to restrain.

Because of the belief in the priesthood of all believers, there was a reduction in ecclesiastic control. Thus because Protestants believed nobody has infallible, unambiguous, or privileged access to divine truth and that congregations should be autonomous with regard to their behaviour, the role of Protestant ecclesiastics was considerably reduced. In this sense the parent of capitalism became its offspring. That is, to follow the analogy, the parent was either ignored or transformed precisely because it had given so much freedom of personal conscience to the believer.

Hampden-Turner (1981) has attempted to summarize and contrast PWE beliefs and what he calls, Anglo-Catholic organicism (see Table 1.2).

Relying heavily on the work of Koestler, among others, Hampden-Turner (1981) argued that PWE beliefs have informed scientific epistemology. He notes:

> It is my contention that modern doctrines of scientism and behaviorism,
> so far from having escaped from religion, 'superstition', and *a priori*
> beliefs, are steeped in Calvinistic ideology, having borrowed even its most
> objectionable characteristic, a devastating lack of self-awareness.
>
> (p. 36)

For the purpose of showing the comparisons between PWE beliefs as positivist epistemology, he contrasts Calvinist and Puritan ideology with behaviourism, positivism, and scientism (Table 1.3).

Many would contest all the above details and relationships both because not all the aspects of the so-called Calvinist/Puritan ideology are found in the PWE nor because behaviourism is always clearly associated with positivism. Nevertheless the comparison is very interesting, not least of which is the clear translation of PWE beliefs into psychological concepts.

Others such as *economists* have attempted to translate or apply Weberian ideas into the language and concepts of today. Ditz (1980), in an interesting essay on the PWE and the market economy, has described the PWE idea of profit making as a calling 'the sacramentalization of acquisition'. He explains in lay economic terms how the PWE affected the market economy (what Marx called capitalism) over the last few hundred years. His key concepts were:

- Inputs to productivity – because pessimistic Calvinists were so concerned with scarcity they stressed the need for productive work to bring about surpluses.

Table 1.2

Anglo-Catholic organicism	v *Puritan atomistic individualism*
The person is part of an organic hier-archy, a Great Chain of Being, rooted in kinship, feudal loyalties, neighbour-hood, animals, and land.	The person is alone, a saintly outcast from corrupt feudalism, but can enter holy leagues or covenants with other upright per-sons.
Communal mediated relationships	v *Private direct relationships*
Salvation is in communal faith, with ac-cess to God mediated by kings, bishops, judges, and lords.	Salvation is a private matter between God and His agents on earth, who have direct access to His will.
Intercessionist God	v *Delegating God*
God is ever-present, interceding in human affairs in miraculous and super-natural ways.	God is distant and delegates his power to chosen human instruments and the laws of nature.
Salvation through communion	v *Salvation through work*
Man is saved less by his own efforts than by faith and partaking of the pas-sion, mercy, forgiveness, and indul-gence of the crucified God in the family of believers.	God is the task-master to his earthly agents, a state of grace they can demonstrate but not alter. Interpersonal emotions are indul-gences of a corrupt order.
God experienced with many senses	v *The Word read, heard, enacted*
God is experienced as mystery in many dimensions, in ritual, community, sacra-ment, awe, asceticism, and participa-tion, by way of Mary and the saints.	God gives unambiguous instructions to man's reason by way of His Objective Words. Mystery, magic, and speculation are vain, when compared with active obe-dience.
Other worldliness	v *This worldliness*
In this vale of tears the greatest respect belongs to those who prepare us for the world to come.	God's Kingdom will be founded in this world by the Saints doing the work to which God calls them.
Human personality cultivated	v *Personality submerged in work*
Virtue is personified by self-cultivation, courtliness, wit, charm, and the flamboy-ant manners of the Cavalier.	Virtue is achieved by self-effacement, and becoming the mere agent of God's objec-tive order (e.g. the Roundhead).

Source: Hampden-Turner, 1981, pp. 33–4.

- Propensity to save – because maximization of productivity and minimiza-tion of consumption were ethically important, saving seemed a most use-ful solution.
- Risk taking investments – saving was more acceptable than spending, and investing more acceptable than saving because charging interest was taboo.
- A calculating orientation – effective efficiency means knowledge of and ability in making calculations of input and output, demand and supply, cost, price, and profits. Quantitative skills became professionalized.
- Profit making as a calling – profit maximization was the prime objective. The acquisition instinct became a utopian ideal.
- From labour costs to profits – anything that increases net profit is good and anything that lowers it is bad. Labour *per se* is only good when it

Table 1.3

Calvinist and Puritan ideology	Behaviourism, Positivism, Scientism
Religious freedom is the means by which the Elect show proofs that they are predestined by God.	'Academic freedom' is the means by which behavioural scientists demonstrate strict psychological determinism.
The individual is primarily alone before God and only through a common subjection does he learn to associate himself.	The operant learns by atomistic responses elicited by his trainer and so learns to form associations and bonds.
The visible world is prior to and of greater salience than the invisible. Self-objectification through visible works is the best evidence of God's grace.	Scientific data must be demonstrable and located in public space. Self-objectification through observable behaviours are the building blocks of science.
The human personality should efface itself for the benefit of manifest orderly and disciplined habits of work.	The 'mentalism' and 'consciousness' of the person should be ignored in favour of his systematic response and reflexive habits.
The individual's relation to God is strictly private and should not be confessed to mediators. Justification being through works, picturesque images are false.	'Mental events' are private and inaccessible to science. Mutual understanding should not be confused with scientific exploration. Homunculi and 'maps' are mistaken.
The objective word of God is unambiguously rendered in the Bible and in activity based thereon. The public scrutiny of sober men will lead to agreement.	An objective science of behaviour is unambiguously rendered in responses to stimuli under schedules of reinforcement. A consensus of dispassionate and disciplined observers will naturally result.
Attention to method, details, and the minutiae of daily life will lead to human self-discipline and perfectibility.	Careful methodology, rigorous testing, and painstaking precision will lead to perfect systems of prediction and control.
There is a permanent inescapable estrangement of man from God, for which the answer is the obedience and total subjection of man to become an instrument of God's will.	There is a permanent dualism between knower and known, for which the answer is that the known must become a part of the knower's behaviour-control technology.
'Forsake unprofitable speculation; avoid mysteries that haveth no daily use.'	Theories, models, and non-operational concepts are unscientific.

Source: Hampden-Turner, 1981, pp. 37.

becomes efficient, cost reducing, and effective.

- Encouragement of marketing – marketing helped the consumer consume more effectively and hence the producer produce more efficiently, hence marketing empathy with the consumer.
- Emergence of new elites – the new 'would-be-saints' were successful entrepreneurs, captains of industry, elected political leaders, certified men of knowledge, and accepted opinion leaders.
- Creation of new democracies – all organizations were turned into meritocratic democracies. Liberty and equality were promoted as was mobility, democratized social structure, etc.
- Resolution of organized conflict – the PWE philosophy was individualistic against government interference, nonconformist, and against conflict and militant behaviour. It tended to retreat from conflict

and be anti-authoritarian.

● Middle class and mass market – PWE endorsers were upward-moving, middle-class oriented, and tried to resolve conflicting claims of merito-cratic elitism and egalitarianism.

● The manipulation of consumers – promotion of products through advertising, etc. – was given ethical support because self and other material improvement was thought of as morally desirable.

However, as Ditz (1980) noted, Weberian glimpses of the future were pes-simistic. Various features would inevitably lead to a decline in the PWE. These included: the waning of religious faith and with it the moral justifica-tions for the market economy; the fact that excessive individualism loosened kinship and ethnic community ties so leading to a weakening of the overall social structure; the emergence of unionism, monopolies, and other anti-PWE ethics; hedonism replacing asceticism; institutional minimizing risk taking replacing individual risk taking; indifference and disrespect for ration-ality and the 'calculating' professions; de-sacramentalization of property, ero-sion of property rights, and indifference to crimes of property; taxation and inflation causing a waning of consumer sovereignty; an increase in egalitarian-ism which inhibits innovation, entrepreneurship, and risk taking.

One way of attempting to understand the nature of the controversy about the PWE is to look at the different approaches in terms of three simple mod-els. Figure 1.1 presents three types of models all looking at the relationship between three variables: religious beliefs, economic forces, and capitalism/the spirit of enterprise.

Mechanistic models

Mechanistic models are the simplest and most misleading. The first illustrates naive theological determinism or the idea that theological beliefs alone were both necessary *and* sufficient to 'cause' the origin of capitalism. Many believe that this is, in fact, a Weberian position (or that of his followers) but nothing could be further from the truth. Weber did not ascribe the rise of capitalism to a single cause – it was not his aim to substitute one-sided materialism for one-sided spiritualism. The one-sided materialism is to be seen in the second posi-tion described as vulgar Marxism. This position sees economic forces alone as being responsible for the origin of capitalism. Although the question remains unanswered as to which economic forces were important, or indeed how one might distinguish an economic from a political or sociological force, the bot-tom-line position here is that material forces alone account for the origin of capitalism. A third possibility allows for both spiritual and economic forces contributing to the origin of capitalism equally but separately. Again how this is achieved is not clear.

The point about mechanistic models is that they may be very useful for pro-tagonists to 'straw-man' their opponents in intellectual argument but few, if

Mechanistic models

Theological determinism   Vulgar Marxism   Naive Weberianism

Intermediate model

Organismic models

P = Protestant/Puritan beliefs
E = Economic and structural forces operating at the time
C = Capitalism/spirit of enterprise

Figure 1.1 Three different models accounting for the origin of capitalism

any, people interested in the origin of capitalism actually take this position.

Intermediate model

The intermediate model acknowledges that both spiritual and material (theological and economic) forces interacted to combine to produce the origin of capitalism. The essence of this position is that (which ever came first) theological beliefs and behaviours associated with Protestantism had effects on economic variables (productivity, taxation, saving), which in turn affected these beliefs. However, the model does not have a feedback mechanism from capitalism back to theological and economic factors. Again, this position is rare: many writers (including Weber) have speculated on the effect of capitalism on the PWE itself (the seeds-of-its-own-destruction hypothesis), while it seems nonsensical to argue that the rise of capitalism does not affect prevailing economic forces.

11

Organismic models

These models come in various 'incomplete' forms but the third example shows the fully integrated, organismic model which suggests each of the three variables in question affect each other variable reciprocally. This is clearly the most likely and sophisticated model but what it does not take into account is *which* theological (P) and which economic (E) forces are involved and more importantly *how*, and by *how much* they interact to produce capitalism (C).

Certainly most thoughtful commentators have accepted the organismic position though they might attribute other positions to their enemies. However, what does appear to be the case is that various ill-informed or casual spectators in the debate tend to assume that mechanistic models are being proposed by major protagonists which is clearly not the case.

Like others, Preston (1987) has tried to point out the relationship between religious *and* economic forces in Weber's thinking, without simplifying the issue:

> Weber's thesis is that there was an 'elective affinity' between the overall motivation in Calvinism with respect to daily work, including the disciplined and austere pursuit of gain, and the attitude appropriate to the growth of capitalism. Contemporaries noted how much more prosperous were Protestant countries, except Scotland, than Roman Catholic ones. The economic centre of Europe moved from the Italian city-states to Antwerp and then, with the Industrial Revolution, to Britain. Weber's aim was to show the part played by Calvinist ethics in this. He never suggested that it 'caused' the rise of capitalism, still less that he was giving a 'spiritual' explanation of it as against a Marxist 'materialist' one. He argued merely that Calvinism contributed an outlook from which elements highly congenial to capitalism could be drawn by Christians in that tradition, and that they were drawn, and were influential. In fact Weber's thesis if anything strengthened a stress on the importance of economic factors. For there was a difference between Calvin and Calvinism of a century or more later. Calvin had more awareness than Luther of what was happening in society, and he had the courage to break away from medieval presuppositions which led both to the banning of interest on loans and to sophistries in getting round the ban. He cautiously agreed to interest at the rate of 5 per cent per year, and later to 6⅔ per cent. But he was not a friend of capitalism as such, and it could not have flourished for long under the restrictions imposed in Geneva. However, much of Weber's evidence came from the century after Calvin, for instance from Richard Baker, and even from Benjamin Franklin in the century after that. Elements in Calvinism congenial to capitalism had been utilized, and those not congenial were not stressed. Capitalism used Calvinists, who on the whole were willing victims.
>
> (pp. 119–20)

However, what should not be forgotten, is that despite the fact that there are sophisticated and reasonable interpretations of Weber's thesis, there remains considerable doubt as to its veridical nature.

What is the PWE?

Despite all the argument and research on the PWE there are relatively few clear statements on the actual constituents of the PWE. Innumerable writers have tried to define or elucidate the components of the PWE. Oates (1971) noted:

> The so-called Protestant Work Ethic can be summarized as follows: a universal taboo is placed on *idleness*, and *industriousness* is considered a religious ideal; *waste* is a vice, and *frugality* a virtue; *complacency* and *failure* are outlawed, and *ambition* and *success* are taken as sure signs of God's favour; the universal sign of sin is *poverty*, and the crowning sign of God's favour is *wealth*.
>
> (p. 84)

Cherrington (1980) listed eight attributes of the PWE. The broader meaning of the work ethic typically refers to one or more of the following beliefs:

1. People have a normal and religious obligation to fill their lives with heavy physical toil. For some, this means that hard work, effort, and drudgery are to be valued for their own sake; physical pleasures and enjoyments are to be shunned; and an ascetic existence of methodical rigour is the only acceptable way to live.
2. Men and women are expected to spend long hours at work, with little or no time for personal recreation and leisure.
3. A worker should have a dependable attendance record, with low absenteeism and tardiness.
4. Workers should be highly productive and produce a large quantity of goods or service.
5. Workers should take pride in their work and do their jobs well.
6. Employees should have feelings of commitment and loyalty to their profession, their company, and their work group.
7. Workers should be achievement-oriented and constantly strive for promotions and advancement. High-status jobs with prestige and the respect of others are important indicators of a 'good' person.
8. People should acquire wealth through honest labour and retain it through thrift and wise investments. Frugality is desirable; extravagance and waste should be avoided.

(p. 20)

Cherrington (1980) has attempted to put the meaning of work on a continuum characterized by two factors: meaning of work and time perspective (Figure 1.2). This offers seven positions. He makes an interesting and important distinction within the PWE: work as a terminal virtue (like honesty or loyalty) which is a good for its own sake; and work as an instrumental virtue as it helps to achieve.

	Point	
Work is extremely desirable		*Workaholic*
	A	Displaced terminal value
		Reward = removal of guilt, fear or uncertainty
		Time perspective = general
		Work ethic
	B	Terminal value – Part of the Character ethic
		Reward = work itself is a positive virtue of good character
		Time perspective = general
	C	Generalized instrumental value
		Reward = service to others: society, community or company
		Time perspective = general
		Worth ethic
	D	Self-Evaluation
		reward = self esteem
		Time perspective = general or specific
	E	Specific instrumental value
		Reward = money, status, recognition, promotion
		Time perspective = specific
		Leisure ethic
	F	Unfortunate Obligation
		Reward = leaving work and using money from work to pursue nonwork activities
		Time perspective = specific
	G	Mind-Numbing violence
Work is extremely undesirable		Reward = none: all work is punishing
		Time perspective = general

Continuum of importance

Figure 1.2 The meaning of work: continuum of importance

Source: Maccoby and Terzi, 1979.

Maccoby and Terzi (1979) found that the term PWE was being used very loosely and actually contained few overlapping ethics:

1. The *Puritan* ethic supporting a highly individualistic character, oriented to self-discipline, saving, deferred rewards, and antagonistic to sensuous culture.
2. The *craft* ethic emphasizing pride in work, self-reliance, independence, moderation, mobility, and thrift.
3. The *entrepreneurial* ethic which emphasized merchandizing not manufacture, the organization and control of craftsmen, growth and zeal to succeed. It makes a bold risk-taking character oriented to exploiting opportunities and using people.
4. The *career* ethic which emphasizes meritocracy, talent, and hard work within organizations leading to success and promotion. This ethic implies an other-directed, ambitious, marketing character.

The authors argued that these four ethics, all related to one another, developed sequentially and that in present-day America the career ethic holds sway but which may be replaced by the self-fulfilment or self-development ethic.

Some have argued that traditional values have not changed a great deal from the time of American independence to the present day. Thus one may compare the values of Benjamin Franklin with those of current America as set out by Williams (1970):

- *Temperance* Eat not to dullness; drink not to elevation.
- *Silence* Speak not but what may benefit others or yourself; avoid trifling conversation.
- *Order* Let all things have their places; let each part of your business have its time.
- *Resolution* Resolve to perform what you ought; perform without fail what you resolve.
- *Frugality* Make no expense but to do good to others or yourself; that is, waste nothing.
- *Industry* Lose no time; be always employed in something useful; cut off all unnecessary actions.
- *Sincerity* Use no hurtful deceit; think innocently and justly; and, if you speak, speak accordingly.
- *Justice* Wrong none by doing injuries, or omitting the benefits that are your duty.
- *Moderation* Avoid extremes; forbear resenting injuries so much as you think they deserve.
- *Cleanliness* Tolerate no uncleanliness in body, clothes, or habitation.
- *Tranquillity* Be not disturbed at trifles, or at accidents common or unavoidable.
- *Chastity* ...
- *Humility* Imitate Jesus and Socrates.

Benjamin Franklin (1784/1970)

- *Achievement and success* as the major personal goals.
- *Activity and work* favoured above leisure and laziness.
- *Moral orientation* that is, absolute judgements of good/bad, right/wrong.
- *Humanitarian motives* as shown in charity and crisis aid.
- *Efficiency and practicality*, a preference for the quickest and shortest way to achieve a goal at the least cost.
- *Process and progress* belief that technology can solve all problems, and that the future will be better than the past.
- *Material comfort* as the American Dream.
- *Equality* as an abstract ideal.
- *Freedom* as a person's right against the state.
- *External conformity* as the ideal of going along, joining, and not rocking the boat.
- *Science and rationality* as the means of mastering the environment and securing more material comforts.
- *Nationalism* belief that American values and institutions represent the best on earth.
- *Democracy* based on personal equality and freedom.
- *Individualism* emphasizing personal rights and responsibilities.
- *Racism and group-superiority themes* that periodically lead to prejudice and discrimination against those who are racially, religiously, and culturally different from the white northern Europeans who first settled the continent.

Williams (1970)

Interesting though these lists are, they do have some very serious problems associated with them. The list of values is bewilderingly mixed, containing personal, political, and economic factors. Many of these values are directly *contradictory* and it would be almost impossible to hold these at the same time (i.e. both freedom and equality). Similarly these values *change* – they wax and wane, disappear and reappear as a function of numerous sociological phenomena and ought not to be thought of as static. More importantly perhaps, they are only conjectures for which there is little mixed or no empirical evidence. That is to say that two people drawing up these lists may come to very different conclusions.

Jazarek (1978) became interested in how the PWE was conceived and measured. He detected in the writings of others a plethora of PWE attributes: thrift, industriousness, capacity for deferred gratifications, work discipline, the success ethic, a competitive spirit, self-reliance, belief in the virtuousness of work, and the centrality of work in life. He argues that three quite different interpretations are implicit in these definitions – a sociopsychological issue, a problem about the centrality of work, or an issue concerned with a person's conformity with certain expectations about job performance. Yet each conception tended to acknowledge the fact that for the PWE the perception of work was of a social obligation towards the society and fellow men, rather than a personal choice.

Understanding this latter point resolves an important paradox. Both popular and academic researchers have lamented the decline in the PWE and there is general agreement that it is in decline. On the other hand, numerous empirical studies have demonstrated that verbal commitments to work remain high among different populations and different age groups.

> Some authors of today are happy to announce that the work ethic is alive and well, because people have a stronger than before desire for meaningful and creative work. This is, of course, a confusion and a misunderstanding. The thrust of the work ethic was that the non creative, menial, unpleasant, untimely work had to be done. The work ethic was from the very beginnings an instrument of social control, an instrument which helped to fill the loopholes of the economy whenever and wherever needed. This is exactly what appears to be missing today. Unless we will be able to produce other equally efficient methods of work motivation, which is somewhat unlikely in the opinion of this author, we may reserve our joy about the death of the work ethic as well as curb our enthusiasm about its presumed health. The question of the work ethic, to be understood, has to be studied, not as a matter of verbal attitudes but as the problem of the structural match between social attitudes of the population and the socio-economic needs of the system. Only such an analysis will help us grasp the socio-economic dilemma of the work ethic in modern society.
>
> (Jazarek, 1978, p. 676)

This lack of definition as to the major definitional distinctions in the PWE is a major handicap to both conceptual and empirical development in the area and will be discussed in Chapter 2.

Interest in the work ethic

One way of tracing popular interest in the PWE is to examine popular articles on the topic. Cherrington (1980) examined the *Reader's Guide to Periodic Literature*, and came up with a graph (Figure 1.3). He pointed out that the peak period occurred between 1930 and 1940 but that the resurgence of articles since 1970 were primarily concerned with the decline or disappearance of the work ethic. Before the mid-point in this century, PWE beliefs were unchallenged and six major justifications were put forward in support of the PWE:

- religious principles, biblical injunctions, and ethical speculations
- the idea that hard work, diligence, honesty, perseverance, and industry led to success

- the idea that work builds character (especially in young people) and is a major source of happiness
- hard work leads to greater physical and emotional health
- work experience enhances the ability to learn and the motivation to excel
- work benefits society as a whole by bolstering the economy and helping to maintain material security.

However, such an analysis neglects to mention *base rates* of published articles and it could well be that interest in the PWE is declining relative to other topics!

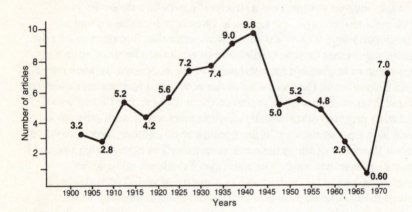

Figure 1.3 Average number of articles published on the work ethic per year, 1900–1975

Source: Cherrington, 1980.

However, as evidence of the increased interest in the PWE among psychologists, the president of the American Psychological Association based her annual address on it in 1985. Spence (1985) argued that *individualism* was central to the American character and the origins lie in the PWE and the philosophy of the enlightenment. The Protestantism of the PWE sought not only to render unnecessary any intervention (i.e. priest) between the individual and their God, but also to distract their loyalties to human social institutions. She attributes the American admiration of success or winners as a manifestation of the PWE. American parents socialize their children (particularly the boys) with a strong *interpersonal competitiveness* which is an integral feature of the PWE and achievement motivation. She attributes *materialism*, an unfavourable self-characterization recognized by Americans, to the PWE, as well as self-actualization movements against it.

Furthermore, the PWE has influenced psychological theories of achievement motivation which are intra-individualistic. Spence believes that the PWE has certain self-evident virtues:

However, a work ethic that has no further justification than work itself and is divorced from other values is susceptible to being driven by narrow self-interest, and it risks that conceptions of achievement will be distorted into forms that are indifferent if not antithetical to the public good.

(p. 1292)

Competitive climates spawn unethical behaviour. Further selfless commitment to one's work, even noble work, that is accomplished at the expense of others can in a large sense become selfish. In other words, PWE individualism that can lead to so much material prosperity does also have within it the seeds of its own destruction or at least decline. Another manifestation of interest in the PWE is the extent to which people use it to 'explain' miraculous economic growth.

One country that has elicited a great deal of admiration in recent years is that of Japan. Various attempts have been made to explain the Japanese economic miracle in terms of the work ethic. Kubota (1983) noted that a combination of Confucianism, the social structure of Japan, and the work ethic provide a unique explanation for the impressive productivity of that country. The quasi family group or social familism helps an intra-group support system and considerable productive competitiveness between groups. Competitiveness is based on the effort of the groups, not solely the individual. Being better educated, more insecure and hence desiring to be more fully accepted, the Japanese tend to work harder and compete more. Precisely because the Japanese PWE is integral to the social structure it is unlikely to significantly alter unless the latter does.

Certainly this address and the current plethora of books and publications on the PWE (see the References) appears to indicate no decline in interest in the PWE.

Explaining everything with the PWE

The PWE has been seen as, and held responsible for, many things. These include:

● An ideological justification of capitalism. Buchholz (1983) maintains that the PWE provided moral legitimacy for the origin and maintenance of capitalism because it provided a moral foundation for productive activity and legitimized the pursuit of profit and accumulation of wealth on the part of those who worked hard and invested their money wisely.

● Sexual repression. Albee (1978) argued that sex was the most repressed and heavily censored by PWE supporters and hence the last to be released. Johnson and Masters (1972) have argued that the PWE stresses the sinfulness of idleness, play, and indulgence. Hence sex is seen as strictly procreative never recreative and non-goal oriented, playful sex is to be shunned. Thus along with sex guilt comes sexual inadequacy which may be directly attributable to the PWE.

- Ecological crisis and destruction. Bruhn (1982) argued that the self-suffi-
cient ethos of early American pioneers with their PWE was responsible
for an over-exploitation and abuse of the environment. To accept nature
and live with it as it is runs counter to the PWE which stresses that the
forces of nature be harnessed and controlled. This, he argues, has led to
considerable abuse and exploitation.

- A spirit of violence and militarism. Aho (1979) in a historical analysis has
argued that Protestant mysticism was characterized by a justified divine
hatred of the ungodly that resulted in a deadly martial enthusiasm. He argues that PWE beliefs in certitude that one has been saved still gives im-
measurable inner strength to the believer and tremendous courage to
fight and zeal to win which could be seen as militaristic.

- Animal psychologists, have even argued that the PWE can be detected in
rats! Stephens *et al.* (1975) tested what they called the Protestant ethic
effect, namely that under certain circumstances, an organism will prefer
to 'work' for a reinforcer rather than receive the same reinforcer 'free'.
Various studies on rats have shown that when food pellets are placed
within the test chamber so that the rat may either 'freely' partake of food
or produce the conditioned (usually bar-pressing) behaviour to receive
food they tend to do the latter. Various explanations have been put
forward to account for this phenomenon: the strong habit strength of
responding; previous deprivation; or that animals are motivated to
actively manipulate their environment. Stephens *et al.* (1975) actually
provided experimental evidence to support their view that rats prefer to
work to control the process of receiving food by operantly responding
(albeit on a non-stringent schedule) to the environment. Indeed this is
supported by other interesting evidence that mice tore down and rebuilt
nests provided for them!

The use of the PWE as a simple-minded explanatory factor for such a range of
diverse sociological phenomena is naive and misplaced. Nevertheless it shows
the extent to which writers acknowledge the power of the PWE to motivate
and change behaviour.

The PWE and science

Sociologists of science have pointed to the close connection between several
facets of Puritan thought and early (especially seventeenth-century) scientists.
Scientific work was seen to promote discipline, work, and serious rather than
idle thoughts. PWE values sanctioned science because understanding how
nature works gave a better insight into the works of God. In this sense there
was a greater end to science than the mere statements and discoveries about

empirical regularity or the mechanisms underlying nature.

Merton (1957) argued that one test of the validity of the PWE would be to find, in the early days of scientific discovery, more Protestant scientists than one might expect on the basis of their representation in the total population. His analysis of seventeenth century as well as current day scientists supports the view that some Protestant denominations are disproportionally over-represented among a list of meritorious scientists.

Merton believed that the relationship between PWE and science was indirect and unintended and that once the empiricist ideology was established would be completely removed from religious modes of thought.

It may be argued (and Weber recognized it himself) that the PWE had within it seeds of its own destruction or decay. Capitalism has become, as Weber predicted, independent of its religious origins. But two factors, both outgrowths of the PWE, may be responsible for its demise (Cuzzort, 1969):

The development of bureaucracies – paradoxically bureaucracies which may be seen as the rational ordering of relations and operations within an organization, routinize charisma and suppress individualism. While files, records, and regulations so characteristic of bureaucratic organizations provide for continuity and efficiency they breed rigidity and impersonal relations. Hence it is the good bureaucrat who paradoxically can learn how to violate the formal system. Thus the spirit of the PWE which led to the proliferation of bureaucracies of all sorts is itself suppressed by the workings of them.

The development of science – the PWE emphasized many scientific virtues like rationality, utilitarianism, and empiricism and there is a close relationship between the PWE and science. However, the irony between the early congruence of PWE and science is that the religious ethic brought into being an ideology that is one of its most serious and intellectual challenges. That is because science is so frequently opposed to religion of all kinds the PWE nursed those who rejected it.

Furthermore, with the growth of wealth that naturally follows from economic development and concomitant increase in discretionary wealth, leisure time, etc, it means that people do not have to work as hard and are enticed with leisure indulgences. Hence the benefit of the PWE is temptation, to which many no doubt succumb. The increase in science, wealth, and bureaucracies then would appear to lead to the decline or at least a change in the PWE. Whether this is true or not will be discussed in Chapter 7.

The PWE as a psychological variable

McClelland *et al.* (1953) were the first to attempt a specifically psychological analysis of the PWE. But it was in his later book (McClelland, 1961) that

McClelland linked it to economic growth which he argued was

> a first attempt by a psychologist interested primarily in human motivation
> to shed some light on a problem of historic importance.
>
> (p. 3)

He rejected biological and economic theories as well as sociological theories, partly because of the paucity of evidence in their favour as well as tautological arguments. He stressed the need for the careful quantification of variables followed by relating them systematically to sensitive and salient dependent variables. He set out what he described as the key hypothesis, notably the effects of the Protestant Reformation on the need for achievement (see Figure 1.4).

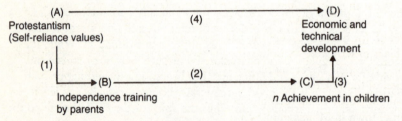

Figure 1.4 Hypothetical series of events relating self-reliance values with economic and technological development

Source: McClelland, 1961.

Weber was chiefly concerned with the linkage between A and D, with the way in which Protestantism led to a change in the spirit of capitalism in the direction of a speeded-up, high-pressure, competitive business economy. But the manner in which he describes this relationship strongly suggests that the linkage by which these two events are connected involves steps B and C, namely a change in family socialization practices which in turn increased the number of individuals with high achievement motivation. Thus a full statement of the hypothesis would be that Protestantism produced an increased stress on independence training which produced higher achievement motivation which produced more vigorous entrepreneurial activity and rapid economic development.

McClelland was heavily influenced by the findings of Winterbottom (1958) who found evidence that need for achievement was related to child-rearing, namely that high-achieving boys had mothers who had stressed self-reliance and independence. McClelland *et al.* (1953) noted that

> In the first place, he (Weber) stresses, as others have, that the essence of
> the Protestant revolt against the Catholic church was a shift from a
> reliance on an institution to a greater reliance on the self, so far as

salvation was concerned....As Weber describes it, we have here what seems to be an example of a revolution in ideas which should increase the need for independence training. Certainly Protestant parents, if they were to prepare their children adequately for increased self-reliance so far as religious matters were concerned, would tend to stress increasingly often and early the necessity for the child's not depending on adult assistance but seeking his own 'salvation'. In the second place, Weber's description of the kind of personality type which the Protestant Reformation produced is startlingly similar to the picture we would draw of a person with high achievement motivation. He notes that Protestant working girls seemed to work harder and longer, that they saved their money for long-range goals, that Protestant entrepreneurs seemed to come to the top more often in the business world despite the initial advantages of wealth many Catholic families had, and so forth....

What then drove him to such prodigious feats of business organization and development? Weber feels that such a man 'gets nothing out of his wealth for himself, except the irrational sense of having done his job well'. This is exactly how we define the achievement motive....Is it possible that the Protestant Reformation involves a repetition at a social and historical level of the linkage that Winterbottom found between independence training and n Achievement among some mothers and their sons in a small town in Michigan in 1950.

(p. 44)

McClelland's major interests were firstly the relationship between the need for achievement (as a psychological individual difference variable) and economic growth; and secondly Protestantism and economic growth. The crucial question he sought to discuss was whether the association between Protestantism and economic activity was mediated by need for achievement.

His first task was to demonstrate the Weberian hypothesis was still currently true, namely that Protestantism was related to economic growth. McClelland (1961) used as one source of evidence per capita electronic power consumption, arguing that this is a good index because the data are available in comparable units between countries, and that modern societies are based on this form of power. His analysis supported the thesis as Table 1.4 illustrates.

However, this sort of data was comparatively easy to obtain compared to being able to demonstrate that need for achievement was related to economic growth, because the former was so difficult to measure. To do this McClelland content-analysed a whole range of written materials and cultural artifacts such as children's books, folk tales, speeches from leaders of countries, songs, and poems. From this sort of analysis he was able to compare the difference between the expected and actual gains in electric power consumption per capita between the years 1929 and 1950 as a function of achievement motivation. This revealed a strongly significant positive correlation of .53. The actual results can be seen in Table 1.5.

Table 1.4 Average per capita consumption of electric power, corrected for natural resources, for Protestant and Catholic countries outside the tropics of Cancer and Capricorn

Countries	Consumption of electricity kwh/cap (1950)	Predicted output kwh/cap	Difference (predicted– obtained)	Rank of difference
Protestant				
Norway	5,310	3,379	1,931	1
Canada	4,120	3,186	964	4
Sweden	2,580	903	1,672	2
United States	2,560	2,328	232	9
Switzerland	2,230	1,253	977	3
New Zealand	1,600	1,526	74	11
Australia	1,160	1,598	− 438	20
United Kingdom	1,115	2,631	− 1,566	24
Finland	1,000	652	348	6
Union S. Africa	890	1,430	− 540	21
Holland	725	724	1	15
Denmark	500	74	426	5
Average	*1,983*	*1,645*	*338*	*10.1*
Catholic				
Belgium	986	1,959	− 973	22
Austria	900	620	280	8
France	790	989	− 199	16
Czechoslovakia	730	1,734	−1,004	23
Italy	535	227	308	7
Chile	484	764	− 280	18
Poland	375	2,007	−1,632	25
Hungary	304	628	−324	19
Ireland	300	154	146	10
Argentina	255	251	4	14
Spain	225	459	−264	17
Uruguay	165	154	11	18
Portugal	110	82	28	12
Average	*474*	*771*	*− 208*	*15.7*

Source: adapted from McClelland, 1961, p.51.

Furthermore he inferred from these data that achievement motivation precedes economic development, hence it may be possible to infer causality. McClelland (1961) however provides many sources which are extensively and exhaustively discussed and described. Others too have provided the same sort of data (see Figure 1.5).

McClelland (1961) believed economic growth was determined, in part, by ideological (*n* Ach) factors. He believed:

- The greater predominance of an ideology emphasizing individuality, the more frequent child-rearing practices that stress self-reliance.
- Greater self-reliance as socialized in childhood, leads to greater need for

Table 1.5 Rate of growth in electrical output (1952–1958) and national *n* achievement levels in 1950 (Deviations from expected growth rate in standard score units)

National *n* achievement levels (1950)		Above expect-ation	National *n* achievement levels (1950)		Below expect-ation
3.62	Turkey	+1.38			
2.71	India	+1.12			
2.38	Australia	+ .42			
2.33	Israel	+1.18			
2.33	Spain	+ .01			
2.29	Pakistan	+2.75			
2.29	Greece	+1.18	3.38	Argentina	− .56
2.29	Canada	+ .06	2.71	Lebanon	− .67
2.24	Bulgaria	+1.37	2.38	France	− .24
2.24	USA	+ .47	2.33	U. So. Africa	− .06
2.14	W. Germany	+ .53	2.29	Ireland	− .41
2.10	USSR	+1.62	2.14	Tunisia	−1.87
2.10	Portugal	+ .76	2.10	Syria	− .25
1.95	Iraq	+ .29	2.05	New Zealand	− .29
1.86	Austria	+ .38	1.86	Uruguay	− .75
1.67	UK	+ .17	1.81	Hungary	− .62
1.57	Mexico	+ .12	1.71	Norway	− .77
.86	Poland	+1.26	1.62	Sweden	− .64
			1.52	Finland	− .08
			1.48	Netherlands	− .15
			1.33	Italy	− .57
			1.29	Japan	− .04
			1.20	Switzerland	−1.92
			1.19	Chile	−1.81
			1.05	Denmark	− .89
			.57	Algeria	− .83
			.43	Belgium	−1.65

High *n* Achievement (top section); Low *n* Achievement (bottom section).

Note: Correlation of *n* Achivement level (1950) x deviations from expected growth rate =. 43, *p*<.01.
Source: McClelland, 1961, p.100.

achievement.
- The greater the level of *n* Ach, the more entrepreneurs in the society.
- The greater number of entrepreneurs, the greater and faster the economic growth.

But despite all the macroeconomic data, McClelland's work is still clearly a socio-psychological analysis. His central variable *need for achievement* is conceived of at the level of the individual and extrapolated to society. He focuses on psychological and sociological factors that determine need for achievement as well as the economic consequences for these beliefs in national figures. His model can be seen quite clearly in an abbreviated and simplified version of the final table in the book (see Figure 1.6). In various places in the book McClelland (1961) seems to argue that his psychological analysis of the

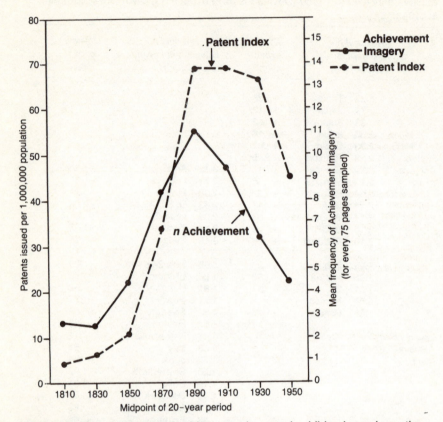

Figure 1.5 Mean frequency of achievement imagery in children's readers – the patent index in the United States, 1800–1950

Source: McClelland, 1961.

n Ach (clearly related to the PWE) provides one with both an analytic tool for socio-economic events in the present, but also a way of influencing the future:

> If man wants to control his destiny, he must learn to deal less in terms of the supposed reasonable consequences of historical events and more in terms of their often unintended or indirect effects on the motives and values of the next generation.
>
> (p. 388)

> The psychologist has now developed tools for finding out what a generation wants, better than it knows itself, and *before* it has had a chance of showing by its actions what it was after. With such knowledge man may be in a better position to shape his destiny. (p. 437)

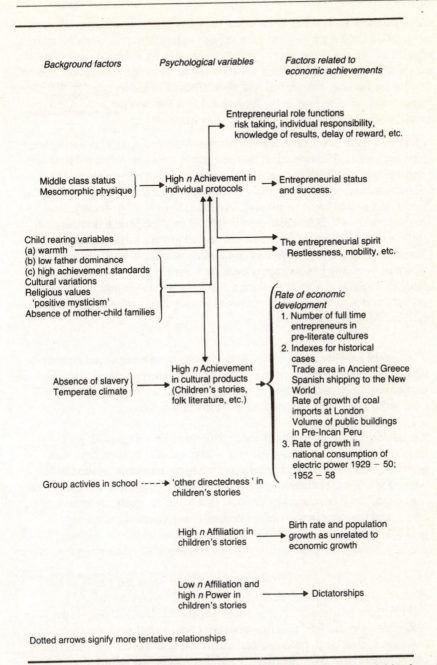

Background factors

Psychological variables

Factors related to economic achievements

Entrepreneurial role functions
risk taking, individual responsibility,
knowledge of results, delay of reward, etc.

Middle class status
Mesomorphic physique

High *n* Achievement in
individual protocols

Entrepreneurial status
and success.

Child rearing variables
(a) warmth
(b) low father dominance
(c) high achievement standards
Cultural variations
Religious values
    'positive mysticism'
Absence of mother-child families

The entrepreneurial spirit
Restlessness, mobility, etc.

*Rate of economic
development*
1. Number of full time
   entrepreneurs in
   pre-literate cultures
2. Indexes for historical
   cases.
   Trade area in Ancient Greece
   Spanish shipping to the New
   World
   Rate of growth of coal
   imports at London
   Volume of public buildings
   in Pre-Incan Peru
3. Rate of growth in
   national consumption of
   electric power 1929 – 50;
   1952 – 58

Absence of slavery
Temperate climate

High *n* Achievement
in cultural products
(Children's stories,
folk literature, etc.)

Group activies in school - - - - ▶ 'other directedness' in
children's stories

High *n* Affiliation in
children's stories

Birth rate and population
growth as unrelated to
economic growth

Low *n* Affiliation and
high *n* Power in
children's stories

Dictatorships

Dotted arrows signify more tentative relationships

Figure 1.6 Flow chart showing interrelationships among the key variables found
to be related to economic achievement

Source: McClelland, 1961.

McClelland's theory has been open to scathing attack (Eisenstadt, 1963; Portes, 1976) but his thesis remains a subject of both discussion and research. For instance, in the three years 1980–2 there were 64 references to McClelland's work in the Social Science Citation Index. However, many attempts to replicate his findings have failed and re-analysis of this data suggests his conclusions were false. Frey (1984b) has argued that the critique of McClelland's seminal work has revolved around three key issues:

1. *Methodological shortcomings* in the measurement of *n* Ach (either by content analysis or questionnaire) because it was unreliable, limited in scope, and unrepresentative; the particular economic indicators chosen; the countries used and the veridical nature of their data. The data were selectively interpreted to show *support* for, rather than *test*, the theory. For instance when GNP is substituted for the electronic production measure, the positive relationship between *n* Ach and growth turns negative! Social context (school, organization, family, neighbourhood) is neglected which of necessity has an impact on *n* Ach. Finally numerous research findings looking at *both* the relationship between *n* Ach and economic growth, and *n* Ach and entrepreneurial activity have failed to provide support for McClelland's thesis.

2. *Theoretical adequacy* in that the thesis fails to specify the social context in which *n* Ach arises and how it is transmitted to entrepreneurial activity and economic growth. Social conditions may induce or limit entrepreneurial behaviour irrespective of individual beliefs.

   'Coupled with the a-structural conception of economic growth is the related limitation of an ahistorical and a-international view of economic growth....This perspective borders on "blaming the victim" since the blame for limited economic growth is placed on traditional values, rather than on colonial conquests of the past that acted to create structural rigidities and limit opportunities for domestic entrepreneurial acting' (p. 130).

3. *Policy relevance* is problematic because policy makers have little or no control over *n* Ach, which according to McClelland is determined by child-rearing practices, religious ideology, etc. McClelland believed *n* Ach courses could lead to entrepreneurial activity but neglected to consider sociological, political, and economic factors that also determine entrepreneurial activity, irrespective of the beliefs and values of individuals.

Put quite simply the major argument against McClelland's approach is that while psychological factors may be necessary, they are not sufficient to foster or sustain economic growth. Structural factors (capital accumulation, population growth, taxation policies) at both the national *and* international level must be taken into account. Lea *et al.* (1987) have suggested that McClelland's thesis may be correct but that the causal chain proposed by him is too long. Also it could well be that high *n* Ach is the product not the cause of economic growth.

But perhaps the strong reaction to McClelland's thesis was precisely because it was psychological rather than sociological or economic. Just as economists and sociologists working at the level of the group/population ignored psychological, individual difference variables, so McClelland tended to underplay sociological or structural variables. This is not to excuse McClelland's oversights, simplifications, and methodological errors. Rather it is to acknowledge that he found a role for psychology in economics. Research on *n* Ach is extensive. A considerable effort has gone into the developing of instruments to *measure n* Ach (Tziner and Elizur, 1985) of which there are many but few of proven psychometric worth (Fineman, 1977). The advancement in the area is crucially dependent on the availability of a psychometrically proven measure. Secondly the *theory* of achievement motivation has received consistent attention. But perhaps the area that has attracted most attention is the *relationship* between the achievement motive and economic behaviour.

Morgan (1966) has argued and demonstrated that need for achievement has real value for improving the explanation of several crucial forms of economic behaviour in a representative cross-section of the population. He was keenly aware of intervening and moderating variables, not to mention the treacherous problem of causal chains and direction of causality. However, taking those into account he demonstrated that *n* Ach *and* the subjective expectation that hard work pays off is related to variables such as completed education of children, plans for education of children, income from saving, hourly earnings, and the extent of planning ahead.

Frey (1984a, b) however is critical of McClelland's thesis. Frey (1984a) attacked McClelland's (1961) hypothesis that a society with a generally high level of need for achievement produces not only more, but more energetic entrepreneurs, who in due course produce more rapid economic growth. Using cross-lagged correlational techniques however he found partial support for the theory that need for achievement is a cause and not a consequence of economic development.

The debate stimulated by McClelland will continue; *n* Ach is clearly a major component of the PWE (see Chapter 2) though these overlapping concepts are not identical. The latter is multi-dimensional, while the former uni-dimensional. Hence the PWE may be found to relate to a wider number of dependent variables.

The PWE and economic growth

One method of ascertaining whether PWE attitudes, beliefs, values, and associated behaviours are linked with financial or career success is to study a group
of highly successful individuals and compare them to a less successful, everyday group. This method attempts to find those factors which discriminate
between the two groups. Of course, it cannot be assumed that these factors
caused the success, indeed they may have been a *consequence* of success. That
is, this method cannot, unless the two groups are considered longitudinally
over time, separate cause and effect but it can at least indicate the extent to
which PWE beliefs and behaviours are associated with success.

This form of analysis has already been done at the institutional or company
level. Both in America (Peters and Waterman, 1982) and Britain (Goldsmith
and Clutterbuck, 1985) researchers have attempted to identify those specific
characteristics of successful companies. The latter identified eight factors:
strong leadership; autonomy to encourage entrepreneurial spirit; tight control on areas that matter; creating high job involvement; market orientation
and quality control; sticking to the fundamental principles of the business;
desire for innovation; passion for integrity. To what extent are these values an
institutional adaptation of PWE values? Certainly many of the features of successful companies – stress on job involvement, autonomy, the cultivation of an
entrepreneurial spirit – could be described as PWE values. It would be equally
instructive to determine whether poor performing or failing companies
showed either the lack of those identified successful features or else they
stressed other quite different values.

A second discriminatory approach has been to study certain individuals,
who are obviously financially very successful, to try and determine how they
achieved their success. There is no shortage of popular books on the rich, the
powerful, and the successful (Davis, 1985; Kay, 1986). For instance, Davis
(1985) in his analysis of the very rich – whether it was earned, won, or
inherited – listed the ingredients of success found most commonly among his
large sample. They were: ability (to create and make use of lucky chances);
contacts with the right sort of people; single-minded determination and con-
centration; an astute use of time and timing; planning and thinking big. Many,
but not all, PWE values like tenacity, determination, and a concern with time
and money seem apparent in this group. Similarly, Kay (1986) in his biographical account of self-made British millionaires found the most consistent
theme running through the thirteen biographies was the theme of perseverance and action: people who started modestly, expanded cautiously, tended to
advocate self-help, and strived for independence. Beyond their drive, acumen,
ability, and beliefs there was no other common feature:

> It is difficult to generalize: some left school early, others are graduates;
> there is a preponderance of only children, and there is one orphan, but
> several have emerged from large and happy families; some of their fathers

had been in business, but with no great success. A few showed signs of their money-making talents in their childhood or early youth, and in some cases that planted the idea of running their own business. But ... none appears to have had much active encouragement from his parents.

(p. 9)

Most of these studies on successful individuals or institutions have been inductive, rather than hypothetico-deductive. The conclusions drawn and the factors listed are not counter intuitive though it may surprise some people that specific factors are not mentioned. No hypotheses-testing exercise has been done using PWE values, and it is difficult therefore to conclude that 'discriminant analysis-type' studies had supported Weber's thesis or more modern psychological speculations. Nevertheless it is probably true to say that the results from these studies probably provide some evidence for the fact that specific PWE values – namely tenacity, perseverance, autonomy, independence, and hard work – are to be found in financially successful individuals and companies alike.

Conclusion

Nearly two decades of intensive psychological work on the PWE belief construct has confirmed its place as an important individual difference variable related to human motivation. Psychologists have been less interested in whether the original PWE thesis of Weber (1905) was correct or not than by translating his ideas into psychological (that is individual) terms. McClelland (1961) performed an analysis as imaginative and broad in its scope as Weber (1905) by emphasizing the concept of need for achievement.

Most psychological studies however have been of more limited scope, yet no less important for that. Psychologists have chosen to conceive of and measure the PWE as a coherent, bi-polar belief system similar to the locus of control or just world belief constructs. Indeed there is a striking similarity between PWE and other individual differences (rather than dispositional) variables such as locus of control, just world belief, need for achievement systems both in their antecedents and determinants (see Chapter 2). However, as in the above related concepts no attempt has been made to delineate the aetiology of the beliefs in individuals or the socio-cultural specificity of these beliefs. McClelland did do this but with specific reference to *n* Ach.

Considerable effort has gone into devising valid, reliable, and robust self-report questionnaires that measure PWE beliefs, and many exist (see Chapter 3). This may account for the fact that studies on the PWE and beliefs are equivocal as beliefs need to be subdivided into their various components.

Most of the research on the PWE has concerned PWE beliefs and work where it has been found to be an only moderately useful predictor of behaviour, values, job satisfaction, etc. However, where the PWE beliefs have been examined in relation to poverty, unemployment, mental illness, it has also been shown to be a more useful discriminatory variable. Perhaps the fact that the construct has been called the *Protestant Work Ethic* has led psychologists to overconcentrate on the relationships between PWE beliefs and aspects of work, rather than looking at a range of related areas such as leisure, economic behaviour, health, etc. (see Chapter 5).

The research relating PWE beliefs to other personality variables has been limited but is encouraging. However, little or no work has looked to aetiology and determinants of these beliefs, their stability over time, or their cultural specificity. If the PWE beliefs are to be conceived of as a personality dimension, as Mirels and Garrett (1971) suggested, there is room for a great deal of further empirical and theoretical research in this field (see Chapter 2).

Finally there remains some confusion as to whether one should talk about the PWE, the Work Ethic (Buchholz, 1976), or the Protestant Ethic (Ray, 1982). The term PWE implies that the concept has been borrowed from the writings of Weber which is clearly not the case as few psychologists appear to have read his many works in detail or paid much attention to the metaphysical aspects of PWE beliefs. The PWE beliefs and behaviours as defined and measured by the many PWE scales appear to be concerned with work values, beliefs, and needs and more particularly 'a person's continuing commitment to paid employment' (Cook *et al.*, 1981, p. 132). Just as it was pointed out that the Holy Roman Empire was not Holy, Roman, nor Empire, so it could be claimed that the PWE is not exclusively Protestant, about only work, nor exclusively concerned with ethics. It may therefore be more accurate to talk about work values and beliefs rather than the PWE itself.

Chapter two

Psychological components of the PWE

It seems to me that a great deal of nonsense is talked about the dignity of work. Work is the drug that dull people take to avoid the pangs of unmitigated boredom.

> Somerset Maugham

The love of money as a possession – as distinguished from the love of money as a means of the enjoyments and realities of life – will be recognised for what it is, a somewhat disgusting morbidity, one of those semi-criminal, semi-pathological propensities which one hands over with a shudder to the specialist in mental disorder.

> John Maynard Keynes

Men do not desire to be rich, but to be richer than other men.

> J.S. Mill

Put not your trust in money, but put your money in trust.

> Oliver Wendell Holmes

To be clever enough to get all that money one must be stupid enough to want it.

> G.K. Chesterton

Introduction

The PWE is nearly always referred to as a set or system of beliefs mainly, but not exclusively, concerning work. It is, of course, much more than that, being multi-dimensional and related to various aspects of social, political, and economic life. This chapter will attempt to refine the definition of the PWE, describe the structure and range of PWE beliefs, and consider the overlapping psychological concepts.

Psychologists and other social scientists have spent many years investigating various processes, belief systems, and individual difference factors that clearly relate to the PWE. Although these concepts originate in extremely diverse research traditions, each informs the PWE in different ways. As has been noted the concept of the PWE had existed in sociology for almost sixty years before it was introduced into psychology, and a further ten years before any test construction had taken place.

However, there were, and remain, a number of specifically psychological concepts that overlap with the PWE as defined in both the classic and modern psychological literature. Each of these concepts measures a specific feature or facet of a person's behavioural repertoire or conceptual schema. Furthermore there are various measures (usually questionnaires) of these overlapping constructs and many correlational studies have been done which demonstrate significant positive correlates with the PWE. In this sense these studies could be seen to demonstrate concurrent validity rather than to illustrate redundancy in one concept or the other. Cherrington (1980) has observed:

> When talking about the work ethic people could be referring to any of these attitudes. The concept is so difficult to understand because so many ideas are thrown together. Although they might be related in the value systems of most people, these ideas need to be studied separately.
>
> (pp. 20–1)

Overlapping psychological constructs

Two functions of the overlapping constructs or facets should be discussed. The first is that in nearly all instances there is clear empirical proof of the association between these constructs and PWE beliefs. In this sense what follows is not merely idle speculation but documented evidence of the relationship between various (themselves related) psychological constructs and the PWE. Secondly, this literature is useful because researchers interested in these overlapping constructs have sought to describe and explain the *aetiology* of these constructs and in some instances how they are maintained. This research is of particular importance as it sheds light into how the PWE beliefs and behaviours are socialized and shaped on an individual level.

Achievement motivation

The considerable psychological work on need for achievement or achievement motivation can be traced back to the personality theorist Murray (1938) who included achievement as one of his twenty basic needs. It was defined thus:

> The desire to accomplish something difficult. To master, manipulate, or organize physical objects, human beings, or ideas. To do this as rapidly and independently as possible. To overcome obstacles and attain a high standard. To excel one's self. To rival and surpass others.
>
> (p. 164)

These needs were seen to be largely unconscious, dispositional tendencies, general in nature and not specifically linked to situations and which tend to be stable over time. Since the Second World War there has been a considerable growth of interest in achievement motivation led by Atkinson (1964) and McClelland (1961). This growth can be seen in Figure 2.1.

There are a number of quite different models, theories, and hypothesized processes concerning the nature of the achievement motivation. While there remains in certain areas a considerable amount of conjecture as well as equivocal findings it is probably true to say that there is some agreement as to the nature of people high vs low in achievement motivation. However, the following are said to be the characteristics of persons high in Need for Achievement (*n* Ach):

1. Exercise some control over the means of production and produce more than they consume
2. Set moderately difficult goals
3. Maximize likelihood of achievement satisfaction
4. Want concrete feedback on how well they are doing
5. Like assuming personal responsibility for problems
6. Show high initiative and exploratory behaviour
7. Continually research the environment
8. Regard growth and expansion as the most direct signs of success
9. Continually strive to improve

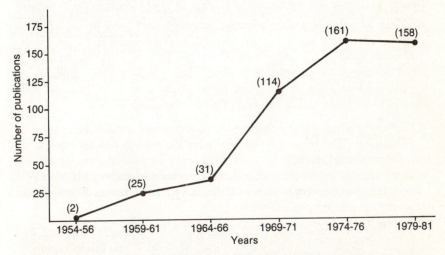

Figure 2.1 Annual number of publications on achievement motivation from 1954 to 1981, as listed in *Psychological Abstracts*, with frequencies averaged over 3-year periods *Source:* Heckhausen *et al.*, 1985.

A great deal has been written about the PWE and achievement motivation (see Chapters 1, 3, and 4). There is no doubt whatsoever, that people who endorse the PWE tend to be those high in achievement motivation and there is empirical support for this thesis (Furnham, 1987a, b). However, there are serious problems and disagreements as to how to define, operationalize, and measure need for achievement (and indeed the PWE). Hence it becomes difficult to define precisely the nature of the relationship between PWE beliefs and need for achievement. However this will be discussed more fully in other chapters.

Authoritarianism

This concept arose from investigators who asked the question in the immediate to post-Nazi period 'Do extremely prejudiced people have unique personality characteristics?' From interviews with specific people they believed to have found an overall system of values and beliefs called authoritarianism (Adorno *et al.*, 1950).

This personality dimension is made up of various parts – see below – which is described in psychoanalytic terminology as having weak egos reflected in the constructs of anti-intraception, superstition, stereotyping, and projectivity. Considerable research on this topic has provided a picture of a person who is generally conservative in political and social attitudes, deferent to authority, and prone to be offended by deviations from the conventional moral orders.

Authoritarians have been shown to avoid situations that involve ambiguity, are reluctant to believe that 'good people' possess both good and bad attributes. However they often appear less interested in political affairs, participate less in political and community activities, and tend to prefer strong leaders. There are a number of measures of authoritarianism; the best known (and hence most widely used) is the California F Scale (Adorno *et al.*, 1950), which attempts to measure prejudice, rigid thinking, etc. Subjects are requested to respond on a 7-point agree–disagree scale to 29 items which attempt to measure various aspects of authoritarianism such as

- Conventionalism: rigid adherence to conventional middle-class values. ('Obedience and respect for authority are the most important virtues children should learn.')
- Authoritarian submission: uncritical acceptance of authority. ('Young people sometimes get rebellious ideas, but as they grow up they ought to get over them and settle down.')
- Authoritarian aggression: a tendency to condemn anyone who violates conventional norms. ('A person who has bad manners, habits, and breeding can hardly expect to get along with decent people.')
- Anti-intraception: rejection of weakness or sentimentality. ('The businessman and the manufacturer are much more important to society than the artist and professor.')

- Superstition and stereotypy: belief in mystical determinants of action and rigid, categorical thinking. ('Some day it will probably be shown that astrology can explain a lot of things.')
- Power and toughness: preoccupation with dominance over others. ('No weakness or difficulty can hold us back if we have enough willpower.')
- Destructiveness and cynicism: a generalized feeling of hostility and anger. ('Human nature being what it is, there will always be war and conflict.')
- Projectivity: a tendency to project inner emotions and impulses outward. ('Most people don't realize how much our lives are controlled by plots hatched in secret places.')
- Sex: exaggerated concern for proper sexual conduct. ('Homosexuals are hardly better than criminals and ought to be severely punished.')

The questionnaire has been criticized on a number of grounds but a wide range of studies have shown that it is theoretically linked to other predicted phenomena such as prejudice towards blacks, intolerance of ambiguity, childhood experiences, obedience to authority and preference for certain politicians.

A number of studies have related the F scale to the PWE and found significant positive correlations (see Table 2.1).

The fact that these correlations are fairly high and positive suggests that

Table 2.1

Author	N	Scale	PWE measure	Correlation
Mirels & Garrett (1971)	117	California F	Mirels & Garrett	.51
MacDonald (1972)	101	California F	Mirels & Garrett	.44
Joe (1974)	183	California F	Mirels & Garrett	.38

people who endorse the PWE have some authoritarian traits though it is not clear which of the particular aspects of authoritarianism they possess more or less of. It is also not clear how these traits or behaviour patterns arose, though it may well be that early socialization experiences of a specific kind led both to development of authoritarian and PWE beliefs. However, studies on the associated beliefs and behaviour patterns of PWE endorsers suggest a clear and close relationship between PWE values and some if not all authoritarian beliefs and practices.

Beliefs in a just world

This belief pattern was identified over 25 years ago and concentrates on the tendency of people to blame victims of misfortunes for their own fate (Lerner, 1980).

The essence of this hypothesis or theory was succinctly summarized by Lerner and Miller (1978) thus:

Individuals have a need to believe that they live in a world where people generally get what they deserve. The belief that the world is just enables the individual to confront his physical and social environment as though they were stable and orderly. Without such a belief it would be difficult for the individual to commit himself to the pursuit of long range goals or even to the socially regulated behaviour of day to day life. Since the belief that the world is just, serves such an important adaptive function for the individual, people are very reluctant to give up this belief, and they can be greatly troubled if they encounter evidence that suggests that the world is not really just or orderly after all.

(pp. 1030–1)

Considerable laboratory evidence has been accumulated in support of the concept most of which has attempted to spell out exactly how and when victims are blamed for their fate, how these beliefs arise, and their correlates.

Rubin and Peplau (1973, 1975) devised a self-report inventory to measure the attitudinal continuity between the two poles of total acceptance and rejection of the notion that the world is a just place. About half the items suggest that the world is a just place where good deeds are rewarded (i.e. 11. 'By and large people deserve what they get'); and half refer to an unjust world where good deeds are no more likely to be rewarded than bad deeds (i.e. 4. 'Careful drivers are just as likely to get hurt in traffic accidents as careless ones').

Many studies have used this scale to examine further the relationship between just world and other beliefs and behaviours (Furnham and Procter, 1989). The measure is not without its difficulties. For instance, Furnham and Procter (1989) have considered the validity of the uni-dimensionality of the concept of a just world. They suggest that there might well be three worlds: *a just* world where people get what they deserve (the good and virtuous are rewarded and the bad punished); the *unjust* world where the opposite occurs (the good go unrewarded and may even be punished while the wicked win out in the end), and the *random* or *a-just* world where neither occur consistently in that some good deeds are rewarded, others ignored, and still others punished. Furthermore, it is possible that people believe that some aspects of their life are just (e.g. interpersonal relations) and others unjust or a-just (sociopolitical happenings).

Nevertheless, the Belief in a Just World measure has been shown to correlate significantly with demographic variables like age, income, and religion but also such personality factors as attitudes to authority, conservatism, and locus of control. Given that studies have shown that Just World Beliefs correlate significantly positively with authoritarianism, conservatism, and internal locus of control and furthermore that these three measures have been shown to correlate significantly positively with the PWE, one might expect positive correlations between Just World and PWE beliefs (see Table 2.2). Indeed, this has been the case in all the studies investigating this topic.

Table 2.2

Author	N	Scale	PWE measure	Correlation
Smith & Green (1984)	233	Just world (16 items)	2 items	.24
Wagstaff (1983)	70	Just world (16 items)	Mirels & Garrett	.21
Lerner (1973)	106	Just world (16 items)	Mirels & Garrett	.35
Ma & Smith (1985)	1,091	Just world (20 items)	Mirels & Garret	.33
Furnham (1989b)	1,021	Just world (16 items)	Mirels & Garrett	.32
			Blood	.19
			Ray	.42
			Ho	.39

These results are sufficiently consistent to suggest overlap between the concepts. Indeed, what is known from PWE believers' reaction to virtues of such things as poverty, unemployment, and mental illness would suggest that PWE believers have the conception of the world as a just place.

Conservatism

A concept closely linked with authoritarianism is that of conservatism. Wilson (1973) has claimed that conservatism is

> a general factor underlying the entire field of social attitudes much the same as intelligence is conceived as a general factor which partly determines abilities in different areas.

> (p. 3)

Wilson's theoretical stance to the conservative attitudes syndrome is that it is intimately related to genetic and environmental factors that determine feelings of insecurity and inferiority. The common basis for all of the various components of the syndrome is assumed to be 'a generalized susceptibility to experience threat or anxiety in the face of uncertainty' (Wilson, 1973, chap. 17). The conservative individual tends to avoid both stimulus and response uncertainty, and this avoidance is reflected in the verbal attitudes that are expressed as well in other aspects of behaviour. Wilson (1973) assumes that conservative beliefs

> serve a defensive function. They arise as a means of simplifying, ordering, controlling, ordering, controlling, and rendering more secure, both the

external world (through perceptual processes, stimulus preferences, etc.) and the *internal* world (needs, feelings, desires, etc.). Order is imposed upon inner needs and feelings by subjugating them to rigid and simplistic external codes of conduct (rules, laws, morals, duties, obligations, etc.), thus reducing conflict and averting the anxiety that would accompany awareness of the freedom to choose among alternative modes of action.

(pp. 261–4)

Furthermore Wilson (1973) provides a 'model' (see Figure 2.2) for this psychological process.

There has been a considerable interest in this variable. For instance Feather (1979) hypothesized and demonstrated that conservative people would emphasize values such as security, cleanliness, obedience, politeness, and salvation which are concerned with attachment to rules, authority, and ego defences while simultaneously devaluating values concerned with equality, freedom, love, pleasure, as well as open-minded, intellectual, and imaginative modes of thought. He also found, as have many others, that older people tend to be more conservative than younger people and females slightly more conservative than males.

Many researchers have been struck by the fact that attributes of psychological conservatism tend to overlap with core PWE beliefs such as religious fundamentalism, insistence on rules and punishments, preference for conventional art and institutions, an anti-hedonic outlook (Joe *et al.* 1981). Indeed Furnham and Bland (1983) have demonstrated that PWE beliefs are positively related to PWE belief scores and hence conclude that it is unlikely that one changes without the other. A number of studies have demonstrated positive correlations between the two (see Table 2.3). However, some researchers have been puzzled by this relationship which they describe as a paradox. Atieh *et al.* (1987) found it surprising that PWE beliefs associated with entrepreneurship and the fuelling of capitalism, were associated with risk averse conservatism and offered a solution: individuals in the private sector are more enterprising than those in the public sector and this economic sector membership moderates the PWE–conservatism relationship. However they did not find evidence for this thesis and concluded that the PWE alone does not adequately gauge people's work orientations. In other words, they appear to doubt the validity

Table 2.3

Author	N	Scale	PWE measure	Correlation
Feather (1984)	140	Wilson & Patterson	Mirels & Garrett	.57
Furnham (1984a)	256	Wilson & Patterson	Mirels & Garrett	.52
Atieh *et al.* (1987)	155	Wilson & Patterson	Mirels & Garrett	.22

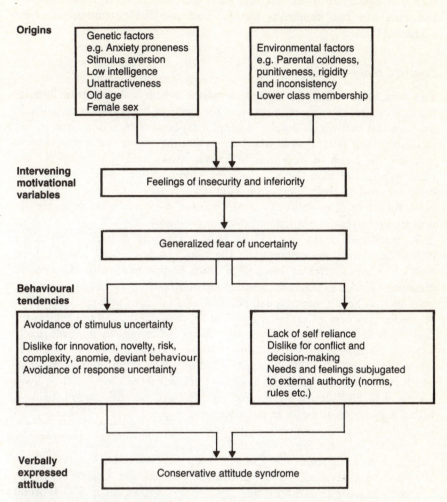

Figure 2.2 A theory of the psychological antecedents of conservatism

Source: Wilson, 1973.

or sensitivity of the PWE measures. Another explanation for the paradox is that the correlations are small, albeit significant, because although there is *some* overlap between conservatism and the PWE there is on the other hand, a good deal associated with PWE beliefs that is not psychologically conservative.

The question remains for conservatism, as it does for all the other overlapping constructs which are themselves multi-faceted, which particular features or facets of conservatism overlap with the PWE and which not. This issue is of course complicated by the fact that the PWE itself is not a unidimensional construct but has numerous specific and specifiable components (see Chapter 3).

Perceived control

This personality variable or dimension relates to beliefs about internal versus external control of reinforcement – i.e. the cause of behavioural outcomes. It assumes that individuals develop a general expectancy regarding their ability to control their lives. People who believe that the events that occur in their lives are the result of their *own* behaviour and/or ability, personality, and effort are said to have the *expectancy of internal control*, while people who believe events in their lives to be a function of luck, chance, fate, God(s), powerful others or powers *beyond their* control, comprehension or manipulation are said to have an *expectancy of external control*.

It is without doubt one of the most extensively measured individual difference dimensions measured in the whole of psychology. Indeed there exist a number of different scales all of which purport to measure this general dimension as well as scales designed to tap beliefs with respect to specific settings such as health, educational, political, and religious settings. In each instance locus of control has been significantly, consistently, and predictably related to beliefs and behaviours nearly always indicating the psychologically adaptive features associated with inner locus of control. Locus of control is related to desire for control, conceived of as a trait reflecting the extent to which individuals are generally motivated to control the events in their lives. People with high desire for control tend to have internal control, to have higher aspirations, to be more persistent and respond more to challenge, and to see themselves as the source of their success (Burger, 1985).

More recently, the locus of control concept has been applied to *behaviour in organizations*. Spector (1982), in a review paper, noted that locus of control is related to motivation, effort, performance, satisfaction, perception of the job, compliance with authority, and supervisory style, as well as an important moderator between incentives and motivation, satisfaction and turnover. For instance, internals tend to prefer piece-rate systems while externals tend to be more satisfied with direct supervision, to comply more with demands of coercive supervisors, and to be more compliant with social demands than internals. Indeed, he concludes that much more organizational theory may be limited to internals. Similar studies on employment and unemployment and labour market discrimination have demonstrated different levels of internality and externality as a function of work experience. Indeed, Hammar and Vardi (1981) found that in organizational settings which encouraged personal initiative in career development (personnel policies and promotion practices), internals more than externals played a more active role in their career progress. However, in situations which do not reinforce self-initiative, locus of control had little effect on career self-management and job experience. They note the existence of a feedback loop from career experience to locus of control such that favourable experiences increase tendencies towards internal control which, in turn, increases a person's initiative in self-development with future favourable outcomes.

Similarly, Lawler (1971) found that the more a person is orientated towards internal control, the more he or she will feel that his or her performance will lead to desired outcomes, while the more he is orientated to external control, the less likely he or she is to have high performance-to-outcome expectancy.

In a large study of nearly 3,000 employed people, Andrisani and Nestle (1976) examined the influence of internal–external control on success in the world of work. Locus of control was significantly related to occupational attainment, hourly earnings, job satisfaction, annual earnings, and perceived financial progress.

> More specifically, the cross-sectional data suggest that internals are in the better and higher status occupations, earn more money, and tend to be more highly satisfied in their work than comparable externals. The longitudinal data further suggest that internals experience more favourable employment circumstances than their external counterparts, namely greater earning and job satisfaction.
>
> (p. 160)

Frantz (1980) looked at the effect of work (labour market experience) upon the internal locus of control of a large group of American young people. He found, as predicted, that increases in hourly earnings, additional labour market experience, and a larger number of years of formal schooling increase feelings of internal control. Public sector employment, however, was associated with increasing external locus of control due to bureaucratic structures tending to restrict opportunities for developing abilities. More recently studies have related locus of control beliefs to economic crises (Chebat and Filiatrault, 1986), while others have attempted to develop a measure specifically of economic locus of control which was demonstrated to be related to the PWE (Furnham, 1986a).

A number of studies have demonstrated a significant relationship between PWE beliefs and locus of control. Because the locus of control dimension is scored in the direction of external (rather than internal) locus of control, the correlations have all been negative (see Table 2.4). Once again these results point in the same direction and suggest that those with PWE beliefs tend to have an internal locus of control.

Postponement of gratification

The concept of postponement or deferment of gratification occurs mainly in the developmental psychology literature and to a lesser extent social

43

Table 2.4

Author	N	Scale	PWE measure	Correlation
Mirels & Garrett (1971)	117	Rotter	Mirels & Garrett	−0.30
MacDonald (1972)	165	Rotter	Mirels & Garrett	−0.35
Waters *et al.* (1975)	146	Rotter	Mirels & Garrett	−0.41
Lied & Pritchard (1976)	146	Rotter	Mirels & Garrett	−0.23

psychologists' studies on middle-class values. Whereas instant gratification is associated with immaturity and lack of social mobility, the ability to postpone gratification is associated with educational and socioeconomic attainment.

Allen (1970) has noted extensive research on postponement of gratification which is a concept akin to impulse control and ego strength. A person's ability to postpone gratification (delay immediate, less valued goals for the sake of later, more valued goals) is supposed to reflect a more mature personality orientation in which the pleasure principle is superseded by the reality principle. In a recent summary of the extensive literature (much of his own work) Mischel (1981) notes:

> Two contrasting patterns of delay and impulsivity have been conceptualized as extreme poles. On one end is the individual who predominantly chooses larger, delayed rewards or goals for which he must either wait or work. This person is more likely to be oriented toward the future and to plan carefully for distant goals. He also is apt to have high scores on 'ego control' measures, high achievement motivation, to be more trusting and socially responsible, to have a high level of aspiration, and to show less uncontrolled impulsivity. This extreme pattern resembles what has been called the 'Puritan character structure'. Socioculturally, this pattern tends to be found most often in middle and upper (in contrast to lower) socioeconomic classes, and in highly achievement-oriented ('Protestant ethic') cultures. This pattern also shows that high ego strength is also related to a relatively high level of competence, as revealed by higher intelligence, more mature cognitive development, and a greater capacity for sustained attention.
>
> At the opposite extreme is the individual who predominantly prefers immediate gratification and declines the alternative of waiting or working for larger, delayed goals. Correlated with this is a greater concern with the immediate present than with the future, and greater impulsivity. Socioculturally, this pattern is correlated with membership of cultures in which the achievement orientation is low, and with indices of lesser social and cognitive competence.
>
> (p. 47)

Funder *et al.* (1983) examined some personality characteristics in gratification postponement in children. Their results seem to support other findings concerning the relationship between ability to delay gratification and other PWE virtues. Boys who delayed gratification were consistently and independently described as deliberate, attentive, reasonable, reserved, and co-operative while girls were thought of as intelligent, resourceful, and competent. Certainly the results suggest PWE values are inculcated at an early age.

Ray and Najman (1985) have in fact developed a self-report measure of deferment of gratification with satisfactory psychometric properties. Using this measure Furnham (1987b) showed that postponement of gratification was indeed linked to PWE beliefs. The study used multiple regression to attempt to establish which of a number of factors best predicted PWE beliefs. Although postponement of gratification was not the most powerful predictor it was significant. Indeed, both Weber (1905) and McClelland (1961) noted that central to PWE beliefs was a valuing of deferment. In fact some like Campbell (1987) have even suggested that the PWE is really a success ethic because at the heart of the ethic is the belief that hard work, saving, wise investment will, *in due course*, lead to success. Mainly because of the lack of a self-report measure of postponement/deferment of gratification relatively little work has been done in this field. But a related topic, notably attitudes to time (discussed later in this chapter), emphasizes the role of deferment in PWE beliefs.

Social values

Researchers on the topic of social values have conceived of them as a system of beliefs concerned with such issues as competence and morality and which are derived in large part from societal demands. These value systems are organized summaries of experience that capture the focal abstracted qualities of past encounters; have a normativeness or oughtness quality about them and which function as criteria or frameworks against which present experience can be tested. Also it is argued that these act as general motives.

Various instruments have been devised to measure a person's value system but the one that has probably attracted the greatest following is that of Rokeach (Rokeach, 1973; Ball-Rokeach *et al.*, 1984), who distinguished 18 terminal and 18 instrumental values. A value is considered an enduring belief that a specific instrumental mode of conduct and/or a terminal end state of existence is preferable. It is argued that once a value is internalized it consciously or unconsciously becomes: a standard criterion for guiding action; for developing and maintaining attitudes towards relevant objects and situations; for justifying one's own and others' actions and attitudes; for morally judging self and others; and for comparing oneself with others.

Research by Feather (1975) and others has demonstrated that these value systems are systematically linked to culture of origin, religion, chosen

Table 2.5 Product-moment correlations relating the terminal and instrumental values to each of the seven work beliefs

	PWE	Work ethic	Organizational beliefs	Marxist beliefs	Humanistic beliefs	Leisure ethic	Work involvement
Terminal values							
Comfortable life	-0.02	0.09	-0.06	-0.04	-0.16**	-0.06	-0.09
Exciting life	0.06	0.23***	0.21***	-0.08	-0.12*	-0.04	-0.01
S.O.A.†	0.03	0.08	-0.10*	-0.11*	0.05	-0.02	0.13*
World at peace	-0.03	-0.12*	0.15**	0.25**	0.07	0.12*	0.05
World of beauty	-0.08	-0.07	-0.13*	-0.01	-0.03	-0.04	-0.05
Equality	-0.30***	-0.17***	0.16**	0.41***	0.07	0.19***	-0.06
Family security	0.06	-0.03	-0.04	-0.15**	0.11*	-0.13*	0.18**
Freedom	-0.02	0.03	-0.04	-0.04	0.04	-0.03	-0.00
Happiness	0.12*	-0.01	0.04	0.00	0.00	-0.07	0.02
Inner harmony	-0.10*	-0.15**	-0.05	0.10*	0.10*	-0.02	-0.05
Mature love	-0.12*	-0.08	-0.11*	0.12*	0.00	-0.06	0.00
National security	0.14**	0.00	0.04	-0.10	-0.03	-0.09	0.00
Pleasure	0.06	-0.17**	-0.03	0.05	-0.24***	0.13*	-0.14*
Salvation	0.17***	-0.06	0.22***	-0.01	-0.02	-0.13*	0.02
Self-respect	0.00	0.00	-0.10*	-0.09	0.00	-0.04	0.00
Social recognition	-0.05	-0.03	0.00	-0.07	-0.04	0.05	0.02
True friendship	0.02	-0.18***	0.03	-0.04	0.02	-0.08	0.12*
Wisdom	-0.02	-0.02	-0.06	-0.03	0.14**	0.05	0.00
Instrumental values							
Ambitious	0.09	0.25***	0.11*	-0.11*	0.00	-0.11*	0.11*
Broadminded	-0.15**	-0.18**	-0.05	0.09	0.09	0.06	0.03
Capable	-0.04	0.02	-0.15*	-0.15*	-0.01	-0.12*	0.04
Cheerful	0.00	-0.06	0.10*	0.04	-0.08	0.03	-0.01
Clean	0.19***	-0.14***	0.10*	0.00	-0.15**	0.00	-0.15**
Courageous	-0.10*	-0.06	-0.07	0.10*	0.04	0.06	-0.05
Forgiving	-0.10*	-0.25***	0.08	0.13*	-0.03	-0.04	-0.00
Helpful	0.04	0.06	-0.09	-0.02	-0.06	0.13*	-0.03
Honest	0.07	0.14*	0.13*	0.05	0.10*	0.03	0.11*
Imaginative	-0.15***	0.04	-0.22***	0.11*	-0.01	0.25***	0.15**
Independent	-0.06	0.19***	-0.16**	-0.08	0.01	0.02	-0.06
Intellectual	-0.14**	0.03	-0.18**	0.00	0.02	0.04	-0.05
Logical	-0.00	0.11*	-0.13	-0.06	-0.09	-0.03	-0.13*
Loving	-0.07	-0.15***	0.00	0.11*	0.13*	0.12*	0.02
Obedient	0.19**	0.02	0.20***	-0.07	-0.07	-0.18***	0.05
Polite	0.15**	0.07	0.10*	-0.16**	-0.09	-0.22***	0.14**
Responsible	0.13*	0.02	-0.02	-0.12*	0.05	-0.11*	0.13*
Self controlled	0.04	0.10*	0.13*	-0.09	0.01	-0.03	-0.02

*** p < 0.001   ** p < 0.01   * p < 0.05   † S.O.A. = Sense of accomplishment   *Source:* Furnham, 1987a.

university discipline, political persuasion, generations within a family, age, sex, personality, and educational background. Feather (1985) has argued that social attitudes precede values which emerge as abstractions from personal experience of one's own and others' behaviour. These values in time become organized into coherent value systems which serve as frames of reference that guide beliefs and behaviour in many situations, such as work. He has argued that values, attitudes, and attributions are linked into a cognitive-affective system. Thus people's explanations of unemployment are

> linked to other beliefs, attitudes and values within a system in ways that give meaning and consistency to the events that occur.
>
> (p. 805)

Thus it may be expected that there are coherent and predictable links between one's general value system and specific work-related beliefs.

Furnham (1987a) looked specifically at PWE beliefs (measured by two different scales), other work beliefs, and human values. It was predicted that Protestant Work Ethic beliefs as measured by two different scales would be associated with values such as *salvation, security, cleanliness, obedience*, and *politeness*; and negative associated with values such as *equality, harmony, love, broadmindedness, imaginativeness*, and being *intellectual*. It was also predicted that work-involvement beliefs would be associated with values such as *sense of accomplishment, security, social recognition, ambitiousness, responsibility*, and *self-control*; and negatively associated with values such as a *comfortable life, pleasure, imaginativeness*, and *loving*. On the other hand it was predicted that Marxist work-related beliefs would be positively associated with values such as *equality, peace, inner harmony, love*, and *forgiving*; and negatively associated with a *sense of accomplishment, salvation, ambition, obedience, politeness*, and *responsibility*. Similarly the leisure ethic was expected to be associated with values such as a *comfortable life, happiness, pleasure, imaginativeness*, and *independence*; and negatively associated with a *sense of accomplishment, salvation, ambitiousness, capability, obedience*, and *politeness*. The actual results are set out in Table 2.5. Thus many of the hypotheses were confirmed, especially with respect to instrumental values. Work-related beliefs thus relate to a whole range of values which, in part, may explain why PWE beliefs are so predictive of such a wide range of behaviours. However, the work on social values has concentrated less on how these values are socialized and maintained in individuals and groups.

The Type-A behaviour pattern

Over 25 years ago psychiatrists became interested in whether heart attack patients shared any psychological traits. Through a number of different studies they did indeed find a pattern, labelled the Type-A pattern, which was initially characterized by excessive and competitive drive and an enhanced sense of time urgency. From the start, however, this behaviour pattern was seen as multi-dimensional, having numerous components such as an intense sustained desire to achieve, an eagerness to compete, persistent drive for recognition, a continuous involvement in deadline activities, a habitual propensity to accelerate mental and physical functions, and consistent alertness. Considerable research has identified other traits associated with this syndrome (see Table 2.6). It is suggested that this behaviour is learnt. Price (1982) has suggested that this behaviour pattern is learnt in open, competitive economies where upward mobility is possible, success is thought to be a function of individual effort and that progress is best defined in terms of material or tangible achievements and related states. Amongst the social and cultural antecedents of the Type-A behaviour pattern such as the educational system, urbanization, and socio-

Table 2.6 Type-A characteristics in research literature from 1959 to 1979: Frequency of citation

Characteristics cited	Frequency of citation		
	Total	1959–1974	1975–1979
Competitiveness	72	27	45
Time urgency	62	24	38
Aggressiveness	44	13	31
Drive [a]	41	22	19
Achievement striving	33	9	24
Preoccupied with/subject to deadlines	28	14	14
Ambition; desire for advancement	26	14	12
Accelerated pace	25	12	13
Impatience	24	9	15
Hostility	19	2	17
Motor mannerisms	18	11	7
Hyperalertness	14	4	10
Speech mannerisms	13	9	4
Struggle	13	6	7
Hard-driving	12	5	7
Restlessness	12	8	4
Job commitment	12	5	7
Involved in too much	11	8	3
Extremely conscientious/responsible	11	6	5
Seek recognition	10	8	2
Coping style to gain control	7	0	7
Job success	3	3	0
High productivity	3	1	2
High activity level	3	2	1
Chronic conflicts; challenge	2	2	0
Neglect of nonjob activities	2	1	1
Perfectionism; high standards	1	1	0
Anxiety	1	0	1
Unwillingness to define limits	1	0	1
Expressiveness	1	0	1
Need for power	1	0	1
Number of articles reviewed	101	44	57

[a] Often used in conjunction with another characteristic, as in 'competitive drive' or 'aggressive drive' (Price, 1982).

economic factors, Price (1982) lists the role of religion. She writes:

> Throughout the early history of the United States, and despite religious
> pluralism in American society, Protestantism exerted a powerful
> influence on people's thoughts and actions. The Protestant work ethic as
> it evolved in America since the seventeenth century asserted that spiritual
> salvation was to be attained through good works (i.e. through striving). In
> one perspective, a vengeful God was seen as meting out punishment in
> the form of eternal damnation to anyone failing to work hard for his
> salvation. The Protestant work ethic continues to exert an influence in
> present day America. To a considerable extent, however, it does so
> outside the context of faith in a supreme being–that is, outside the
> context of spiritual values. It unreflectively assumes hard work is good for
> the material benefits and personal recognition it affords. A godless
> Protestant work ethic combined with the lack of emphasis of guiding
> moral principles appears to constitute important social and cognitive
> antecedents of Type-A behaviour.
>
> (pp. 45–6)

She also argues that schools and the television act as a transmitter of Type-A
beliefs and expectations. Unlike most other researchers in the field she does
provide a model or theory underlying the Type-A behaviour pattern (see
Table 2.7).

The Type-A behaviour pattern has been linked with a whole range of other
psychological variables and the validity of the construct proven. However,
despite occasional reference to the links between the Type-A behaviour pattern and the PWE few studies have investigated it empirically. Tang (1986)
has however demonstrated that Type-As do not distinguish between work and
leisure, being achievement-orientated and competitive in both. In this sense,
Type-As tend to spill over their coronary behaviour pattern to leisure activities. More recently, however, Furnham (1989a) has provided some empirical evidence for a modest, but significant association between PWE beliefs
and Type-A behaviour patterns.

Entrepreneurship

Surprisingly little psychological research has been conducted on the determinants or the process of entrepreneurship (Wortman, 1987). Either because,
like the word, the concept is foreign or alien to many of the social sciences, or
because as a group they seemed so heterogeneous, almost no attempt has been
made to systematically study them and see if they could be identified by any
particular behavioural or belief system. Sampson (1981) has argued that the
British have a distaste for aggressive entrepreneurs, hence the fact that most
successful British entrepreneurs are outsiders, foreigners, or people who have
not been socialized into rejecting these values. This may, in part, account for

Table 2.7 Proposed beliefs and fears related to the Type-A behaviour pattern

Social and cultural antecedents: prevailing social beliefs	Personal cognitive antecedents: personal beliefs or constructs about one's relationship to the world	Personal fears or anxieties
Since upward mobility in an open economy is theoretically unlimited, if one tries hard enough he will be successful. The criteria of success are material accomplishments and related status	I must constantly prove by my accomplishments that I am successful (worthy of esteem, love, approval)	Fear of insufficient worth, of being considered unsuccessful (i.e. fear of disapproval)
There is no universal moral principle to regulate the process and outcome of human endeavours. The end justifies the means	There is no universal moral principle, no orderly (predictable) relationship between the intention of my actions and their consequences	Fear that right actions may produce negative consequences and that wrong actions can produce good consequences (i.e. nice guys finish last)
Hard-driving and competitive achievement striving is necessary and to be highly valued	All resources are scarce, therefore, your win is my loss, and I must strive against everyone to get what I need	Fear of an insufficient supply of life's necessities (e.g. time, achievements, recognition)

the lack of research. On the other hand, researchers have preferred to look at entrepreneurial working culture rather than the psychological factors in entrepreneurs' make up (Kanter 1983).

Most researchers have found it difficult to define what an entrepreneur actually is or indeed the motives that drive entrepreneurs (e.g. a desire for independence, an opportunity for achievement). The most common way of dealing with both of these problems has been to categorize entrepreneurs into a list, or, more rarely, a manageable typology.

Gray (1986) has identified eighteen types of entrepreneur: *soloist* (who is self-employed); *key partner* (semi-autonomous individual in a partnership); *grouper* (who works in small to medium sized groups); *professionals* and consultants (with specialist knowledge); *inventor–researcher* (who creates, markets, and produces bright ideas); *high-tech* (intelligent and competitive analyst); *work force builder* (astute hirer, delegator of and organizer of others' ability); *inveterate initiator* (perpetual initiator of new enterprises); *concept multiplier* (franchiser, licensor, or expander of others' ideas); *acquirer* (person who takes over existing businesses); *speculator* (those who buy and sell land, property, art, etc.); *turn-about artist* (people who specialize in identifying business weaknesses and turning them into strengths); *value manipulator* (acquires assets and then manipulates financial features of them to improve their worth); *lifestyle entrepreneur* (a middleman whose business involves putting together deals); *committed manager* (someone totally committed to a particular business or product); *conglomerator* (a person who attains companies to create larger groupings); *capital aggregator* (a raiser of large sums of money through investors), or the *matriarch/patriarch* of a family-owned business

As if this exhaustive and non-empirical taxonomy were not enough, Gray (1986) lists forty-four common characteristics of (presumably successful) entrepreneurs and provides a 220 item questionnaire to measure them! This list includes physical factors (health); demographic variables (age, education, ethnicity, employment, and family history); ability factors (thinking and selling); circumstantial factors (access to financial resources as well as technical and industrial knowledge), but by far the most characteristic were psychological in nature. They included continuous goal setting, perseverance, ability or style in dealing with failure, self-determination, initiative, drive and energy, tolerance of uncertainty, competitive, self-confident, versatile, independent, achievement oriented, flexible, innovative, strong in self-esteem.

There are a number of problems with this 'popularist' approach. First of all it is not empirical, being based on 'person experience'. Secondly, it is uncertain which characteristics are more important than others or indeed how they relate to one another. There is also the important question of whether all great entrepreneurs need to have *all* of these attributes or merely some of them. Furthermore it is not clear whether the different types of entrepreneurs described earlier have different characteristics. Most importantly it is not clear which PWE beliefs and values are important in the aetiology and maintenance of entrepreneurial behaviour.

Some empirical work has, however, been done on industrial entrepreneurs (Venkatapathy and Subramanian, 1984). For instance Venkatapathy (1983) attempted to determine the biographical characteristics of first and second generation entrepreneurs, the former being individuals who enter into ventures of their own accord for which there is no family precedence, while the latter take over or adapt family ventures. As well as important differences between these two groups of entrepreneurs, there were important similarities between the behaviour of their parents, particularly the father. In another study Venkatapathy (1984) found first-generation entrepreneurs more social and enterprising but less conventional than second-generation entrepreneurs. Winfield (1984) in a more considered review of the psychology of entrepreneurs has distinguished between cultural and social psychological factors involved in entrepreneurship. He quotes researchers who found two different types of cultural factors likely to encourage entrepreneurial behaviour. The first was reactivity to major change – the idea that most entrepreneurs began as result of personal loss, social upheaval, job loss, death, or famine – suggesting that it is frustration and misfortune which provides the initial spur. The second was that personality factors are important *only* if the culture is pro-entrepreneurship by providing social contacts and not if the culture does not support that sort of empathy.

However, in a review of the psychological determinants of entrepreneurs, Winfield (1984) detected a fairly important disparity between research done in India which stresses the role of fathers in carefully instilling entrepreneurial values in their sons, and research done in Europe which stresses the role of the mother in nurturing entrepreneurial values within the family. De Vries (1980) has argued that entrepreneurs are basically anxious and angry individuals who seek to overcome their anxiety by the accumulation of wealth. He found that both parents tend to be rejecting but whereas fathers exercise little control over their offspring, mothers tend to be firmer and stronger on control. Psychologically, then, they appear to be non-conformist, anti-authority, and lacking in confidence which is made up for in the ceaseless dedication to work and money-making at the expense of warm and lasting personal relationships. They therefore never fit comfortably in other people's organizations preferring to create and run their own.

Despite the fact that many entrepreneurs appear to adhere to many PWE principles – hard work, postponement of gratification, time consciousness, ambitions – it is quite clear that very many are not conventionally conservative or risk averse. Indeed other entrepreneurs' attitudes to morality and leisure fly in the face of PWE beliefs. Added to this is the point that it is the lower-middle classes more than the rich (self-made or inherited) that endorse the PWE more closely. Clearly, there is a complex, ambiguous, even paradoxical relationship between PWE beliefs and entrepreneurial behaviours that merits future research.

Attitudinal correlates

As well as various 'traits' that overlap with the core PWE beliefs and behaviours, there appears to be a number of attitudinal correlates or composites. Indeed there are potentially a high number of attitudinal correlates which include theological, political, and economic beliefs. However, some attitudes seem much more central to the PWE as conceived by psychological and sociological writers. Four of these will be discussed. These are attitude to leisure (free-time discretionary behaviour or hobbies and pastimes); attitudes to all aspects of money (a taboo and hence neglected topic); attitudes to time, a topic of increasing interest to psychologists; and attitudes to success.

Attitudes to leisure

Calvin's view was that for the most part leisure was a form of idleness (synonymous with mischief and the devil's work). He considered dancing, gambling, and card games immoral but did not disapprove of all recreational activities. If leisure activities recuperated power or kept one fitter to sustain the physical and mental faculties necessary at work, they were to be tolerated. Thus just as one had a deserving and non-deserving poor, so one had good and bad leisure.

Leisure has been seen as the primary site of all desirable experiences, it offers freedom from bosses and supervisors, choice in spending one's time, the fulfilment of the needs for rest and recreation, and the potential for self-articulation and self-expression. But beyond their picture the desirable goal of leisure has, for most people, been dependent on the confines of employment – the compensation has to be earned through work. Wilson (1980) has suggested a number of important political functions of leisure which may be important in understanding the work and leisure ethic. Leisure can have a very important impact on socializing immigrants into dominant cultural norms, values, and moves. Leisure is also a great 'leveller' in the sense that it provides people with the opportunity for people of very unequal socioeconomic status to meet and interact at the same level. To some degree then, leisure could be seen to be useful as a tool of nationalism.

Despite the obvious difficulty in defining leisure there are no shortages of theories about leisure. These include theories about surplus energy, preparation for life, spill-over and compensation theory, discretionary time activity, and state-of-mind theories, etc. Similarly there are numerous writings on the conceptual distinctions between play, recreation, rest, leisure, idleness, hobbies, etc. Although there is no agreed upon definition there appears to be sufficient agreement about the definitional dimensions, if not the functions, of leisure.

Over the past twenty years there has been a growth of studies looking at the measurement of leisure using different methods including time and money-budgeting, free-time activities, the perceptions of the meaning of leisure. It may indeed be possible to infer attitudes to leisure from the data we have on leisure behaviour, rather than is more frequently the case, namely inferring behaviour from attitudes.

Neulinger (1978) got over 300 working people to complete a 323 leisure-item questionnaire. He found five factors in this measure: a person's affinity for leisure (their perceived liking and capacity for leisure); society's role in the control, regulation, support, or interference with leisure planning; the extent to which people define themselves either through their work or leisure; the amount of, and satisfaction with, the leisure time a person has; and finally the balance between the amount of work or vocation desired. Using this measure Neulinger (1978) and colleagues examined various correlates of the five factors. For instance, young people appear to have a greater affinity for leisure than older people. Higher educated people seem to have a higher affinity for leisure yet tend to identify more with work. The higher people's income, the less likely they appear to identify through leisure, but professionals express higher affinity with leisure compared to tradesmen. True to the PWE hypothesis the Protestants compared to Agnostics (but not Catholics) showed stronger preferences for work compared to leisure. Few of the other variables – race, country of origin, birth-order, or personality variables – appear to relate to leisure attitudes.

Table 2.8 Leisure Satisfaction Scale factors

Subscale	Item

I. *Psychological*
1. My leisure activities are very interesting to me.
2. My leisure activities give me self-confidence.
3. My leisure activities give me a sense of accomplishment.
4. I use many different skills and abilities in my leisure activities.

II. *Educational*
5. My leisure activities increase my knowledge about things around me.
6. My leisure activities provide opportunities to try new things.
7. My leisure activities help me to learn about myself.
8. My leisure activities help me to learn about other people.

III. *Social*
9. I have social interaction with others through leisure activities.
10. My leisure activities have helped me to develop close relationships with others.
11. The people I meet in my leisure activities are friendly.
12. I associate with people in my free time who enjoy doing leisure activities a great deal.

IV. *Relaxation*
13. My leisure activities help me to relax.
14. My leisure activities help relieve stress.
15. My leisure activities contribute to my emotional well-being.
16. I engage in leisure activities simply because I like doing them.

V. *Physical Activity*
17. My leisure activities are physically challenging.
18. I do leisure activities that develop my physical fitness.
19. I do leisure activities that restore me physically.
20. My leisure activities help me to stay healthy.

VI. *Aesthetic*
21. The area or places where I engage in my leisure activities are fresh and clean.
22. The areas or places where I engage in my leisure activities are interesting.
23. The areas or places where I engage in my leisure activities are beautiful.
24. The areas or places where I engage in my leisure activities are well designed.

Source: Beard and Ragheb, 1979.

Neulinger (1978) speculated not only on the personal, social, and cultural determinants of leisure attitudes but also on the development of these attitudes. He asserts that there may be a developmental sequence akin to Erikson's stage paradigm in which adolescents play an important part informing and fixing leisure attitudes and behaviours. This measure has been criticized by Crandall and Slivken (1980) on a number of grounds – the scale has poor validity; is difficult to score; the factor structure is not replicable. Nevertheless, they recognize the importance of this first attempt.

One measure that has attempted to investigate multidimensional aspects of attitudes towards leisure is the Leisure Satisfaction Scale (LSS) (Beard and Ragheb, 1979). This scale has six dimensions each with impressive internal reliability. The items are set out in Table 2.8.

Ragheb (1980) has argued both that leisure attitudes are important predictors of behaviour, but also that there remains many unanswerable questions. These include:

> What is the relationship among parents' attitudes and values and their children's choices and participation in leisure activities? Are leisure attitudes a function of skill and knowledge of leisure activities? What is the relationship between pre-retirement leisure and work attitudes and post-retirement leisure attitudes, adjustment and mental health? What is the relationship between being unemployed and leisure attitudes?
>
> (p. 45)

Part of the problem in this area lies in the fact that it is pre-taxonomic in the sense that there is no consensus as to the fundamental types or dimensions underlying leisure pursuits. Nor are there any robust or well used instruments. Generally it is agreed that all parts of leisure (leisure activities, leisure satisfaction) have various components – psychological, educational, social, relaxational, physiological, aesthetic (Ragheb and Beard, 1980).

Put crudely, one could define attitudes to work and leisure as broadly in favour, or broadly against. Figure 2.3 sets out the four possible positions.

Four possible combinations exist which may be categorized thus:

AB Work hard/play hard – the idea that both work and leisure are desirable characteristics and that, when no doubt properly distinguished, should be highly enjoyable.

AD Puritan – the idea that work (in all its forms) is good and equally leisure (whichever course that takes) is bad.

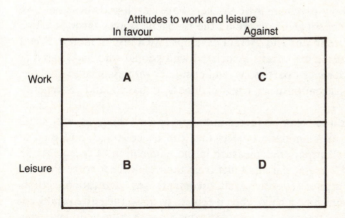

Figure 2.3 Attitudes to work and leisure

CB   Hedonist/Idle rich -- this position is largely against all forms of work (particularly if they are not immediately enjoyable or worthwhile) but in favour of most, particularly preferred form of leisure.
CD   Alienated – people who are against work and leisure seem particularly alienated perhaps with concomitant feelings of powerlessness, normlessness, and meaninglessness.

Clearly, the strict Calvinistic position is AD though it is quite conceivable for PWE believers to endorse AB. It all depends on the nature of leisure-time pursuits. No doubt all PWE believers would be against idle, self-indulgent leisure such as drinking but be in favour of educational or health-promoting leisure. Indeed many leisure pursuits, such as do-it-yourself, amateur science, and fitness-training, seem the very embodiment of PWE virtues. By virtue of the fact that both leisure behaviours and beliefs are very diverse, it is difficult to arrive at any simplistic conclusion. However depending on the nature of the leisure time activity, it is quite conceivable that it could be strongly approved of by those who endorse the PWE.

Attitudes to money

An essential part of the PWE refers to attitudes to money and wealth which is a topic widely neglected in the social sciences, especially psychology. Lea and Webley (1981) have pointed out that for economists and politicians money is something which measures the value of everything but which itself cannot be measured while psychologists of various persuasions, from psychoanalytic to behaviouristic, have long understood that money is a complex symbol imbued with meaning and symbolism.

In an essay entitled 'Character and Anal Eroticism', Freud (1908) first drew attention to the relationship between adult attitudes to money as a product of anal eroticism. Many psychoanalytic thinkers have developed these notions. For instance, Ferenczi (1926) described the ontogenic stages through which the original pleasure in dirt and excreta develops into a love of money. Freud (1908) identified three main traits associated with people who had fixated at the anal stage: orderliness, parsimony, and obstinacy with associated qualities of cleanliness, conscientiousness, trustworthiness, defiance, and revengefulness.

The child's first interest in his faeces turns first to such things as mud, sand, stones, thence to all man-made objects that can be collected, and then to money. Children all experience pleasure in the elimination of faeces. At an early age (around 2 years) parents toilet train their children – some showing enthusiasm and praise (positive reinforcement) for defecation, others threatening and punishing a child when it refuses to do so (negative reinforcement). Potty or toilet training occurs at the same stage that the child is striving to achieve autonomy and a sense of worth. Often toilet training becomes a source of conflict between parent and children over whether the child is in control of his sphincter or whether the parental rewards and coercion compel submission to their will. Furthermore the child is fascinated by and fantazises over his faeces which are, after all, a creation of his own body. The child's confusion is made all the worse by the ambiguous reactions of parents who on the one hand treat the faeces as gifts and highly valued, and then behave as if they are dirty, untouchable, and in need of immediate disposal.

If the child is traumatized by the experience of toilet training, he or she tends to retain ways of coping and behaving during this phase. The way in which a miser (like Silas Marner) hoards money is seen as symbolic of the child's refusal to eliminate faeces in the face of parental demands. The spend-thrift, on the other hand, recalls the approval and affection that resulted from submission to parental authority to defecate. Thus some people equate elimination/spending with receiving affection and hence felt more inclined to spend when feeling insecure, unloved, or in need of affection. Attitudes to money are then bimodal – either they are extremely positive or extremely negative.

Evidence for the psychoanalytic position comes from the usual sources – patients' free-association and dreams. However, Freudians have attempted to find evidence for their theory in idioms, myths, folklore, and legends. There is also quite a lot of evidence from language particularly from idiomatic expressions. Money is often called 'filthy lucre', and the wealthy are often called 'stinking rich'. Gambling for money is also associated with dirt and toilet training: a poker player puts money in a 'pot'; dice players shoot 'craps'; card players play 'dirty-Girty'; a gambler who loses everything is 'cleaned out'.

Families, groups, and societies which demand early and rigid toilet training tend to produce 'anal characteristics' in people, which include orderliness, punctuality, compulsive cleanliness, and obstinacy. Hence one can be miserly about knowledge, time, and emotions as much as money. These effects may be increased or reduced depending on whether the child grows up in a socialist or capitalist country, in times of comparative expansion or depression, or whether one is part of a middle- or working-class family.

The extent to which money is imbued with psychological meaning is clearly apparent from the following quote by Wiseman (1974):

One thinks of kleptomaniacs, or of the women who drain men of their resources, to whom money, which they are always striving to take away, symbolizes a whole series of introjected objects that have been withheld from them; or of depressive characters who from fear of starvation regard money as potential food. There are too those men to whom money signifies their potency, who experience any loss of money as a castration, or who are inclined, when in danger, to sacrifice money in a sort of 'prophylactic self-castration'. There are, in addition, people who – according to their attitude of the moment towards taking, giving, or withholding – accumulate or spend money, or alternate between accumulation and spending, quite impulsively, without regard for the real significance of money, and often to their own detriment every man has, and the pricelessness of objects, and the price on the outlaw's head; there are forty pieces of silver and also the double indemnity on one's own life.

Behind its apparent sameness lie the many meanings of money. Blood-money does not buy the same thing as bride-money and a king's ransom is not the same kind of fortune as a lottery prize. The great exchangeability of money is deceptive; it enables us to buy the appearance of things, their physical form, as in the case of a 'bought woman', while what we thought we had bought eludes us.

(pp. 13–14)

There have been both speculation and empirical attempts to categorize or taxonomize different attitudes to money. For instance Goldberg and Lewis (1978) who were particularly interested in the paradoxes, hypocrisies, inconsistencies, and lies associated with money, identified four forms of 'money madness':

1. Security collectors such as compulsive savers, self-deniers, and fanatic collectors who distrust others and find having money reduces anxiety because one is less dependent on others.
2. Power grabbers who might be business empire builders or 'godfathers' tend to see money as a form of strength and power and its loss as being rendered helpless, weak, scorned, and humiliated.
3. Love dealers who buy, sell, and steal love either see love as money, or money as symbolic of love or as commonly a commodity that can be bought or sold.
4. Autonomy worshippers who hope to buy or fight for freedom that they see money providing.

They stress the many emotions such as greed, fear, envy, anger, contentment and that money neither be worshipped nor denounced. Money behaviour frequently involves unconscious motivation, but people have the ability to control rather than be controlled by it.

A rather different, but overlapping, taxonomy has been proposed by Forman (1987) who listed five money complexes! He too points out that money is frequently equated with love, self-worth, freedom, power, and security. His five types are:

1. The miser who hoards money that is itself completely fascinating. They tend not to admit being niggardly, have a terrible fear of losing funds, and tend to be distrustful, yet have trouble enjoying the benefits of money.

2. The spendthrift who tends to be compulsive and uncontrolled in their spending and do so particularly when depressed, feeling worthless and rejected. Spending is an instant but short-lived gratification that frequently leads to guilt.

3. The tycoon who is totally absorbed with money making which is seen as the best way to gain power status and approval. They argue that the more money they have, the better control they have over their worlds and the happier they are likely to be.

4. The bargain hunter who compulsively hunts bargains even if they are not wanted because getting things for less makes people feel superior. They feel angry and depressed if they have to pay the asking price or cannot bring the price down significantly.

5. The gambler feels exhilarated and optimistic by taking charge. They tend to find it difficult to stop even when losing because of the sense of power they achieve when winning.

Forman considers in some detail some of the more fascinating neuroses associated with everyday financial and economic affairs like saving, paying insurance and taxes, making a will, using credit cards. For instance he looks at the issue of borrowing and the occasional obsessive, persistent, unrealistic, and intense phobia surrounding this. He gives examples of the fear and avoidance of lending institutions, partly from fear of dependence or punishment if loans are not repaid. The essence of this work, as with so many other books on this topic, is that because money is imbued with so much meaning there are a large number of neuroses and compulsions associated with it. Furthermore, as with all self-help approaches, the author attempts to help people recognize and change the nature of their behaviour. Forman (1987) concludes with such a table (p. 235), set out here in Table 2.9.

As well as 'speculative clinical' taxonomies, various empirical studies have attempted to classify people's different reactions to money. Wernimont and Fitzpatrick (1972) used a semantic differential approach to attempt to understand the meaning that different people attach to money. In their sample of over 500 subjects they had such diverse people as secretaries and engineers, nursing sisters and technical supervisors. Factor analysis revealed a number of interpretable factors which were labelled shameful failure (lack of money is an indication of failure, embarrassment, and degradation), social acceptability, pooh-pooh attitude (money is not very important, satisfying, or attractive), moral evil, comfortable security, social unacceptability, and conservative business values. The subjects' work experiences, sex, and socioeconomic level appeared to influence their perceptions of money. For instance employment status showed that employed security groups view money much more positively and as desirable, important, and useful, whereas the unemployed seemed to take a tense, worrisome, unhappy view of money.

Yamanchi and Templer (1982), on the other hand, attempted to develop a fully psychometrized Money Attitude Scale (MAS). A factor analysis of an original selection of 62 items revealed five factors labelled Power-Prestige, Retention Time, Distrust, Quality, and Anxiety. From this a 29-item scale was selected which was demonstrated to be reliable. A partial validation–

Table 2.9 They money sanity transition from neurotic to well

From *'Money as Inner Tormentor'* *(neurotic)*	To *'Money as Inner Mentor'* *(non-neurotic)*
You use money to impress and influence other people. To feel powerful and to gain status, you flaunt your wealth.	You are comfortable and at ease in the world. You know that power and status come from within.
You amass money as an end in itself. You like to have money for its own sake.	You value money for what it can do. You can distinguish between worldly desires and emotional needs.
You feel anxious, tense, worried, when you think about money.	You are relaxed about money and can think about it in a logical way.
You distrust other people around your money and you suspect that they are trying to take advantage of you.	You are self-confident and have a good self-image. You know your friends like *you,* not your money.
You hoard money in an attempt to protect yourself.	Your desire to save is healthy.
You have trouble controlling your spending and you tend to buy things impulsively. You like to gamble.	You are a good money manager.

Source: Forman, 1987.

correlations with other established measures such as Machiavellianism, status concern, time competence, obsessionality, paranoia, and anxiety – showed that this questionnaire was related to measures of other similar theoretical constructs:

> The correlations are in agreement with ostensibly suggested motives such as power and prestige. And, the evidence is viewed as congruent with less surface psychodynamic formulations such as the relationship of money retention to the obsessive-anal character structure.
>
> (p. 528)

Most interestingly the authors found that money attitudes were essentially independent of a person's income.

More recently Furnham (1984c) both developed a Money Belief and Behaviour scale and related it to PWE beliefs and a range of other variables. Factor analysis showed the 60-item inventory to have six dimensions labelled obsession, power/spending, retention, security, inadequacy, and effort/ability. As regards the PWE, high scorers more than low scorers were more obsessed by money, more money retentive, more security minded, and believed wealth to be obtained by effort and ability. The fear of losing all one's savings was also felt significantly more by high rather than low PWE scorers. Sex, age, education, income, and conservative beliefs all tended to relate significantly and predictably to money beliefs and behaviours.

Although there has been limited research in this field three important facts emerged. The first is that there is considerable overlap between theoretical and empirical typologies of people's attitude to money. The second is that both a historical review of the writings on the PWE and what limited empirical work that there has been, suggests that PWE beliefs are associated with security, collecting, miserliness, and saving, but also with autonomy and power. At the heart of the PWE is an obsession with money as a sign of success (and grace) and hence a powerful psychological indicator of PWE beliefs. Thirdly, all writers in this field have emphasized that money beliefs and behaviours are established fairly early in childhood and maintained in adult life. If this is indeed the case, and PWE beliefs are closely associated with money, this provides an interesting and important insight into the early socialization practices of PWE parents who, no doubt, inculcate the belief in their children. However, a problem in interpretation may arise here because either too much or too little specific parental behaviour may be associated with money. For instance there is some evidence that people with either very insecure or extremely secure childhoods tend to look to money for security in later life. However, PWE values and practices like training in postponement of gratification and the stress on autonomy and the necessary contingency of all behaviour, are more likely to relate to later monetary beliefs and behaviours.

Finally, it is possible to look at PWE attitudes to money in a similar format as attitudes to work and leisure. Figure 2.4 shows four possible patterns:

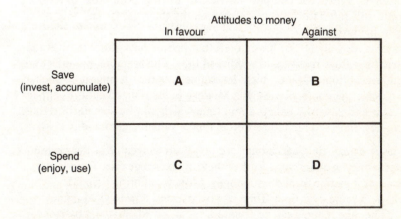

Figure 2.4 Attitudes to money

AB In favour of both spending and saving money, no doubt following some rule such as the spending of discretionary rather than borrowed cash.

AD In favour of saving but against spending. This is the Puritan position.

CB Against saving and in favour of spending. This somewhat profligate position may however be purely rational depending on interest rates, inflation, etc.

CD People against both saving and spending might not have any money or store rather than save it.

Clearly, the Calvinist position is AD but, given that certain rules apply, the PWE position could also be AB. Just a simplistic categorization takes no account of the fact that saving or spending attitudes are multi-dimensional! Nevertheless it provides a useful way to look at PWE beliefs as they relate to some money-related behaviours.

Attitudes to time

> Waste of time is thus the first and in principle the deadliest of sins.
> (Weber 1905)

Benjamin Franklin and Max Weber both mentioned the importance of certain attitudes to time: punctuality, the ability to defer gratification, the undesirability of procrastination. One would therefore presume that PWE beliefs are related to the way in which people perceive, understand, feel threatened or liberated by time. There is a long and fairly extensive, but very fragmented literature on different aspects of time, some of which are closely related to PWE beliefs.

Scott (1970) noted that just as regular bells summoned monks to pray, so they sounded in factories to summon 'worldly monks' to their labour. This time-conscious, somewhat compulsive, view of work is noticeable in the fact that people still refer to their 'trade manual' as their 'bible' and talk about working 'religiously'.

McGrath and Kelly (1986) have noted that people have different attitudes to the structure, flow, reality, and validity of time. Furthermore, cultures have dominant conceptions of time which determine how time is measured such as through clocks, calendars, diaries, etc. Modern industrialized cultures appear to hold clear and powerful beliefs about time which may be summarized thus: time is money, time is a limited resource; time a valuable commodity.

> To a large extent, time and money are not interchangeable as the phrase 'time is money' would imply. Rather they are exchangeable. Time is not money, but it can be turned into money. Money can bring time. Money increases in value over time. Time can be invested now to yield money later. Time, like money, can be counted, spent, saved, wasted, possessed, invested, budgeted, used up, borrowed, lost, left over and valued.
> (p. 108)

With organizations, McGrath and Kelly (1986) note there are three major time-related problems: because the environment is inherently uncertain, time plans have to be flexible; because of conflicting interests co-ordination and synchronization must occur; and because time is a scarce resource, careful temporal priorities must be established.

Dapkus (1985), on the other hand, found three major dimensions to people's experience of time: change and continuity (becoming in time); limits and choices (doing in time); and tempo (pacing in time). It is probably the limits and choices part of this three-fold categorization that relates most clearly to the PWE. Certainly a consistent psychological theme on time, closely related to the PWE, is delay of gratification.

Two contrasting patterns of delay and impulsivity have been conceptualized as extreme poles. On one end is the individual who predominantly chooses larger, delayed rewards or goals for which he or she must either wait or work. This person is more likely to be orientated towards the future and to plan carefully for distant goals. He or she also is apt to have high scores on 'ego control' measures, high achievement motivation, to be more trusting and socially responsible, to have a high level of aspiration, and to show less controlled impulsivity. Socioculturally, this pattern tends to be found most often in middle and upper (in contrast to lower) socioeconomic classes, and in highly achievement-oriented cultures. This pattern of high ego strength is also related to a relatively high level of competence, as revealed by higher intelligence, more mature cognitive development, and a greater capacity for sustained attention.

At the opposite extreme is the individual who predominantly prefers immediate gratification and declines the alternative of waiting or working for larger, delayed goals. Correlated with this is a greater concern with the immediate present than with the future, and great impulsivity. Socioculturally, this pattern is correlated with membership in the lower socioeconomic classes, with membership in cultures in which the achievement orientation is low, and with indices of lesser social and cognitive competence.

In other words, this dimension is concerned with the planning of, and receiving the rewards from, short, middle, and long-term goals. Clearly those people who show difficulty in postponing their gratification will show a preference for short term goals which are not always appropriate. The ability to delay gratification is associated with future time perspective. There are some 'four-legs-good two-legs-bad' suggestions in this work suggesting that ability to postpone gratification is always a good thing – far from the case. Furthermore, it is possible that people have both personal and work-related patterns of postponement, the one 'compensating' for the other. In other words, people who are forced to delay gratification for long periods at work may attempt to compensate for this frustration by indulging in very immediate gratification activities.

Ray and Najman (1985) devised a self-report measure for delay of gratification which includes questions such as 'Do you enjoy a thing all the more because you have had to wait for it and plan for it?'; 'Would you describe yourself as often being too impulsive for your own good?'; 'Do you agree with the philosophy – eat, drink and be merry for tomorrow we may all be dead?' Furnham (1987) used this questionnaire and found postponement of gratification to be a small, but significant predictor of PWE beliefs.

A second very important aspect of individual differences with respect to time and the PWE is need for order. This may simply be a very high need or may be pathological obsessionality. In order to describe this phenomenon, Freud identified three main traits associated with people who had fixated at the anal stage: orderliness, parsimony, and obstinacy with associated qualities of cleanliness, conscientiousness, trustworthiness, defiance, and revenge-fulness.

A number of important points need to be made here. First, although anality is associated with obsessive behaviours they need not necessarily be so. Secondly, there are different types of anal characteristics – associated with holding on and letting go (accumulative vs expulsive). Thirdly there are different characteristics associated with anality many of which are relevant to time keeping: need for regularity to the point of rigidity; concern with order of all facets of behaviour; frugality in all things; concern with time keeping; the idea that time is a precious resource.

To some extent the opposite of the anal personality is the oral character but to a larger extent there is no opposite – either one is non-anal or anal to some degree. Like nearly every other concept anality has both good and bad points and there are jobs well suited to, and highly appropriate for, the anal type. To a large extent PWE behaviours are associated with anal traits which are valued by parents and hence socialized in children. The problem mainly lies with the non-anal type whose life is highly disordered, erratic, and irregular. There have been a number of empirical attempts to look at personality and the subjective experience of time (Wessman, 1973) and healthy adaptive as well as maladaptive time perspectives (Wolf and Savickas, 1985).

A third important time-related theme of relevance to the PWE is that of procrastination. Procrastination is the tendency to postpone that which is necessary to reach a goal. It appears that the tendency to procrastinate can occur for a number of reasons. These include:

Neurotic disorganization – being so disorganized that certain goals have to be postponed because they cannot be faced or achieved.

Low self-esteem and high anxiety which means that never achieving a goal (such as taking a test) means that one cannot fail it. In other words doubt about one's ability leads to procrastination.

Low energy levels which means that people attempt to cope by spacing out various activities so that there is sufficient energy to use on each occasion.

It is quite possible that procrastination is a coping strategy but it may also be associated with other traits and work-related behaviours. Lay (1986) is one of the few people to have done psychological research on the concept of procrastination. He concludes from this work that:

> Part of the irrationality of the procrastinator (as opposed to the irrationality of the act), may be in their failure to maintain priorities over a series of ongoing and upcoming tasks and goals. The procrastinator may be as likely as the non-procrastinator to make plans in conjunction with the importance of tasks in one's life, and in conjunction with time considerations about those tasks. That is, they may equally be able to prioritize ongoing tasks on a day-to-day basis. On the other hand, during periods of the wait stage, they may be less able to keep these priorities sorted and cognitively available to them through the course of the day and the week. Or they may actively engage in behaviour which does not correspond to their priorities. This link between priorities and goal-associated behaviour may be viewed as an inherent part of the defining of procrastinatory behaviour. The premise here would be that one should spend the most time, or the most adequate time, on tasks that are viewed as most important. Failure to do so would constitute procrastinatory behaviour, viewed in both the short-run and the long-run as a failure to act on one's priorities. Spending less than adequate time on important projects is deemed to be procrastination. Among other things, this conceptualization will take into account the high energy individuals who, completing few of their most important tasks, claim not to procrastinate, but simply to be over-burdened.
>
> (pp. 493-4)

No doubt for a variety of reasons there have appeared a large number of books on personal time management, and the widespread sale of diaries that attempt to improve a person's ability to plan, control, and prioritize their time. What is most striking about so many of these books is the extent to which they endorse PWE values of parsimony, control, and work and warn against procrastination and time wasting. Take, for instance, the popular book by Lakein (1974) which boasts sales over 2 million. In this book he warns against wasting time through escapism, poor habits, and following the demands of others, preferring to stress the need for personal control, planning, and promoting. He stresses, for instance, that one should not 'waste' time but use 'transition times' such as commuting time, coffee breaks, waiting time, even sleep, to work more profitably. The book warns about the price of procrastination and offers as techniques for improvement: 'maintain a positive attitude in spite of previous failures' and 'resist doing a very easy (but unimportant) task that is right in front of you'. Although the book could not be said to completely endorse PWE beliefs, the theme of most chapters certainly concurs with PWE beliefs and values.

The same is true for books on time management. Garratt (1985) noted in her practical manual that the best managers are those who respond 'Yes' to questions like: 'Do you regularly take work home in the evenings or at weekends?'; 'Do you prefer doing things yourself rather than giving them to members of your staff?'; 'Do you ever leave the building to work elsewhere if you have something important to do?' Of course, it may be true that the very concern with time itself is a PWE characteristic and no surprise that self-help time-related books endorse the PWE values.

One final point needs to be stressed and concerns time-keeping for appointments. Keeping appointments and not being late are PWE values partly because keeping an appointment is seen as a *contract*, not an *estimate* of arrival. People who see an appointment time as a contract may feel guilty for being late (or in some cases early), while they might experience anger and outrage at others who failed to keep to their contract for whatever reason. For those who see appointment times merely as an estimate, no such emotions are likely to follow. PWE time attitudes and behaviours then are complex but not ambiguous. Just as for Type-A individuals, time is seen as a valuable commodity not to be squandered or misused.

Attitudes to success

PWE attitudes to success seem somewhat ambiguous. On the one hand it seems the case that the PWE should allow the unselfconscious celebration of success. After all success, in monetary terms, meant being one of the elect and hence one could rejoice in this state of grace. Secondly, success was a matter, not of good fortune, but hard work and it seemed natural to celebrate the inevitable and justified outcome of effort. On the other hand, the ascetic nature of the PWE means that this success was not to be enjoyed selfishly or indulgently. Success then was to be enjoyed as a just reward.

Some of the most outspoken and well-known proponents on some PWE values such as Phineas Barnum and Andrew Carnegie (both born in Great Britain, but 'rags to riches' immigrants to America) endorsed the gospel of success. Rischin (1965) has traced themes in the belief in success in America through the writings of extremely successful American entrepreneurs who could trace clear endorsement of most PWE virtues. Success ideology couched in highly individualistic terms would be found everywhere.

Consider the advice of Andrew Carnegie:

Aim for the highest; never enter a bar-room; do not touch liquor, or if at all only at meals; never speculate; never endorse beyond your surplus cash fund; make the firm's interests yours; break orders always to save owners; concentrate; put all your eggs in one basket and watch that basket; expenditure always within revenue; lastly, be not impatient, for as Emerson says 'no one can cheat you out of ultimate success but yourselves'.

Certainly the PWE taught that one should admire rather than be jealous of success, because it was a sure sign of God's grace. On the other hand, failure could be seen as a lack of grace, due simply to idleness and hence able to be despised.

Demographic and belief correlates of the PWE

How do PWE beliefs relate to mental and physical health, education, etc.? Two important points need to be made with regard to this section. First, that there is a paucity of reliable representative data on many of these issues. That is large, representative surveys have tended to use unreliable, simplistic, or naive measures of the PWE, while smaller-scale studies that have used robust and valid measures have tended not to examine large representative populations. Hence much of the data is somewhat speculative. Secondly, it cannot be assured that correlation is the same as causation. If PWE beliefs, for instance, are shown to be significantly related to educational attainment it is unclear whether education modifies or is modified by educational experiences (or indeed both). Of course, common sense and intuition would lead to various assumptions about the direction of causality but these must be recognized for what they are – speculative.

PWE and age

Do people tend to endorse PWE beliefs more as they get older? Are PWE beliefs related to generational effects such that they are socialized into one generation, but to a far lesser extent the next? There are both good theoretical grounds and empirical evidence for the fact that PWE ideals and values tend to be more endorsed as people get older. Theoretically it has been argued and observed that as people get older they tend to become more conservative in their social, economic, and political outlook. This point has been nicely observed in the well known phrase that if one was not a socialist at 20 one had no heart, but if one was a socialist at 40 one had no head. Because PWE beliefs are, in essence, so conservative one may imagine they too increase over the life span. Indeed there is empirical evidence for this hypothesis.

Both Aldag and Brief (1975) and Furnham (1989a) found a significant positive correlation between PWE beliefs and age. However, it should be pointed out that not all studies have found the relationship: Buchholz (1978a) and Furnham (1982) found no significant positive relationship but this may well be due to a restricted age range in the sample. Certainly if the PWE is significantly associated with conservatism, n Ach, and perceived control all of which increase with age, it might be imagined that PWE beliefs do likewise. However, it should be borne in mind that many things co-vary with age (like wealth), and it could quite easily be that it is some other variable that determines PWE beliefs over time. Secondly it may also be that the relationship between PWE beliefs and age is not linear but curvilinear with a peak between 40 and 50 years followed by a slow decline (see Figure 2.5, later on in the chapter).

But nearly all these studies have been cross sectional rather than longitudinal, and hence it has not been possible to determine whether these are the result of a motivational or a generational effect or both. It could be that older people – say for instance those born between 1910 and 1940 – were powerfully 'indoctrinated' with the PWE, which has remained largely unaltered and that cross-sectional correlational studies are simply demonstrating this effect. Preston (1987) has put arguments in favour of the generational effect:

> Remnants of the Protestant Work Ethic, with its horror of being
> beholden to anyone else, remain among the elderly. Many are reluctant to
> claim benefits to which they are entitled. Some have a horror of debt.
> They were brought up to save, and to wait until they had the money
> before buying anything, even a house when there were so many to rent;
> now there are very few. The world of Hire Purchase and of the Credit
> Card is alien to them. Low take-up of benefits is more of a problem than
> the attempt to secure them by fraud. The public is slow to realize this.
>
> (p. 124)

Of course it is most probable that there is both a maturational *and* a generational effect. However, if the post-war, and more particularly the 1970s, generation have been less imbued with the PWE, one may expect that older people in the future will not hold to the PWE as much as their parents or grandparents.

PWE and education

Taking into consideration (partialling out) all other salient variables, is there a relationship between the quality and quantity of education and PWE endorsement? There have been some studies which have somewhat serendipitously looked at this relationship but have been flawed for a number of reasons: salient other variables have not been partialled out or controlled; nearly always it has been the quantity (i.e. length) of education that has been examined rather than quality or type; often sampling has been inadequate in terms of size and homo/heterogeneity.

It is no doubt for the above reasons that the results have been somewhat equivocal. For instance, Ray (1970) found a significant negative correlation ($r = -.17$) between the PWE and education in a sample of 120 young army conscripts. Once again, however, the studies have been done on people with both a restricted age and educational range. Furthermore, it is extremely difficult to control for all the other variables (such as intelligence, socioeconomic states) that co-vary with education.

However it seems much more likely that PWE beliefs are related to education in an inverse U-curve with the least and most educated (as defined by years of primary, secondary, and tertiary education) adhering *least* to PWE beliefs, and those in-between (say with 'O' levels or 10th grade) endorsing the PWE most. However, as has been mentioned above, there is a dearth of careful extensive and non confounded research to support this point.

Do PWE values still exist in our schools? How are they presented or discredited? Indeed, is the school where PWE beliefs and behaviours are most clearly and importantly formulated?

Hodgkinson (1969) has noted:

> The Protestant Ethic, as applied to the sphere of work, is not so much dead as it is obsolete. It was a marvellous motivational structure in an economy based on scarcity and individualistic competition but does not seem appropriate to the development of mass, bureaucratic, industrial complexes. However, this should not be interpreted to mean that the motivational patterns implicit in the Protestant Ethic are of no value in our lives *outside* of the occupational sphere. Social mobility, after all, refers to a change in social status as perceived by the individual and the groups to which he refers. If reference groups outside of the occupational area increase in importance, it may well be that some aspects of the Protestant Ethic are still very relevant to our lives, if not to our jobs.
>
> (p. 30)

His argument is that as secular society becomes more hedonistic, now-centred, and dominated by the leisure–pleasure ethic it presents crucial problems for educators at all levels. Yet certain PWE values are still crucial for success like effort sustained in work. Furthermore it seems the case that people still value things most that they have suffered or worked hard for. One problem for the educator is not the decline of the PWE but a lack of consensus in the ethic which has replaced it (Gilbert, 1973). Again, reliable factual information of the PWE in the educational system is alas missing.

PWE and political preference

There are good reasons to suppose that PWE beliefs are linked to political preference because PWE beliefs are closely aligned to the goals of the business community which, in time, are related to party politics.

In a series of studies in the 1960s, Johnson (1962) investigated the effects of ascetic Protestantism on political party preference in America. His thesis, with replicated findings, was that for people exposed to Protestant fundamentalist teachings, religious involvement would co-vary with (right-wing) Republican party preference, whereas for people exposed to liberal teachings the opposite would occur. In other words, liberal Protestants preferred left-wing, and fundamentalist Protestants preferred right-wing parties but this was also affected by class.

Though this seems an implicitly reasonable hypothesis, the research by Johnson has been criticized, primarily on methodological grounds, by Rojek (1973). In a much more sophisticated study Rojek (1973) found *no* evidence of any relationship between religious and political preference. The problems were essentially two-fold: all Protestants were treated as a unified homogeneous group; the confusion of religion and church attendance; the fact that both religious and political beliefs are multidimensional.

It should, of course, be pointed out that these sociological studies did not actually look at the association between the PWE itself and political preference. A few studies, mainly done by psychologists, have. For instance, an American study by Beit-Hallahmi (1979) found a significant difference between the PWE scores of people of different political persuasions. Similarly, in a series of studies with different populations, Furnham (1984 b, c, d) found that PWE beliefs were associated with right-wing, free-enterprise, anti-welfare beliefs. This, of course, has been well documented, particularly by Feagin (1972).

As one may expect given the relationship between PWE beliefs and authoritarianism and conservatism, empirical studies and conceptual analyses appear to suggest that PWE beliefs would be closely linked to political beliefs and practices (voting, support for parties, newspaper readership, etc.).

PWE and religious denomination

There has been surprisingly little good, recent, empirical research on the relationship between the PWE and religious beliefs and practices. Bouma (1973) is correct in criticizing much PWE research for being too simplistic and not testing the links in the detailed causal chains as discussed by Weber. Apart from a lumping together of all Protestant sects, Bouma (1973) is quite rightly concerned that few sociological researchers ever considered the actual beliefs of people grouped by demographic or religious variables:

> Although lip service is often paid to the Weber thesis, no researcher has taken it seriously enough to measure actual beliefs and to then determine the impact of these beliefs on behaviours.
>
> (p. 147)

That is, it has not been established that Protestants actually hold stronger PWE beliefs than do Catholics!

Kim (1977), in reviewing the extensive but highly equivocal literature on religion and occupational success, has quite rightly pointed out that these studies looked at religious denominational identification rather than specifically Calvinist beliefs and values and their effect. Therefore a measure of PWE values (the Calvinist index) which he found, correlated significantly positively with occupation and education. He also found that fathers' occupation constitutes a significant variable, intervening in the relationship between Calvinist beliefs and values and occupational states, while the Calvinist beliefs and values have an independent effect on occupational status. Yet his results showed there to be no significant difference between Protestant denominations, Catholic, and Protestant sects and was forced to conclude that the use of religious affiliation as a measure of the PWE 'is less than adequate'. In other words, any study of behavioural correlates of religion should abandon the use of religious affiliation as a measure of the PWE.

In Australia, however, Ray (1970) tested two hypotheses relating the PWE to believers and non-believers: practising Protestants should show higher need for, and actual, achievement than unbelievers; and among unbelievers, the more Protestant ideals are accepted the more they should show higher need for, and actual achievement. He found the PWE was positively related to achievement orientation but negatively related to education. Ray concluded that he had evidence for the fact that what Weber said of the difference between Protestants and Catholics was today true of the difference between Protestants and agnostics. His argument is that actual belief is not so important as in adhering to PWE values which do indeed relate to desire for actual material and occupational achievement.

More recent empirical results looking at the association between PWE beliefs and empirical results are equivocal. Ray (1982) in Australia, Beit-Hallahmi (1979) in America, and Ma (1986) in Taiwan found no significance between the PWE scores of Protestants and Catholics. Similarly, Chusmir and Koberg (1988) found no significant correlations between work-related attitudes and specific religious affiliation or degree of conviction. However, they did find religious conviction was significantly linked to organizational rank, with non-managerial employees reporting a higher degree of religious conviction than managerial employees. Protestants had higher PWE scores than non-Protestants and persons with no religious affiliation had higher need for power than Protestants and Catholics. However, the relationship between religion (qualitatively and quantitatively) and work seems non-existent or washed out by more powerful factors.

Rather than give up trying to test whether the PWE is today currently true, others have called for better, less inadequate tests of theory. More importantly, it is necessary to control for the salient non-religious determinants of achievement and occupational success of different religious groups.

Cohen (1985) argued that although Protestants' religion (and presumably PWE) may well provide them with various socioeconomic advantages, those advantages may well be neutralized, or even reversed by socioeconomic, non-religious factors. In a large, careful, longitudinal study he sought to provide a good test of the PWE in current America. He found a weak ($r < .10$) significant relationship between Protestant affiliation and the PWE but a weak negative correlation between Protestant affiliation and occupational attainment. Using a regressional analysis he found the work ethic effect on economic success is slight and that where there is an effect is *indirect*. For instance, the PWE appears to affect educational attainment and 'grade-point average' which, in turn, affects the PWE. He argues that his results have three solid conclusions:

> First, the Protestant ethic affects early status-attainment; second, the Protestant ethic affects educational performance and attainment; and third, the Protestant ethic has an indirect effect on economic success....If the work ethic can be tied to religious beliefs on the one hand, and to economic success on the other, support can be obtained for the American Protestant ethic hypothesis despite the absence of socio-economic differences between Protestants and non-Protestants.
>
> (pp. 56–7)

The PWE and pathology

Over the last 25 years a number of popular books, nearly all written by psychiatrists, have discussed what might be thought of as pathological correlates of PWE values in the work place. For instance, Rohrlich (1980) has identified a great amount of aggression in the work place, particularly the terms used in everyday language: *'tackling* new problems'; *'grappling* with new ideas'; *'wrestling* with the data'; *'sinking one's teeth into* work'; 'making a *killing* on the stock market'; 'choosing people with more *punch'*. He has identified considerable amounts of aggression and rage in the work place as a result of having one's goals blocked, or one's desires unfulfilled. It is suggested that work provides a sense of self; feelings of security; victorious feelings of competence, power, and self-respect when interacting with the external world; the conquest of time and the feeling of progress. However, where there is an imbalance between work and love, unfortunate psychopathological consequences are likely to occur. These include:

- *Addiction to Work* due to a predilection for skill development (and discomfort with emotion, fantasy, and spontaneity); a need for order and analysis; an opportunity to manipulate and control the environment; an obsession with achieving future goals; and the need for efficiency and effectiveness. Various types of work addicts are identified.
- *Angry* and *Hostile* where work is socially acceptable means to discharge aggressive energy.
- *Ashamed* who has low self-esteem and can only salvage the sense of self worth in the work place.
- *Competitive* because work provides a forum for scoring the world and winning the game.
- *Defensive* where work protects one from unpleasant feelings and helps avoid needs, desires, and wishes that cause pain.
- *Friendless and Lonely* because work functions to bind people into larger groups, beyond the nuclear family, and give a sense of belonging.

- *Guilty* because some work harder and harder to repudiate the pleasure they derive from their work.
- *Latent Homosexual* who enjoy being kept in submission by other men or enjoy the hypermasculinity of the environment.
- *Narcissist* who compulsively depend on work to compensate for an other-wise unremitting sense of inadequacy.
- *Obsessive* because work provides an ideal environment for organizing, categorizing, and defining.
- *Passive Dependent* because in the work place people are taken care of and told what to do.
- *Pre/Post Psychotic* who lose their bearings after work where personal relationships are diffused and leisure time too vague.
- *Impotent* because work provides an area for flirtation and pseudo-intimacy.

The author also considers fear of success a potential problem particularly among women. After the potential problems at work, the core of the author's thesis is that one should achieve a *balance* between love and work.

> Work confirms and defines the self; loving dissolves and obliterates it. Work is structure and order; love is freedom. Work is oriented to the future, to goals; love demands the present. Work is domination and mastery; love is receptivity and submission. Work is mind; love is feeling.
>
> (pp. 231–2)

This approach is a curious mixture between the self-evident and common-sensical such as the idea that we need balance in our lives, with the highly counter-intuitive seeing work as the area whereby a high number of patho-logies can be 'worked out'. Of course the evidence for this comes from case histories, not large scale empirical research, and may therefore simply repre-sent a small group of people who are not happily adjusted but hard-working.

More recently psychiatrists have been intrigued by another curious and counter-intuitive phenomenon – the success syndrome and why success brings unhappiness. Berglas (1986) notes America's obsession with success and the assumption that it brings pleasure, prestige, freedom, and control. Success is derived from three interrelated factors: comparative ranking, rewards, espe-cially money, and social status and prestige. But success can lead to stress because with success come certain expectations and obligations, that may frequently exceed the successful person's capacity to perform. Because of the reactions of others to success, once a person has become so, he or she must make many painful adjustments in terms of living arrangements, inter-personal relationships, and internal standards of behaviour. Furthermore, Berglas (1986) offers the following equation:

$$\text{Self-esteem} = \frac{\text{What has been accomplished}}{\text{What is possible or expected}}$$

Thus what a successful person offers is the unwanted, unfounded, and unshakeable expectations to succeed. Hence the frequent problems of children of the famous who have had educational privileges where because much has been given, much is expected. It is furthermore assumed that if one is successful one is intelligent, if attractive then good, etc. Compliments and positive feedback then may be a two edged sword. Success, in other words, leads to various types of losses such as actual rewards, of reinforcing interpersonal relationships, or control over reinforcers. Worse still, success sufferers are denied sympathy and even receive criticism for expressing their distress.

The cruel paradox of success depression is that successes are often the root cause of the disease-producing losses.

(p. 151)

As a result of these problems people attempt to cope with success stress in a number of characteristic ways: deliberate under-achievement, depression, or drug abuse. Hence therapy is aimed at gaining appropriate expectancies about competence and how to cope with the problem of giving the encore to successful performance; about directing challenges to the expectations derived from success; and about redirecting attention to the process of succeeding as opposed to the products of success.

To what extent do success-driven PWE believers suffer burdensome expectations, jealousies, losses, and difficulties in forming intimate relationships? The answer must lie both in the extent to which they achieve success and the beliefs of those that admire them. For the PWE believer, success is a sign of God's grace and being about to invoke metaphysical powers might actually help people in coping with the problem. The ability to attribute one's success partly to the workings of the Holy Spirit may in fact have many advantageous consequences.

The PWE and health

Are PWE beliefs in any way associated with mental or physical health? In a very interesting and illuminating essay, Abraham (1983) has looked at the PWE underpinnings of current-day therapeutic, self-help movements that stress the rationalization of the psyche. These groups encourage the individual to interpret his or her predicament pre-eminently as a moral predicament whose origins seem to be in ascetic Protestantism. He argues that post-Freudian lay therapies have sought to enhance one's ability to evaluate prospective guides for personal agency in interpersonal contexts. Further, the religious foundations of the modern movements (especially EST) can be found in the writings of Weber with its stress not just on a 're-ordering' of human personality, but of human interests generally towards the problem of possessing and maintaining a calm, controlled, and, above all, rational personality. Although Abraham (1983) does not believe *all* modern self-help therapies are linked with the ascetic, utilitarian spirit of the PWE he does provide convincing evidence of Weberian ideas in our times. One implication of this finding is that PWE endorsers are fairly well adjusted.

On the other hand, there is some evidence to suggest that PWE components are linked with heart attacks. Chusmir and Hood (1986) found Type-A individuals (those likely to have elevated levels of serum cholesterol and have an increased risk of heart disease) higher in need for achievement, need for power, job commitment, and managerial responsibilities. In a more direct test of this hypothesis, Furnham (1989a) found PWE beliefs and the Type-A behaviour pattern significantly positively correlated.

In a review, Flannery (1984) has pointed out that because both internal locus of control and belief in hard work have been shown to be associated with physical health, we may expect the PWE to act as a powerful moderator between life stress and physical illness. Indeed, he presents evidence to this effect. Other studies have come up with much the same result. For instance, Wiener, Muczyk, and Gable (1987) found a linear relationship between work commitment (organizational, job, and career) and personal well-being as measured by affective symptoms, self-esteem, life-satisfaction, and over-all well-being. They suspected the relationship would be curvilinear in that 'over-commitment' would be associated with poorer well-being, but that hypothesis was not supported.

On the other hand, one may suspect that if PWE beliefs are related to Type-A behaviours, they are associated with illness rather than health. Clearly people may be able to 'sublimate' in their work which might be a healthy reaction to their personal problems, but if they are too work obsessed (workaholic) their health might deteriorate. It is unclear, however, which PWE beliefs are most crucial in this relationship or indeed which types of illness (mental vs physical) are likely to be affected. There is sufficient evidence now that personality and belief systems have clear relationships to physical illness, so it would be of considerable surprise if PWE beliefs did not affect a person's health.

Conclusion

This chapter has been dedicated to 'translating' the PWE into psychological terms. Originally defined as a theological and sociological variable, the PWE clearly overlaps with a number of well-established psychological variables, themselves interrelated. A number of possible overlapping variables were mentioned and frequently there was correlational evidence for empirical studies to support this view.

However, three important caveats need to be mentioned. First it is unclear if the nine variables mentioned in this chapter are the only *psychological* variables that 'overlap' with the PWE. There may well be others more important than those mentioned here. Secondly, the relevant importance of these overlapping variables has not been considered, due to the lack of evidence. That is, could it be said for instance that personal control, conservatism, and postponement of gratification are more central or fundamental to PWE beliefs than achievement motivation, or social values? This is a theoretical and empirical question which awaits further analysis. Thirdly, if all these variables overlap with the PWE, does it have any unique variance? In other words, is there any necessity to retain the concept from a psychological point of view? Some may argue that it is utterly redundant and can only lead to ambiguity to introduce a concept so debatable, and overused in an area of research already somewhat overburdened with concepts. Others, however, may see it as an extremely important and useful summary variable that captures important unique variables and, furthermore, helps to unite the social sciences.

Finally it may be worth speculating on the relationship between some of the variables mentioned in this chapter. Table 2.9 shows the strength of relationship between the various overlapping 'traits' and 'attitudes' and the PWE, as well as the five specified behaviours. It should be pointed out that this table is highly speculative and not based on hard empirical data, although the findings from this chapter were used in its formulation. Another way of looking at these and other variables is to be found in Figure 2.5 which shows graphically the possible relationship between the PWE and other variables. Table 2.10 may indeed act as a possible agenda for testable hypotheses.

Table 2.10 Hypothetical table indicating the 'possible' relationship between some of the variables mentioned in this chapter.

Components of the PWE	PWE	Age	Education	Politics	Health	Pathology
Traits						
1. Achievement motivation	+++	++	++	+	+	+
2. Authoritarianism	++	+++	+	+++	+	++
3. Beliefs in a just world	+	++	+	+++	+	+
4. Conservatism	++	+++	+	+++	+	++
5. Personal control	+++	++	++	+	+++	+++
6. Postponement of gratification	++	+	++	+	++	+
7. Social values	++	++	++	++	+	+
8. Type-A behaviour pattern	+	+	+	+	+++	+++
9. Entrepreneurship	+	+	+	+	+	+
Attitudes						
1. Leisure	+++	+	++	+	++	+
2. Money	++	+	+	++	+	+
3. Time	+++	+	+	+	+	+
4. Success	++	+	+	++	+	+

The + sign indicates the *strength* rather than the *direction* of the relationship.

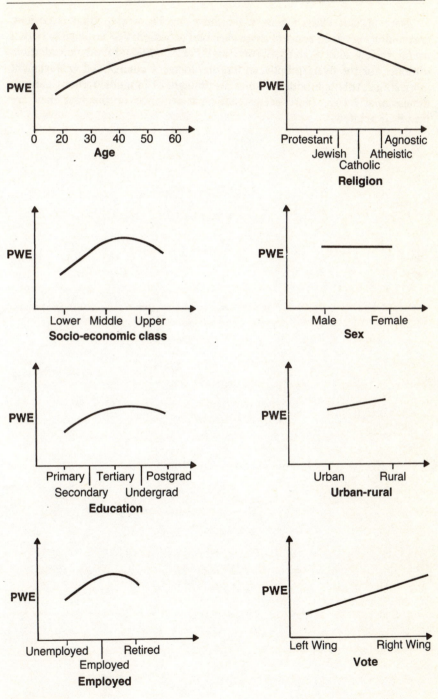

Figure 2.5

There already exists extensive literature on the overlap (that is positive correlation) between some of these variables specified. For instance in both a useful review and a study, Erwee and Pottas (1982) found considerable evidence for the overlap between internal locus of control and achievement motivation. Although both variables are thought of in multi- rather than uni-dimensional terms, there seems sufficient evidence of the fact they are positively related.

Chapter three

The measurement of PWE beliefs

If the facts don't fit the theory, change the facts.

Albert Einstein

Whatever exists, exists in some quantity and can (in principle) be measured.

E.J. Thorndike

Introduction

The problem of the measurement of attitudes, beliefs, and behaviours has long concerned social scientists from various disciplines. However, it is not until comparatively recently that psychologists and sociologists have attempted to devise subtle, scientific instruments and methods to measure PWE beliefs and values.

There are two basic questions that one must ask before setting about either choosing an existing questionnaire or devising a new method of measurement. The *first* refers to *what* one is attempting to measure. This, of necessity, dictates which type of method to use. For instance, consider the following:

Beliefs vs. Behaviour: Is one interested in measuring PWE beliefs (attiudes and values) of PWE-type behaviours? There is a complicated literature on the relationship between beliefs/attitudes and behaviours that cannot be considered here. Suffice it to say that methods appropriate for behavioural analysis (observations and experiment) are not necessarily the most appropriate to assessing belief systems, and vice versa.

Present vs. Past: Is one interested in measuring current PWE beliefs in a living individual or a group or is one interested in these beliefs during a specific historical period (i.e. at the beginning of the Industrial Revolution; during the reign of Queen Victoria, etc.)? Of course, it is impossible to interview historical characters so archival sources must be considered. These techniques may vary considerably in what they focus on and what data they provide, which may give a rather different picture of

PWE beliefs and behaviours at the time.

Individual vs. Group: Is one interested in measuring beliefs or behaviours of a specific, probably famous and influential person (i.e. a prominent self-made man or powerful political figure) or the beliefs/behaviours of a group? The sort of autobiographical technique appropriate to the former analysis is quite impractical for the latter.

General vs. Specific: Is one interested in measuring general PWE beliefs concerning various aspects or facets of the PWE – attitudes to money, saving, and consumption; attitudes to leisure, pleasure, etc. – or is one interested in measuring one specific aspect of the PWE belief system, for instance the psychopathology of people who do and do not endorse the PWE?

There may be various other questions that may be asked which dictate the choice of a particular methodology, not to mention the particular epistemological bias of the researcher.

The *second* important question is clearly related to the first. This concerns the *quality* of the research instrument and is usually asked in terms of the two most salient criteria: reliability and validity. Reliability refers to consistency – to obtaining the same results again (with similar groups at the same period in time; or with the same group or individual over time). Validity refers to whether the test actually measures what it is supposed to measure, and may take various forms. For instance, there is *content* validity (*face* validity which concerns whether the test looks as if it measures what it is supposed to measure and *sampling* validity which concerns whether a given population of questions and behaviours is adequately sampled by the measuring instrument in question); *empirical* validity (*predictive* validity is characterized by prediction to an external measurement referred to as the criterion and by checking a measuring instrument against some outcome) and *construct* validity (this involves relating a measuring instrument at an overall theoretical framework in order to determine whether the instrument is tied to the concepts and theoretical assumptions that are employed).

Ideally, whichever particular technique one wishes to use, one would hope that they are both valid and reliable. Both psychologists and sociologists have been interested in measuring PWE beliefs though the former, with a long psychometric tradition, have devoted more attention to measurement than the latter. Indeed, though it is rarely articulated one does notice something of a disagreement between psychologists and sociologists over theory and measure of PWE (or any other belief). Psychologists tend to stress the importance of measurement, arguing that one can only test general theories or specific hypotheses derived from them by first devising valid and reliable measures. Sociologists, on the other hand, see psychometrics as merely the technology that follows from the more important business of theory building.

It is, of course, necessary to point out that both are important, though possibly at different points of the scientific discovery process. Nevertheless, one may suspect that it is the psychologists of the psychometric tradition that have spent most time on the development of measures of the PWE.

The measures

There are two popular ways of measuring PWE beliefs. These are by *self-report* – nearly always questionnaire, which may be administered in an interview format – or by *unobtrusive* measures available in 'archives'.

Self-report (questionnaire) methods

A number of attempts have been made by scholars from different backgrounds to develop a robust and sensitive measure of the PWE. Some measures are better than others (in terms of their psychometric assessment) and are more popular in research. Seven such measures (eight scales) are briefly described as they were developed in chronological order.

1. *Protestant Ethic Scale* (Goldstein and Eichhorn, 1961)

A. *Items*
(1) Even if I were financially able, I couldn't stop working.
(2) I've had to work hard for everything that I've gotten in life.
(3) The worst part about being sick is that work doesn't get done.
(4) Hard work still counts for more in a successful farm operation than all of the new ideas you read in the newspapers.

B. *Scale*
Agree (1)   Disagree (2)
Range 0–4

C. *Reliability*
None

D. *Validity*
Face Validity – Acceptable
Predictable Validity – Theoretically linked to other social, religious, and work beliefs.

2. *Pro-protestant Ethic Scale* (Blood, 1969)

A. *Items*
(1) When the work day is finished, a person should forget his job and enjoy himself (R).
(2) Hard work makes a man a better person.

(3) The principal purpose of a man's job is to provide him with the means for enjoying his free time (R).
(4) Wasting time is as bad as wasting money.
(5) Whenever possible a person should relax and accept life as it is, rather than always striving for unreachable goals (R).
(6) A good indication of a man's worth is how well he does his job.
(7) If all other things are equal, it is better to have a job with a lot of responsibility than one with little responsibility.
(8) People who 'do things the easy way' are the smart ones (R).

(R) Reversed Item

B. *Scale*
Disagree completely (1) to Agree completely (6)
Range 8–48
Mean = 20.10 for each of the two scales (Pro, Non Protestant Ethic)

C. *Reliability*
Spearson-Brown .70 for Pro-Ethic (Wanous, 1974)

D. *Validity*
Face Validity – Acceptable
Concurrent Validity – Correlated with Job Satisfaction (Aldag and Brief, 1975).
Predictive Validity – Predicts work-related behaviour while in transit.

E. *Studies using the scale*
Aldag and Brief (1975), Armenakis *et al.* (1977), Filley and Aldag (1978), and Rim (1977).

3. *Protestant Work Ethic Scale* (Mirels and Garrett, 1971)

A. *Items*
(1) Most people spend too much time in unprofitable amusement.
(2) Our society would have fewer problems if people had less leisure time.
(3) Money acquired easily (e.g. through gambling or speculation) is usually spent unwisely.
(4) There are few satisfactions equal to the realization that one has done one's best at a job.
(5) The most difficult college courses usually turn out to be the most rewarding.
(6) Most people who don't succeed in life are just plain lazy.
(7) The self-made man is likely to be more ethical than the man born to wealth.
(8) I often feel I would be more successful if I sacrificed certain pleasures.
(9) People should have more leisure time to spend in relaxation (R).
(10) Any man who is able and willing to work hard has a good chance of

succeeding.
(11) People who fail at a job have usually not tried hard enough.
(12) Life would have very little meaning if we never had to suffer.
(13) Hard work offers little guarantee of success (R).
(14) The credit card is a ticket to careless spending.
(15) Life would be more meaningful if we had more leisure time (R).
(16) The man who can approach an unpleasant task with enthusiasm is the man who gets ahead.
(17) If one works hard enough he is likely to make a good life for himself.
(18) I feel uneasy when there is little work for me to do.
(19) A distaste for hard work usually reflects a weakness of character.

(R) Reversed Item

B. *Scale*
Strongly Disagree (1) to Strongly Agree (7)
Range 19–133: Mean = 85.6 SD (15.7)

C. *Reliability*
Kuder-Richardson .79 (N = 222) (Mirels and Garrett, 1971);
Spearman-Brown .67 (Kidron, 1978); Cronbach's Alpha coefficient .70 (Lied and Pritchard, 1976); .75 (Ganster, 1980)

D. *Validity*
Face Validity – Acceptable
Concurrent Validity – Correlated with sex guilt, morality conscience guilt, California F Scale, internal locus of control.

E. *Studies using the scale*
Lied and Pritchard (1976); Merrens and Garrett (1975); Greenberg (1977, 1978a, b); Kidron (1978); Ganster (1980); Furnham (1982, 1983, 1984a,b,c,d,e, 1985a, 1986a, 1987a,b).

4. *Spirit of Capitalism Scale* (Hammond and Williams, 1976)

A. *Items*
(1) Time should not be wasted: it should be used efficiently.
(2) Even if I were financially able to do so, I still wouldn't stop pursuing my occupation, whatever it might be at the time.
(3) Hard work is a good builder of character.
(4) A person without debts who inherits $5,000 should invest it for the future rather than spend it.
(5) Regardless of what a person does, the most important issue is how successful he or she is in doing it.
(6) People should be responsible for supporting themselves in retirement and not be dependent on governmental agencies like social security.

B. *Scale*
Strongly Disagree (–3) to Strongly Agree (+3)
Range –18 to + 18

C. *Reliability*
None

D. *Validity*
Face Validity – Acceptable
Concurrent Validity – Correlated with measures of worldly
asceticism .28

5. *Work and Leisure Ethic Sub-scale* (Buchholz, 1976)

A. *Items*

Work Ethic (5a)
(1) By working hard a person can overcome every obstacle that life presents.
(2) One must avoid dependence on other persons wherever possible.
(3) A man can learn better on the job by striking out boldly on his own than
he can by following the advice of others.
(4) Only those who depend on themselves get ahead in life.
(5) One should work like a slave at everything he undertakes until he is
satisfied with the results.
(6) One should live one's own life independent of others as much as
possible.
(7) To be superior a man must stand alone.

Leisure Ethic (5b)
(1) Increased leisure time is bad for society (R).
(2) The less hours one spends working and the more leisure time available
the better.
(3) Success means having ample time to pursue leisure activities.
(4) The present trend towards a shorter working week is to be encouraged.
(5) Leisure time activities are more interesting than work.
(6) Work takes too much of our time, leaving little time to relax.
(7) More leisure time is good for people.
(8) The trend towards more leisure is not a good thing (R).

(R) Reversed Item

B. *Scale*
Strongly Disagree (1) to Strongly Agree (5)
Range WE (7–35) LE (8–40); WE: Mean = 16.24, *SD* 5.18;
LE: Mean = 24.72, *SD* 5.60

C. *Reliability*
None

D.   *Validity*
     Face Validity – Acceptable
     Concurrent Validity – Theoretically linked to various other social and
     work beliefs.

E.   *Studies using the scale*
     Buchholz (1978a); Dickson and Buchholz (1977, 1979); Furnham
     (1984a, 1985a, 1986a, 1987a, b).

6.   *Eclectic Protestant Ethic Scale* (Ray, 1982)

A.   *Items*
(1) Eat, drink and be merry, for tomorrow we may be dead (R).
(2) Too much attention today is given to pleasures of the flesh.
(3) There is some great plan for the affairs of men, the end of which no
     mortal eye can foresee.
(4) If you've got it, why not spend it? (R).
(5) You can't take it with you, so you might as well enjoy yourself (R).
(6) Saving always pays off in the end.
(7) The only way to get anything worthwhile is to save for it.
(8) I believe in God.
(9) I believe in life after death.
(10) Once you die, that's all there is (R).
(11) The spirit of God lives within every man.
(12) Predestination is a myth (R).
(13) For girls to keep themselves virgins before they are married is old-
     fashioned and unnecessary (R).
(14) You should never speak lies about other people.
(15) Stealing is alright as long as you don't get caught (R).
(16) There's nothing wrong with having sex with another man's wife (R).
(17) There is no such thing as absolute right or wrong (R).
(18) If one works hard enough, one is likely to make a good life for oneself.
                                                        (R) Reversed Item

B.   *Scale*
     Strongly Disagree (1) to Strongly Agree (5)
     Range = 18–90: Mean = 62.38, *SD* (19.24)

C.   *Reliability*
     Cronbach's Alpha .82, .78 (Ray, 1982)

D.   *Validity*
     Face Validity – Acceptable
     Concurrent Validity – Correlated with Mirels and Garrett (1971)
     Scale .36
     Predictive Validity – Score predicts church attendances and religious

belief

7. *Australian Work Ethic Scale* (Ho, 1984)

A. *Items*
(1) People who work deserve success.
(2) Hard work is fulfilling in itself.
(3) Nothing is impossible if you work hard enough.
(4) If you work hard you will succeed.
(5) You should be the best at what you do.
(6) By working hard an individual can overcome most obstacles that life presents and make his or her own way in the world.
(7) Hard work is not a key to success (R).

(R) Reversed Item

B. *Scale*
Strongly Disagree (1) to Strongly Agree (4)
Range 7–28: Mean = 18.11, *SD* (4.12)

C. *Reliability*
Cronbach's Alpha Coefficient 0.76 (Ho, 1984)

D. *Validity*
Face Validity – Acceptable
Convergent Validity – Correlated positively with other scales (.65 with Mirels and Garrett, 1971; .59 with Blood, 1969)
Concurrent Validity – Subjects who scored highly on the scales tended to make more internal attributions and less external attributions for many by most, and were less willing to help the unemployed.

E. *Studies using the scale*
Ho (1984).

These seven questionnaires are summarized in Table 3.1

Relationship between these measures

All seven of the measures reported above purport to measure the PWE. Although these are of different lengths, ranging from 4 to 19 items, and completed on different answering scales from 2 to 7 points, they should all correlate highly and positively. That is, if they are all measuring the same thing they should be very closely related.

A number of individual studies have correlated two measures at a time – for instance, Ray (1982) reports that his measure correlates .36 with the well established Mirels and Garrett (1971) Scale, while Ho (1984) found his measure correlated .65 with the Mirels and Garrett (1971). However, there have been a number of attempts to compare and correlate more than two measures at a time.

Table 3.1 The seven questionnaires used to measure the work ethic

	Scale	Number of items[a]	Response scale	Reliability	Validity	Studies using the scale[c]
1.	Protestant Ethic (PE) (Goldstein & Eichhorn, 1961)	4 (0)	Agree–disagree 1 or 2	None	None	None
2.	Protestant Work Ethic (PWE) (Mirels & Garrett, 1971)	19 (3)	Agree–disagree 7 to 1	SB. 67[b] KR.79 C.70	Concurrent Predictive	Merrens and Garrett (1975), Greenberg (1977, 1978a, b), Kidron (1978), Ganster (1980), Furnham (1982, 1983, 1984, 1985a, 1986a)
3.	Pro-Protestant Ethic (PPE) Scale (Blood, 1969)	8 (4)	Agree–disagree 6 to 1	SB.70	Concurrent Predictive	Aldag and Brief (1975), Armenakis et al. (1977), Filley and Aldag (1978), Rim (1977)
4.	Spirit of Capitalism (SoC) Scale (Hammond & Williams, 1976)	6 (0)	Agree–disagree +3 to –3	None	Concurrent	None
5a.	Leisure Ethic (LE) (Buchholz, 1977)	8 (2)	Agree–disagree	None	Concurrent Predictive	Buchholz (1977), Dickson & Buchholz (1977, 1979), Furnham (1984b, 1985a, 1986a)
5b.	Work Ethic (WE)	7 (0)	7 to 1			
6.	Eclectic Protestant Ethic (EPE) Scale (Ray, 1982)	18 (9)	Agree–disagree 5 to 1	C.82	Concurrent Predictive	Ray (1982)
7.	Australian Work Ethic (AWE) Scale (Ho, 1984)	7 (1)	Agree–disagree 4 to 1	C.76	Convergent Concurrent	Ho (1984)

[a] Items in brackets indicate the number of reversed items.
[b] SB Spearman-Brown; KR Kuder-Richardson; C Cronbach.
[c] This list is not exhaustive.

Table 3.2 Correlations between measures of work and the work ethic

		AP	JI	PW	SS	US	AE	PWE
Intrinsic	Activity Preference (AP)							
	Job Involvement (JI)	.52*						
	Pride in Work (PW)	.71*	.64*					
	Social Status of Job (SS)	.15	.20	.14				
Extrinsic	Upward Striving (US)	.24*	.34*	.36*	.50*			
	Attitude to Earning (AE)	−.11	−.11	−.15	.45*	.34*		
Blood PWE (PWE)		.49*	.35*	.45*	.36*	.48*	.27*	
Mirels and Garrett (MGPWE)		.49*	.37*	.47*	.35*	.47*	.26*	.70*

* $p < .01$
Source: Waters, Bathis, and Waters, 1975.

Waters, Bathis, and Waters (1975) administered a number of self-report measures to 165 university students. These results are set out in Table 3.2. The authors made little attempt to explain their findings which seemed pretty much in line with what one may expect. It is particularly interesting to note the extent to which the PWE scales correlate similarly with the other six measures. Iso-Ahola and Buttimer (1982) correlated two measures of the PWE, two of the leisure ethic, and a measure of leisure satisfaction together. They also used students, but a far larger number (N = 398) – see Table 3.3.

In that the work and leisure ethic are antithetical one may have expected large positive correlations between measures of the same thing but large negative correlations between measures of opposite beliefs. Although the correlations were in the predicted direction they were not particularly large and, in some instances, not significant. The authors explained the results in terms of the specific items included in the various questionnaires.

Table 3.3 Correlations between PWE and leisure ethic beliefs

		LE1	LE2	LS	PWE1
Crandall and Slivken (1980)	Leisure ethic (LE1)				
Buchholz (1978a)	Leisure ethic (LE2)	.48*			
Ragheb and Beard (1980)	Leisure satisfaction (LS)	.32*	.11*		
Buchholz (1978c)	PWE (PWE1)	−.03	−.09	.09	
Mirels and Garrett (1971)	PWE (PWE2)	−.12*	−.31*	.18 *	.33*

* $p < .01$
Source: Iso-Ahola and Buttimer, 1982.

Clearly, then, the negative correlation between work and leisure ethic can be increased by selecting two instruments that contain statements about the opposite constructs, especially if the items explicitly put work against leisure. It may be that such scales awaken subjects into the dialectical

Table 3.4 Correlational analysis between the seven different measures; the correlations in brackets represent the range of partial correlations with age, sex, nationality, religion, and occupational status partialled out

	1	2	3	4	5	6	7
1. Goldstein & Eichhorn							
2. Mirels & Garrett	.52 (50–52)						
3. Blood	.30 (29–30)	.46 (45–48)					
4. Hammond & Williams	.53 (52–53)	.60 (58–61)	.42 (41–43)				
5a. Buchholz (Leisure)	-.28 (-27–29)	-.36 (-37–37)	-.28 (-28–29)	-.22 (-21–22)			
5b. Buchholz (Work)	.28 (25–27)	.45 (42–45)	.22 (22–23)	.45 (42–45)	.00 (01–62)		
6. Ray	.29 (26–29)	.37 (33–39)	.32 (32–33)	.36 (32–37)	-.19 (-16–19)	.17 (17 + 18)	
7. Ho	.42 (41–43)	.60 (58–66)	.37 (36–38)	.59 (58–59)	-.09 (06–09)	.55 (54–55)	.37 (34–32)

thinking pattern in which work becomes contradictory, rather than complementary to leisure.

(p. 433)

Table 3.5 Higher order factor analysis of the eight scales

	Scales		Loading Factor 1	Factor 2
1.	Goldstein & Eichhorn (1961)	(PE)	.80	−.06
2.	Mirels & Garrett (1971)	(PWE)	.58	−.68
3.	Blood (1969)	(PPE)	.76	.22
4.	Hammond & Williams (1976)	(SoC)	.88	−.06
5a.	Buchholz (1977): leisure	(LE)	.14	.89
5b.	Buchholz (1977): work	(WE)	.75	.10
6.	Ray (1982)	(EPE)	.72	.22
7.	Ho (1984)	(AWE)	.87	−.07
Eigenvalue			4.22	1.42
Variance			52.9%	17.8%

More recently Furnham (1989) has administered all seven questionnaires reviewed in the previous sections to large groups of subjects from different nationalities. The results of the English subjects are presented in Table 3.4. Predictably, all the correlations were positive, though radically different in size. The questionnaire which correlated most highly with all the others was the well known Mirels and Garrett (1971) scale, while that which showed the lowest correlations was the Buchholz (1976) scale. In all, 26 of the 28 correlations were significant at the $p < .05$ level. These results were confirmed by a higher order factor analysis of the different questionnaires.

It should be pointed out that these correlations in Table 3.4 were partial correlations which, if anything, strengthens the case for conceptual and empirical overlap. Because the N was so large (over 100) it is not surprising that so many of the correlations were significant, but then this was predictable given that all were supposed to be measuring the same thing.

The question remains why the correlations are not higher if all seven scales were supposedly measuring the same thing. Three possible explanations, which are not mutually exclusive, are relevant. First, each questionnaire focused on different aspects of the PWE and hence tapped attitudes to, and beliefs about, different dimensions of this multifaceted concept. Secondly, the reliability of the questionnaires themselves differed considerably; hence, low correlations may simply reflect the poor psychometric qualities of some questionnaires as opposed to others. Finally there are always errors in test measurement which may account for some discrepancies in correlations.

Thus, although all the questionnaires are positively correlated, the size of the correlation suggests that they are tapping rather different aspects of the scale. This has been demonstrated by Furnham (1987a) who regressed two sets of 18 values (terminal and instrumental) ranked by the same subjects onto the Mirels and Garrett (1971) and the Buchholz (1976) PWE Scale. Although there was some overlap it was demonstrated that different values were significantly predictive (in the regression analysis) of the two different PWE Scales.

> Certainly these results do serve to caution researchers about not only the generalizability of findings across populations and time, but across different measures of the same thing.
>
> (Furnham, 1987a, p. 635)

The content of the measures

It has been suggested that the existing questionnaires that have been devised to measure the PWE differ primarily in the dimensions of facets of the PWE they measured.

Furnham (1990) included a content analysis of the seven measures reviewed earlier. In all, seven dimensions were reflected in the 93 items from different questionnaires.

It is quite clear from Table 3.6 that the different questionnaires focus their questions unevenly on very different aspects of the PWE. Whereas all seven questionnaires have some, and in two cases most, of their questions to do with 'hard work and success', only two have questions concerned with independence or self-reliance and two with spiritual or religious issues.

One can make predictions from Table 3.6 as to which scales are likely to correlate most highly (e.g. 3. Protestant Work Ethic and 7. Australian Work Ethic) and which to a very limited extent (1. Protestant Ethic and 6. Eclectic Protestant Ethic). The results presented in Table 3.4 show that to a large extent these predictions are confirmed.

Finally, this table shows the fairly limited number of dimensions that current PWE scales measure. Certainly, compared with the psychological facets of the PWE spelt out in Chapter 2, only a restricted range are considered. For instance, attitudes to time (e.g. procrastination or gratification), prudence, and asceticism are missed from nearly all of the measures.

It seems that most psychometricians concerned with devising PWE measures have been more concerned with reliability than validity measuring the PWE as conceived by Weber.

Factor structure of the PWE measures

Nearly all researchers have looked upon the PWE as a unidimensional construct. However, studies that have factor-analysed the extant measures have found that they certainly contain more than one clearly identifiable factor. For instance Heaven (1989) factor analysed both the Mirels and Garrett (1971)

Table 3.6 Content analysis of the seven work ethic scales – seven coding categories

	Scales	Items	Work as an end to itself	Hard work and success	leisure	Money/efficiency	Spiritual/religious	morals	Independence/self-reliance
1.	Protestant Ethic (PE) (Goldstein & Eichhorn, 1961)	4	2 (50%)	2 (50%)					
2.	Protestant Work Ethic (PWE) (Mirels & Garrett, 1971)	19	2 (10.5%)	8 (42.1%)	5 (26.3%)	2 (10.5%)	1 (5.2%)	1 (5.2%)	
3.	Pro-Protestant Ethic (PPE) Scale (Blood, 1969)	8	2 (25%)	1 (12.5%)	3 (37.5%)	2 (25%)			
4.	Spirit of Capitalism (SoC) Scale (Hammond & Williams, 1976)	4	1 (16.6%)	2 (33.3%)		2 (33.3%)			1 (16.6%)
5a.	Leisure Ethic (LE)	8			8 (100%)				
5b.	Work Ethic (WE) (Buchholz, 1977)	7		2 (28.5%)					5 (71.4%)
6.	Eclectic Protestant Ethic (EPE) Scale (Ray, 1982)	18		1 (5.5%)		4 (22.2%)	6 (33.3%)	7 (38.8%)	
7.	Australian Work Ethic (AWE) Scale (Ho, 1984)	7	1 (14.2%)	5 (71.4%)				1 (14.2%)	

and the Ray (1982) scales. Whereas the former appeared to be unidimensional, having one major factor labelled *striving*, the latter had three factors labelled *belief in God*, *hard work*, and *thrift and enjoyment*. When these four factor scores were inter-correlated, only one of the six correlations was significant providing yet further evidence of the multi-dimensional structure of the PWE measures.

Furnham (1989b) gave all seven PWE questionnaires to over 1,000 subjects and factor analysed the 78 questions.

Table 3.7 shows the results of the factor analysis including the mean standard deviation and loading of each item over .30 on the factor. In all five factors emerged, accounting for over a third of the total variance. The first factor had 27 items loading > 0.30 on it which is just over a third of all items. Items from all seven PWE scales loaded on it, including one item (25%) of the Goldstein and Eichhorn (1961) scale; 10 items (52%) of the Mirels and Garrett (1971) scale; 2 items (25%) of the Blood (1969) scale; 2 items (33%) of the Hammond and Williams (1976) scale; 2 items (28%) of the Buchholz (1977) work scale; 3 items (16%) of the Ray (1982) scale, and all 7 items (100%) of the Ho (1984) scale. Clearly all the scales tap what is considered to be the fundamental dimension underlying the PWE – respect for, admiration of, and willingness to take part in, hard work.

The second factor was bipolar and accounted for seven and a half per cent of the variance. All three leisure items from the 19-item Mirels and Garrett (1971) loaded along with all 8 items (100%) of the Buchholz (1977) scale. Those items loading positively were against leisure while those loading negatively were for it. The fact that these items loaded on a separate orthogonal factor suggests that being pro-leisure is not the opposite of being in favour of hard work.

The fourth factor contained all 7 items (100%) from the Buchholz (1977) scale. What distinguishes this from those of others appears to be their stress on independence from others, indeed a theme which can be found in the work of Weber (1905). All three highest loading items (49, 51, 52) stress the avoidance of dependence.

The final factor contained 5 items (26%) of the Mirels and Garrett (1971) scale, one item (25%) from the Goldstein and Eichhorn (1961) scale, and one item (12%) from the Buchholz (1977) leisure scale. This factor tends to have items loading on it which stress asceticism – the damages of having too much time and money. This theme too can be found in the work of Weber (1905).

The five factors emerging from the orthogonal factor analysis of all 77 items then appeared to reveal factors not unlike those found in Weber's (1905) original work: belief in hard work, the role of leisure, religious and moral beliefs, a stress on independence from others, and asceticism.

The factor analytic results confirmed both the content and correlational analysis. Indeed, five clearly interpretable factors emerged which *all* seem to be fundamental to the PWE. Yet not all scales consider attitudes to leisure (e.g. Ho, 1984), and it is primarily the Ray (1982) scale that considers any aspects of theological beliefs. Further, it is primarily the Buchholz (1977) work ethic subscale that taps beliefs about independence and self-reliance which are almost totally ignored by the other scales.

Table 3.7 Factor analytic results showing loadings from PWE questionnaires (A–G)

		Loading	Mean	SD
1. The worst part about being sick is that work does not get done.	A	0.30	3.56	1.79
2. There are few satisfactions equal to the realization that one has done his best at a job.	B	0.38	5.17	1.49
3. The most difficult college courses usually turn out to be the most rewarding.	B	0.33	4.07	1.70
4. Most people who do not succeed in life are just plain lazy.	B	0.38	2.81	1.65
5. The self-made man is likely to be more ethical than the man born to wealth.	B	0.40	3.68	1.82
6. Any man who is able and willing to work hard has a good chance of succeeding.	B	0.61	5.20	1.41
7. People who fail at a job have usually not tried hard enough.	B	0.40	3.29	1.44
8. Hard work offers little guarantee of success.	B	0.44	4.53	1.53
9. The person who can approach an unpleasant task with enthusiasm is the person who gets ahead.	B	0.56	5.04	1.40
10. If one works hard enough he or she is likely to make a good life for him/herself.	B	0.72	4.85	1.39
11. A distaste for hard work usually reflects a weakness of character.	B	0.33	3.72	1.63
12. Hard work makes one a better person.	C	0.48	4.14	1.57
13. A good indication of a person's worth is how well they do their work.	C	0.37	3.97	1.67
14. Hard work is a good builder of character.	D	0.52	4.81	1.35
15. A person without debts who inherits a lot of money should invest it for the future rather than spend it.	D	0.30	4.50	1.66
16. By working hard a person can overcome every obstacle that life presents.	F	0.60	2.99	1.62

		Loading	Mean	SD
17. One should work like a slave at everything he or she undertakes until he/she is satisfied with the results.	F	0.31	3.09	1.56
18. Saving always pays off in the end.	G	0.36	4.56	1.55
19. The only way to get anything worthwhile is to save for it.	G	0.30	4.32	1.61
20. If one works hard enough, he or she is likely to make a good life for him/herself.	H	0.75	4.67	1.53
21. People who work deserve success.	H	0.57	5.17	1.38
22. Hard work is fulfilling in itself.	H	0.52	4.31	1.47
23. Nothing is impossible if you work hard enough.	H	0.67	4.04	1.82
24. If you work hard you will succeed.	H	0.75	4.10	1.56
25. You should be the best at what you do.	H	0.47	4.61	1.79
26. By working hard an individual can overcome most obstacles that life presents and make his or her own way in the world.	H	0.73	4.36	1.53
27. Hard work is not a key to success.	H	0.46	4.09	1.65
		Eigenvalue	13.33	
		Variance	17.3%	
28. Our society would have fewer problems if people had less leisure time.	B	0.40	2.57	1.50
29. People should have more leisure time to spend in relaxation.	B	− 0.74	3.23	1.37
30. Life would be more meaningful if we had more leisure time.	B	− 0.68	3.90	1.43
31. Increased leisure time is bad for society.	E	0.52	5.08	1.49
32. The less hours one spends working and the more leisure time available the better.	E	− 0.57	3.76	1.42
40. Success means having ample time to pursue leisure activities.	E	− 0.35	3.86	1.72
41. The present trend towards a shorter working week is to be encouraged.	E	− 0.67	4.32	1.60
42. Leisure time activities are more interesting than work.	E	− 0.38	4.23	1.59
43. Work takes too much of our time leaving little time to relax.	E	− 0.60	4.10	1.41
44. More leisure time is good for people.	E	− 0.78	4.57	1.31

		Loading	Mean	SD
45. The trend towards more leisure is not a good thing.	E	0.70	4.68	1.37
		Eigenvalue	5.78	
		Variance	7.5%	
46. There is some great plan for the affairs of men, the end of which no mortal eye can foresee.	G	0.59	3.96	1.84
47. I believe in God	G	0.84	4.77	2.27
48. I believe in life after death.	G	0.88	4.53	2.20
49. Once you die, that's all there is.	G	0.85	4.92	2.13
50. The spirit of God lives within every man.	G	0.74	4.30	2.23
51. Predestination (idea that some people have been chosen for salvation) is a myth.	G	0.30	3.08	2.07
52. For girls to keep themselves virgins before they are married is old-fashioned and unnecessary.	G	0.33	6.01	1.50
53. There is nothing wrong with having sex with another man's wife.	G	0.33	6.01	1.50
		Eigenvalue	3.98	
		Variance	5.2%	
54. By working hard a person can overcome every obstacle that life presents.	F	0.31	2.99	1.62
55. One must avoid dependence on other persons wherever possible.	F	0.63	4.33	1.71
56. A person can learn better on the job by striking out boldly on their own than by following the advice of others.	F	0.58	3.23	1.54
57. Only those who depend on themselves get ahead in life.	F	0.72	3.62	1.58
58. One should work like a slave at everything he or she undertakes until he/she is satisfied with the results.	F	0.45	3.09	1.58
59. To be superior a person must stand alone.	F	0.68	2.72	1.64
		Eigenvalue	2.53	
		Variance	2.3%	
60. Hard work still counts for more in a successful business operation than all of the new ideas you read in the newspapers.	A	0.43	4.59	1.51

		Loading	Mean	SD
61. Most people spend too much time in unprofitable amusement.	B	0.58	3.18	1.57
62 Our society would have fewer problems if people had less leisure time.	B	0.58	2.57	1.50
63. Money acquired easily (e.g. through gambling or speculation) is usually spent unwisely.	B	0.64	4.17	1.69
64. I often feel I would be more successful if I sacrificed certain pleasures.	B	0.30	4.19	1.78
65. The credit card is a ticket to careless spending.	B	0.30	4.10	1.78
66. Increased leisure time is bad for society.	E	– 0.37	5.08	1.49
	Eigenvalue		2.28	
	Variance		2.2%	

It is therefore no surprise that different PWE scales show a rather different and sometimes dramatically different set of correlations with other variables (Furnham, 1984c). Indeed in a recent study looking at the relationship between PWE beliefs and values, Furnham (1987a) used the Buchholz (1977) *and* Mirels and Garrett (1971) scale to correlate them with instrumental and terminal values. Although 6 of the 18 correlations between the Buchholz (1977) scale and terminal values were significant and a similar number between the Mirels and Garrett (1971) scale and the terminal values, there was only any overlap on two (i.e. under a third). In other words, depending on the PWE scale that is used rather different results will occur. This of course makes a review of the literature complicated (Furnham, 1984c, 1989b) because if there is evidence of non or poor replication of experimental findings using different and clearly non-equivalent measures of the PWE one cannot be sure whether the findings are more robust or indeed whether the scales are not measuring the same thing. By contrast, of course, the replication of a finding using different PWE measures is a testament of their robustness.

Psychologists' major contribution to the PWE literature has been to provide psychometrically sound measures of the PWE to be used in empirical research. Although these measures are themselves open to fairly serious psychometric criticism particularly with respect to the inadequate or indeed poor validity data they have been used successfully in a number of research programmes. Nor should it be imagined that empirical results are free from paradox (Atieh, Brief, and Vollrath, 1987) or that PWE beliefs alone capture a person's total work orientation (Nord, Brief, Atieh, and Doherty, 1988). However, for work to progress in this area it seems that a number of facets of the questionnaire measures need to be considered. First, that instead of yielding a unidimensional single measure of PWE beliefs, a multi-dimensional scale be created which measures such things as attitudes to, and belief about, asceticism, independence, time, leisure, and work. Indeed, the items from the seven scales reviewed and the aforementioned factor-analytic results provide a useful beginning. Secondly that the measure be shown to have not only concurrent but also predictive validity. Finally, that the domain in which PWE belief subscales are salient to work and other behaviours are specified.

Criticism of the measure

Two types of criticisms may be placed at the door of these questionnaire measures of PWE – or any other work-beliefs. The first are general objections that may be made against any (or all) self measures. These include:

- The possibility that respondents are deliberately showing a 'fake' response for a number of reasons (i.e. to please or displease the investigator).
- The possibility that respondents' answers are not truthful, not because they are deliberately faking but rather because they cannot accurately recall their behaviours or cannot accurately report on their beliefs, needs, etc.
- The possibility that beliefs in no way reflect actual behaviours so what ever people say about their work beliefs, these do not correlate with or predict their actual behaviours.
- The possibility that one is limited to certain samples who can read and write – in other words, a bias to the articulate and literate.
- The possibility that people do not understand or find unclear the wording of the questions given to them and respond to different meanings than were meant by the deviser of the test.

Each of these objections has an element of truth in them but there is a sufficiently large literature on these topics to suggest that although these problems make for less efficient or accurate measurements, they in no way invalidate the use of these questionnaires (Furnham, 1986b).

Secondly, specific criticisms of the PWE measures may be made. Many of the scales have more items in favour of the work ethic than against it, so introducing the possibility of bias. Furthermore, it is not entirely clear whether the opposite of strong work ethic beliefs are weak work ethic beliefs or strong leisure ethic beliefs. An important criticism of nearly all the scales is that PWE beliefs are multi-dimensional, yet nearly all the questionnaires provide a simple single total score. Subscale scores would substantially improve measurement as it would show how consistent or inconsistent people were in their various PWE beliefs. A further criticism concerns the fact that too often PWE measures have been validated on students who are for the most part inexperienced in the world of work and fairly unrepresentative of the population as a whole (being younger, more intelligent, etc.). It may well be that the psychometric properties of these questionnaires may be less reliable and valid with non-student respondents.

Finally, many of the individual scale items appear to be rather extreme and unsubtle, and very few refer to religious or theological beliefs. A measure which is more like the original Weberian thesis should have questions concerning not only work and pleasure, but religion, money, nationality, etc. Yet as Furnham (1984c) has stressed:

> Nevertheless it should be pointed out that they are probably no better or worse than numerous other measures in this area of work beliefs, attitudes and behaviour.

(p. 93)

Projective techniques

Projective tests usually consist of such things as inkblots, pictures, and other ambiguous stimuli that a person has to describe. They are deliberately vague and ambiguous so that rather than give a simple veridical description, people project something of themselves onto the stimulus. They are thus seen by advocates of this methodology, to provide a rich measure of idiodynamics (innermost thoughts and feelings).

Critics of these techniques, and there are many, argue that these measures have poor reliability (over time *and* between scorers); show very little validity evidence; are subject to experimenter effects (like sex or race); that there is no adequate theory to account for the claims of users; that it is doubtful whether a single (somewhat simple) measure can tap a large number of variables, as claimed, etc. One response to this attack has been to develop a method for objective, reliable scoring and analyses.

Although projective techniques have not been used to measure the PWE *per se*, they have been used to measure such things as need for achievement (see Chapter 2) and related issues like anxiety over failure. The most popular projective technique used in this regard is that developed by Murray (1938) and called the Thematic Apperception Test. This consists of a set of pictures, mainly containing people, that the subject is asked to describe.

McClelland *et al.* (1953) used the TAT to assess need for achievement and claimed that their scoring method led into inter-rater reliability of .90. Customarily a subject is shown 4–6 of the pictures and asked to write or tell a story about it bearing in mind the questions: What is happening? What led up to the situation? What is being thought? and what will happen? The task of the scorer is first to decide whether there is any achievement-related imagery about such things as unique accomplishments, inventions, long-term achievements, wanting life-success. If the story does contain such imagery, the stories receive a score of 1.00 and ten other subcategories are analysed for particular kinds of achievement-related content. The test is presented to people as a test of 'creative imagination'. Some idea of this scoring can be seen from Table 3.8.

Table 3.8 Typical stories written when achievement, affiliation, and power motives have been aroused to a picture of a man at a drawing board

Achievement Arousal	Affiliation Arousal	Power Arousal
George is an engineer who (need, +1) *wants to* win a competition in which the man with (achievement imagery: standard of excellence, +1) *the most practicable drawing* will be awarded the contract to build a bridge. He is taking a moment to think (goal anticipation, +1) *how* happy he *will* be if he wins. He has been (block, world, +1) *baffled* by how to make such a *long span strong,* but remembers (instrumental act, +1) to *specify a new steel alloy* of great strength, submits his entry, but does not win and (goal state, negative, +1) is *very unhappy.*	George is an engineer who is working late. He is (affiliation imagery, +1) *worried that his wife will be annoyed* with him for neglecting her. (block, world, +1) She has been *objecting* that he cares more about his work than his wife and family. (block, personal, +1) He seems *unable* to satisfy both his boss and his wife, (need, +1) but he *loves her* very much, and (instrumental act, +1) will do his best to *finish up fast* and get home to her.	This is Georgiadis, a (prestige of actor, +1) *famous architect,* who (need, +1) wants to win a competition which will establish who is (power imagery, +1) *the best architect in the world.* His chief rival, Bulakovsky, (block, world, +1) *has stolen his best ideas,* and he is dreadfully afraid of the (goal anticipation, negative, +1) *disgrace of losing.* But he comes up with (instrumental act, +1) *a great new idea,* which absolutely (powerful effect, +1) *bowls the judges over,* and wins!
Thema + 1, Total *n* Achievement score = +7	Thema + 1, Total *n* Affiliation score = +6	Total *n* Power score = +7

Source: David C. McClelland, *Assessing Human Motivation*, Morristown, N.J.: General Learning Press, 1971.

Indeed it is because the test is presented as one of creative imagination that it may be that it has low reliability but high validity because the vast majority of the individuals taking the test are classified identically on two occasions if a dichotomous high–low subject separation is used. But along with this controversy others exist concerning the TAT: the pictures are outdated and it would seem relevant to find some match between the age, race, and sex of the respondents and the pictures. Also the conditions in which one takes the test are important as it has been shown that in conditions that arouse a need for achievement, such as an emphasis on doing well or being assessed, one typically obtains a higher score than when people are tested in neutral or relaxed conditions.

The debate over the validity of projective techniques is a long-standing and fairly complex one. The intricacies cannot be discussed here. Suffice it to say that those researchers who have chosen to use this technique claim impressive evidence for it. Of course it has its limitations and drawbacks but used in conjunction with other, perhaps better validated measures, it appears to offer a dynamic depth approach to the evaluation of the PWE. It should be noted, however, that this seems particularly paradoxical that a belief system that prides itself on rationality should be measured in such a way.

Content analysis of writings

Another method, akin to textual analysis, designed to investigate beliefs is content analysis. Essentially the idea of this approach is that the content of written materials reveals the beliefs of the writer. Usually the method involves devising either a number of specific categories or criterion concepts that are the focus of the investigation and counting their incidence in a given set of writings. Of course the number, nature, and sensitivity of the categories or concepts vary from study to study. However, as a measure of reliability it is usually required that more than one content analysis is done of the same material (using the same scheme) and the results compared. Further it may be possible to provide some evidence of validity by comparing the content analysis with other measures of the same phenomena or ideally with objective behavioural criteria.

Through content analysis the beliefs of both individuals and groups can be studied. While the PWE beliefs of certain historical figures may be of interest because, for instance, of their own prodigious working habits, the fact that they were important opinion-leaders, great statesmen, or authors, it is much more interesting to ascertain, where possible, the beliefs of whole groups.

It was McClelland (1961) who developed perhaps the most extensive and sophisticated method to content analyse the PWE. He argued that children's stories contain sufficient information to assess the motivational levels among contemporary nations. He suggested that these stories had various theoretical and practical advantages:

- They derive from the same oral tradition presented in folk tales.

- They have existed for at least a generation (and often much more) enshrined in school books.

- The stories are simple, short, and imaginative but do not deal with factual or historical events or political problems.

- They represent popular culture, considered appropriate for all children to read, not merely those from a specific class.

- The stories are less subtle and more direct in their 'message' than many other forms of literature.

McClelland (1961) assembled collected stories from 23 countries for the periods 1920–9 and 1946–55. The stories were then content analysed at two

101

Table 3.9

Impulse Control: + or –. The meaning of this category is the Ego is inhibiting the desire for self-indulgence as an end in itself, or as an anti-social behaviour. This suppression has either positive or negative consequences for him in terms of the outcome of the interaction sequence.

> *Example:*
> While Peter is lying in bed, he is frightened by shadows in the corner of the room. He decides to investigate himself, rather than calling his mother, who has a headache and should not be disturbed. Peter conquers the situation himself and is glad that he did not call his mother. Thus the situation has positive consequences for him.

This category of impulse control + is exemplified by the Christian ideology of turning the other cheek where the rewards for not expressing hostile impulses are great in the long range view.

> *Example:*
> Impulse control –. The good hearted straw takes pity on the ember and swims back to ferry him across the river. In the process, the straw catches fire and the ember drowns. In this case, inhibition of the impulse to let the ember get across on his own steam results in negative consequences for Ego.

Impulse Expression: + or –. The meaning of this category is that Ego is expressing impulses aimed at self-indulgence and gratification (egocentric) either in direct rejection of the feelings of others or in indirect neglect of the feelings of others. This expression has either positive or negative consequences for him in terms of the outcome of the interaction sequence (pride-before-a-fall, selfishness are also scored).

> *Example:*
> Impulse expression +. In the story of the mistletoe, the bad fairy dislikes the good fairy and wants to do him in. He manages this by getting a blind fairy to throw a harmful piece of mistletoe at the good fairy. The good fairy falls dead while the bad fairy gets away with his hostile purposes. Here then, impulse expression had positive results in terms of the goals of the bad fairy.

> *Example:*
> Impulse expression –. 'As they reached the middle of the water, the good hearted straw caught flame and the ember drowned. When the bladder saw that, he laughed so hard he burst. It served him right. Why was he so malicious?'

Achieved Status: The meaning here is to change one's rank in the social order, relative to other persons, or to gain recognition, by accomplishing some end, i.e., by doing something. The individual is evaluated in terms of his accomplishments or achievements, rather than in terms of his fixed characteristics, given by birth.

> *Example:*
> 'The sheep, in contrast to the goats, are blessed of God and know neither hunger nor cold, because they sheltered the Saint when he was in trouble and the goats did not.'

Source: McClelland, 1961.

levels, specific and general.

Table 3.9 gives examples of the specific coding categories and the other stories from which they were derived. He found these stories could be very reliably coded and that each country could be given a numerical score, the higher the number the more *n* Ach in the story. Furthermore, stories from the same country tended to correlate highly in terms of their actual scores so giv-

Table 3.10 Comparison of *n* achievement scores from children's readers (1950) and from stories written by groups of male students

Country	Mean n Ach. score from readers N=21 stories	SD	A. College level samples (percentage of students telling stories with achievement imagery)				Per cent of stories achievement related	Mean n Achievement scores	
			N	Picture				Verbal	Graphic
				#2 (%)	#8 (%)	#1 (%)			
US (general)	2.24	2.48	207	69	51	28	49		
US (Catholic)	3.62	3.14	146	63	56	21	47		
Lebanon	2.71	2.68	51	29	27	10	22		
India	2.71	2.46	50	56	44	18	39	3.79	—
Japan	1.29	1.77	50	62	82	22	55	8.33	+ .28
Germany	2.14	2.34	300	34	43	21	33	4.54	− .413
Brazil	1.14	1.96	50	62	64	4	43	5.22	+ .095
			B. Less selective high school samples						
US (general)	2.24	2.48	123	41	53				
Australia	2.38	2.34	c.50	41	50				

Picture #2 is of two men working at a machine in a shop; #8 is of a boy at a desk with an open book in front of him; and #1 is of an older man talking to a younger one (usually interpreted as a father and son).
From the mothers and sons study, verbal *n* achievement scores are based on stories written to pictures #2, #8, #1, #9 (man at a desk). (See Atkinson, 1958, Appendix III.)
Source: McClelland, 1961.

ing one confidence in this approach. Table 3.10 shows the results of an attempt to compare estimates of need for achievement level scores obtained from the content analysis of children's stories with those obtained by testing representative samples of individuals from the country concerned. The correlation over the seven samples was not only non-significant but negative, which may throw doubt on the validity of the *n* Ach scores. Yet McClelland (1961) argues that this is the result of a sampling and methodological error rather than an actual unreliability and goes on to show that the *n* Ach scores do predict economic growth as hypothesized.

This work illustrates most of the important problems associated with a content analysis of written (or spoken) material. Apart from the problem of giving sensitive coding categories and getting reliable scores from different coders, the major question concerns the representativeness of the material chosen. That is if the material is published stories, are the readers and writers representative of the group from which they come? Or if people are asked to tell stories about pictures they are shown, are the people and stories representative? Content analysis can yield interesting and right thematic insight into the beliefs, motives, and values of an individual or a group but unless it is properly done, results can be highly misleading.

Archival research

Archival or desk research is almost by definition historical in nature. It consists in going to some source of data about the past and extracting valid and reliable information that answers the questions that one has posed. This material may be published or not, verbal or numerical, written or spoken (in sound archives). The problems with archival research in general are threefold. First there often remains crucial gaps in archive records, or more importantly, the data were recorded in such a way that critical information was left out. Secondly there remains the question of the reliability of the data that is stored. Often impressive-looking tables on such things as unemployment, suicide rates, or church attendances are based on highly dubious or 'guesstimated' data. Thirdly that data gathered and recorded in different groups or countries that one might wish to compare, are tabulated quite differently. For instance, economic indicators such as growth, inflation, or unemployment may be measured and recorded differently (though reliably), hence it becomes highly difficult if not impossible to undertake comparisons.

However, archival research does have a number of advantages. First it allows one to test hypotheses over wider ranges of time and over many more societies than would otherwise be possible. Secondly, archival research is non-reactive and there is little chance that factors such as demand characteristics or evaluation apprehension will pose problems.

How might one use archival research to investigate the PWE? Both McClelland (1961), and Kelvin and Jarrett (1985), make extensive use of archival data to support their argument. For instance, the latter use many quotes from historical documents to show how frequently people in the seventeenth and nineteenth century complained about the laziness of workers, their poor time keeping, and their frequent absenteeism.

> In terms of its psychological characteristics, the concept of an 'ethic' refers to a system of values which the members of a group, sect, or society have internalised, so that actions based upon it may be regarded as acts of choice. In other words, acts based on an ethic are acts which the individual wants to do in their own right, and not because they are forced upon him by an external circumstance. Bearing in mind, then, that the great bulk of our society is supposed to have been permeated by a Work Ethic for generations, the essential facts seem to be these. The sixteenth and especially the seventeenth centuries saw the economic rise of a *section* of the middle class which was genuinely inspired by a sense of the religious significance of work, and of frugality in their personal lives – what Weber called 'asceticism'; and so the profits from work were not to

be used to indulge in luxuries, or to retire from work, but to create more work and thereby more opportunities for serving God. On that basis alone, anyone who believes that ours is, or ever predominantly was, a society rooted in the Protestant Work Ethic has failed to understand its most essential teaching; for one thing which the Protestant Work Ethic would not have tolerated is that productivity should increase the profits, wages, and luxuries of some, at the cost of unemployment for others. However, these values and sentiments were never more than those of a minority, and of middle-class rather than working- or upper-class origin. The notion that the generality of English workers were imbued with this Ethic just does not survive examination. For at least the last five hundred years, there is steady and consistent evidence of late coming to work, long breaks at work, early leaving of work, downing of tools at the first opportunity, and the like disdain for work.

(pp. 102–3)

McClelland (1961) too relies heavily on archival material, not only of the children's stories and folk tales that he content analysed but also of economic data which constitute the dependent variable in his hypotheses. These archival records are used to gather information on the number of patents taken out (1810–1950) in America, coal imports in Britain (1550–1800), etc., all of which are shown to be systematically related to n Ach.

More recently journalistic speculation about the decline of the PWE has tended to use, rather casually, some archival data on such things as absenteeism, hours worked, strikes, etc. The problem with these analyses, apart from those mentioned, is the assumption that they are, of themselves, *indications* of the PWE. That is, absenteeism rates may be a function of numerous factors as well as of work alteration and declining PWE beliefs. Similarly, increases in productivity may have as much to do with automation as with an increase in PWE beliefs. The danger then with using some types of archival data is to over-interpret what they mean in terms of the PWE.

Conclusion

This chapter has been concerned with the measurement of PWE beliefs and behaviour. Four different types of measures have been mentioned but the all-important question of *what* one is measuring has been ducked.

Is the PWE an unconscious need with various motivational tendencies such as 'hope of success' and 'fear of failure' as some have conceived of need for achievement? Can one distinguish between the PWE motive which is a stable personality trait and motivation which is thought of as a tendency aroused by a specific situation? Is the PWE a conscious structure, an organized belief system that is acquired in the process of socialization? How do PWE beliefs relate to general behaviour like risk taking, persistence, etc.? Is the PWE an attributional style that allows one to attribute blame and praise to self and others?

The above, and many more highly salient questions regarding how psychologists have approached the PWE, have not been asked. They have, however, been asked of similar and overlapping constructs, and it may, as a result, be possible to at least begin to answer them. Since the 1970s when researchers have favoured interactive (personality and situation) process explanations for phenomena, three principal factors of motivation have been distinguished:

- *Personality/Motive* – this is usually subdivided into various subgroups, for instance, success and failure motives which can be further subdivided, for instance, fear of failure might be further subdivided into fear of failure based on self concept of low ability vs that based on a fear of failure based on social consequences. Furthermore, other related concepts such as attribution style and future time perspective may be included.
- *Expectance* – these are situation-outcome expectancies which describe the subjective degree of probability that a current situation leads certain outcomes given the intervention of some action. This idea is that part of any construct are a set of specific expectations based on a particular causal attribution of the event. Thus, for instance, one may specify instrumentality such that people have generalized and specific expectations for positive and negative results (e.g. success vs failure; poverty vs wealth) given certain actions (hard work, investment, etc.).
- *Incentives* – the consequences of action outcomes have definitive incentive values like improved self-evaluation, positive evaluation by others, a better chance of approaching a superordinate goal. Because different incentives appeal to different people it is important to specify what acts as an incentive to different people.

Should one conceive of the PWE as a trait, a belief system, an unconscious motive, an expectancy construct, or an incentive value? Clearly it has been conceived of quite differently by different researchers which may, in part, account for why so varied measurement techniques have been used.

Zealots would no doubt argue strongly for one method such as self-report and specify clearly the criteria to be used in the selection of a specific instrument. Eclectics on the other hand might argue that no one method is superior to any others but it depends most specifically on the nature of the research question. Perhaps because it is manifestly apparent that different methods have their different problems, each may be profitably used in different circumstances.

Chapter four

The aetiology and distribution of PWE beliefs

The 'work ethic' holds that labour is good in itself; that a man or woman becomes a better person by virtue of the act of working. America's competitive spirit, the 'work ethic' of this people, is alive and well on Labour Day, 1971.

Richard Nixon

Work is the refuge of people who have nothing better to do.

Oscar Wilde

Term, holidays, term, holidays till we leave school and then work, work, work till we die.

C.S. Lewis

There is no substitute for hard work.

Thomas Edison

Calvinists and Jews have the religious fervour necessary for capitalistic enterprise.

Werner Sambart

Introduction

This chapter is primarily concerned with two issues – the origin and maintenance of PWE beliefs and behaviours in the individual; and the distribution of these beliefs and behaviours in a culture, sub-culture, or country. The aetiology of these beliefs will be considered primarily at the level of the individual, that is psychologically. The origin of these beliefs in a group (religious or otherwise), their spread, and maintenance is essentially a sociological question, indeed part of the great PWE debate. The central aetiological question is how do individuals come to hold and value PWE beliefs and values. How are they socialized into the child? Who is most responsible for their origin? How do schools build on or destroy PWE values inculcated by parents? In short what child-rearing patterns are most clearly responsible for people holding PWE beliefs? Secondly how are PWE beliefs distributed in this and other societies? There are numerous and constant speculations about changes in the PWE but what do the available data indicate? Of course, as we shall see, the available data, usually based on survey findings, are fairly problematic and cannot always be used to answer questions posed of them. This occurs for a number of reasons:

● Measures of the PWE are incomparable either because they are different (overlapping but not equivalent) or because different groups have been measured at different times in different countries and it is uncertain which factor accounts for the results.
● Sampling differences, error, and limitations mean it is highly dubious to generalize from available results to the population as a whole.
● Only limited dimensions of the PWE have been measured (see Chapter 3) and indeed different studies have focused on different aspects of the PWE.

Despite these and other problems, the studies actually examining the PWE make fascinating reading. Furthermore, they do provide partial evidence for those interested in speculating about changes in the PWE.

Socializing children into the work ethic

How and when do children, adolescents, and adults learn, acquire, and internalize PWE beliefs and manifest PWE behaviours? A great deal of research has been undertaken on children's socialization, much of which could be applied to the PWE though this has rarely been done. Although McClelland (1961) stressed the importance of child rearing patterns on the aetiology of *n* Ach (see Chapter 1), there are actually very few studies on how young children acquire work beliefs.

There remains, however, considerable interest in religion and parental child-rearing orientations. For instance Alwin (1986) in a major reanalysis and gathering of more data concluded:

> (1) substantial change has occurred among some religioethnic groups in their expressed preference for behaviour in children; (2) these changes have resulted in a general convergence of parental values among major religioethnic categories; (3) these changes are reflected in a variety of data sets, as well as across measures of parental values and parental reports of their habits of child-rearing; (4) few, if any, differences exist among major religioethnic groups in their orientation to the extended family; and (5) parental child-rearing orientations are linked more strongly to forms of religious participation than they are to denominational differences.
>
> (p. 436)

Specifically Alwin (1986) showed that Catholic–Protestant differences in values and orientations declined dramatically. However, educational and socioeconomic parental differences do apparently lead to differences in child-rearing patterns.

Despite this paucity of research there is a plethora of studies on the development of the various over-lapping constructs, set out in Chapter 2, which could inform one directly about the PWE. Consider, for instance, locus of control which is clearly a component of the PWE. People who believe in the PWE tend to have an internal locus of control which is itself linked to achievement. For instance internals tend to work harder at intellectual and performance tasks; their efforts tend to be more rewarded by better school and university grades; they receive more desirable reinforcements by delaying gratification; they seek out more information and resist social influence, and tend to attribute responsibility to themselves rather than others.

How are internal–external loci of control beliefs socialized? There is some evidence that warm, protective, positive, and nurturant child-rearing patterns are related to the subsequent development of internal locus of control. However, children exposed to inconsistent parental discipline, either by one or between parents, often see the world as capricious and unpredictable and tend to have external beliefs. Similarly early experiences of little access to power, restricted social mobility, opportunity, or material advantages tend to lead to external belief systems. Some studies have actually examined the antecedents of locus of control. Levenson (1973), who divided external loci into two factors – powerful others and chance – noted:

> The rationale between this tripartite differentiation came from the reasoning that people who believe the world is unordered (chance) behave and think differently from people who believe the world is ordered but that powerful others are in control. In the latter case a potential for control exists.
>
> (Levenson, 1973, p. 261)

In fact, Levenson's (1973) study throws considerable light on this study as she found that high perceptions of control by powerful others are associated with low parental nurturance, high paternal and maternal affective punishment and achievement pressures, and high paternal protectiveness and high maternal physical punishment for males only. Thus, parental behaviours that are associated with powerful other beliefs include punishing and controlling behaviours, while inconsistent and depriving others are most associated with chance locus of control beliefs. Curiously, none of the parental behaviours were associated with internal locus of control beliefs.

Three interesting points arise out of this study by Levenson (1973) and others in the area. Firstly, that parental behaviours and childhood experiences may influence males and females differently and that paternal vs maternal behaviours may have different effects. Secondly that childhood experiences may

109

relate to one pole of a dimension and not the other. That is, parental practices may prevent or encourage external locus of control (i.e. low PWE scores) but not actually affect internal scores. There may be a two-factor phenomenon in operation whereby some experiences prevent external beliefs, while a different set of factors actually encourages internal beliefs.

Finally, parental practices may be reinforced or extinguished by secondary experiences at school or in other social groups, suggesting that parental practices and childhood experiences may as well serve to cancel each other out as to replicate each other.

Although both somewhat speculative and dependent on a rather limited number of studies, McClelland (1961) spelt out in his terms how child-rearing practices lead directly to *n* Ach (and PWE beliefs). He placed heavy reliance on Winterbottom's (1958) findings which showed that mothers of high, as opposed to low, achieving sons expected 'self-reliant mastery' at an earlier age. Boys were encouraged to master something, and once they had done so, held to do it by restrictions on regressive behaviour. Low achieving sons tend to have mothers with lower expectations, and who encourage more dependency. McClelland (1961) recognized that attempts to replicate and extend these findings were not always successful because of the role of other intervening variables like social class. He solved some problems of contradictory findings by noting that early mastery training promotes *n* Ach, provided it does not reflect generalized restrictiveness, authoritarianism, or rejection of parents eager for the child to look after himself and not be a burden.

> The boy can be put on his own either too early, as in the predominantly lower-class, early caretaking families, or too late, as in the predominantly middle class families that expect achievement and independence quite late. Neither condition is optimal for producing high *n* Achievement. Instead what is desirable in somewhat idealized terms, is a stress on meeting certain achievement standards somewhere between the ages of six and eight (at least according to the mothers' reports), neither too early for the boy's abilities nor too late for him to internalize those standards as his own.
>
> (p. 345)

This idea of an optimal or critical period is frequently found in the child development literature and one that, quite clearly, may be applied to PWE beliefs and behaviours.

Three other findings from McClelland's (1961) work and review on the socialization of *n* Ach are particularly worth mentioning. Firstly, there seemed to be an inverse *U* curvilinear relationship between a son's and mother's *n* Ach so supporting the optimal idea. Secondly, studies comparing parent–child interaction for boys with high and low *n* Ach seem to show the former were characterized by higher set standards of excellence, greater warmth, and lower authoritarian behaviours. Thirdly, in a variety of countries, compared to Protestant values, more traditional Catholics do appear to have values and attitudes associated with lower achievement. There are therefore a number of consistent findings which suggest that PWE beliefs or at least their component parts are clearly and systematically related to early socialization.

The transmission of PWE beliefs and behaviours

Most parents attempt to transmit to their offspring their own beliefs and values and are concerned about the role of schools, the media, and other adolescents in frustrating or assisting them in this endeavour. Parents are also extremely eager to know how to communicate these values. Hence there have been a large number of studies on the communication of values such as political, educational, or religious values. For instance, in a recent study Clark *et al.* (1988) examined the transmission of religious beliefs and found strong evidence for the fact that mothers and fathers functioned differently in transmitting religious values to their children.

Furnham (1987b) has argued that it is entirely reasonable to expect children's work-related behaviours to correspond with those of their parents as the latter communicate their beliefs, attitudes, and values in the way they perform activities in the home, discuss their job experiences, reinforce their work habits and achievements. Some highly relevant work has already been done in this field. Feather (1978) set out to investigate the hypothesis that children with highly conservative (on social, moral, and political issues) parents would themselves be relatively conservative compared to children whose parents are less conservative in their social attitudes. He found, as predicted, that parents were more conservative than their children; females more conservative than males; fathers and mothers most alike in conservative beliefs, followed by fathers and daughters then wife and daughters. However, in interpreting his results Feather (1978) noted:

One should remember that many other factors may influence attitudes apart from the socializing effects of the family. For example, the relatively high degree of father/wife resemblance in the present study could be due to a mutual socializing influence between husband and wife within the family context, so that each comes to resemble the other in the attitudes they hold as they learn to live with one another and as they work out solutions to common problems. But the resemblance could also be an outcome of mate selection, husbands tending to marry wives with attitudes similar to their own (and vice-versa). Both husband and wife may subsequently be interested in and exposed to similar types of information (e.g. through the mass media, friendship groups, social and political memberships, etc.), information that might buttress their shared attitudes, even perhaps increasing some initial similarities. Again, the low degree of son/daughter resemblance could be due to differences in the ways boys and girls are socialized within families. But it could also relate to differences in the nature of peer group pressures as between the sexes, and to other wider social influences that move the sexes along somewhat different paths corresponding to normative expectations about how males and females 'typically' differ.

(p. 274)

In a larger study of generational differences in work values Wijting, Arnold, and Conrad (1978) investigated parental transmission of work values. They tested children and their parents in the sixth, ninth, tenth, and twelfth grade and found that at earlier ages there is great similarity in values between children and their like-sexed parent but older boys and girls are most similar to their fathers. Thus, although there is some disagreement as to which parent holds beliefs like which child at which age, there is general agreement about generational similarities in work-related values.

Furnham (1987b) actually set about comparing the PWE and related beliefs of parents and children. The results are shown in Table 4.1. The correlation results from the psychographic factors are particularly interesting. Fathers and mothers had significantly similar economic beliefs, PWE, and internal locus of control scores, all of which were correlated. Fathers and children had significant positive correlations on economic beliefs, need for achievement, chance locus of control, and powerful others, while mothers and children had a similar pattern for economic beliefs and external locus of control scores but did not show a positive correlation with need for achievement yet did for the PWE. Thus, parents were most like their children with respect to economic beliefs.

The findings from this study are nearly all predictable in terms of the original theory (McClelland, 1961), the previous study, and other research in the field (Feather, 1978). The results are like Feather's (1978) in three respects: first, there were consistent highly significant correlations between parents and

Table 4.1 Correlations between parents and children on all variables ($n = 63$)

	Fathers & mothers	Fathers & children	Mothers & children
Age	0.62***	0.40***	0.54***
Education	0.50***	0.11	0.14
Vote	0.39**	0.23*	0.25*
Economic beliefs	0.70***	0.34**	0.43***
Postponement of gratification	−0.01	−0.05	−0.01
Need for achievement	−0.03	0.29**	−0.01
Protestant Work Ethic	0.32**	0.14	0.24*
Internal locus of control	0.34**	−0.02	0.13
Chance locus of control	0.20	0.24*	0.22*
Powerful others	0.00	0.25*	0.28**

*** $p < 0.001$; ** $p < 0.01$; * $p < 0.05$

children in the conservatism measure (economic beliefs); secondly, that daughters are more like their parents than sons; thirdly, parents' correlations with each other were higher than between parents and children. These results also suggest that parents were influencing their children towards various beliefs – particularly economic beliefs, locus of control, and to a lesser extent PWE beliefs – similar to their own, but that there was a small discrepancy between the sexes with daughters being more like parents than sons.

Apart from measurement problems and error variance parent/child differences of this sort are difficult to interpret because various factors such as life-cycle effects, social and historical trends, and other socializing agents such as schools, the media, etc., are confounding and/or mediating variables. It might be expected that parents with certain beliefs about work would attempt to control their children's secondary socialization by ensuring they attend specific schools, take part in select extracurricular activities, etc. Nevertheless by the age they have reached university many of these students have questioned or rejected the belief-system of their parents. Hence one may expect correlations between parents and children to be lower at this age than at various previous ages (Wijting *et al.*, 1978).

As predicted there was a significant positive correlation between parents and children and PWE beliefs, though the correlation between fathers and children was low and not significant. It was chance and powerful other locus of control beliefs that – along with economic beliefs – showed the strongest relationship between individual parents and children. This confirms the finding of Levenson (1973) that both parents share *equally* in fostering their children's generalized expectations of control by powerful others.

Interesting though these results are they do not enlighten one as to *how* these transmissions occur. To know that there are significant sex differences for instance gives one some indication of how the socialization process occurs, yet the precise nature of the transmission mechanism remains to be elucidated.

Pocket money and economic education

To what extent are parents still encouraged to induce PWE beliefs about thrift, saving, budgeting into their children? There are a number of 'Guides for Parents' books that do just that, and what is most apparent about the majority of them is the extent to which they present PWE beliefs, attitudes, and behaviours as most desirable.

Consider, for instance, Davis and Taylor's (1979) work which argues that every child should have a job and that they should be taught money skills like spending, budgeting, saving, and borrowing as well as how to earn money, take risks, and understand competition. They review the range of possible, allowance or 'pocket money' systems and the 'commission system' where allowances are tied to responsibility. However, they recommend a system that has thirteen basic points:

1. The system you will use should be explained to the child at the time it is started.
2. The allowance is initiated at around 6 or 7.
3. The amount should be a reasonable one, and increased as the child grows older when it is expected to cover a wider range of child's expenses.
4. The parent and child should agree in advance on the kinds of expenses the allowance will cover.
5. The allowance should be paid weekly on the same day each week to younger children, and monthly to kids in their mid-teens.
6. The allowance should always be paid and should not be based upon performance of chores; it should never be withheld as discipline or to influence the child's behaviour.
7. Once the amount of the allowance has been established, the child should not be given more money just because he has spent all he had.
8. The child should be allowed to make his own spending decisions.
9. The child should be assigned an agreed-upon chore (or chores), which he will be responsible to do for the benefit of the entire family.
10. No pay is to be expected or received for doing the job.
11. Failure to do the assigned chore must not result in reduction or elimination of the allowance.
12. Parents who are able to pay their kids for doing extra jobs around the house should do so.
13. An annual review should be held yearly on the child's birthday to set the allowance and chores for the coming year.

(p. 50)

Apart from the education derived from a child's allowance or pocket money, Davis and Taylor (1979) also recommend explicit education in such things as profits (why they are necessary); jobs (where they come from); competition (is it good for us?); taxes (do they need to be so high?); saving (can a nickel be worth a dime?); investing (now that you've saved it, what's next?) etc. Most importantly they recommend that a child obtain a job and list six benefits of this:

1. Once they get a job, they have to show up on time. In order to keep most jobs, they are forced to develop promptness and dependability. The principal skill they will acquire is that of planning their time.
2. They will find that the world is competitive. This will be an important discovery in terms of their future ability to understand the adult world. The degree of competition they encounter will, of course, depend upon the job and their age. There may be no competition to run errands for a neighbour at age 8. There will be plenty of competition for a job at McDonald's. Your hope is that they acquire the ability to compete

effectively in the business and job world.

3. Depending on what approach they use to make their money, they might discover that a lot of money can be made with the right idea. This discovery can have a very positive effect on their attitude and stimulate their creativity as they search for even better job ideas in the future. If they can acquire the ability to apply their imagination to the practical problems they will confront later on, they will have a substantial head start on their contemporaries.

4. They'll find that they must make choices – that they cannot do and have everything all at once. Youngsters typically want to make their own decisions. At least they want to until they have to make the difficult ones. Then they probably expect you to make those for them. If you are able to hold back and force them to decide things for themselves, they will develop decisiveness. The ability to choose between alternatives is something that many adults have never quite mastered.

5. With some help from you, they can find that failures along the way are normal, expected events and should be viewed as lessons rather than disasters. If this lesson can be learned and accepted, they will never lack courage to attempt something for fear they will fail, and they will develop the determination to succeed at whatever they try. If, rather than giving up, they acquire the ability to analyse their mistakes, see what went wrong and why, they will be able to avoid those mistakes in the future.

6. A job can expand their horizons. It's very easy for any kid to assume that the whole world is just like the one he knows if he has had no experience outside that world. Many of the jobs kids can do will bring them into contact with a wide range of people, people who live differently from the way they were raised and who have different backgrounds and interests.

(pp. 157–8)

Some studies have attempted to investigate how parental economic beliefs and practices affect children's economic behaviours. Marshall and Magruder (1960) specifically investigated the relationship between parents' money education practices and children's knowledge and use of money. Amongst the many hypotheses that they examined were: 'Children will have more knowledge of money use if their parents give them an allowance' and 'Children will have more knowledge of the use of money if they save money'.

They found, as predicted, that children's knowledge of money is directly related to the extensiveness of their experience of money – whether they are given money to spend; if they are given the opportunities to earn and save money and their parents' attitudes to, and habits of, money spending. Thus it seems that socialization and education would have important consequences on a child's or adolescent's understanding of economic affairs. However, they did *not* find any evidence for a number of their hypotheses. These were: children will have more knowledge of money use if their parents give them an allowance; if children are given allowances, less of the family's money, rather than more, will be taken for children's spending money; if children are given opportunities to earn money, they will have more knowledge of money use than children lacking this experience; children will have less knowledge of money use if money is used to reward or punish their behaviour; and children will have the attitudes about the importance of money and material things that are expressed by their parents.

The ways in which children are socialized into the economic world are numerous but perhaps the most direct method is by the use of pocket money (allowances). Research on children's pocket money has found interesting and predictable differences: age (children get more as they get older); class (working-class children are given more money and more irregularly). Newson and Newson (1976) found that most of their sample of 7-year-olds received a basic sum of pocket money, sometimes calculated on a complicated incentive system. Some children were given money which is instituted for the express purpose of allowing the possibility of fining (confiscating); while others had to 'work' for it. Over 50 per cent of the sample earned money from their parents beyond their regular income but there was no sex or social class differences in this practice. Hence it was difficult to determine how much money children get per week as it varies. They did, however, find social class differences in children's unearned income and savings; middle-class children received less (18 vs 30 per cent) than working-class children, and saved more (90 vs 48 per cent). That is 52 per cent of class V children *always* spend their money within the week, whereas only 10 per cent of class I or II children do so. The authors conclude:

> Having cash in hand is equated with enjoying the good life; the relationship between money and enjoyment is specific and direct ... the working class child already begins to fall into this traditional pattern of life in his use of his pocket money.
>
> (Newson and Newson, 1976, p. 244)

Others have less evidence of class difference. Furnham and Thomas (1984a) tested over 400 children of different sex, class, and age. They found that as children got older they tended to get more money (11 to 12 year-olds got almost twice that which 7 to 8 year-olds received per week, and birthdays and Christmas presents of four times as much) and to spend it rather differently. There were, however, few sex and class differences, although it was hypothesized that working-class children would be given more money than middle-class children, but that it would be given more erratically and that they would be more used to shopping for their parents than middle-class children. It was suggested that the reason for the lack of significant differences could be three-fold: (a) they simply do not exist; (b) the classification into the two classes was too crude; (c) class differences are more apparent as children get older. The authors favour the last explanation, which was supported in a review by Stacey (1982), who argued that:

> In the first decade of life, economic socialization of children does not appear to be strongly influenced by their own social backgrounds, with the exception of the very rich and possibly of the very poor. In the second decade of life, social differences in the development appear to be more pronounced.
>
> (p. 172)

Furnham and Thomas (1984b) looked specifically at adults' beliefs concerning the economic socialization of children through pocket money or allowances. They found evidence of age and sex differences but also class differences. Middle-class adults were more in favour of giving children pocket money and of starting to give pocket money at an earlier age than working-class adults. Over 90 per cent of the middle-class adults believed that by the age of 8 years children should receive pocket money while just over 70 per cent of working-class adults believed that children of 8 years should receive pocket money. All 100 per cent of middle-class adults believed that by the age of 10 the pocket money system should be introduced yet only 84 per cent of working-class adults agreed. Indeed, some working-class respondents did not believe in the system of pocket money at all. A similar class difference was revealed by the question concerning when children should receive their pocket money. Whereas 91 per cent of the middle-class believed that children should receive it weekly (and 4 per cent thought when they need it), only 79 per cent of working-class adults believed children should receive their pocket money weekly (and 16 per cent when they need it). Furthermore, significantly more working-class adults believed that boys should receive more pocket money than girls.

These class difference findings are in line with previous studies on childhood socialization (Newson and Newson, 1976), and with figures on class differences in general (Reid, 1977); that is, working-class adults introduce pocket money later and more erratically than middle-class parents.

These studies on how adults teach their children about money, the virtues of thrift and saving, the association between effort and reward certainly relate to, even if they have not been directly related to, the PWE beliefs of adults and children, certainly reflect on them. There seems to be sufficient evidence that parents with PWE beliefs stress the importance of postponement of gratification and saving; the planning of the use of money; and that money has to be earned. PWE parents also no doubt encourage accounting procedures (however elementary), and stress the virtues of asceticism rather than indulgence.

The PWE in the post-war world

One way of validating some features of Weber's thesis is to see to what extent it applies today. This of course has a number of problems: firstly, finding that it does not apply today does not necessarily invalidate Weber's historical hypothesis; secondly it is almost impossible to confirm or validate the PWE 'hypothesis' as it is by its very nature complex and multifaceted so that confirmation of one aspect may well lead to disconfirmation of another; thirdly there are very many serious and difficult methodological problems to be overcome in the measurement of all the variables.

Crude though it is, an analysis by some economists even compared the GNP of different countries which showed an impressive lead for Protestant countries in the middle half of this century. Of course it is obvious to point out that religion could be a consequence rather than a cause of economic success or even epiphenomenal.

Nevertheless a number of very interesting studies were conducted mainly by sociologists in the 1950s and 1960s. Some were relatively small scale such as that by Goldstein and Eichhorn (1961) who found evidence for PWE high work drive and low spending propensity in rural America. Others have been large scale, both in terms of the countries and subjects used, and these give useful data on the distribution of PWE beliefs in the population.

America

Given their obsession with PWE it is perhaps not surprising that many extensive studies have been done in America. Definitely the two most famous studies on the distribution of PWE beliefs in America were by Greeley (1964) and Lenski (1961, 1971).

Lenski's (1961) major study done in the late 1950s was an attempt to investigate the religious factor prevailing in post-war America. Lenski hypothesized that *religion plays a significant part in determining how people behave* economically, politically, and in their family life. The following hypothesis

Table 4.2 Median per capita income for groups of nations classified by dominant religious tradition, 1957

Type of nation (i.e. dominant religious tradition)	Median income ($)	No. of nations
Protestants	1,130	11
Mixed Protestant–Catholic	881	6
Eastern Orthodox	365	5
Roman Catholic	329	33
Moslem	137	20
Primitive religions	88	15
Eastern religions (Hinduism, Buddhism, etc.)	75	16
Others (including mixed types)	362	7
All nations	224	113

Source: Compiled from data presented in Bruce Russett *et al. World Handbook of Political and Social Indicators,* (New Haven, Conn.: Yale, 1964) Tables 44 and 73–5. Nations with Communist governments are classified on the basis of their traditionally dominant faith.

could therefore be tested: Protestants compared to Catholics are more inclined to view work as important in and of itself. Therefore, they are more likely to have small families so that they will be freer to move about and take better jobs. They are more likely to avoid instalment buying, to save money, to vote right-wing, to deplore the national trend towards a welfare state, and to emphasize individual achievement and intellectual autonomy. In order to test this hypothesis, Lenski divided the Detroit community he studied into four major religious groups based on religion and colour: white Protestants – 41 per cent of Detroit, 267 cases; white Catholics – 35 percent of Detroit, 230 cases; black Protestants – 15 per cent of Detroit, 100 cases; Jews – 4 per cent of Detroit, 27 cases.

Individuals in each of these groups were interviewed about personal background, religious beliefs, church attendance, economic behaviour, political attitudes and behaviour, and family life. Graduate students in sociology, closely supervised by a professor, conducted the interviews and participated in the analysis of the findings. Analysis of the data indicated that a white Protestant is *more likely* than a white Catholic to:

- Consider his work important and have a small family.
- Avoid instalment buying and save money for the future.
- Vote Republican and question the welfare state.
- Take a liberal view of freedom of speech but hesitate to push for racial integration in the schools.
- Migrate and leave close family ties in order to obtain education, a better job, and a higher position in the class system.
- Develop a commitment to the principles of intellectual autonomy.

Lenski's findings also indicate that white Protestants are more upwardly mobile than Catholics even when social class is held constant. Jews tend to be the most successful and black Protestants the least, whilst white Protestants and Catholics fall between these extremes.

The Detroit respondents were asked to rank the following in order of importance in a person's job: high income; no danger of being discharged; working hours short; lots of free time; chances for advancement; the work is important and gives a feeling of accomplishment. Nearly half of those interviewed ranked feelings of accomplishment as the most important aspect of their job. This response could be taken to show what a strong hold the classical Protestant ethic has on all segments of the American population. It is especially evident among middle-class Americans and has impacted across all racial and religious lines.

In fact 52 per cent of white Protestants compared to 44 per cent of white Catholics rated this as top of their list. The opposition to the PWE were the attitudes towards work expressed in items 2 (job security) and 3 (short hours) which most of the respondents did not put at the top of the list; in fact, only 4 per cent of all respondents ranked 'short hours' first.

Lenski also distinguished between white Catholics and white Protestants according to whether they are active or marginal in their church attendance. He then divided each of these four groups into two other categories, according to whether they come from the middle or the working class. Lenski then measured the difference in degree of influence or the spirit of capitalism for each of the eight possible groups. These findings are shown below and reveal that active middle-class Protestants were found to be most influenced by the spirit of capitalism; active working-class Catholics, least influenced. In addition, religiously active Protestants were more influenced than marginal Protestants; active Catholics were less influenced than marginal Catholics. Thus, being active, Protestant, and middle class led one to accept the spirit of capitalism, while being active, Catholic, and working class led one to reject the spirit (see Table 4.3).

The results from the results on political preference and family relations also tended to confirm the PWE. White Protestants were more apt to be Republicans and to take more status quo attitudes towards social change. For instance, white Protestants tended to resist school de-segregation, as well as other direct-action programmes in the realm of civil rights. This resistance is in keeping with the ethic of individual striving and a reluctance to have government interfere with a person's freedom to achieve through individual initiative. There was also evidence for differences in child rearing between Protestants and Catholics. The former were apt to value programmes that emphasize self-direction, perseverance, and intellectual autonomy over those that emphasize popularity and obedience.

Lenski concluded that, in view of the evidence from both his study and elsewhere, apparently the strict environmental or materialist position, which explains economic, political, and family behaviour solely in terms of one's social situation, is untenable. This is not to deny that social conditions, especially those of an economic nature, are powerful forces influencing one's behaviour.

Table 4.3 Degree of influence of the spirit of capitalism for white Protestants and Catholics by religious involvement and social-class origin

Degree of influence	Rank order	Religious group	Religious involvement	Social class
Most	1	Protestants	Active	Middle
	2	Protestants	Marginal	Middle
Moderate	3	Protestants	Active	Working
	3	Catholics	Marginal	Middle
	4	Catholics	Active	Middle
	5	Protestants	Marginal	Working
Least	6	Catholics	Marginal	Working
	7	Catholics	Active	Working

Source: Lenski, 1961.

However, other factors (especially religion) still exercise a significant influence. In short, it still makes a difference whether a person is Protestant or Catholic, even in a modern city where secular trends have eroded religious involvement. In concluding Lenski (1961) wrote:

> Asceticism is rare among modern Protestants, and the distinctive
> Protestant doctrine of 'the calling' has largely been forgotten. However,
> the Protestant concern for intellectual autonomy seems to play an
> increasingly important role, facilitating scientific and technical advance.
> The Protestant small family norm (a relatively recent innovation)
> provides a new end to capital formation, since when families are large,
> more of the income must be spent on consumer goods. The ... orientation
> of Protestants seems to facilitate the channelling of energies into the
> world of work. In short, although the primary concern of Protestantism
> (like Catholicism) is the attainment of spiritual values, material advance
> continues to be a by-product of the Protestant effort.
>
> (pp. 351–2)

As one may suspect this research has been open to considerable criticism. The criticisms are of three basic types: *Sampling* – the sample was not representative, included too few blacks and Jews but ignored other groups, and large subgroups (i.e. Protestants) were lumped together and not divided up; *Measurement* – attitude measures and crude 'more or less' adaptation to occupational careers are far too crude measures of the PWE; *Causality* – the methodology could not disentangle cause from correlation and it is unclear whether religion is the cause or consequence of other social behaviour. Lenski (1971) did however revisit his research and attempt to answer his critics.

Other criticisms of Lenski have been vigorous. Bouma (1973) has talked of the 'simplistic derivations of poor hypotheses' from Weber's richly analytic work. But as Bouma pointed out, Lenski's work not only rekindled interest in the PWE hypotheses but led to numerous more attempts to test Weber's thesis. This research he divided into three areas depending on the hypothesis tested:

- Protestant beliefs and norms lead to greater social mobility and hence social status compared to people of other religions (especially Catholics). Bouma (1973) reviewed 16 studies which showed equivocal results and negligible Protestant–Catholic differences.
- Protestant beliefs and norms produce higher achievement motivation than that among Catholics. Again there were equivocal and sometimes contradictory results with no reliable indication of a relationship between religion and achievement orientation.
- Protestant beliefs predispose them to make more effectual use of educational opportunities than Catholics. Again, few results support this thesis and Catholic education does not appear to produce negative intellectual attitudes or low rates of achievement.

Table 4.4 Socioeconomic composition of religious groups, Detroit, 1954–9

Religious group and race	Median Income $2,000 and above (per cent)	Self- employed (per cent)	High-status occupations (per cent)	Median school year completed
White				
Catholic	27	7	19	10.0
Episcopalian	35	9	42	12.5
Lutheran	30	6	28	12.2
Calvinist	35	11	37	12.5
Methodist	32	8	27	12.3
Baptist	21	6	15	9.8
Small sects	16	11	17	9.5
No denomination	29	11	26	12.0
Semi-Christian	24	15	39	12.4
Jewish	42	41	62	12.5
Eastern Orthodox	35	15	13	9.3
No preference	23	9	28	10.0
Negro				
Catholic	6	4	7	10.0
Methodist	7	5	6	9.8
Baptist	8	3	3	9.1
Other	12	10	15	9.8

Source: Mayer and Sharp, 1962.

Another study by Mayer and Sharp (1962) done in Detroit appears to support the PWE hypothesis (see Table 4.4). Two points need to be made about this data. First, various completely different explanations could be preferred for these results: Belonging to a Protestant sect that encourages hard work and diligence makes members more likely to achieve success; members of certain sects have historically a competitive advantage over members of other sects; successful individuals convert to high prestige Protestant sects after they have achieved success. Secondly the authors tried to account for the differences in terms of such things as parentage, length of residence in Detroit, but could not account for all the variance suggesting that religion is not a summary, intervening, or epiphenomenal variable but an important factor to consider in occupational success.

More recent studies have also attempted to document the extent to which Americans believe in the PWE. Cherrington (1980) reports on a study of 3,053 workers in 53 companies in America (see Table 4.5). He found, somewhat to his surprise, that overall intrinsic features were thought of as more important than extrinsic features. He then divided the concept of the work ethic into two subscales: pride in craftsmanship and the moral importance of work (see Tables 4.6 and 4.7). He found that people tended to believe that occupational success was a function more of effort than knowledge or luck. He concluded:

Table 4.5 Desirability of 13 work outcomes: average responses of 3,053 American workers

Extremely undesirable					Neutral				Extremely desirable		
0	10	20	30	40	50	60	70	80	90	100	

Intrinsic rewards
Feeling pride and craftsmanship in your work	86.6
Feeling more worthwhile	80.4
Being recognized and gaining the respect of others	78.7
Being of service to others	78.3

Extrinsic rewards
Getting more money or a larger pay increase	81.2
Receiving more fringe benefits	68.9
Being promoted more quickly	68.0

Other work outcomes
Having your supervisor compliment you	71.4
Being chewed out by your supervisor	18.6
Being given more responsibility	70.6
Having leisure and free time	58.7
Feeling tired from a day's work	43.3
Being fired	7.9

Table 4.6 Pride in craftsmanship: average responses of 3,053 American workers

Strongly Disagree			Neutral			Strongly Agree
1	2	3	4	5	6	7

A worker should feel a sense of pride in his work	6.61
A worker should do a decent job whether or not his supervisor is around	6.60
There is nothing wrong with doing a poor job at work if a man can get away with it	1.51
An individual should enjoy his work	6.36
Even if you dislike your work you should do your best	6.00
Getting recognition for my own work is important to me	6.00

Table 4.7 Moral importance of work: average responses of 3,053 American workers

Strongly Disagree			Neutral			Strongly Agree
1	2	3	4	5	6	7

A good indication of a man's worth is how well he does his job	5.82
Working hard makes a man a better person	5.46
Work should be one of the most important parts of a person's life	4.92
Rich people should feel an obligation to work even if they do not need to	4.08
An unproductive worker is not loyal to his country	3.96

Source for Tables 4.5, 4.6, and 4.7: Cherrington, 1980

These findings indicate that the work ethic continues to be a significant force in the lives of many American workers. Work *per se* does not possess the strong moral imperatives that was characteristic of the pronouncements of early American moralists. But pride in craftsmanship is still highly valued and generally associated with doing a good job; the road to success is still largely paved with dedicated efforts; and work is still a fairly important part of workers' lives.

(p. 40)

Although this was a cross-sectional rather than a longitudinal study, Cherrington (1980) hoped to establish whether the PWE was on the decline by comparing the beliefs and attitudes of young (17–26), middle aged (27–40), and older (41–65) workers. He found evidence that even young people shared PWE ideals but that younger workers, compared to older workers: were more interested in money and job enrichment; did not believe in hard work and pride in craftsmanship as much; have less favourable attitudes to their jobs, the company, and top management; are less committed but believe more in welfare and are more concerned that other workers like them.

This 'generation gap' in work values is illustrated by Tables 4.8 and 4.9.

Cherrington (1980) attempted to explain these results by three plausible and non mutually exclusive hypotheses:

Table 4.8 Pride in craftsmanship

	Age			
	17–26	27–40	41–65	
If you do an especially good job what are the chances	5.69	6.02	6.09	Male
that you will feel greater pride in craftsmanship? [a]	5.84	6.22	6.12	Female
If you do an especially good job what are the chances	5.51	5.93	5.98	M
you will feel more worthwhile and be a better person? [a]	5.75	6.17	6.04	F
If you do a rather poor job what are the chances you	5.23	5.73	5.79	M
will feel guilty? [a]	5.74	5.91	5.79	F
Feeling pride in craftsmanship in your work? [b]	83.7	86.8	87.3	M
	84.2	87.7	88.8	F
Being of service to others? [b]	75.3	77.3	78.6	M
	78.2	80.7	80.4	F
A worker should do a decent job whether or not his	6.36	6.56	6.61	M
supervisor is around [c]	6.66	6.72	6.73	F
A worker should feel a sense of pride in his work [c]	6.36	6.60	6.66	M
	6.57	6.70	6.75	F
Even if you dislike your work you should do your best [c]	5.72	5.85	6.11	M
	5.84	6.20	6.36	F
There is nothing wrong with doing a poor job at work	1.88	1.51	1.38	M
if a man can get away with it [c]	1.57	1.44	1.34	F

[a] 7-point scale: 1 = never; 7 = 100% certain
[b] 100-point scale: 0 = undesirable; 100 = desirable
[c] 7-point scale: 1 = disagree; 7 = agree

Source: Cherrington, 1980.

Table 4.9 Moral importance of work

	Age			
	17–26	27–40	41–65	
Working hard makes a man a better person	5.08	5.38	5.64	Male
	5.25	5.51	5.82	Female
A good indication of a man's worth is how well he does	5.39	5.67	6.04	M
his job	5.67	5.94	6.20	F
Rich people should feel an obligation to work even if they	3.91	4.09	4.44	M
do not need to	3.80	3.73	4.16	F
Work should be one of the most important parts of a	4.75	4.88	5.38	M
person's life	4.30	4.62	5.30	F
An unproductive worker is not loyal to his country	3.39	3.75	4.54	M
	3.44	3.89	4.60	F
I would quit my job if I inherited a lot of money	4.05	3.62	3.81	M
	4.22	3.80	3.90	F

Note: 7-point scales where 1=disagree and 7=agree.

Source: Cherrington, 1980.

- Maturity – differences in work values result from the process of growing older.
- Historical events – the great depression and the Second World War shaped the beliefs of older workers.
- Training – the PWE was taught in the homes and schools of older people but is not being done so among the young.

Perhaps the most interesting findings from Cherrington's (1980) study concerned PWE beliefs, job satisfaction, and productivity and also the major determinants of PWE beliefs. He found, as predicted, a positive correlation between moral importance of work and pride in craftsmanship and various dimensions of job satisfaction. There were also significant positive correlations, albeit very small ones, between work values and productivity. Most interestingly, Cherrington (1980) performed two regional analyses on the 3,632 responses. These results are given in Table 4.10. These showed biographical factors to be better predictors than job attitudes. The author concluded that children develop a strong work ethic when parents exert firm discipline, delegate work assignments, encourage personal responsibility, establish standards of personal conduct, and encourage religious commitment. He also suggested that job enrichment, participative management, and job autonomy do not promote the work ethic.

There have been other, and more recent studies on PWE beliefs in America. Yankelovich's work has been frequently debated though he is mainly concerned with *change* in PWE beliefs which will be dealt with in Chapter 7. Certainly, from these American studies it seems to be the case that there remains class, regional, and religious determinants of the PWE and that education, sex, and age are consistently related to it.

Table 4.10 Multiple regression analysis predicting two work values

Independent Variables	Moral importance of work		Pride in craftsmanship	
	Beta	F Ratio	Beta	F Ratio
Personal Background				
Discipline in socialization	.233	128.5	.150	56.4
Importance of family life	.049	6.8	.070	14.9
Internal locus of control	.104	29.4	.181	94.2
Acceptability of individual initiative	.100	28.2	.129	50.3
Acceptability of welfare	−.049	6.4	−.120	40.6
Race				
Black	.038	2.0	−.032	1.5
Chicano	−.044	4.5	.010	.2
White	−.184	32.1	.085	7.4
Oriental	.008	.1	−.026	1.5
Religion				
Catholic	.038	.2	−.025	.1
Protestant	.049	.3	−.004	.0
Mormon	.130	4.8	−.015	.0
Oriental Christian	−.008	.0	−.043	1.6
Far East	.044	2.0	−.024	.6
No Religion	.013	.0	−.069	.8
Demographic Data				
Age	.161	56.4	.090	18.9
Educational level	−.024	1.4	a	
Father's education	.026	1.3	.001	.0
Mother's education	−.047	4.5	a	
Population of hometown	.012	.4	−.043	5.4
Occupation	−.034	2.2	.011	.2
Income	.017	.7	−.005	.1
Job Attitudes				
Effort leads to performance	.028	2.3	.052	8.2
Performance leads to extrinsic rewards	.029	1.7	−.037	2.9
Performance avoids punishment	.011	.3	.018	1.1
General satisfaction	.003	.0	−.062	5.5
Personal skill	.018	.6	.070	10.1
Pay satisfaction	−.012	.3	.009	.1
Pay equity	a		−.012	.3
Pay adequacy	−.009	.1	−.025	1.2
Interpersonal attraction	−.036	2.3	.039	2.8
Satisfaction attributed to co-workers	.004	.0	−.065	7.2
Supervisor consideration	−.072	8.1	.049	4.0
Supervisor competence	.028	1.3	−.008	.1
Job attractiveness	a		.053	4.9
Job complexity	a		a	
Job security	−.012	.3	.015	.5
Satisfaction with company	.106	14.0	.086	9.9
Organizational effectiveness	−.005	.0	.058	6.0
Company commitment	.200	89.9	.015	.5
Job enrichment	.039	2.5	.061	6.1
Discrepancy in job expectations	.044	3.8	.137	39.1
Work group cohesiveness	−.015	.5	.040	3.5
Adjusted R^2	.32		.36	
Degrees of freedom	41;2150		40;2151	

a F level was too low for this variable to enter the equation.
Source: Cherrington, 1980.

The work ethic in Great Britain

There seems to be a consensually held view, both within and outside the British Isles that British workers are less hard-working and hence productive than many of their peers from comparable countries. Furthermore this view has been generally held at least since the turn of this century as can be seen from popular records and reports. Despite frequent invectives against the British worker for having no signs of the PWE, there is little substantial evidence to support this view (Nichols, 1986; Thompson, 1982).

The question remains: Is the long-established conventional wisdom about the British worker true? If it is when did this decline occur? What caused it particularly in Britain? The first fact to point out is that although there is a wealth of macro-economic statistics on Britain's relative economic decline, there is precious little empirical evidence on worker attitudes. Furthermore, many studies that have compared productivity in different European countries (and found Britain lagging behind) have tended to invoke attitudes and the PWE post-hoc as an explanation without actually testing for it. Thirdly, as Nichols (1986) has pointed out, even if it is firmly and unambiguously established that British productivity is significantly lower than most other competitors, this may have a number of possible valid explanations that has little or nothing to do with worker attitudes. It may be that management practices, lack of investment in the work place, or indeed the declining PWE of the managers (and not the workers) is the prime cause of decline. Hence it may be possible to witness the paradoxical situation of a maintenance or increase in worker PWE, while simultaneously see a comparative decline in productivity. Nichols' (1986) position is thus:

It has been seen that there is a tendency at work among students of labour productivity to implicate British workers in deficiencies that could sometimes just as well derive from management. High inventories are attributed to strikes. Lack of planning is attributed to the amount of time British managements have to spend on the shop floor; to no investment; to an anticipation of what British workers might do in future, and to the idea that their level of effort does not justify the cost of further outlay. We have come to look at things differently: to suggest that British workers give like for like, inefficient management fostering less than helpful workforces. At the very least, it really is high time this possibility is given something more like equal prominence, and also the proposition upon which it depends, that British management may be deficient in its organisation – in the work of co-ordination in planning, and in its functional integration – as it tends to be in some respects on the technical side.

(p. 68)

Surprisingly perhaps, despite Nichols' (1986) insistence on getting empirical

Table 4.11 Employees' commitment to work by social class

	I & II %	III Non-manual %	III Manual %	IV & V %
Respondent would work even if no financial need	73	72	73	70
Respondent feels work is more than just earning a living	87	68	65	54
Respondent would do best work possible, regardless of pay	66	58	59	57

Source: Mann, 1986.

data on attitudes, his thesis remains unsupported by evidence for poor management practices being responsible for the PWE decline. There are very few studies which yield any actual data on the extent to which the PWE is held among the general population.

An exception is the work of Mann (1986) though it is unclear if he actually measured PWE beliefs.

Amongst many other questions put to this representative population of 1,769, they were asked to choose between three statements:

1. Do you put in only the work you get paid for?
2. Do you make a point of doing the best job you can, regardless of pay?
3. Do you work hard but not so that it interferes with the rest of your life?

As previous questions indicated, there was a strong commitment to work. Whereas 62 per cent took the second option, 30 per cent took the third, but only 7 per cent the first. But this was class related as Table 4.11 shows. In other words the middle class claimed to be more committed to work – higher on the PWE – than the working class. Other results show a similar pattern:

> Whereas 87 per cent of owners, managers and professionals said their job was much more than a means of earning a living, only 54 per cent of semi- and unskilled workers claimed this. In responses to the question about work ethic, there was a clear relationship with age, with only the under 25s (men and women) failing to produce a majority in favour of the 'Protestant' option. Those in public services, the higher socio-economic groups, and (unexpectedly) the poorest, claimed slightly more commitment. But on this measure few deviated much from the norm of a strong work ethic. Even if work is boring or low-paid, it is central to most people's notion of their own moral, as well as material worth.
>
> (Mann, 1986, pp. 2–4)

A close look at Table 4.12 reveals the amount of commitment to work currently prevailing in Great Britain.

Table 4.12 Commitment to and feelings about work: by sex and age within sex

| | Total | Sex | | Age within sex | | | | | | | |
| | | | | Male | | | | Female | | | |
		Male	Female	18–24	25–34	35–44	45+	18–24	25–34	35–44	45+
If without having to work, you had what you would regard as a reasonable living income, would you . . .											
Still prefer paid job:	72	75	68	76	78	74	73	76	69	74	52
Wouldn't bother:	27	23	31	22	22	20	27	22	29	26	44
Other answer:	*	1	1	–	–	6	–	–	1	–	3
Don't know:	*	*	*	1	–	–	–	–	–	–	1
Present job is . . .											
Just a means of earning a living:	30	30	30	33	27	23	36	34	30	26	31
It means much more than that:	70	70	70	67	73	77	64	66	70	75	69
Feelings about work . . .											
Work is only a business transaction. The more I get paid the more I do; the less I get paid the less I do:	7	8	6	9	8	8	8	11	4	4	6
I make a point of doing the best work I can, regardless of pay:	61	59	62	44	53	61	70	42	56	70	75
I want to work hard, but not so that it interferes with the rest of my life:	30	28	30	43	35	30	20	46	40	23	17
None of these:	2	3	2	4	3	1	2	2	–	3	2
Base: all employees											
Weighted	830	467	363	70	117	121	157	83	79	104	97
Unweighted	857	476	381	71	117	123	164	83	82	108	108

Note: All figures represent percentages
Source: Mann, 1986.

Interesting though these results are from a reasonably sized population, it should be pointed out work-commitment alone is not itself an index of the PWE. As was pointed out in Chapters 1 and 2, the PWE has a number of belief and behaviourial (ideological and consequential) facets which include ideas about morality, reward, leisure, etc. Commitment to work is central to the PWE though it is possible for someone to be highly committed to work, while at the same time not sharing other PWE beliefs. Nevertheless, the above results provide useful empirical evidence against the assumption that the PWE is on the sharp decline, indeed even dead in Great Britain. A second, and an important source of comparative evidence for the distribution and spread of PWE beliefs in Great Britain, is the European Value Systems study group. Abrams, Gerard, and Timms (1985) reported on British attitudes to work. They had comparative data from other European countries and set to test various hypotheses such as:

> Working people in Britain, by comparison to others in Europe, are strong
> on the qualities of a reliable subordinate, but weak on the critical and
> dynamic aspects which favour improvement in work, either as a personal
> experience or in its productivity.

(p. 173)

From the data of Table 4.13, it can be seen that the British appear committed to their work, are exceptionally proud of and satisfied with their work, and look forward to it. What was distinctive about the British was their relatively strong emphasis on work as an interesting and satisfying way of life. Though relatively satisfied with their work, British workers find points of criticism like being taken advantage of and not sufficiently free to make decisions. On the positive side, the survey showed the following: commitment to and satisfaction in work; readiness to accept the existing pattern of ownership and management; a strong responsiveness to strong management; and grow-

Table 4.13 Work and life in the EEC

	Percentages or score		
	Britain	West Germany	Ten European countries
Takes a great deal of pride in own work	79	15	36
Job satisfaction (average score: scale 1–10)	7.72	7.05	7.29
Looks forward to work/enjoys both work and weekend	72	57	60
Good if work played a smaller part in our lives	26	30	33
if a simpler and more natural life style	76	69	82
if less emphasis on money and material possessions	62	56	65
if more emphasis on the development of technology	61	55	57
In long run, scientific advances will help mankind	48	33	38

Note: All figures are percentages except for Job satisfaction score
Source: Abrams, Gerard, and Timms, 1985.

Table 4.14 Work attitudes by left–right orientation

	Percentages Position on left–right scale				
	1/2 (left)	3/4	5/6	7/8	9/10 (right)
Dynamic features of a job: average of percentages thinking each of these features important	37	42	45	45	41
If 3-day week without loss of pay, would use extra time to run own business	7	12	16	17	12
Fair to pay according to individual performance	41	55	71	69	73
Works voluntarily for a union	7	2	0	0	0
Often/sometimes seeks to persuade where holds a strong view	33	55	45	40	32
Ownership and management of business and industry: owners should run and appoint managers	26	30	52	60	57
Owners and employees should select managers	42	55	37	33	36
Employees should own and select managers	17	9	7	3	3
State should own and appoint managers	9	3	2	2	0
Orders at work should be followed only if first convinced, or 'it depends'	45	57	54	36	37
Good if: less emphasis on money and material possessions	60	69	62	68	66
work played a smaller part in our lives	35	36	24	26	22
more emphasis on the development of technology	26	30	52	60	57

Source: Abrams, Gerard, and Timms, 1985.

ing interest in information and explanation as a basis for authority. On the other hand they tend to be critical of many aspects of work, have a wide range of activities that are alternatives to work, and ambivalent about the usefulness of unions.

Though religion did not very clearly relate to work attitudes political orientation did (see Table 4.14).

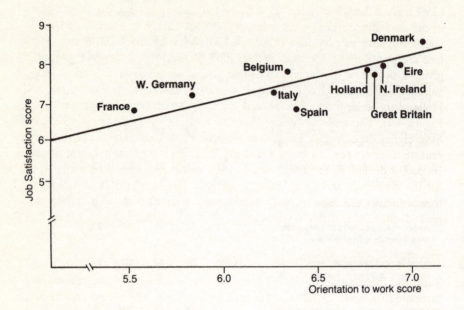

Predictably people with left-wing views place a stronger emphasis on employee involvement and reject traditionalist capitalistic ownership and systems of authority. They also believe that work should play a smaller part in their (our) lives and tend to place less emphasis on dynamic features of work, equity-performance based rewards, and new technology.

Harding, Phillips, and Fogarty (1986) using the same data base looked at West European attitudes to work. They found that over all groups three factors seemed to come out as the most important features of work – the opportunity for intrinsic personal development, pleasant working conditions, and extrinsic features associated with security and reward. Endorsement of these three factors at work tended to be related to age, political beliefs, and socioeconomic states. Interestingly, these factors were also closely related to religious beliefs specifically that Protestants tended to rate almost all the job characteristics as more important more frequently than either Catholics or those of no religious denomination. However, as the authors point out, this cannot be taken as evidence for the PWE as Protestant values may encourage certain aspects of work and work activity, but they inhibit other motivating features like the enjoyment of work and its rewards.

Harding *et al.* (1986) combined the responses to four questions to examine orientation to work. They were: Do you really look forward to your work when the weekend is over or do you regret it? (27% look forward; 33% regret; 33% enjoy both); How much pride, if any, do you take in the work that you do? (36% a great deal; 37% some; 15% a little); Thinking of your job, do you often or occasionally feel that you are being taken advantage of or exploited, or do you never have this feeling? (17% often; 36% sometimes; 42% never); How free are you to make decisions in your job? A composite index was computed giving a profile of the individual's general orientation towards work. The results showed workers from Denmark, the island of Ireland, Great Britain, and Holland to be high and France and Germany to be comparatively low (see Figure 4.1). The authors believe that Germany is low because the Germans have higher expectations which remain unfulfilled. Certainly the available literature does not tend to suggest that the PWE does not exist in Great Britain. Indeed, a decline in the PWE may be seen as a rather simplistic explanation for the numerous and complicated economic, historical, political, and sociological factors that have actually accounted for Great Britain's *relative* economic decline for nearly 100 years.

The PWE in different cultures and countries

Since the formulation of the PWE hypothesis at the turn of the century, anthropologists, psychologists, and sociologists have attempted to examine PWE beliefs among different groups. These comparisons have been both theoretical and empirical, and some historical.

Various attempts have been made to trace PWE beliefs in other cultures and religions, and attempt to ascertain if there is any association between these beliefs and economic growth. For instance, Kennedy (1962) examined the PWE among the Parsees of India – followers of Zoroastrianism – who are a conspicuously economically successful minority religious group. He found evidence for two crucial values – the desire to accumulate rather than to consume material goods, and the desire to maximize one's material prosperity – which were conducive to economic and technical pursuits. Hence he concluded that the commercial bent and values of the Parsees are similar to those of the PWE described by Weber and may, in part, account for their economic success. Similarly, Bellah (1963) found evidence for PWE beliefs in traditional Japanese society and hence questions the 'Protestant' exclusivity of the term. Jonassen (1948) attempted to compare and contrast a Marxist vs. Weberian account for the origin of capitalism in Norway and found more support for the latter.

More recently Munroe and Munroe (1986) found evidence for the Weber–McClelland type thesis among a group of East African natives who had been converted and socialized by Quaker missionaries at the turn of the century. The protestantized Africans tended to put emphasis on education, had socialization practices that down played physical punishment, had realistic beliefs about the factors bound up with success in their socio-cultural system, and health patterns similar to those of educated individuals in developing countries.

According to Weber (1905), Calvinism encouraged man to value highly the rational and methodological mastery of the social and economic environment. On the other hand, the great Oriental religions did not offer an encouraging cultural framework for the rational pursuit of economic gain. Yet how does one explain the phenomenal rise in economic activity, output, and productivity in numerous Asian countries?

- The PWE has been introduced in Asia. Recent work by Hafsi (1987) looked at three different ethnic groups, all Muslim, and suggests that within that faith there is a close connection between religious involvement and work centrality. People with strong religious convictions tended to work more in their free time and have stronger non-financial commitments to work. That is, with a religious group there are significantly different PWE attitudes linked to more actual religious beliefs and practices.
- Asian countries have developed social and economic structures that support the PWE. It could be argued that with the industrialization and westernization of various Asian countries, standard scientific and accountancy practices have been introduced which promote PWE behaviours.
- The Neo-Confucian or post-Confucian Ethic found in many oriental countries that have proved enormously successful (the five dragons of Taiwan, Korea, Hong Kong, Singapore, and Japan) has functioned in the same way as the PWE. That certain Confucian virtues like self-control, duty, gentlemanly conduct, and conformity, which are closely linked to the PWE, have in part led to the recent phenomenal economic rise. Post-Confucian economic culture stresses such things as meritocratic achievement and is profoundly anti-individualistic. Virtue with regard to one's tasks in life consists of trying to acquire skills and education, working hard, not spending more than necessary, being patient and persevering. Moderation in all things is enjoyed.
- The economic culture of Japanese management. Some have argued that the corporate culture imposed by Japanese management has been the key to success. This seems to incorporate some PWE values but is quite antithetical to others. Howard *et al.* (1983), comparing Japanese and American managers, found the former attached greater importance to socially beneficial values and showed greater valuation of accomplishments and more interest in advancement, money, and forward striving. They suggest achievement and advancement motivation may be one reason for Japanese productivity, and collective actions in method for disciplining and rewarding it. Similarly England and Misumi (1986) found work centrality – the generalized and importance of working to individuals – much higher in Japan, than in the United States. Weisz *et al.* (1984) suggested that a major difference between Japanese and American work behaviours

lies in the psychology of control. Whereas Americans are highly individualistic, seeking primarily personal control to achieve ends, the Japanese
stress collective secondary control. America values the self-made man,
loyal to their own careers, while the Japanese are loyal to the organization, believing their team can win everything, as individuals, cannot.

Whilst there is a lot of speculation about the work ethic in non-European
countries there is not a great deal of data. However, albeit that they are on a
small scale, there is increasing evidence from psychological studies done in
different cultures. Psychological studies using self-report measures of Protestant Work Ethic beliefs have been done in many countries though few have
compared results. By far the most popular has been the Mirels and Garrett
(1971) questionnaire which has been used in *Africa*: Heaven (1980), Philbrick
(1976), Vandewiele and Philbrick (1986); *America*: Beit-Hallahmi (1979),
Dorst, Leon, and Philbrick (1978), Eisenberger and Shank (1985), Ganster
(1980, 1981), Goitein and Rotenberg (1977), Gonsalves and Bernard (1983),
Greenberg (1977, 1978a, b, 1979), Hooker and Ventis (1984), Iso-Ahola and
Buttimer (1982), Kidron (1978), Lied and Pritchard (1976), MacDonald
(1971), Merrens and Garrett (1975), Rasinski (1987), Stake (1983), Waters,
Bathis, and Waters (1975); *Australia*: Feather (1982, 1983 a, b, 1984, 1985);
Belgium: Rosseel (1985); *Britain*: Breakwell *et al.* (1985), Furnham (1983,
1984 a, b, c, d, 1985a, 1986a, 1987a, b), Wagstaff (1983); *Israel*: Shamir (1985,
1986); *Malaysia*: Furnham and Muhuideen (1984); *Taiwan*: Ma (1986). Table
4.15 illustrates some of these studies.

Less well known and frequently used measures have also been used in different countries such as the Blood (1969) measure – *America*: Aldag and Brief
(1975), Armenakis *et al.* (1977), Iso-Ahola and Buttimer (1982), Greenberg
(1978), and Wanous (1974); *Britain*: Furnham (1987a); *Israel*: Rim (1977).

A great number of the above studies have used student subjects. Nevertheless, it is very difficult to compare results from studies for three reasons. First,
a minority rather than a majority of studies report on PWE score means and
standard deviations. Secondly, there is a problem of equivalent samples because the age, education, and class of university students differs fairly considerably from one country to the next. Thirdly these studies have been conducted at different times, as much as fifteen years apart, and as beliefs may
change in a country over time it is impossible to compare studies from different countries done at different times.

What empirical predictions would one make when comparing PWE beliefs, as defined and measured by psychological tests?

• PWE beliefs would be *lower* in more liberal, less conservative or authoritarian cultures. Because PWE are so closely aligned with conservative
  views of all types, one would imagine conservative cultures (that is socially but not necessarily economically conservative) would yield higher
  scores.

Table 4.15 Means and Standard Deviations of PWE scores published in papers categorized by country

Country	Author	Subjects	Scores		Quotes
(a) Africa					
East Africa	Philbrick (1976)	60 Black Students Age 20.7 years. All males	x = 103.57	SD 11.03	'An examination of responses suggests a strong identification with hard-work, enterprise, ambition, goal-directed activity, competition, success-orientation and achievement need. This "African elite" are manifestly out-Protestanting the Protestant' (p. 175).
South Africa	Heaven (1980)	99 White Students Age 16.7 years. All males	x = 91.48	SD 9.71	'Earlier research in which University students had a very high mean score cannot be generalized to West Africa' (p. 446).
West Africa	Vandewiele & Philbrick (1986)	163 Black School Children Age 19.6 years. Half Male	x = 85.0	SD 13.71	
(b) America					
	Mirels & Garrett (1971)	54 Male Students	x = 85.7	SD 15.5	'Results for the female sample parallel the findings for males and support a similar attribution of characteristics to women who are inclined to accept the Protestant Ethic' (p. 44).
		55 Female Students	x = 85.5	SD 16.2	
	Merrens & Garrett (1975)	40 Male and Female Students	x = 86.57	SD 13.55	'The high Protestant Ethic group spent significantly more time working on a task and produced significantly more output' (p. 125).
	Greenberg (1978)	128 Female Students	x = 79.21	SD 9.85	

Country	Author	Subjects	Scores	Quotes
	Dorst, Leon, & Philbrick (1978)	Students from: 126 – California State 184 – Arizona State 63 – University of Hawaii 92 – New Mexico State	x = 81.3 SD 14.6 x = 79.0 SD 15.1 x = 82.3 SD 14.6 x = 86.3 SD 15.5	'Behaviour seems to be situation specific – the subject does not appear to rigidly manifest a preoccupation with, preference for and disposition to work, and to allow this tendency to generalize across situations' (p. 190).
	Gonsalves & Bernard (1983)	22 Afro-Americans 20 Afro-Caribbeans	x = 84.80 SD 13.51 x = 80.46 SD 13.40	'Such findings underscore the need for additional research on specific class related endorsement of the Protestant Ethic thesis and larger groups of subjects' (p. 646).
	Hooker & Ventis (1984)	76 Retired People Age 69.6 years	x = 92.12 SD 13.33	
(c) Australia	Feather (1984))	144 Students (66 male) Age 20.45	x = 82.28 SD 13.7	
	Feather (1982)	39 Employed Males 32 Unemployed Males 39 Employed Females 37 Unemployed Females	x = 82.72 x = 72.41 x = 82.62 x = 84.65	'Unemployed male subjects had lower Protestant Ethic scores and reported that good and bad outcomes across a range of situations were less important to them when compared with employed male subjects'.
(d) Taiwan	Ma (1986)	707 Students (Age 20.34) 312 Males 395 Females	x = 70.73 SD 7.95 x = 69.68 SD 7.18	'The lack of significance of religious variables for the PWE scale is interpreted as indicating that the Protestant Ethic is nor uniquely Protestant among college students in Taiwan, rather, it may represent a general work orientation setting across all groups, including religious groups' (p. 219).

Table 4.16 Comparing the scores from thirteen cultures on eight measures

	Countries	N		Protestant Work Ethic Measures						
			PE	PWE	SoC	LE	WKE	EPE	AWE	PPE
1.	America	172	16.96	79.44	28.27	36.25	26.38	84.59	35.34	32.56
2.	Australia	93	17.32	76.95	25.99	30.62	22.07	84.06	30.10	30.99
3.	British	189	15.72	76.90	25.97	33.82	24.94	74.64	31.10	30.97
4.	Ciskei (SA)	122	22.59	89.50	24.29	30.00	32.18	92.29	40.55	37.00
5.	Germany	154	14.40	66.44	34.28	33.53	24.00	73.57	24.12	29.98
6.	Greece	97	18.17	83.68	33.13	35.85	34.02	88.32	34.69	12.27
7.	Hong Kong	117	18.60	79.77	28.13	33.90	36.32	86.48	33.41	32.11
8.	India	144	21.96	102.88	35.95	28.00	39.53	88.62	42.52	35.15
9.	Israel	224	15.01	70.25	27.31	33.84	35.29	69.78	30.75	31.83
10.	New Zealand	180	16.51	73.80	25.76	35.94	22.52	75.75	30.62	30.71
11.	South Africa	93	16.72	80.93	28.93	30.62	25.46	80.09	33.32	34.65
12.	West Indies	125	16.70	76.30	36.20	32.27	30.17	84.03	34.04	37.70
13.	Zimbabwe	101	19.68	86.67	31.98	29.05	28.06	94.05	38.11	36.11
	F level		52.64	24.57	59.42	18.78	89.31	39.10	58.08	24.57
	Probability		.001	.001	.001	.001	.001	.001	.001	.001

PE   Protestant Ethic (Goldstein & Eichhorn, 1961)
PWE   Protestant Work Ethic (Mirels & Garrett, 1971)
SoC   Spirit of Capitalism (Hammond & Williams, 1976)
LE   Leisure Ethic (Buchholz, 1977)

WKE   Work Ethic (Buchholz, 1978)
EPE   Eclectic Work Ethic (Ray, 1982)
AWE   Australian Work Ethic (Ho, 1984)
PPE   Pro-Protestant Ethic (Blood, 1969)

- PWE beliefs would be lower in more 'scientific' countries and those with bigger bureaucracies. To a larger extent the PWE had the seeds of its own destruction within it because it encouraged science and empiricism which rejected metaphysical beliefs and also favoured bureaucratization which stifled individual enterprise. Thus countries that value science and have well established bureaucracies will have lower scores.
- Countries that stress power distance, uncertain avoidance, and individualism would score higher on PWE beliefs than those which do not. This is based on the ideas of Hofstede (1984).
- Countries which have large inequalities between the rich and the poor, the haves and have-nots, will show strong PWE scores, at least on the part of those that have.

Many of these ideas were examined by Furnham (1989b) who gathered data from thirteen different countries. All of the above hypotheses received some support. Table 4.16 illustrates the results from the student sample. Overall Indians and Africans seemed to have the highest scores and Germans the lowest. Furnham (1989b) has speculated on the possible reason for these results but also pointed out their limitations which are in sampling (in terms of size and equivalence) and in the differential results of the different questionnaires. Nevertheless they prove useful for examining certain specific hypotheses.

Conclusion

This chapter has examined research on the individual aetiology of PWE beliefs – the factors that seem to lead to individuals, as representatives of groups or cultures, adhering to PWE beliefs. Although the research has been somewhat equivocal and occasionally problematic in that few really good and extensive longitudinal (as opposed to cross-sectional) studies have been done, there seems sufficiently reliable evidence that child-rearing patterns do have an effect on components of the PWE like need for achievement, locus of control, etc. In other words, early experiences seem to 'lay-down' behaviour patterns that are maintained throughout life.

Therefore if a particular method of child-rearing is seen to dominate in a culture or subculture, such as that advocated by Dr Benjamin Spock, it may be predicted that a large group of people who shared similar early learning experiences held similar PWE beliefs. Hence psychological phenomena become sociological and vice versa. This research left a number of issues tantalizingly unresolved: is there a critical or optimal period in the socialization practice that affects PWE beliefs; do mothers and fathers have differential effects on their sons and daughters; precisely how are beliefs and values transmitted; can all the 'good work' done by parents be wiped away by inappropriate or opposite experiences at school? Certainly there is enough research evidence for one to formulate clear hypotheses about these issues.

This chapter also examined studies which attempted to look at the distribution of PWE in various countries, particularly the United States and Great Britain. It is difficult to evaluate and compare these studies. No doubt psychometricians would be concerned about the so-called measures of the PWE while methodologists would criticize the sampling frames of these studies. Suffice it to say that it appears to be the case that many people over a number of countries seem to still endorse PWE beliefs and practise PWE behaviours. Secondly, that the determinants of these beliefs (age, sex, class) seem pretty robust and consistent across cultures. However, there remains a number of unique and complexly interwoven factors in each and every society making the prediction of the distribution of these beliefs somewhat problematic.

Chapter five

The work ethic at work

I am a great believer in luck, and I find the harder I work the more I have
of it.

Stephen Leacock

The only place where success comes before work is in the dictionary.

Vidal Sassoon

Nothing great was ever achieved without enthusiasm.

Ralph Waldo Emerson

Perfect freedom is reserved for the man who lives by his own work, and in
that work does what he wants to do.

Collingwood

Introduction

Poets and politicians, novelists and economists, philosophers and psychologists have speculated about the nature, meaning, advantages, and disadvantages of work. There are many famous advocates of the benefits of work: *Voltaire* believed work banished the three evils of boredom, vice, and poverty. *Carlyle* thought it was the grand cure for all the major miseries and maladies of this life; while *Freud* believed love and work were the most meaningful acts of all people. But the Greeks and Romans did not value work, especially manual work, which they saw as a curse, suitable only for slaves.

Historical evidence shows how the meaning of work has changed over the centuries, no doubt adapted to fit, explain, or support contemporary social structure. Thus the Greeks distinguished between creative (leisure) work for the elite and physical toil for slaves. The Hebrews thought it an honourable necessity for all, imposed on men because of the sins of their fathers. However, twentieth-century theorists have also speculated on the nature of work though they have differed on a number of grounds: the *extent* to which they see work as necessary for psychological growth; the stress on the *content* of work tasks vs organizational structure; their emphasis on individual differences. Kahn

(1981) has argued that there are three faces of work characterized by the terms affliction, addition, and fulfilment. People's feelings about work are characterized by passionate ambivalence, but by and large all people (and young people in particular) show a strong attachment to work. Weber's (1905) conception of the PWE was that it was a self-imposed willingness of the individual to identify and conform with the goals of society and to volunteer his or her services to the abstract ethic of industrial acquisition, effort, enterprise, and growth. It was in this sense irrational because work was done for no obvious reason but for its own value. Hence it was in, and of, itself satisfying. Thus there were no external extrinsic characteristics that determined job satisfaction, but this was similarly a function of how much one believed in the PWE.

The nature, purpose, and benefits of work have been debated by all the great modern writers: Freud, Marx, Morris, Ruskin, etc. Sociological thinking about work is highly political and frequently utopian. Various implicit assumptions and personal values appear to determine, in part, writers' ideas on work (Salaman, 1986). There are many famous essays on work like Bertrand Russell's 'In Praise of Idleness' published in *Harper's Magazine* in 1932; William Morris's 'Useful Work versus Useless Toil' published by the Socialist Platform in 1885. Anthony (1984) has suggested that the ideology of work has taken two forms – an official view, representing the employer's injunction that work should be well done, and a radical view that work should be re-organized. What is the role in a person's life? Fraser (1962) put it thus:

Ought (the individual) to find in (work) his principal means of self expression? Ought it to be the cause of his deepest satisfaction? Should it be the biggest thing in his life? This is to demand a great deal both of the individual and the job, and it is unlikely that more than a small proportion of any community will ever approach such standard. Nor may it be desirable that they should, for the number of individuals who have this level of motivation to pour into their work is limited, while the number of jobs into which it would be worth pouring it is similarly restricted. On the other hand, ought work to make as few demands as possible on the individual? Ought it to offer only a limited sense of achievement or identification? Ought it to become a means of putting in part of the day quite agreeably while at the same time providing the wherewithal to finance his home and leisure pursuits? There are individuals to whom a job like this would make a strong appeal and who might find their real satisfaction in other areas of their life. Between these extremes there will be jobs and individuals with different levels of expectation and satisfaction to offer and receive, and if we were to match up each with the other we might claim to have achieved the ideal industrial community. Those who expected a great deal from their work and were prepared to put a lot into it would be in jobs which utilized all their potentialities to the full and gave them in return a deep sense of personal achievement. Those who neither expected nor were prepared to contribute very much would be in the comfortable, undemanding jobs where they would be reasonably occupied, well paid and contented.

(pp. 176–7)

Whilst everybody might not agree with this very psychological approach, it raises many important questions. Central to this idea, and many other in I/O psychology, is the idea of 'fit' between person and job. Cherrington (1980) has provided a simple but useful matrix (Table 5.1) within which to conceive of work. This matrix emphasizes the relationship between work and non-work, a point discussed in detail later. The central idea is that work beliefs, attitudes, and motivations cannot be separated from those not strictly pertaining to work.

Hall (1986) offered as his definition of work:

Work is the effort or activity of an individual performed for the purpose of providing goods or services of value to others; it is also considered to be work performed by the individual.

(p. 13)

Whereas many would be unhappy with this definition because of the omission of any comment about pay, occupational role, etc., he does attempt a taxonomy of work by looking at different types of work: professions, managerial and professional occupations, white-collar work, skilled blue-collar work, semi-skilled blue-collar work, and unskilled work as well as farm work and house work. He does, however, try to come to terms with the meaning of work

Table 5.1 Matrix of meanings

	Work Is Meaningful	*Work Is Meaningless*
	I	**II**
Life Is Meaningful	Strong work ethic. Happy and productive workers. Work is a terminal and/or instrumental value. 50% of workforce.	Work is an obligation that is not consistent with the meaning of life. Solution: inculcate work values, redesign the job, or change jobs. 20% of workforce.
	III	**IV**
Life Is Meaningless	Work is a displaced terminal value. Work is the reason for existence. Solution: enforced rest, re-assessment of priorities, diversification of interest. 10% of workforce.	Work is soulless, mind-numbing drudgery. Welfare is preferred to work. Solution: 'right actions' and 'contributing to life'. 20% of workforce.

Source: Cherrington, 1980, p.268.

to individuals, and in doing so holds three assumptions: people vary hourly/ daily in their orientations to work; work varies widely in what it provides the individual; there is no ordering/hierarchy in terms of how people respond to or are motivated by their work. This seems to imply complete individual and transient phenomenology and yet he identifies various dimensions of work shared by all. This is certainly a problem for the meaning of work concept – how is it acquired and how idiosyncratic is it?

A terminological note is in order here to try to distinguish between work and employment. Whereas *leisure* is a goal-based activity aimed at maximizing enjoyment, *work* is any activity that is directed to goals possibly beyond the enjoyment of the activity itself. Work may be long or short term, may be done alone, or linked to an institution with social roles. *Employment*, on the other hand, it is worth noting, of necessity involves a contractual obligation and a salary – in other words a relationship based on the exchange of economic rewards for labour. Housework, volunteer work, and honoraria are then truly work rather than employment.

Different conceptions of work

Popular books on the topic of work have portrayed work very differently. There are few eulogies in favour of work but there are two distinct kinds of popular books: *Negative* (Thank God it's Friday). One of the most celebrated texts is based on interviews with dozens of working people by Terkel (1975). It begins:

> This book, being about work, is, by its very nature, about violence – to the spirit as well as to the body. It is about ulcers as well as accidents, about shouting matches as well as fist fights, about nervous breakdowns as well as kicking the dog around. It is above all (or beneath all), about daily humiliations. To survive the day is triumph enough for the walking wounded among the great many of us. The scars, psychic as well as physical, brought home to the supper table and the TV set, may have touched malignantly, the soul of our society....It is about a search, too, for daily meaning as well as daily bread, for recognition as well as cash, for astonishment rather than torpor; in short, for a sort of life rather a Monday through Friday sort of dying.

(p.1)

Terkel argues that the questioning of the PWE by the young has touched off grievances in others previously silent. He appears to claim that all the signs of job dissatisfaction – absenteeism, poor production – is a result of dehumanizing, humiliating work. Though it is true to say not all the biographic interviews portray work as negative, the vast majority do and few talk of their work as liberating, absorbing, fulfilling.

Positive (Thank God it's Monday). A second popular response recognizes that work is sometimes unpleasant but advocates ways of reducing stress (Lucas *et al.*, 1986) or increasing job satisfaction (Cameron and Elusorr, 1986). One approach aims to eradicate negative aspects of the job while another to increase positive aspects. Cameron and Elusorr (1980) talk about the concept of optimal work. Essentially they advocate a careful, explicit, and detailed analysis of people's current job followed by an exploration of their personal skills and aptitudes which maximize passion and delight. They claim their approach is simply a collection of commonsense ideas that are forgotten under the pressure of money, success, and other work constraints.

> Many people, even those who are fairly creative and imaginative in their approach to their personal life, allow any sense of vision to lapse when they think about work and money. Lacking a lyrical or imaginative approach to work, they find themselves working at jobs that talk lyricism and imagination. To help you integrate the imaginative and the realistic, the pragmatic and the visionary faculties in your approach to work, this book suggests techniques through which you can find work which is as acceptable to your highest vision as to your most basic needs and requirements; as practical and grounded in the mundane realities of the market place as it is playful and inspirational.

(p. 8)

These two popularized images of work differ not only in terms of valence (i.e. positive vs negative) but other dimensions. For instance the former view is pessimistic, and fatalistic, seeing individuals as victims of powerful organizational and economic forces beyond their control while the latter view is optimistic, and instrumental, believing people are able to change aspects of work they do not like. For the former work is a jailer of the human spirit, for the latter a liberator.

But there are also quite different 'academic' conceptions of work like Freudian, Marxist, and Humanist approaches. In Freudian theory work fulfils many functions:

- When asked what were the basic requirements of human existence, Freud said psychoanalysts have tended to see work as part of the reality principle that fights the pleasure principle (Neff, 1965). Work can provide sublimatory activities through which one can gratify sexual and aggressive impulses.
- Prevents uninhibited satisfaction of sexual and aggressive instincts.
- Imposes rules of conduct which require people to live by the reality and not the pleasure principle.
- It encourages transactions with the physical environment which strengthens ego inner control mechanisms.
- It curbs inborn tendencies to carelessness, irregularity, and unreliability.

Thus the task of work was to socialize and mature people by providing the necessities for survival but also encourage socially acceptable co-operative activities. Thus work has overt and covert functions but the emphasis is not on the *content* of different jobs so much as on the psychological significance of work as a whole.

But in accordance with Freud's hydraulic view of libido, one could as much invest too much or too little energy in work. He has the concept of an optimal division between energy investment in work and non-work, but this is not spelt out in any detail:

> Freud (1962) argued that 'laying stress upon importance of work has a greater effect than any other technique of living in the direction of binding the individual more closely to reality', since 'in his work he is at least securely attached to a part of reality, the human community'.
>
> (p. 34)

> Freud also noticed that... as a path to happiness work is not valued very highly by men. They do not run after it as they do after other opportunities for gratification. The great majority work only when forced by necessity, and this natural human aversion to work gives rise to the most difficult social problems.
>
> (p. 34)

Yet work was invaluable for the maintenance of mental health:

> Work is no less valuable for the opportunity it and the human relations connected with it provides for a very considerable discharge of libidinal component impulses, narcissistic, aggressive and even erotic, than because it is indispensable for subsistence and justifies existence in a society.
>
> (p. 34)

Neff (1977) argued that the psychological baggage which people bring to work is described in the language of personality theory: motives, needs, feelings, coping mechanisms, defences, etc. Is it not possible then to maintain that work behaviour is not mediated through personality characteristics. Relying heavily on neo-psychoanalysts like Erikson, Neff (1977) suggested that one could trace the development of the work personality whose critical components are formed in middle adulthood and adolescence. The central feature of this developmental process is how children react to the demand to achieve – to acquire competence:

> Certain basic components of the work personality appear to be laid down in the early school years – the ability to concentrate on a task for extended periods of time, the development of emotional response patterns to supervisory authority, the limits of cooperation and competition with peers, the meanings and values associated with work, the rewards and sanctions for achievement and non achievement, the affects (both positive and negative) which become associated with being productive.

School is thus a precursor of adult work and provides a set of models for it. It may be gratifying, even beneficial, if the child enjoys his homework, but enjoyment is not the purpose of the process. Basically, he is required to be productive, to be serious, to meet standards, to turn out the required amount of work at a desired level of quality, to meet certain responsibilities.

Of course, school is not the only force which prepares the child to cope with the demands of work. Parents also play a prominent role, but child–parent relationships now begin to differ from those in early childhood. Although parent-child interactions continue to be centred chiefly around nurturance and love, new elements begin to appear in middle childhood. In many ways, the parents begin to convey the impression that it is expected or desired that the child be something when he grows up. School achievement may be encouraged or discouraged to variable extents. The parents act to reinforce or to counteract the authority of the teacher. Children begin to become dimly aware that their parents are not only important to them because they are the primary sources of love and nurturance, but also because they are models – good, bad, or indifferent – of how grown-ups behave in the outer world. During middle and later childhood the child begins to develop a set of values concerning work and achievement and probably the initial sources of these developing ideas are his parents. As powerful as parental influence may be, however, it is only one source among many. The larger society also plays its part, through countless and often contradictory messages conveyed by way of the mass communication media and through its public figures. A significant role also is played by the teen-age subcultures in which the child increasingly becomes embedded, the values of which are often incongruent with the goals either of the school or the parents. Depending upon the variable strength and congruence among all these influences, the child develops his individual set of attitudes to work.

(pp. 188–9)

From the perspective of the self-actualization theorists one has to distinguish between good and bad work. Work is only psychologically beneficial if it develops healthy self-esteem and the feeling of control by allowing people to use their skills, make responsible decisions, and provide variety.

In many ways these views stress the negative functions of work. According to Marx, man had become alienated from his work, his workers, and his own identity by the dehumanization of work in industrial capitalistic society.

What, then, constitutes the alienation of labour? First, the fact that labour is external to the worker, i.e., it does not belong to his intrinsic nature; that in his work, therefore, he does not affirm himself but denies himself, does not feel content but unhappy, does not develop freely his physical and mental energy, but mortifies his body and ruins his mind.

147

The worker therefore only feels himself outside his work, and in his work feels outside himself. He feels at home when he is not working, and when he is working he does not feel at home. His labour is therefore not voluntary, but coerced; it is forced labour. It is therefore not the satisfaction of a need; it is merely to satisfy needs external to it.

(Marx, 1844, pp. 70–1)

There are, then, radically different conceptions of work that could be classified on various dimensions. However these conceptions are too general (and too zealously argued) to be of much use and a more systematic approach needs to be undertaken.

The meaning and functions of work

Most researchers have noted that working is more than just a means to an end for the vast majority of employed men, and that it serves a function other than economic in both middle- and working-class people (Morse and Weiss, 1955). A great deal has been written about the meaning and functions of work. This is both interesting and important because it reveals *why* the PWE stresses the moral as well as the psychological and physical benefits of work. Calvin and his followers stressed that work should be methodical, disciplined, rational, and uniform, not casual or occasional. Fineman (1987) claims that middle-class work is portrayed as:

- A key source of identity, self-respect, and social status.
- The most central life activity, more important than leisure.
- Intrinsically valuable and rewarding as much as, even more than, what it 'buys'.
- Difficult to separate from other aspects of life.
- Providing secure, predictable, and increasing rewards for effort.
- Allowing for the development and acquisition of discretion, power and control over people, things, and processes.

Others have attempted to list the most crucial factors contributing to the psychology of work. In summarizing about eight other authors who have written on this topic Fagin and Little (1984) listed seven major functions of work:

- Work as a source of identity – the work people do classifies them in terms of class, status and influence, and established hierarchies and groupings from which people derive a sense of security, recognition, belonging, and understanding. Work-identity may be transferred to children or other family members but may be lost on retirement or unemployment.
- Work as a source of relationships outside the nuclear family – work allows emotional outlets in family relationships as well as enriching the scope of interpersonal relationships, which in turn has benefits on family life.

- Work as a source of obligatory activity – work provides a very useful framework of regular, purposeful activity. Despite the fact that this function is largely imposed and often resented, when it is taken away it can cause considerable difficulty and hardship.
- Work as an opportunity to develop skills and creativity – although work can satisfy sensual and aggressive instincts, as well as allay fears or anxieties, it can allow for the mastery, control, or altering of the environment. There is considerable satisfaction in the integrity and co-ordinating of intellectual and motor functions which lead, over time, to the development of skills.
- Work as a factor which structures time – because work structures time into regular, predictable time periods involved with rest, refreshment, and actual work, it provides a useful temporal framework within which people can become maximally active and happy.
- Work as a source of sense of purpose – at best work prevents classic signs of alienation such as feelings of powerlessness, self-estrangement, isolation, and meaninglessness while at best, work ensures interdependence with others which helps in the development and achieving of life goals.
- Work is a source of income and control – work means putting oneself in the hands of employers during working hours so long as it provides sufficient money to assure oneself of independence and free choice of leisure and future outside the work-place.

The meaning that people attach to work is important on an individual, organizational, and social level. The meaning that PWE supporters give, develops over time for individuals and groups and can affect such things as mobility, conflict, productivity, absenteeism, etc.

A research team, M.O.W. (1987), developed a heuristic model with three antecedent or conditional variables – personal/family history, present job/career, macro-economic environment; and five central meanings of work variables – centrality of work, societal norms, valued working outcome, importance of work goals, and work-role identification. The group carried out a high eight-nation study that in many ways could be seen as a modern, partial test of the PWE. They found evidence of considerable attachment to work – 86 per cent of the combined sample (of about 15,000) said they would continue to work even if they had enough money to live comfortably for the rest of their life without working. Over a quarter placed work above all four of the following roles: family, community, religion, and leisure.

They found no association between religion and work attitudes, with work centrality being highest in Japan and Yugoslavia. Hence they believe work centrality is primarily a function of industrialization. Yet the importance of demographic and psychographic variables was undervalued, particularly as time spent planning, training, and preparing for work (that takes 1/3 of adult working hours) starts at a very early age. Sex, age, educational, occupational, and organizational variables were all apparent in the centrality of work, underscoring the importance of early socialization. Extensive research on individual samples (Harpaz, 1985, 1986) tends to support the general conclusions.

Various writers have attempted to identify the major functions and benefits of work (Shepherdson, 1984; Shimmin, 1966). Indeed most of the researchers in this field have studied the effects of unemployment on individuals and by seeing their various deprivations have inferred the possible benefits of work.

Based on her work dating from the 1930s Jahoda (1982) has developed a theory based on the idea that what produces psychological distress in the unemployed is the deprivation of the latent functions of work. These include:

- *Work structures time.* Work structures the day, the week, and even longer periods. The loss of a time structure can be very disorienting. Feather and Bond (1983) compared the structure and purposeful activity among employed and unemployed university graduates. They found, as predicted, that the unemployed were less organized and less purposeful in their use of time, and reported more depressive symptoms than the employed.

- *Work provides regularly shared experiences.* Regular contact with non-nuclear family members provides an important source of social contact. There is a vast literature on social-skills deficits which suggests that social isolation is related to disturbed mental states. There is now a growing interest in the social support hypothesis which suggests that social support from family and friends buffers the major causes of stress and increases coping ability, so reducing illness. If one's primary source of friends and contacts is work colleagues then the benefits of social support are denied precisely when they are most needed. There are also a wealth of studies in organizational psychology which suggest that one of the most frequently cited sources of job satisfaction is contact with other people.

- *Work provides experience of creativity, mastery, and a sense of purpose.* 'Both the organization and the product of work imply the interdependence of human beings. Take away this daily experience and that efforts must be combined, and the unemployed are left with a sense of uselessness, of being on the scrap heap.' Work, even not particularly satisfying work, gives some sense of mastery or achievement. Creative activities stimulate people and provide a sense of satisfaction. A person's contribution to producing goods or providing services forges a link between the individual and the society of which he or she is a part. Work roles are not the only roles which offer the individual the opportunity of being useful and contributing to the community but, without doubt, for the majority they are the most central roles and consequently people deprived of the opportunity to work often feel useless and report that they lack a sense of purpose.

(Jahoda, 1979, p. 313)

- *Work is a source of personal status and identity.* A person's job is an important indicator of his personal status in society – hence the often amusing debates over job titles such as sanitary engineer for street cleaner! Furthermore it is not only to the employed person that the job gives certain status but also to his family. The employed person therefore is a link between two important social systems – family and home. An unemployed person has lost his employment status and hence identity. Not unnaturally there is a marked drop in self-esteem following unemployment.

- *Work is a source of activity.* All work involves some expenditure of physical or mental effort. Whereas too much activity may induce fatigue and stress, too little results in boredom and restlessness, particularly among extraverts. People seek to maximize the amount of activity that suits them by choosing particular jobs or tasks that fulfil their needs. The unemployed however are not provided with this possibility and have consistently to provide stimulation to keep them active.

This 'deprivation theory' has had its critics (Fryer and Payne, 1984). Fryer (1986) has offered three kinds of criticism:

- Pragmatic – the theory is very difficult to test
- Methodological – one cannot be sure which or how the deprivations are caused by unemployment; people *not* deprived do not necessarily enjoy, appreciate, or acknowledge this state
- Empirical – the theory does not take into account changes over time and undivided difference in reaction

In a sense, Jahoda (1982) argues that people are *deprived* while Fryer (1986) argues that institutions *impose* things on people (like stigma). Further, whereas the former underplays individual choice and personal control, the latter tends to underplay social identity and interdependence of people at work.

An alternative model has been proposed by Warr (1987) called the 'vitamin' model, which assures that mental health is assumed to be influenced by the environment in a manner analogous to the effects of vitamins on physical health:

> The availability of vitamins is important for physical health up to but not beyond a certain level. At low levels of intake, vitamin deficiency gives rise to physical impairment and ill-health, but after attainment of specified levels there is no benefit derived from additional quantities. It is suggested that principal environmental features are important to mental health in a similar manner: their absence tends towards an impairment in mental health, but their presence beyond a required level does not yield further benefit. In addition, however, certain vitamins become harmful in very large quantities. In these infrequent cases the association between increased vitamin intake and health becomes negative after a broad range of moderate quantities.
>
> (p. 10)

Table 5.2 Environmental categories and subcategories within the vitamin model, in its application to job settings

1. Opportunity for control
   Opportunity for intrinsic control, over job content and procedures
   Level and type of pacing
   Opportunity for extrinsic control, over employment conditions and company policies
   Control over other environmental features within the model

2. Opportunity for skill use
   Opportunity to use current skills
   Opportunity to acquire new skills

3. Externally generated goals
   Intrinsic job demands: level and pattern
   Conflicts between demands
   Task identity
   Traction and flow
   Time demands: level and pattern

4. Variety
   Intrinsic variety, within job tasks
   Length of cycle time
   Extrinsic variety, in respect of job contexts

5. Environmental clarity
   Information about the consequences of actions (feedback)
   Information about future developments (job future ambiguity versus clarity)
   Information about role requirements and performance standards (role ambiguity versus clarity)

6. Availability of money
   Income relative to need (deprivation/adequacy)
   Income relative to other people (inequity/fairness)

7. Physical security
   Temperature, noise, illumination, vibration
   Absence of danger
   Good equipment design

8. Opportunity for interpersonal contact
   Amount of interaction which is possible (level of contact)
   Quality of available interaction (friendship opportunities, social support)
   Privacy and personal territory

9. Valued social position
   Esteem from roles
   Personal meaningfulness of job

Source: Warr, 1987.

For Warr (1987) there are nine basic vitamins, the benefits of work, or the principal features of the environment. These are set out in Table 5.2.

Warr is aware of a number of problems with this approach. First, that his list of nine vitamins may be enlarged (subdivided) or reduced (reclassified)

Table 5.3 Possible matching characteristics for each environmental category

	Category	Possible matching characteristics
1.	Opportunity for control (AD)	High growth-need strength (ES) High desire for personal control High need for independence (ES) Low authoritarianism (ES) Low neuroticism High relevant ability
2.	Opportunity for skill use (AD)	High growth-need strength (ES) High desire to use/extend skills (ES) Relevant skills which are unused Low neuroticism
3.(a)	Externally generated goals: Level of demands (AD)	High growth-need strength (ES) High desire for high workload (ES) Type-B behaviour High need for achievement Low neuroticism High relevant ability (ES)
3.(b)	Externally generated goals: Task identity (AD)	High growth-need strength (ES) High desire for task identity
4.	Variety (AD)	High growth-need strength (ES) High desire for variety (ES)
5.(a)	Environmental clarity: Feedback (AD)	High growth-need strength High desire for feedback
5.(b)	Environmental clarity: Role clarity (AD)	High need for clarity/intolerance of ambiguity (ES) External control beliefs (ES?) Low need for achievement (ES?)
6.	Availability of money (CE)	High desire for money
7.	Physical security (CE)	High desire for physical security
8.	Opportunity for interpersonal contact (AD)	High sociability Lack of contact in other environments High desire for social support
9.	Valued social position (CE)	High desire for social esteem

'ES'= empirical support is available for a significant person-situation interaction in respect of job satisfaction. 'AD'= vitamins that at high levels cause decrement in mental health. 'CE'= vitamins that at high levels do not cause decrement.

Source: Warr, 1987

but believes that in the interests of parsimony, inclusiveness, and complexity it seems sufficient. Secondly, that when looking at the relationship between these features at work and mental health, it becomes progressively more difficult to define the latter which has itself many different components and conceptualizations. Thirdly, there is a paucity of empirical evidence in favour of certain features of the model. Fourthly, that the model is certainly a situation- or environment-centred model in that it looks at the effects of job characteristics on mental health.

However, Warr (1987) does offer some insights into personal characteristics and mental health in jobs and unemployment, which may relate to PWE beliefs. More important perhaps, he notes that there is certain empirical support for his thesis. These results overlap in part with work on the PWE. Table 5.3 shows, for instance, some of the variables mentioned in Chapter 2, hence one may be able to infer the relationship between PWE beliefs and individual differences. Thus externally generated goals seem important to PWE beliefs but opportunities for feedback not. Warr's (1987) thesis requires empirical support and further investigation yet remains a useful source of hypothesis.

The relationship between work and leisure

Despite difficulties with both definition and measurement, researchers are agreed that the concepts of work and leisure are multidimensional although there is no clear consensus what the dimensions are. Nor is there any agreement about the relationship between work and leisure despite the fact that it has been discussed since the time of Plato (O'Leary, 1973), or conceived of as a relationship between job and life (rather than simply leisure) satisfaction (Steiner and Truxillo, 1987). Since Wilensky (1960), it has been customary to divide the relationship between leisure and work into three possibilities:

- *Spillover* – Leisure is an *extension* of work, hence they are similar, the demarcation is weak, and work is the person's central interest.
- *Compensation* – Leisure is an *opposition* to work in which leisure is apart from and counter-posed to work.
- *Neutrality* – Leisure and work are somewhat *different* and while the demarcation is not strong, the person is probably more interested in leisure.

Wilensky (1960) describes two of these as follows:

> The *compensatory leisure hypothesis:* ... the Detroit auto-worker, for eight hours gripped bodily to the main line, doing repetitive low-skilled, machine-paced work which is wholly ungratifying, comes rushing out of the plant gate, helling down the super-highway at 80 miles an hour in a second-hand Cadillac Eldorado, stops off for a beer and starts a bar-room brawl, goes home and beats his wife, and in his spare time throws a rock at a Negro moving into the neighbourhood. In short, his routine of leisure is an explosive compensation for the deadening rhythms of factory life.
>
> The *'spillover' leisure hypothesis:* Another auto-worker goes quietly home, collapses on the couch, eats and drinks alone, belongs to nothing, reads nothing, knows nothing, votes for no one, hangs around the home and the street, watches the 'late-late' show, lets the TV programmes shade into one another, too tired to lift himself off the couch for the act of selection, too bored to switch the dials. In short, he develops a spillover leisure routine in which alienation from work becomes alienation from life; the mental stultification produced by his labour permeates his leisure. (p. 544)

Table 5.4 Types of work–leisure relationship and associated variables (individual level)

Work–leisure relationship variables	Extension	Opposition	Neutrality
Content of work and leisure	similar	deliberately different	usually different
Demarcation of spheres	weak	strong	average
Central life interest	work	–	non-work
Imprint left by work on leisure	marked	marked	not marked
Work variables			
Autonomy in work situation	high	–	low
Use of abilities (how far extended)	fully ('stretched')	unevenly ('damaged')	not ('bored')
Involvement	moral	alienative	calculative
Work colleagues	include some close friends	–	include no close friends
Work encroachment on leisure	high	low	low
Typical occupations	social workers (especially residential)	'extreme' (mining, fishing)	routine clerical and manual
Non-work variables			
Educational level	high	low	medium
Duration of leisure	short	irregular	long
Main function of leisure	continuation of personal development	recuperation	entertainment

Source: Parker, 1972, p. 103.

Parker (1972) has attempted to look at the consequences of these three relationships, which he calls extension, opposition, and neutrality, in a range of relationships (see Table 5.4). Each of these possibilities, particularly the former two, suggest a wide variety of hypotheses that may be tested – work satisfaction is correlated with leisure satisfaction; types of work are correlated with leisure activities; the degree of role involvement in work might be related to the degree of role involvement in leisure. Naturally a clear-cut hypothesis-testing opportunity such as this has attracted a good deal of research as well as review and conceptual clarification (Wilson, 1980; Staines, 1980). According to Wilson (1980) who reviewed a number of studies in this area both the *kinds of activity* and the *satisfaction derived* at work tend to spill over into leisure. Staines (1980) concludes similarly:

> Data from relevant studies support the motives of spillover and compensation under different conclusions but, overall, offer more evidence of spillover than compensation. Support for spillover, for example, is reflected in the positive correlations between general types of activities engaged in at work and corresponding types of activities in non work.

Support is also shown in the positive correlations between subjective reactions to work and to leisure and family life. The most important exceptions to this pattern of spillover concern physical effort on the job. Workers who expend a relatively great amount of physical effort at work are less involved in nonwork activities and less likely to be physically active away from their jobs.

(p. 111)

Recent evidence can be found for the spillover hypothesis, for instance in the leisure patterns of retired workers (Kremer and Harpaz, 1982). However, there is both argument against and evidence for the compensation hypothesis. Miller and Weiss (1982) argued that it cannot be assumed that different leisure activities (writing, poetry, gardening, motor mechanics) have different significances for the people engaging in them (they are all forms of creativity). Equally, it cannot be assumed that the same activity has the same meaning for all individuals. They argued that individuals themselves sometimes compensate for work deficiencies through leisure activities. By examining organized league bowling, they found individuals in low status jobs stressed the importance of prize winning in leisure more than people with high status jobs, to compensate for their lack of achievement at work. Their argument was that since low- and high-status individuals did not differ in their abilities actually to win prizes, the results are attributed to the desire of low-status individuals to compensate for lack of occupational status through leisure achievement. Various attempts to examine the relationship between work and leisure have attempted to break down factors on either side of the equation.

The literature on the relationship between work and non-work has been examined in many ways. Shamir (1983) looked at the 'conflict' between the two as a function of aspects of a person's *work schedules*. Elizur (1984), on the other hand, used facet analysis to divide work–non-work relations into three different categories: cognitive, affective, and instrumental. In this sense the relationship between work and leisure could be compensatory, spillover, and segmentationary all at the same time, because each could refer to the relationship in one of the three domains. This, of course, complicates the picture but probably reflects the somewhat complex nature of reality. Yet another approach has been that of Shaffer (1987), who argued that patterns of work and non-work satisfactions are moderated through individual differences. He found six different profiles including work and non-work compensations, maternally dissatisfied individuals, and dissatisfied isolates.

One additional complication regarding the model for the association between work and leisure is that it is quite possible that different models or theories apply to different work/leisure phenomena. For instance, Parker (1983) considered the relationship between:

● Work and leisure *involvement*.
● Work and leisure *activities*.

● Work and leisure *attitudes*.

Thus it is possible that regarding activities there is some evidence of spillover, while involvement shows evidence of compensation, while attitudes support the neutrality position. In other words depending on what aspect of the work–leisure relationship is being considered, different models may simultaneously apply.

More than others, Kabanoff and colleagues (Kabanoff, 1980; Kabanoff and O'Brien, 1980, 1982) have attempted a clear empirical *and* theoretical analysis of the relationship between work and non-work. They proposed a *task attribute* analysis where people described their jobs in five task attributes – autonomy, variety, skill-utilization, pressure, and interaction. Leisure activities could be rated on the same dimensions. Thus it was possible to test which model – compensation, generalization, or segmentation – applied on which attribute. A variety of patterns emerged, though the general lack of correlations between attributes of people's work and leisure activities suggests that segmentalist ideas tend to be correct. Further, both sex and socioeconomic factors affected the relationship.

Kabanoff (1980) suggests four distinct work/leisure patterns exist:

● Passive generalization – low levels of both the work and leisure attribute (predominantly males with low income, education, and intrinsic work motivation).
● Supplemental compensation – low levels of an attribute in work, but a high level in leisure (predominantly older, low income, internally controlled, low extrinsic work motivated people).
● Active generalization – high levels of an attribute in both work and leisure (these tended to be better educated, high income, intrinsically, rather than extrinsically, motivated people).
● Reactive compensation – high levels of an attribute at work and a low level in leisure (predominantly males, job centred, and those with intrinsic motivation).

He concludes:

In future we should abandon oversimplified, undirectional models of work and leisure that offer little or no account of the processes that underlie interactions among different life spheres. The time for creating ad hoc typologies is past, and the future must see a concern with deriving empirical evidence dealing with rather than ignoring undoubtedly complex interchange between the individual's work and non-work life.

(p. 74)

Wilson (1980) has identified four major problems in this area of research:

● 'Work' is often measured by occupational group rather than what people actually do. In other words occupational groups or even professionals with similar titles do very different activities at work and it should not be assumed that they are homogeneous.

- Because it acknowledged that both work and leisure are multi-dimensional, it could be that both compensation and spill-over hypothesis are operating at the same time. Hence similar effects may arise from different causes and vice versa.
- Intervening variables such as one's position in the life cycle may change the nature of the relationship between work and leisure. It is just as important to demarcate which possible intervening variables are important as defining the nature of the relationship between work and leisure.
- In examining the relationship between work and leisure one cannot ignore the effect of the occupational milieu. That is shared, consensually defined, and strongly work-related leisure functions, function to replenish the labour force and legitimate working arrangements.

Clearly, the relationship between work and leisure is important for the PWE (see Chapter 2). It is quite possible that the rather simplistic view of the PWE being pro-work and anti-leisure is misleading. From the above it may be seen that PWE believers may indeed partake of spillover leisure pursuits. However, as yet, few researchers have looked at the association between PWE beliefs and leisure activities, hence only speculations are possible.

The PWE and workaholism

Oates (1971) claimed to have invented the neologism workaholic meaning the addiction to work and the compulsion or the uncontrollable need to work incessantly. But unlike other forms of addiction which are held in contempt, workaholism is frequently lauded, praised, expected, and even demanded. Signs of this 'syndrome' according to Oates (1971) include boasting about the hours of work, invidious comparisons between self and others on the amount of work achieved, inability to refuse requests for work, and general competitiveness:

> The workaholic's way of life is considered in America to be one and the same time (a) a religious virtue, (b) a form of patriotism, (c) the way to win friends and influence people, (d) the way to be healthy and wise. Therefore the workaholic, plagued though he be, is unlikely to change. Why? Because he is a sort of paragon of virtue.... He is the one chosen as 'the most likely to succeed'.

(p. 12)

From a Christian perspective Oates (1971), a professor of the psychology of religion, looked at 'Sunday neurosis' or the difficulty for a workaholic of coping with a work-free weekend. He offers six pieces of advice to the workaholic:

- Admit that you are a workaholic, powerless to do anything about it without help beyond yourself.
- Make a fearless inventory of all the busy-work you do which is not essential or part of your job and throw it overboard.
- Make a plan to spend part of each weekend in meditation.
- Remember something that you enjoyed doing when a teenager, and do it again.
- If you read at all, find something you do not have to read as part of your job.
- Meet some new people you have not met before, and renew contact with some old acquaintances with whom you have lost touch.

Other advice includes re-evaluating the whole economy, pattern, productivity, and purpose of holidays. The dangers of workaholism are seen to be not only the physical and mental health of the workaholic him or herself, but also of the spouse who might become hyperactive or alcoholic, and the children of workaholics.

As is customary with popularist expositions of a psychological variable, a taxonomy is provided by Oates (1971) who listed *five types of workaholic*:

- Dyed-in-the-Wool – with five major characteristics: high standards of professionalism; tendency to perfectionism; vigorous intolerance of incompetence; overcommitment to institutions and organizations; considerable talent with marketable skills.
- Converted – a person who has given up the above but may behave like a workaholic on occasions for the rewards of money or prestige.
- Situational – workaholism not for psychological or prestige reasons but necessity within an organization.
- Pseudo-Workaholic – someone who may look on occasion as a workaholic but has none of the commitment and dedication of a true dyed-in-the-wool character.
- Escapist as a workaholic – these are people who remain in the office simply to avoid going home or taking part in social relationships.

Finally, Oates (1971) considered the religion of the workaholic. He argues that they are worried by the future with its meaninglessness and hopelessness. Workaholics tend to be unforgiving, lacking in a sense of irony and humour as well as wonder and awe. For the author once these are renounced, a workaholic experiences a much better quality of life.

It has been suggested that people become helplessly addicted to work, just as some become addicted to drugs. They are prepared to forsake everything in their desire to work. Is this a latter-day manifestation of the PWE?

Machlowitz (1980) has defined workaholics as people whose desire to work long and hard is intrinsic and whose work habits almost always exceed the prescriptions of the job they do and the expectations of the people with whom, or for whom, they work. She quotes Galbraith on the first page of her book, who noted that 'No ethic is as ethical as the work ethic'. Throughout her book she assumes that the workaholic is the embodiment of the PWE.

According to Machlowitz (1980) all true workaholics share six *traits*, some more paradoxical than stereotypic:

- Workaholics are intense, energetic, competitive, and driven.
- Workaholics have strong self-doubts.
- Workaholics prefer labour to leisure.
- Workaholics can – and do – work any time and anywhere.
- Workaholics make the most of their time.
- Workaholics blur the distinctions between business and pleasure.

All workaholics have these traits, but may be subdivided into four distinct types.

- The *dedicated* workaholic. These are quintessentially the single-minded, one-dimensional workaholics frequently described by lay people and journalists. They shun leisure and are often humourless and brusque.
- The *integrated* workaholic. This type does integrate outside features into the work. Thus, although work is 'everything' it does sometimes include extracurricular interests.
- The *diffuse* workaholic. This type has numerous interests, connections, and pursuits which are far more scattered than those of the integrated workaholic. Furthermore they may change jobs fairly frequently in pursuit of their ends.
- The *intense* workaholic. This type approaches leisure (frequently competitive sport) with the same passion, pace, and intensity as work. They become as preoccupied by leisure as work.

Machlowitz (1980) has developed a 10-item scale to measure workaholism. Though she provides no psychometric assessment of the scale she does note that if a person answers 'yes' to eight or more questions, they too *may* be a workaholic (see Table 5.5).

Farnsworth (1987) has devised a non-psychometrically assessed test, which also purports to measure the extent to which a person is a workaholic. Each item has a three-point scale which for most, but not all, questions is 'frequently', 'very rarely', 'never' (see Table 5.6).

To some extent it is thought that workaholism is an obsessive-compulsive neurosis characterized by sharp, narrowed, focused attention, endless activity, ritualistic behaviours, and a 'strong desire to be in control'. However, the aetiology of this 'syndrome' is seen to lie in childhood where workaholism is fairly easily recognized. Machlowitz (1980) argues that some children are driven from within, but others are pushed by parents, for example by reinforcement. That is, parents threaten to withdraw love if ever-increasing expectations are not fulfilled:

Table 5.5 Machlowitz's Workaholism Questionnaire

1.	Do you get up early, no matter how late you go to bed?	Yes	No
2.	If you are eating lunch alone, do you read or work while you are eating?	Yes	No
3.	Do you make daily lists of 'things to do'?	Yes	No
4.	Do you find it difficult to 'do nothing'?	Yes	No
5.	Are you energetic and competitive?	Yes	No
6.	Do you work weekends and holidays?	Yes	No
7.	Can you work any time and anywhere?	Yes	No
8.	Do you find vacations 'hard to take'?	Yes	No
9.	Do you dread retirement?	Yes	No
10.	Do you really enjoy your work?	Yes	No

Seeing paternal love as contingent on achievement instead of unconditional surely spurs progress, but it may also be the source of self-doubts ...
success is self-perpetuating, but the promise of failure is even more pro-
pelling and compelling.

(pp. 41–2)

Further, parents may encourage workaholism by providing a model for their
children. But because the parents are so busy they may be poor parents in that
they are inattentive or simply exhausted when at home. To find workaholics at
play may simply be an oxymoron. Machlowitz (1980) offers a number of rea-

Table 5.6 Farnsworth's Workaholism Questionnaire

1.	Do you work before breakfast?
2.	Are you usually the first to arrive at the office?
3.	Do you work through your lunch break?
4.	Are you usually the last to leave the office?
5.	Do you work at home during the evening?
6.	Do you telephone your staff during the evening or at weekends to discuss work problems?
7.	Do you lie awake at night thinking about work problems?
8.	Do you ever get up during the night and begin working?
9.	Do you take work home at weekends?
10.	Do you ever come into the office on Saturdays and Sundays?
11.	Do you take your full annual holiday entitlement?
12.	Have you ever cancelled a holiday because of work?
13.	Have you ever cancelled a family outing or anniversary celebration because of work pressure?
14.	Do you take work with you on holiday?
15.	Do you ever contact the office while you are on holiday?
16.	Do you read material unrelated to work in your spare time?
17.	Are you reluctant to delegate, preferring to do the important jobs yourself?
18.	Have you ever refused to attend training programmes because of pressure of work?
19.	Have you ever been advised by a doctor to take things easier?
20.	Have members of your family ever complained about the hours you work?

sons why workaholics shun vacations and time-off: they have never had a good experience of holidays either because they have expected too much or chose the wrong type; as their jobs are their passion they do not feel that they need to get away from it all; traditional forms of recreation seem like a waste of time and incomprehensible to them; the preparation for and anxiety that precedes taking a holiday are more trouble than they are worth; and, finally, workaholics are afraid that they would lose complete control of their jobs if they left for a holiday.

However, workaholics do report being remarkably satisfied and content with their lives. Machlowitz (1980) found little difference between workaholic men and women's source of joy and frustration. These were fourfold: whether in their home life the workaholic felt free of the responsibility for supervising or performing household duties; whether their job offered them autonomy, control, and variety, whether the job needed the workaholic's 'particular' skills and working styles; whether the workaholics felt healthy and fit for work. Though they appear to never feel successful many non-frustrated workaholics do report happiness. Finally, Machlowitz (1980) offers some advice for workaholics, maximizing the pleasures and minimizing the pressures of that particular life-style:

- Find the job that fits – that exercises one's skills and abilities.
- Find the place that fits – that provides the most convivial environment.
- Find the pace that fits – that allows one to work at the most desirable speed.
- Create challenges in your work – to deal with pressures effectively.
- Diversify each day – because of short attention spans.
- Make sure that every day is different – to improve levels of stimulation.
- Use your time; don't let it use you – establish your own circadian rhythm and plan your day around it.
- Don't deliberate excessively on decisions that don't warrant the attention.
- Let others do things for you – learn how to delegate.
- Work alone or hire only other workaholics – to prevent intolerance and impatience with others.
- Become a mentor, teacher, guide, and counsellor to others.
- Make sure you make time for what matters to you – such as your family, leisure pursuits.
- Get professional help – if you have a job, home, or health crisis as a function of your life.

The crucial question remains whether workaholism is a present-day manifestation of the PWE. Certainly, workaholic attitudes to work, time, success, denial, of leisure/pleasure would seem to be closely linked to PWE beliefs. However, some workaholic traits seem counter-productive such as the inability to delegate or relax, and thus workaholism is unlikely to lead to success. Furthermore, the idea that workaholics are neurotic obsessionals full of self-doubt suggests that their beliefs and behaviours are pathological, which is not the case with PWE beliefs and behaviours as currently conceived. Yet there is quite clearly a high degree of overlap between the PWE (as described by Franklin, Weber, and others) and the life style of the workaholic (as described by psychologists).

The PWE and vocational preference

Are PWE believers attracted to certain sorts of jobs like accountancy, research science, or medicine? Given that the people who endorse the PWE have specific values, beliefs, and behaviour patterns do they as a result have specific vocational choices? Are PWE believers more attracted to certain jobs compared to others? Although there are a number of theories that have attempted to specify why people choose certain occupations and the consequences of ideal vs non ideal, or good (person – job) fit vs bad fit jobs, without doubt the theory that has attracted most attention is that of Holland (1973).

Holland (1973) suggested that one can characterize people by their resemblance to each of the six personality types: realistic, investigative, artistic, social, enterprising, and conventional, which are the product of characteristic interaction among a variety of cultural and personal influences. The environments in which people live and work can also be characterized according to their resemblance to six model environments corresponding to the six personality types. Because the different types have different interests, competencies, and dispositions, they tend to surround themselves with people and situations congruent with their interests, capabilities, and outlook on the world. People tend to search for environments that will let them exercise their skills and abilities and express their personality, i.e. social types look for social environments in which to work.

Along with many attempts to demonstrate the positive consequences of the P-E fit such as job satisfaction and negative consequences such as psychological distress (Furnham and Schaeffer, 1984), various researchers have examined individual differences and personality correlates of the hexagonal types. Using 16 PF, Peraino and Willerman (1983) found, as predicted, that Social and Enterprising occupations (ones that require sociability, enthusiasm, and adventurousness) were more closely associated with extraverted behaviour than was found in Investigative and Realistic occupations. Similarly Costa, McCrae, and Holland (1984) looked at the relationship between neuroticism, extraversion, and openness and Holland's types. The results showed strong significant associations between Social and Enterprising vocations and extraversion, as well as significant correlates between Investigative and Artistic interests and Openness to Experience. Similarly, individuals interested in Conventional vocations tended to be closed to experiences.

How are high and low PWE scores related to Holland's (1973) six vocational types? The most direct and useful source of evidence for this relationship is a study by Mirels and Garrett (1971) in which subjects with measured PWE beliefs rated their preference for a number of different occupations from the Strong Vocational Interest Blank (SVIB). High PWE scores preferred conventional and realistic occupations (banker, dietician, farmer, policeman, office-worker, pharmacist, veterinarian), and disliked social and artistic occupations (advertising man, author, artist, architect, music teacher, psychologist).

They concluded that endorsement of the PWE values is associated with interest patterns characteristic of people in occupations demanding a 'concrete, pragmatic orientation' towards work. In general the quality and quantity of products associated with these occupations can be evaluated according to basically extrinsic, objective, and easily specifiable standards (such as farmer's crop yield). These standards, highly related to earned profit, carry much 'consensual validity' and are the ones most likely to be used by the worker as a measure of his own success. The service occupations (Holland's 'Realistic' type) associated with endorsement of the PWE are also very amenable to objective evaluation. Typically, occupations associated with endorsement of the PWE place a premium on conventional adherence to prescribed role-appropriate behaviour, and conversely require little innovativeness or creativity and make relatively few demands on emotional sensitivity or close interpersonal skills. These primarily 'social' dispositions would be important for success in most of the occupations with interest patterns that correlate negatively with the PWE.

More recently Furnham and Koritsas (1989) looked at the relationship between the PWE and Holland's (1973) hexagonal models of vocational preference. It was predicted that PWE measures would be positively correlated with realistic, enterprising, and conventional types but not social, investigative, or artistic. The hypotheses were supported but the PWE measures, themselves all correlated, were also positively correlated with the artistic type.

The PWE was found to be associated with four vocational types (Realistic, Conventional, Enterprising, and Artistic) but this may either imply that there is an association with four separate groups of people, or, if these types were all found within the same person, that there is an association with a certain group of people having a combination of vocational types. These two alternative explanations would each account for a differing number of individuals since the first would involve four different groups of people, and the second only one or two groups of people.

The results from this study suggest that measures or tests of occupational or vocational preferences – such as that of Holland – could be usefully supplemented by PWE measures or any other work-related attitude variable. It is not only the type of work that attracts people but their very attitude to work (their PWE) that may determine why certain jobs are found to be more or less attractive than others. One implication of this study then is that just as people may be dimensionalized in terms of the extent to which they adhere to the

PWE, so jobs or occupations may be equally described. Hence vocational guidance may benefit from the use of work values and orientation measures in addition to measures focusing on preferences.

However, it should not be assumed that the direction of causality is one way – i.e. that belief patterns determine occupational choice. As Kohn and Schooler (1973) have clearly pointed out there are reciprocal effects – occupational experiences affect *and* reflect psychological functioning. Hence some job experiences might increase and others decrease PWE beliefs.

The PWE and tedious work

There is certainly sufficient evidence to suggest that PWE beliefs are associated with hard work. But do people who endorse the PWE work hard at all tasks, even those that are tedious, boring, and have low rewards?

A few empirical studies have addressed this topic but have come up with somewhat equivocal results. In one study Merrens and Garrett (1975) administered the Protestant Ethic Scale to a class of 333 psychology students. Later in the term 20 students with the highest scores and 20 students with the lowest scores were asked to participate in a simple study testing eye–hand co-ordination. The students were seated alone at a table with 100 sheets of paper and asked to draw an X in each circle on the paper with their non-preferred hand (usually the left hand). Each sheet had 250 circles on it, and the students were told to keep filling out sheets until they became tired. The students with high Protestant ethic scores spent an average 23.00 minutes at the task and completed 4.10 sheets, while students with low Protestant ethic scores spent only 16.85 minutes and completed 2.55 sheets. Students with high Protestant ethic scores not only worked longer and accomplished more work but they also worked at a much faster rate. They reported that their feelings were replicated with a different population at a different institution but with similar results.

Ganster (1981) re-examined this finding using a different, more realistic and meaningful electronic sorting task. The results showed no statistical relationship between the PWE scores and either performance at, or satisfaction with, the task. Hence the author questions the usefulness of the PWE scale as an indicant of work attitudes and behaviours. But, of course, Ganster's study can also be criticized and it may be unwise to generalize these results to all work circumstances.

All work provides both extrinsic and intrinsic rewards and hence it seems reasonable to talk about people being extrinsically or intrinsically motivated. Given the nature of the PWE it is likely that believers have higher intrinsic motivation than non-believers. That is intrinsic motivation is a function of personal values but also of how tasks are presented. Following this logic, Tang and Baumeister (1984) found that when given a task called 'work', high PWE scorers were more motivated to do it than low scorers. Tang (1985) also showed that PWE scorers seem less affected by positive *or* negative feedback than low scorers. On the other hand low PWE scorers showed greater intrinsic motivation when given negative feedback.

Then important implication of the work lies in two spheres. First, how a task is presented to someone presumably affects how he or she approaches it. Some people present 'work' or a chore as potential fun but though this strategy may be successful with low PWE scorers, it may have precisely the opposite effect on PWE believers whose values would lead them to be more committed to work than play. Secondly, the fact that feedback has less impact on high than low scorers may have implications for how one attempts to shape behaviour. For instance one might use more positive feedback with low PWE scorers and more negative feedback with high PWE scorers, though it is uncertain whether there are optimal amounts of different types of feedback or whether the effect is linear. Certainly, this research attests to the importance of PWE beliefs in the work place.

Job enlargement (scope) and the PWE

Although researchers have found no close relationship between job scope and job satisfaction, there appears to be some evidence that this relationship is modified by individual difference factors. For instance Hulin and Blood (1968) hypothesized that there would be a *positive* relationship between job satisfaction and scope for people with middle-class work values, but a *negative* relationship for people who are alienated. It was also hypothesized that this relationship would only be true for *blue-collar* workers.

There has been equivocal support for the idea that PWE values moderate between job scope and satisfaction. In two studies Stone (1975, 1976) found, using subgroup analyses, no support for the hypothesis that job scope and satisfaction would be negatively correlated for the alienated workers. Stone (1975) was specifically concerned with the role of the PWE as a moderator variable. However, he found that neither the PWE nor any of its subscales (as measured by Wollack *et al.*, 1971 scale) appeared to moderate the job scope–satisfaction relationship.

Wanous (1974) looked at three possible moderators of this relationship – higher order needs, the PWE, and urban–rural background. The PWE was shown to have a significant moderator effect on a third of the satisfaction measures, but not at all with respect to global satisfaction. He concluded:

> The fact that higher order need strength yielded the clearest results seems reasonable because it is closest to the employee reactions it moderates. Thus it is not surprising that the PWE showed moderate usefulness as a moderator and urban–rural differences the least, because each is increasingly farther removed from on-the-job attitudes and behaviour.
>
> (Wanous, 1974, p. 622)

More recently Peters and Rudolf (1980) not only criticized previous studies on the topic but also tested the relationship between job scope and satisfaction as moderated by the PWE. They found that blue-collar workers had significantly lower PWE scores compared to white-collar and managerial levels. But whereas they found no evidence of the PWE as a moderator variable it did correlate significantly with several dependent variables. However, they were able to draw some very interesting conclusions from their study, namely that PWE beliefs have more direct influence for lower, rather than higher organizational levels, in that PWE correlates positively with satisfaction, internal motivation, and self-evaluated performance. They conclude:

> Thus, persons with strong PWE beliefs should perform better than their low PWE counterparts (and experience corresponding more positive affective reactions) at low, less ambitious organizational levels than at high, more ambiguous organizational levels.

> (p. 250)

Thus it may well be that the effect of the PWE is felt more strongly or differently at different levels in an organization. This may be because of a number of reasons: people at certain levels are nearly always likely (or unlikely) to endorse the PWE and hence there is insufficient variance; PWE values have more impact on certain types of work (dull, repetitive job) than others; or finally PWE beliefs are often closely related to motivation and effort which have a more powerful and noticeable effect at certain levels of an organization compared to others.

The PWE and competitiveness

The profile of the PWE believer is of an independently minded, hard-working individual who is prepared to persevere at a task to achieve desirable ends. The fact that PWE believers are highly individualistic implies that they are more likely to be competitive than co-operative. Furnham and Quilley (1989) in fact used two versions of the well-known prisoner's dilemma game to investigate the co-operation/competition strategies of PWE believers; their predictions were empirically supported. They argued that these results are most important for further work on the PWE. Many studies have shown, for instance, that the PWE is associated with a strong desire to succeed, persistence at work tasks, and a strong resistance to cheating (Eisenberger and Shank, 1985). Yet, as this study demonstrated, the competitiveness associated with an endorsement of the PWE can be disadvantageous. In this study, because of their competitive rather than co-operative tactics high PWE scorers actually achieved lowest scores, thus winning least reward. What PWE high scorers therefore need to do is to be able to distinguish those solutions in which competitiveness is the best strategy from those in which it is the worst. However, given the often replicated finding that PWE beliefs are closely associated with inflexible and simple conservative thinking, it is possible that co-operative strategies are

167

fairly antithetical to PWE beliefs in general and, indeed, may threaten them. In this then may lie the Achilles heel of PWE beliefs – namely the idea that competition as opposed to co-operation is the best strategy.

The PWE and fair rewards

At the heart of many PWE beliefs is the concept of equitable or distributive justice. It appears that the layman, like social scientists, follows the Aristotelian distinction between equity and equality. These two concepts are quite different particularly when one considers the relationship between input and output, effort and reward. A preference for *equity* indicates that a person believes that rewards (for 'work') should be distributed in direct proportions to their effort or reward, i.e. the harder you work, the more you get. A preference for *equality* indicates that a person believes that rewards should be distributed equally to all regardless of input and effort. Of course, perceptions of justice based either on the equity, equality, or any other principle relate to perceptions of fairness and presumably relate to motivation. Other principles include giving to somebody according to need, regardless of input or other's share.

There is an extensive literature on equity theory and social change (McClintock *et al.*, 1982) and procedural justice (Folger and Greenberg, 1985) which concerns various theories of justice and related issues. Whereas some studies have shown quite specific and predictable cultural differences in procedural justice (Leung and Lind, 1986), far fewer have considered individual differences in understanding and preferences for certain reward systems. It would however not be difficult to predict the perceptions and preferences of PWE endorsers. Given their emphasis on personal effort, and contingency based upon individual work, one may suppose that people who believe in the PWE strongly support the equity rather than the equality norm.

There have been quite a few studies on equity and the PWE. In an experimental study Greenberg (1978b) found that when a competition was perceived to be fair, high PWE scorers chose to distribute rewards according to the equity principle, but when the competition was unfair (and to their advancement) high PWE scorers attempted to re-establish fairness by compensating the former with the unfair disadvantage. Low PWE scores followed the equality principle fairly strictly, keeping approximately half the available reward whether they won or lost. Overall then the major hypothesis regarding PWE beliefs and perceived justice was supported.

Greenberg (1979) reported on two further studies which threw light on this topic. In one study, respondents whose PWE scores had been assessed were asked to allocate salary amounts (to hypothetical workers) based on the duration and quality of their performance. Predictably, high PWE scorers paid on an equity basis by taking into account both quantity and duration of work, while low scorers ignored quality, paying workers equal amounts, but did take duration into consideration. The result suggests that PWE endorsement is associated with the acceptance of *different types* of inputs: inputs perceived to be under the control of workers (performance quality) were more closely related to PWE beliefs than those not so easily within the control of workers. A second study set out to test the assumption that people supporting the PWE would believe it to be fair to pay workers in proportion to their personal performance (effort and ability), but reject the fairness of basing rewards on externally based inputs. The results clearly demonstrated this point, namely that people who believe in the PWE are highly sensitive to feeling that workers should be rewarded for performance for which they were personally responsible, and not successes attributable to external, fortuitous factors. Stake (1983) replicated this result on a group of students who allocated bonus pay and salary increases in a hypothetical business setting. She found that high PWE endorsers rewarded more on the basis of worker-controlled inputs than low endorsers. In other words, it is not the actual output alone – measured in terms of duration or productivity – that is perceived of as being important so much as the control the worker has over that output.

> These findings suggest that high-PWE subjects may have more sympathy than low-PWE subjects for the slower, less capable worker who is willing to put in time, but who produces less.
>
> (p. 417)

Greenberg's work has demonstrated the importance of PWE beliefs in the perception of fair and unfair rewards at work and in other settings. In Australia, Feather and O'Driscoll (1980) found consistent findings though they did not use a PWE measure. They noted:

> The results imply that the ambitious, hard-working person who values accomplishments and who believes in the virtues of rationality and intelligence will also be likely to believe that higher levels of performance that reflect these characteristics should be rewarded more than lower levels, where these characteristics may be absent. The person for whom these values are not so important, but for whom other values are presumably more dominant, will be less likely to prefer the equity norm as a basis for allocation and more likely to favour an allocator who distributes payments equally.
>
> (p. 125)

However, in another similar study, Feather (1983b) did examine the relationship between PWE and equity/equality allocations and distributions. The results showed some predictable results: PWE scores were positively related with ratings of effort under two conditions but generally the PWE effects were minor. The author believed this to be due to the fact that individual difference variable effects were relatively minor compared to the very powerful effects of the task and situational variables.

More recent American studies have tended to confirm earlier findings (Rasinski, 1987). Stake (1983) set out to examine how high and low PWE endorsers were allocated rewards as a function of an internal, worker-controlled variable like number of hours worked versus a non-worker-controlled variable like ability (workers in the study were described as volunteering overtime hours, but differing in their ability to produce work units). As predicted, high PWE scorers tended to distribute more rewards on the basis of worker-controlled inputs (be it time or ability) compared to low scorers. The findings suggest that high PWE scorers may have more sympathy than low scorers for slower, less capable workers, who are willing to work harder.

Along with the concept of equity in reward is the idea of equity in effort. A number of researchers have demonstrated the phenomenon, no doubt long suspected by PWE endorsers, of *social loafing* whereby people expect less effort when working in groups than when working alone. A number of possible explanations for this fairly well established phenomenon include: people get away with poor performance in a crowd because their individual outputs are not identifiable; people reduce their own efforts to establish an equitable division of labour. Indeed Jackson and Harkins (1985) found evidence for the latter hypothesis. However, the hypothesis has interesting implications for the PWE hypothesis. It may be that people who believe in the PWE are particularly poor group members because in order to attain an equitable position they regularly under-perform. On the other hand, if put in a group who appear to be more productive than themselves, they may well over-extend themselves.

A PWE corporate culture?

The PWE has been conceived by psychologists as an individual difference belief variable while sociologists have often written about it as a consensually held ethic. But could it be conceived of at the intermediate level as, say, a corporate culture?

According to Deal and Kennedy (1982) a corporate culture has a number of identifiable characteristics: a widely shared philosophy, shared values, a consensually held recognition of heroes, and a systematic routine of rites and rituals. Strong corporate cultures, it is argued, provide a system of informal rules that specifies how people should behave and tends to make people more satisfied. Organizations forge a value system with various slogans that establish this culture, but there may be disadvantages to the organization in the long run if the environment changes and the culture does not, or if the values are contradictory. Tribal habits of a corporate culture dictate dress, housing, sports preferences, language use, etc.

It is through the company heroes and their elaborate and often functional rites and rituals that cultures express themselves. Deal and Kennedy (1982) have identified four generic cultures. The second one they specify – the 'Work Hard, Play Hard Culture' – may have been inspired by the PWE. The values are that success comes with persistence. The American Hamburger giant's values of *quality, service, cleanliness,* and *value* offer a good example, so does Hewlett-Packard's *try* it, *fix* it, *do* it. The heroes of this culture are very successful salesmen and all the rites and rituals are intense and competitive. Of course this culture has disadvantages – adherents have a short-term perspective, failure rapidly turns into disillusionment.

However, the work hard/play hard culture infringes some PWE beliefs. Indeed it might seem an oxymoron that one would have a PWE *culture* because, by definition, the PWE is so individualistic. That is because of the extreme individualism of endorsers of the PWE, it might be difficult to imagine a PWE *culture*. But as was pointed out in Chapter 2, it is possible to identify a constellation of values around the PWE that would dictate that culture. Certain educational institutions probably have a strong PWE culture.

According to Deal and Kennedy (1982) one can recognize a corporate culture from the outside and the inside – the physical layout; annual reports and press releases and how strangers are greeted, are all external forms of a culture. One can also get a good idea about corporate culture by looking at the career path progression of employees, how long people stay in a job, and the sort of anecdotes frequently heard in that culture.

But the main point of corporate cultures is how they select and socialize a particular pattern of beliefs and behaviours. Over time, the people inside strong cultures become more homogeneous and of a 'like mind'. In this sense corporate cultural values rather than the beliefs of individuals like the PWE are the primary determinants of work- *and* non-work-related behaviour. It might be, then, that in some organizations the reason why PWE beliefs are not particularly predictive of behaviour is because corporate cultural values 'wash out' or 'overlay' the traditional PWE virtues and values.

The application of anthropological insights and methods to the work-place is to be greatly welcomed. Some recent attempts have resulted in taxonomies. For instance, examining cheating in the work-place, Mars (1984) identified four different types:

- Hawks – individualistic entrepreneurs who tend to be innovative professionals and small business men and 'perch unhappily in organizations'.
- Donkeys – are people highly constrained by externally imposed rules and isolated one from the other.
- Wolves – these are 'pack' or group oriented individuals who have and prefer hierarchies, order, and internal controls.
- Vultures – they are supported by colleagues but competitive, isolated, and challenging in their work.

Mars (1984) shows how these occupational cultures have different influences on economic productivity and industrial relations. It is quite possible to conceive of a corporate culture imbued with PWE values. Despite the individualistic, competitive nature of the PWE it is possible that an organization take the fundamental tenets of the PWE, inculcate them in the work-staff, and consciously shape and reward them in the corporate culture.

The PWE after work

There has been considerable interest in age-related differences in work attitudes and behaviour. In an extensive review of the area, Rhodes (1983) found three studies which found a positive and one a negative relationship between PWE beliefs and age but believed the best studies showed clear evidence for a positive effect (with all salient variables controlled for). How then does the PWE affect retirement?

McGoldrick (1973), interviewing 1,800 early-retired men and their wives, grouped the possibilities in an interesting way. She identified the following types:

- 'Rest and relaxers'. These people, mostly the older ones in the sample, were content with the traditional pastimes of newspapers, TV, walking, gardening, and trips in the car.
- 'Home and family men'. These enjoyed spending more time with their wives, looking after and helping in the home.
- 'Hobbyists'. For many the hobby has become the focus of their lives. Hobbies ranged from DIY, philately, birdwatching, golf, and fishing, to music and art.
- 'Good timers'. Social life, travel, and going out in the evenings were the choice of some.
- 'Committee and society men'. Twenty-four per cent of the sample found that they were able to devote more time to societies and committees that they had been interested in before.
- 'Volunteers'. Nineteen per cent of the sample had done voluntary work after ending employment. This ranged from helping friends and neighbours to full-time work for a local charity.
- 'Further education'. Nine per cent enrolled on courses at universities, among them the Open University, and at local colleges.
- 'Part-time jobbers'. Twenty-four per cent did some extra work, a few because they needed the money, but most because of the interest it gave them. More intended to do some part-time work when their year of unemployment benefit ended.
- 'New jobbers'. This includes the 'easier jobbers' who took a lower and slower job for less pay, the 'other job men' who looked for equivalent jobs, the 'second-career men' who wanted the chance to move into another career, usually after a period of retraining, and the 'entrepreneurs', who used early retirement as a chance to start their own business with redundancy money as capital.

Certainly, one could predict that PWE beliefs would be associated with a likelihood of becoming a part-time or new jobber. What would be particularly interesting, is to determine which type or pattern of adjustment is most adaptive for retired people given their work beliefs or attitudes. In other words this is not to argue that one type or behaviour pattern is most healthy or adaptive, but rather that it best 'fits' with other characteristics of the person, such as their PWE beliefs. In this sense the idea is alien to that proposed by Holland (1973) on vocational preference.

Conclusion

This chapter has considered the role of PWE beliefs in the work place. There has been extensive sociological and psychological research on the meaning, function, and conception of work, not to mention the relationship between work and leisure. Although it has not been explicitly discussed as such, it is probable that people who endorse the PWE have significantly different conceptions of work than those who do not endorse, even actively reject, the PWE.

There are many ways of approaching the issues of the needs satisfied by work. One method, proposed by Sales and Strauss (1966), was to have three higher order factors – physical and security needs; social needs; and egoistic needs – and then describe the constituents of each. Thus primary physical and security needs fulfil desires for money, security, and advancement. Social needs include friendship, the sense of identification with other groups, and teamwork. Primary egoistical needs include feelings of accomplishment (use of skill, productivity), feelings of autonomy, and the increase of knowledge. Underlying all these classifications of needs is the assumption about a hierarchy. But there are other important questions such as the relationship among needs; the possibility of substituting one need for another. More important, however, is the question concerning the role of job satisfaction and its relationship to productivity. Some have argued that job satisfaction is a crucially important determinant of the meaning of work, others that it is completely irrelevant. Sales and Strauss (1966) summarized those arguments (see Table 5.7).

This dichotomous approach is too simplistic but helpful in understanding the role of PWE belief at work. It has been suggested that PWE beliefs are related to vocational choice; the ability to endure tedious work; characteristic reactions to job enrichment; the amount of competitiveness at work and the reactions to reward structure. In this sense PWE may be conceived of as a multi-dimensional, but powerfully predictive individual difference measure in the work-place. Much of the material reviewed in this chapter suggests that PWE beliefs are highly predictive of work-related behaviours.

However, many of the studies in this field are small-scale experimental studies. Studies, ideally done longitudinally over time, with large, varied heterogeneous populations, could allow numerous hypotheses to be properly

Table 5.7 Summary of the argument

Job Satisfaction Important	Job Satisfaction Unimportant
People who want self-actualization.	Some people prefer unchallenging work.
Those who don't obtain job satisfaction never reach psychological maturity.	Individual personality becomes fixed before people start working. Work is not to blame.
Those who fail to obtain job satisfaction become frustrated.	Most people have relatively low levels of aspiration for job satisfaction and expect only routine work.
The job is central to man's life.	This is a professor's value. Many people focus their lives on family and community.
Those without work are unhappy. People want to work even when they don't have to.	Even though there are social pressures to have a job, this does not mean the job must be challenging, etc.
Lack of challenging work leads to low mental health.	Poor mental health may be due to low income or low status of routine jobs. Anyway, research findings are not conclusive.
Work and leisure patterns spill into each other. Those with uncreative jobs engage in uncreative recreation.	A new bohemianism off the job will make up for increasing boredom at work.
Lack of job satisfaction and alienation from work lead to lower morale, lower productivity, and an unhealthy society.	We can provide challenging work for everybody only at the cost of eliminating our mass production technology and high standard of living – and society is unwilling to pay this price.

Source: Sales and Strauss, 1966.

tested. The PWE is an individual difference variable conceived around the world of work. It would indeed be surprising if it did not relate directly to a whole range of work-related behaviours.

Chapter six

The work ethic and worklessness

Work is the price you pay for money.

Anon

Work spares us from three great evils: boredom, vice, and need.

Voltaire

But though we had plenty of money,
  there was nothing our money could buy,
And the Gods of the Copy Book Headings said
  'If you don't work, you die'.

Kipling

And that thou, Lord, art merciful: for thou rewardest every man according to his work.

Book of Common Prayer

It is impossible to enjoy idling thoroughly unless one has plenty of work to do.

Jerome K. Jerome

Introduction

This chapter concerns the relationship between PWE beliefs and the condition of not being at work by choice or by chance. It compares both PWE beliefs of people in and out of work to those in the same or the other condition (namely working or not). However, there are a number of possible states of worklessness. For instance, a person may be unemployed or retired, or simply not working – at leisure – because they are rich or of independent means so that they are not required to work and choose not to do so. The relationship between PWE beliefs and work-related behaviours has been considered in the previous chapter. This chapter will consider the relationship between PWE beliefs and unemployment; retirement, psychotherapy, and Christian ethics.

The PWE and unemployment

It is an obvious and straightforward hypothesis that employed people with high PWE beliefs would be highly unsympathetic to the unemployed. People with PWE beliefs would, according to the original hypothesis, probably see unemployment as voluntary (that is chosen in some sense) rather than the result of uncontrollable structured or cyclical factors in the economy. People without work would be viewed quite unsympathetically as the damned and the undeserving poor.

At the heart of PWE is that God achieves things through the labour of man and that work is a means of discipline, a prescription against sexual temptation and religious doubt, and a moral necessity – the purpose of life. Laziness and idleness – any condition of worklessness – must therefore be a source of evil and the failure to impose discipline. If people are unemployed yet having presumably been endowed by God with equal capability to work as other people, his or her condition must be due to individual improvidence and vice, and hence it may be unwise, even dangerous, to pamper those who fail. Despite the widespread beliefs that 'the poor are different' and have a PWE-rejecting culture of poverty, there is no evidence that the work-motivation of the poor is different from the non-poor (Davidson and Gaitz, 1974). Yet beliefs persist in the 'damnable' status of the poor.

This section will consider two things – the first is the attitudes and beliefs the PWE endorses who are themselves in work, and secondly the reaction and coping strategies of PWE believers to their own unemployment will be considered.

Welfare and the work ethic

There is both speculative, conceptual, and empirical work on the relationship between PWE beliefs – held by people at work – to the poor, the unemployed, and those in receipt of state or charitable help. One of the early manifestations of the PWE was to distinguish between the *deserving* poor – the widowed, the orphaned, the ill, the aged (who had been prevented from saving), and the physically handicapped who were innocent victims – and the *undeserving* poor such as alcoholics, neurotics, and slothful individuals whose indolence and inefficiency was immoral and who could be exploited, condemned, or discarded with impunity. It has been argued by Williamson (1974) and others that beliefs about the motivation of the poor (i.e. this PWE) and attitudes to public policy are a function of economic self-interest and PWE beliefs. Indeed, he showed in a regressional analysis that PWE beliefswere the best predictor of attitudes to the poor.

Hence, the welfare and social work system, at least as it developed in America, sought to inculcate middle-class PWE values of thrift, sobriety, self-improvement, etc. However, there was (and possibly still is) a gulf between welfare aims and ideals, and the practices of welfare workers and agencies.

Paradoxically it is the recipients of welfare more than the dischargers of welfare who have to live according to the PWE – not build up debts, use credit carefully, budget and plan ahead, be prompt for appointments, avoid alcohol, indulge in non-conspicuous consumption. But according to Segalman (1968) the PWE disappeared with the Depression and mass unemployment – the idea that a quarter of all Americans were sinners was too incredible to believe. Hence there arose the belief in the right to public assistance.

The PWE was therefore also applied to what Rotenberg (1975) has called the people-changing sciences like psychiatry and psychotherapy. He argued that the Calvin-attributed concept of predestination was seen to imply that the elect were predestined to have the psychological 'symptoms' of righteousness, while the damned were seen to suffer the unchangeable 'symptoms' of wickedness. Whereas most PWE scholars have concentrated on the successful, predestined righteous, few have looked at societies' reactions to the unsuccessful predestined damned. The PWE allowed that the unsuccessful were born criminals or alcoholics, and because they were hopelessly damned, they could be 'put away' and 'relieved from competing for survival'.

Hence it becomes both normal and acceptable to express little compassion and waste minimal help on the 'unsuccessful'. Furthermore, it makes the treatment of those who have internalized the PWE particularly problematic as they are, presumably, imbued with feelings of powerlessness and guilt. There appears to be a major paradox for the PWE believer in that no amount of effort or striving would apparently help those who have been predestined to fail. The social fatalism and notion of an unchangeable human nature makes the concept of change highly problematic for the PWE believer.

Because the PWE is opposed not only to impulsive living, magical or festive entertainments, but also sexual enjoyment, a great deal of psychological meaning is attributed to sexual behaviour. Sexual restraint was founded on the concept of bowel control and because of the equating of semen with money, it meant that sexual urges and the temptations of the flesh should be denied, controlled, and repressed. Albee (1977) argued that various forms of psychopathology resulted primarily from the guilt arising from the lack of sexual control. These included hysteria, and manic depressive psychosis. Yet he believes that this phase has ended with the death of the PWE. Albee (1977) concludes thus:

> The emerging epic struggle now going on in psychology between the hard-nosed experimental scientists and the 'humanists' is reflective of conflicts within the larger society between still-powerful, last-ditch defenders of the Protestant ethic (most of whom are obsessive personalities) and revolutionaries advocating the primary importance of sensory experience, sexual recreation, and encounter (many of whom are hysterics).
>
> The sciences and professions, in particular, have been a last stronghold of an obsessive-compulsive, and therefore Protestant-ethic oriented,

elite. By setting up all sorts of admission prerequisites based on intellectual effort and achievement, the professions have been kept relatively pure. The more scientific the field, or the greater its earning power, the more carefully are neophytes selected to insure continuation of the proper obsessive personality characteristics. For example, to get into medical school, it is necessary to make a career choice fairly early and to prepare from high school days, at least, in order to have the prerequisites to take the courses that are prerequisite to other required courses. Medical schools insist on a year of organic chemistry, physics and calculus, and many add a required year of physical chemistry, genetics, comparative anatomy, etc. While these prerequisites are not essential to later successful performance as a physician, they insure that most students earning their required A's in these courses will be obsessive compulsive grinds. Humanistically oriented students, members of the Pepsi Generation, cannot discipline themselves to get through these prerequisites. Psychology requires statistics, research design, history and systems, and physiological approaches for majors, and only majors have been admitted to the Boulder-Model, scientifically oriented departments of psychology. But many of the new schools and humanistic programs have relaxed these entrance requirements.

(p. 158)

However, in the 1980s many industrialized countries, especially Britain and America, have been returning to some of the original PWE values like ambitiousness, hard work, and self-reliance. As a result more recent observers of social welfare have begun to condemn PWE-based beliefs. For instance Goodin (1986) has described the doctrine of 'self-reliance' at the heart of much PWE thinking as a 'pernicious doctrine' that does nothing to prevent vulnerability and dependency but rather serves only to increase it. He argues, as do others, that welfare is a moral obligation and that welfarism is not the cause of dependency.

There have also been over the years a number of empirical studies examining the relationship between the PWE and attitudes to welfare and the poor. For instance, Goodwin (1973) interviewed five groups of people some of whom were, and others who were not, recipients of welfare, about such things as their aspirations as well as the work ethic. They were required to rate such statements as 'Getting recognition for my own work is important to me'; 'I feel good when I have a job'; 'Success in an occupation is mainly a matter of how much effort you put into it'. The results were very interesting. Among the poorer respondents, many of whom were on welfare, those with a high PWE score showed greater lack of confidence presumably because inability to succeed in the working world lowers their feelings of self-worth such that they are unable to participate in an important activity. Yet the middle class perceive the precise opposite, namely that the work ethic is seen to lead to strong confidence in self and conversely that middle-class people mistakenly tend to see a great lack of confidence among poor people as an indication of their low work ethic. Similarly they see those who accept or condone the notion of state welfare as having a low work ethic. The major point here is that a high PWE belief is maladaptive among the poor and those on welfare as it leads to lack of confidence and apathy, which in turn mitigates any occupational success that may help them break out of the trap. Most recipients of welfare therefore do not need to be inculcated with the work ethic, rather they desperately need the experience of success at work. This is a challenging and counter-intuitive finding that may warrant both replication and explanation.

MacDonald (1971) argued and demonstrated that people who do *not* endorse the work ethic tend to believe in the ethics of personal conscience, seeing any and all sources of injustice as residing in society's established institutions, while those who believed in the PWE endorsed the ethics of social responsibility which locates the source of injustice as residing in people rather than society's institutions. In a second study MacDonald (1972) demonstrated that PWE beliefs were associated with negative attitudes to the poor. Thus people with high PWE scores tended to agree with statements such as: 'I can't understand why some people make such a fuss over the disadvantaged state of the poor, most of them could improve their condition if only they tried'; 'Although we don't like to face it, most people on welfare are lazy'; 'In this country, almost everyone can make it if he tries hard enough'; 'By pouring money into poverty programs we are destroying the very thing that made this a great and prosperous country: competition' etc. These results have been successfully replicated in England by Wagstaff (1983).

In a series of papers, Furnham (1982, 1983, 1985a) examined attitudes to, and explanations for, unemployed people on social security (welfare in Britain). Furnham (1982) has argued that explanations for poverty, wealth, and unemployment, as beliefs about social security and the importance of work, form a coherent whole; and that three different belief systems can be distinguished. These are: *individualistic* beliefs which place responsibility for economic success or failure on the behaviour of individuals; *societal* beliefs which place responsibility on external societal or economic forces; and *fatalistic* beliefs which place responsibility on chance, luck, or fate. It is likely that high PWE scorers would believe in individual explanations for unemployment, suggesting that people are unemployed due to laziness, lack of effort, unwillingness to take on certain jobs, or move to places of work, etc. High PWE scorers are also likely to believe that social security (welfare) recipients who are unemployed should be working, as welfare encourages idleness.

The results largely substantiated these hypotheses. Table 6.1 shows five individualistic, three societal, and two fatalistic items showed significant differences. Each showed high PWE scorers endorsed the items as more true than low PWE scorers. Despite the fact that some items were societal they were fairly reactionary and this may have caused high PWE scorers to agree with them. The attitudes to recipients showed even clearer findings. There

Table 6.1 Means and F values for the explanations for unemployment offered by the three PWE belief groups, and factor loadings after varimax rotation

Explanations	Low PWE	Middle PWE	High PWE	F value	Factor 1	Factor 2	Factor 3
Individualistic							
1. Unemployed people can earn more money on social security.	5.17	4.28	4.22	3.59*	0.78	0.11	−0.09
4. Lack of effort and laziness among unemployed people.	5.00	4.29	3.85	4.18**	0.81	0.10	0.05
7. Unemployed people don't try hard enough to get jobs.	5.05	4.03	3.80	5.09**	0.68	0.16	0.03
9. Lack of intelligence or ability among the unemployed.	5.00	5.07	4.57	1.02	0.15	1.13	−0.42
10. Unemployed people are too fussy and proud to accept some jobs.	5.42	3.85	3.78	3.78*	0.60	0.41	−0.18
12. Poor education and qualifications among unemployed people.	4.05	3.44	3.52	1.51	0.06	0.25	0.09
13. Unwillingness of unemployed to move to places of work.	3.72	3.62	3.00	3.43*	0.55	0.45	0.14
Societal							
2. The policies and strategies of the present government.	2.20	2.74	2.69	1.23	0.09	0.07	0.02
5. The policies and strategies of previous British governments.	2.52	2.66	2.67	0.13	0.00	0.10	0.36
11. Inefficient and less competitive industries that go bankrupt	3.05	3.00	2.95	0.05	0.00	0.15	0.75
14. Inability of unemployed people to adapt to new conditions.	4.10	3.88	3.26	2.75	0.24	0.69	0.09
15. An influx of immigrants have taken up all available jobs.	5.47	5.44	4.11	7.29***	0.74	0.03	−0.13
16. Trade unions have priced their members out of a job.	3.73	3.18	2.83	2.98*	0.13	0.82	0.14
17. Overmanning in industry which has occurred for too long.	3.27	2.77	2.54	2.54*	0.00	0.81	0.24
18. Incompetent industrial management with poor planning.	2.65	2.70	2.69	0.02	−0.08	0.24	0.18
20. Weak trade unions that do not fight to keep jobs.	5.25	5.51	5.21	0.35	0.14	−0.31	0.05
Fatalistic							
3. Sickness and physical handicap among unemployed people.	5.37	5.88	4.83	3.68*	0.15	−0.18	−0.00
6. Just bad luck	5.77	5.87	5.02	2.96*	0.21	0.03	0.27
8. Worldwide recession and inflation.	1.85	2.11	1.59	1.71	−0.06	0.13	0.67
19. The introduction of widespread automation.	3.60	3.70	3.16	1.12	0.17	−0.31	0.68
				Eigenvalue:	4.62	2.89	1.94
				Variance (%):	23.1	14.5	9.7

*$p < 0.05$; **$p < 0.01$; ***$p < 0.001$.
Note: These numbers represent the mean on the following scale: important 1 2 3 4 5 6 7 unimportant.
Source: Furnham, 1982.

Table 6.2 Means and F values for the attitude statements concerning social security by the three PWE belief groups, and factor loadings after varimax rotation

Explanations	Low PWE	Middle PWE	High PWE	F value	Factor 1	Factor 2	Factor 3
1. There are too many people receiving social security who should be working.	4.00	3.90	2.52	6.40***	0.68	−0.06	−0.27
2. Many people getting social security are not honest about their needs.	4.17	3.77	3.00	3.78*	0.61	−0.24	−0.39
3. Many women getting social security are having illegitimate babies to increase their allowances.	6.35	6.18	5.61	2.65*	0.72	−0.16	0.13
4. Generally, we are spending too little money on social security.	3.80	4.59	4.80	3.42*	−0.15	0.17	0.78
5. Most of the people on social security who can work try to find jobs so that they can support themselves.	2.87	3.07	3.21	0.48	−0.18	0.72	0.25
6. One of the main troubles with social security is that it doesn't give people enough money to get along.	3.97	4.14	4.73	2.03	−0.13	0.33	0.75
7. A lot of people are moving to this country from other countries just to get the social security here.	5.22	4.48	4.00	3.77*	0.55	−0.20	−0.34
8. Many of the people on social security have very little talent, ability, or intelligence.	6.40	4.96	4.72	11.54***	0.02	−0.15	−0.17
9. People are often ashamed of being on social security.	2.57	2.44	2.26	0.43	−0.18	0.75	−0.04
10. Many people in this country who are entitled to social security are too proud to claim it.	3.62	3.07	3.50	0.82	−0.04	0.27	0.08
11. A country's compassion and humanitarianism can be judged by its social security payments.	4.02	3.37	4.21	1.46	−0.24	0.42	0.44
12. Nobody can possibly enjoy living on social security for a long time.	3.32	3.22	3.07	0.18	−0.18	0.72	0.11
13. There would be fewer people on social security if there were more jobs.	2.22	2.33	2.23	0.04	−0.20	0.74	0.18
14. There is no reason why a person who is able to work should receive social security.	5.57	5.66	5.04	1.37	0.47	−0.22	−0.03
15. Social security is a right not a privilege.	2.51	2.60	3.64	4.29**	0.28	−0.07	0.65
16. Too many people on social security spend their money on drinking.	4.42	4.45	3.55	2.59	0.69	−0.17	−0.32
17. Having a social security system only encourages idleness.	3.97	3.07	2.41	6.15**	0.73	−0.24	−0.34
Eigenvalue:					5.97	1.63	1.23
Variance (%): 35.2						9.62	7.32

*$p<0.05$; **$p<0.01$; ***$p<0.001$.   Note: These numbers represent the mean on the following scale: agree 1 2 3 4 5 6 7 disagree. Source: Furnham, 1982.

were significant differences on nearly all the items that suggested social security recipients were dishonest about their various needs and do immoral things to acquire welfare payment. Other studies have been concerned with the structure of the beliefs about social security (welfare) recipients.

Two more recent British studies are worth mentioning. Furnham (1983) examined the effect on sex, education, and voting pattern on over 170 normal subjects' attitudes towards (unemployed) people receiving unemployment benefits. Both education and vote (but not sex) appeared to be important factors in predicting people's attitudes. A factor analysis of the 12-item questionnaire revealed three clearly interpretable factors which indicated that attitudes centred around the difficulty of coping with the amount of benefit provided; beliefs about people being dishonest about their needs and abusing benefit payments; and the loss of self-esteem and stigma associated with being on social security. The results showed that in Britain, as in America, people not on social security tend to have more negative attitudes towards those that are, although they may appreciate some of the problems of the unemployed on social security.

More recently, Furnham (1985a) replicated the above study but found four clearly interpretable dimensions underlying attitudes to social security requests. In all the factor analytic (empirical or conceptual) work, similar factors arise with regard to attitudes to those on social security: dishonesty/idleness/prodigality – referring to the *undeserving nature* of the recipients; difficulty/poverty referring to the *economic deprivation* of those attempting to cope on the amount of benefit provided; stigma (shame)/self-esteem referring to the *social consequences* of being the recipients of 'charity'. Other less important factors from this work appear to concern fatalism or future needs for social security. Similar studies have found similar results.

Golding and Middleton (1983) found four clear factors which they called prodigality (being to do with wasteful spending patterns, financial ineptitude, imprudent breeding habits, and sheer fecklessness or lack of motivation of the poor on welfare), injustice (exploitation or unfair distribution of financial rewards), bad luck (cycle of deprivation thesis), and individualistic fatalism (sheer unpredictable, undeserved personal as opposed to structural misfortune). Furnham (1985a) also looked at PWE beliefs as they related to the few factors identified above. Predictably those who believed in the PWE tended to see those on social security as idle and dishonest, did not believe that it was particularly difficult existing on social security, and felt recipients suffered little stigma and shame while on the dole. Feather argued that attributions or explanations for unemployment were not simply products of neutral information processing, but linked to the cognitive-affective system. PWE values influence the way people explain a widely different range of events, including the causes of unemployment. Thus the PWE can be seen as an organizing cognitive system through which the social world is perceived and 'explained'.

The work ethic of the unemployed

People become unemployed for a wide variety of reasons: they may be made redundant because their place of work is closing or the product/service they are providing is no longer demanded; or they may never have got a job after leaving school. How do PWE beliefs and other work-related beliefs affect the beliefs and behaviours of the unemployed? A number of possible hypotheses would be suggested some of which are complementary, others contradictory. For instance:

● Unemployed people with strong PWE beliefs would become more depressed, anxious, and apathetic than unemployed people who did not believe in the work ethic.
● Unemployed people with strong PWE beliefs would participate more frequently in a greater range of non-work (but work-like or work-substitute) activities than people who did not believe in the PWE.
● Unemployed people with strong PWE beliefs would persevere with more effort and over a longer period to get a job than unemployed people who did not believe in the PWE.
● Belief in the PWE would gradually decrease the longer a person remained unemployed.

Work in this area appears to fall into two areas: studies done on adult unemployed people noting the effect of the PWE on their adaptation; and studies done on school leavers and young people attempting to ascertain whether the PWE led to adaptive or maladaptive qualities.

Shamir (1985) examined over 400 adults in Israel all of whom had been employed. Contrary to his hypothesis, however, he found that individuals with a high PWE turn to non-work activities more frequently while unemployed and derive more psychological benefit from such activities than individuals low on PWE beliefs. Thus it appears that PWE beliefs contribute to, rather than hinder, coping strategies useful while unemployed. There may be some sort of 'spillover' principle where stable, intellectual, and motivational coping styles associated with the PWE in the occupational role get transferred to non-work activities. 'In summary, the results of this study raise some doubts concerning the claim that a reduction in the PWE would automatically lead to coping better with unemployment. In fact, the opposite might be true. Rather than fighting the Protestant work ethic, a more realistic strategy would be to harness it and channel it to non-employment related work and to other non-work activities which have the potential for answering individuals' needs for activity structure, social meaning and intellectual stimulation' (p. 344).

In a related study, Shamir (1986) tested various hypotheses about the psychological well-being of unemployed individuals focusing on the moderating effects of the PWE. Contrary to predictions, the PWE did not moderate the relationship between employment status and psychological state, though various methodological problems could account for them. Thus Shamir (1986) concludes: 'There is also no evidence in our study that the Protestant work ethic hinders the processes of coping with unemployment in any way or that individuals who "free" themselves of the ethic find unemployment easier to bear' (p. 36). Furthermore, using the same data, Shamir (1987) was able to demonstrate that people's belief in, and adherence to, the PWE is *not* influenced by their change in work status in and out of work. This implies both that the PWE is a relatively stable dispositional factor but also that the experience of unemployment does not lead to work inhibitions.

Shamir's work would appear to indicate that PWE beliefs do not adversely affect people who are unemployed, indeed they may even make adjustment to worklessness better. However, it should be pointed out that these results are based on a limited sample of middle-class Israelis. It is quite probable that other variables as well as the PWE mediate between unemployment and psychological reactions such as class, self esteem, attributional style, coping strategies, etc. In fact the studies on young people – school-leavers – have tended to examine those other factors and, as a result, come up with a rather different set of findings concerning the moderator effects of the PWE.

There are a host of studies which have examined differences in, and behaviours of, the unemployed (O'Brien and Kabanoff, 1979). Some have looked specifically at the moderating effect of work commitment, clearly closely akin to the PWE. For instance Jackson *et al.* (1983) found that the effect of change in employment status (getting or losing a job) on the levels of distress is a function of employment commitment such that those with high commitment showed greater change in distress scores as a result of change in employment status. But the authors note the possibility of other important variables such as the person's activity level, social support, recent negative life events, socio-economic status, financial resources, vulnerability to stress.

Some studies, both cross-sectional and longitudinal, have looked at the PWE and other moderators between unemployment and psychological well-being in young people (Lynn *et al.*, 1984). Feather (1982), in a cross-sectional study, showed unemployed young males had lower PWE scores than employed male subjects and that active pursuit of employment tended to be more frequent among those with higher self-esteem, stronger PWE values, and lower apathy. However, it is only by longitudinal studies that it is possible to separate cause from correlation. Feather and O'Brien (1986a, b) in fact reported on a longitudinal study of nearly 3,000 Australian school-leavers. They found that those young people who did not find work, compared to those who did, tend to see themselves as less competent, pleasant, and active; to report more stress and depressive affect but less satisfaction with life; to have lower PWE scores and to rate their need for a job as less important. But the PWE scores did not change in time such that the high scores of the employed remained much the same and significantly higher than the unemployed at both time periods. However, Feather and O'Brien (1986b) showed that for those who changed their status there were significant changes – those who were employed and then became unemployed tended to show a decrease in their PWE score, while those who went from unemployment into employment showed a significant increase in their PWE score. They also found that PWE beliefs in both the employed and unemployed were correlated with feelings that one needed a job, the perceived attractiveness of work, self-perceptions of competence, life satisfaction, and the perception that the unemployed lack motivation. More recently in a study of 320 young unemployed people, Feather and O'Brien (1987) found their perceived desirability of being employed was positively related to their endorsement of the PWE.

The PWE and retirement

In most western industrialized countries there is both the expectation and practice that people will 'retire' from work at or near a specific age – frequently between 60 and 65 years. This may differ enormously as a function of health, job, etc. (some sportsmen have to retire in the mid-30s; politicians, it appears, have no formal retiring age). People may take early or premature retirement as well as late or delayed retirement. Work appears to be so important for some individuals that they find it almost impossible to retire, continuing to work (for little or no stipend) till they die. Others take on different, albeit frequently menial, work just so that they have the rewards of work.

Men and women who continue to work over the age of 65 or 70, tend to be drawn from the extremes of the occupational ladder – the lower unskilled end through financial necessity, but also at the higher end because of certain benefits accrued. Why is it that healthy, financially secure individuals choose to work after retirement? Fillenbaum and Maddox (1974) listed a number of potentially important factors:

- Negative attitudes to retirement.
- Inappropriate or no plans for retirement.
- Amount of intrinsic vs extrinsic work commitment.
- Personality factors such as need for achievement.
- The influence of peers.

They found that all these factors, but least of all the personality dimensions that were measured, were direct predictors of work after retirement. Continued working appears to be a function of personal dislike of retirement, intention to work after retirement, active pre-retirement involvement in work, and the presence of younger friends who are themselves working.

How do PWE beliefs relate to work after retirement states/active with retirement, etc.? Clearly PWE beliefs are related to leisure and non-work, hence it is possible to entertain a number of testable hypotheses such as the following: High, as opposed to low, PWE believers will:

- Tend to resist early retirement and opt for delayed retirement.
- Tend, if possible, to continue working at the same job.

- Find alternative 'employment' if available.
- Report lower retirement satisfaction if unable to work.
- Adapt a life style particularly in terms of time-keeping closely akin to that of working people.

Hooker and Ventis (1984) in fact examined the relationship between PWE beliefs, retirement satisfaction, and the daily activities of those who were retired. They found, as predicted, that PWE beliefs were inversely related to satisfaction in retirement. This may have been because high PWE scorers tended to have fewer non-work-related activities which are usually related to work satisfaction, but are in any case under-valued being leisure. Least satisfied retirees were those with high PWE beliefs who did not perceive their activities as useful, and vice versa. The authors feel that pre-retirement counselling should be aimed at helping to relinquish the strong work-orientation of some people, but that work-like activities remain a source of satisfaction for high PWE scorers.

The work ethic, social security/welfare support

At first glance it may seem that there is a simple and obvious relationship between the PWE and attitudes to welfare. If it were the case that the PWE maintained that efforts were rewarded and idleness punished, and that wealth was the fruit of the former and poverty the latter, it may be assumed that the PWE would be against welfare to the poor. Rather than assisting the indolent, they would be put into work-houses which were an institutional means of containing the idle and instilling the work ethic. Literally hundreds of quotes would be sought to demonstrate that from the fifteenth century to the present day people have been obsessed by the indolent, idle, work-shy.

However, from earliest times the distinction has been made between the deserving and the non-deserving poor. Hence the existence in the sixteenth and seventeenth centuries of houses of correction for vagrants, work-houses for the able-bodied paupers, and poor houses for the aged, the sick, widows, and orphans. Again the 1834 Poor Law Amendment Act was aimed at ending a bounty of indolence and vice, seen to be the major causes of poverty. Golding and Middleton (1983) outlined four tenets of the moral theory:

- The notion that what the poor needed was remoralization.
- There is perfidious exploitation of the good intentions of benefactors.
- Pauperism needed to be contained, eliminated, and repressed.
- The poor needed to be classified into the small minority of blamelessly indigent and a larger group of the 'vicious' and indolent.

Later there were many distinctions made such as those who *will, can't,* or *won't* work; the workless, thriftless, and worthless.

Royal commissions, 'professional' social reformers, and journalists in the mid to late nineteenth century spent a great deal of time and effort debating the causes, consequences, and alleviation of poverty. Throughout this work is a constant source of references to work and the worthiness of PWE values and ideals. According to Golding and Middleton (1983) three themes re-occurred in popular understanding of, and attitudes to, poverty, welfare, and worklessness: the efficiency of the labour market and economic forces; the morality of the work ethic and self-sufficiency; and the pathology of individual inadequacy. Of course, all three may be seen to be necessary and none sufficient. More recently, attitudes to the workless and those on welfare have had a number of themes: there is widespread abuse of welfare and those caught are simply the tip of the iceberg; welfare scroungers are abusing the rights of citizenship; the welfare (nanny) state has been extended over too wide a range of clients, at great social and economic cost; many recipients belong to the undeserving poor; welfare benefits which have become too easy to get have become excessively generous, encourage indolence, and insult the honest worker. Golding and Middleton (1983) found that journalists believe in the work ethic and individualism and are hence unsympathetic to those on welfare. 'Nevertheless, the self-made journalist committed to the work ethic and individualistic self-reliance, will find in the occupation a well-formed occupational ideology to support these values and much to lend weight to the equally well-nourished scepticism in British culture about the concerns of the welfare services and the motivation of their clients' (p. 143). They argue that currently there is a strong spirit of acute welfarism and the reassertion of basic values of national unity, the work ethic, self help, traditional family life, and moral rectitude.

The PWE and psychotherapy

How do PWE believers react to the mentally ill and the deviant? How do they explain the origins of mental illness and how do these theories of aetiology relate to what they believe to be the cure or 'management-strategy'? In a robust attack on the PWE, Rotenberg (1978) argued that over the past centuries there had been discernibly different attitudes to mental illness and deviance. The presumed aetiology, treatment, and metaphor for illness and deviance in our present time is to see it as caused by innate, internal factors which are frequently irreversible, hence the treatment is primarily stigmatization and incarceration. To a large extent he blames this unsympathetic view on the PWE. In doing so he presents both a model and a set of propositions set out below:

1. To the extent that the Protestant Ethic had a general impact on the Western world in terms of economic and scientific development, it is equally responsible for the belief in man's inability to change, since both effects are traceable to Calvin's influential doctrine of predestination.
2. The Protestant Ethic, which is characteristically associated with such referents as 'striving', 'achieving', 'individuality', and 'rationalism', fitted and facilitated the development of a scientific model that held nature to

be changeable by man. The arbitrary extension of this model to a people-changing technology, however, appears to be paradoxical and self-defeating, since it is rooted in the doctrine of predestination which holds that man himself is unchangeable.

3. According to modern interpretations of the concept of predestination, a person's ultimate success (mainly material) serves as *a priori* proof that he belongs to the 'elect', whereas the absence of success indicates that he is numbered among the 'damned'. It is thus possible that the traditional preference of Western psychotherapists for treating neurotics while shunning psychopaths and psychotics is due not so much to a lack of effective and measurable treatment methods but rather to the therapists' underlying belief that the neurotic is treatable ('elect') while the others are unchangeable ('damned').

4. In psychopathology it is not so much the medical-scientific labelling system *per se* that causes stigma and its detrimental social consequences but rather the *dualistic nature and origin* of the diagnostic labelling procedures, which produce the dichotomous classification of people as 'sick-damned' or 'healthy-elect'.

5. While the continuity between medieval demonology and the contemporary mental-health movement has often been pointed out, the historical factors accounting for the augmented persecution of deviants during the Renaissance and the following period have been largely ignored. This phenomenon can be explained by the advent of Calvinism at that time.

6. Behaviour-disorder models, such as 'demon possession' or 'pacting with the devil', imply an external cause that could be removed or a voluntary act that could theoretically be avoided. These models, which are perpetually blasted in modern texts, leave more room for change than a predestinal model, which includes *a priori* any human intervention capable of changing 'the damned'.

(Rotenberg, 1978, pp. 2–3)

Rotenberg (1978) makes much of the PWE concept of predestinal dualism and the way people understand the 'born criminal type' and the 'people-changing sciences' (see Figure 6.1). He believes that in countries where the PWE was not influential, the rejection of the mentally disordered was not as noticeable though not very persuasive evidence is put forward. This attack is strident but not always factually based. Indeed the author appears to lay all modern problems, including loneliness, at the base of the PWE. Nowhere are competing political, economic, or theological explanations examined as to their validity for explaining attitudes to the mentally ill. Nevertheless it is important and worthwhile to point out the association between PWE beliefs and attitudes to deviants and mental illness. However, much more current empirical work will need to be done to determine the exact relationship between PWE beliefs and beliefs about psychopathology.

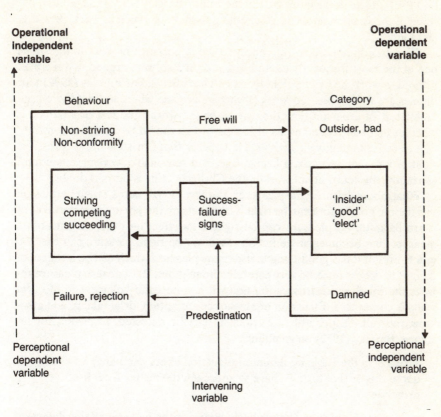

Figure 6.1 The Calvinist success–failure scheme

Christian ethics and the PWE

As has been noted there is considerable debate in theology surrounding the PWE thesis. Debates in this area have included the following sorts of attack:

- Selectivity – Weber tended to ignore theological beliefs and practices which did not fit his theory.
- Constructionism – the PWE was an ideal construct or concept which did not fit the facts.
- Oversimplification – the discovery of a simple, un-causal construct tended to ignore other equally or more important mutually influencing phenomena.
- Generalization – what may have occurred at a certain period in time among a small sect was over-generalized across groups and time.

However, there remains the question of New Testament teaching on PWE-related issues such as work, money, time, and leisure. To what extent does one find PWE ethics in the latter part of the Bible? Barclay (1972) has pointed out some of the fundamental Christian ethics about issues such as work, pleasure, and money.

There are innumerable references to the importance of work in the Bible, one of the most frequently quoted is that of St Paul who argued that if a man refused to work, he had no right to eat (2 Thess. 3:10). For Barclay (1972) four themes are detectable: our work is what we are and where we are; there is no better test of a person than the way he or she works; the test of a person is whether he or she deserves his or her pay; work should be seen as a contribution to the community as a whole. He believes that Christian ethics stress the right of a person to work, a living wage, and reasonable working conditions. Certainly, the centrality of work in the Christian ethic is beyond doubt.

What about leisure and pleasure? Barclay (1972) notes crucial ethics on this theme: no pleasure can be right if its effects on the person who partakes of it are harmful; no pleasure can be right if its effect on others is harmful; a pleasure that becomes an addiction can never be right; pleasure can cost too much, even if it is a good thing in itself; any pleasure which can be a source of danger to others must be very carefully thought out. But because pleasure relaxes the mind and refreshes the body, it is a necessary element in life. Yet when it comes to a discussion of alcohol consumption, drug taking, and gambling the full disapproval of Puritanism can be detected. Consider, for instance, Barclay (1972) on gambling:

> There is in the Bible no definite instruction about gambling; we cannot quote this or that text; we have to approach the matter from first principles.

   i. The gambler had better begin by facing the fact that all the chances are against him. His chances of losing are far greater than his chances of winning, and his chances of a really big win are very slim indeed.

   ii. There are few activities which gain such a grip of a man. It is a common saying of wives that they would rather that their husbands drank than that they gambled. Gambling can become a fever which can leave a man penniless. To go into a casino and to watch professional gamblers at work is a grim experience. There is a bleak and deadly silence and a look on faces which have nothing remotely to do with what we would ordinarily call pleasure.

   iii. It is not irrelevant to remember the effect of gambling on sport. Horses and dogs can be doped; more rarely, players can be bribed. Gambling is often allied to crime.

   iv. From the point of view of the Christian ethic, the case against gambling can be based on two things.

   (a) Basically, gambling is an effort to gain money without working. It is an attempt to become wealthy with no contribution whatever to the common good. The gambler produces nothing and hopes to gain much. Gambling is a deliberate attempt to bypass the essential social principle that reward should go to productive labour. Gambling literally attempts to get money for nothing.

(b) In gambling all winning is based on someone else's losing. In order that one should win another must lose. One person's good fortune is based on another person's ill fortune. One man's winnings are paid out of another man's losses, losses that all too often the loser can ill afford.

It may be argued that the harmless 'flutter' which a man can well afford, that the raffle, the sweepstake and so on can do no harm. They are the very things which can start a man on a way of excitement which can end in very serious harm. It would be well that the Christian and the church should have nothing whatever to do with gambling, which has reached the proportion of a social menace.

(pp. 129–30)

A third topic is that of money. There is no shortage of biblical teachings on money or indeed commentaries on these teachings (Fuller and Rice, 1966; Barclay, 1972). Many writers have been impressed by the fact that the apparent wealth of a country is often associated with increased, rather than decreased, social problems such as mental illness, drug and alcohol addiction, delinquency. There are a number of parables concerning money:

1. The Rich Man and Lazarus (Luke 16:19–31): the rich man was punished in the world to come for being complacent and doing nothing to help the poor. The sin was not so much the possession of wealth but the diminished sense of responsibility for those less fortunate.
2. The throwing of the moneychangers out of the Temple (Mark 11:15–16): Jesus threw the moneychangers out of the Temple because they were exploiting honest pilgrims' credulity, trust, and more importantly their basic needs.
3. The rich young ruler (Matthew 19:16–30): Jesus tells a rich young ruler to give all of his considerable wealth to the poor. The sin of the rich man was not his money *per se* but his possessiveness.

It is not money that is condemned but a particular attitude towards it. The more money a person has the more temptations he has and thus the more he needs God. The dangers of money are manifold: it creates a false sense of independence and invulnerability; it can be most easily acquired immorally and hence encourages bad habits; the more people possess in this world, the more difficult it becomes for them to leave it; and paradoxically instead of satisfying people that they have enough, it does the opposite, making people more greedy.

Barclay (1972) concludes with five general principles which supposedly save people from the dangers of wealth:

1. Money should be honestly acquired so that it harmed or injured no one, but helped and enriched the community.
2. Money should be regarded as something to be shared, not hoarded. It should be used to help others.
3. Money should not be used selfishly but should be given away.
4. People are more important than things; men are more important than money; workers are more important than machines.
5. Sometimes giving money is not enough but an evasion of a greater responsibility – a gift of self.

But along with issues *related* to the work ethic, modern theologians and ethicists have considered current ethical thinking on the PWE. Preston (1987) has noted that long-term structural changes have led to unemployment and general changes in employment which raises interesting and important issues. For instance, he argues that 'It is inhuman to say to them (the young unemployed) in effect, "You have nothing to contribute to society which we think worth paying for; but we will pay you to be idle at a rate which will feed and clothe you at a very modest level, if you use your money with exceptional care; and we hope you will find ways of making a contribution to the community by some kind of voluntary work"' (p. 128).

Where does this leave the Protestant Work Ethic? Obviously the boundary between work and leisure becomes blurred if a basic citizen wage is instituted, and if there is a shorter working week and life. Work cannot have the same commanding place that it had in the Protestant Work Ethic. Education will be seen as a lifetime enterprise. Enjoyment will be seen not merely as an interval of relaxation necessary to enable us to work better. Creativity in personal choices will be stressed. Celebrations will be encouraged. Contemplation will be an element in Catholic spirituality which needs cultivating to complement the active stress of the Protestant ethic. Workaholics will have to be weaned from the boredom which afflicts them when not working. Both work and leisure will need better liturgical expression.

Nevertheless work will remain as a prime requirement in human life, and it will still be needed as a key element in a person's social significance. Those who have good reasons for taking the basic citizen wage and doing no more will be like the conscientious objector who makes a point which has substance but which can be valid only as a minority reminder to the majority, in this case that there are values in life which far transcend work. The scrounger will have to be left to public opinion. The work which is needed should be properly paid and organized, with proper participation in its running by all involved in it, and it needs to be well done and not scamped. The merit of the Protestant Work Ethic is its stress on efficiency. Waste is an offence to it. Efficiency is the economist's virtue. He is constantly exercised by the relative scarcity of our resources as compared with the many uses we might make of them, and he thinks it a pity if we do not do as much with them as we might when we keep costs artificially high, and cling to obsolescence. Of course there are other virtues besides efficiency. To pursue that to the exclusion of all others quickly leads to inhumanity. Nevertheless vested interests often cause us to pay too little attention to it, or to fudge the issue. The Protestant Work Ethic has a perennial relevance in its stress on diligence in the job on hand and avoidance of waste as a way of glorifying God. But it needs to be communalized in terms of the way society orders its affairs, and not thought of in purely individual terms; and it needs to be balanced by an ethic of celebration. That we must make the best we can, other things being equal, of our relatively scarce resources is the strong point of those who emphasize the creation of wealth. How it is created, what is to count wealth, and how it is distributed are the underlying issues of social, economic and industrial politics. The mistake was to exalt the Protestant Work Ethic to a solitary eminence. It has become discredited, and we are left with a secularized and rather unpleasant residue. It needs to recover more of its gospel basis.

(Preston, 1987, pp. 133–4)

Conclusion

This chapter has concentrated particularly on the moral dimension of the PWE as it relates to worklessness. Because the virtue of hard work is so central to the PWE, it is no surprise that in general people who endorse the PWE are unsympathetic to those out-of-work, or at least attempt to distinguish between the deserving and undeserving poor. There is substantial literature to support this point of view.

On the other hand, the effect of the PWE on those unemployed for whatever reason has tended to yield some interesting findings. On the one hand it seems PWE values tend to make some workless people (unemployed, retired, etc.) better adapted to that state, while the opposite is true for others. Clearly other, possibly interesting variables account for these discrepant findings. These variables may include personality and ability variables associated with the individual (like temperament and personality); as well as the range and type of non-work activities available. It is very difficult to distinguish between work and leisure, but presumably the more the non-paid activities approximate regular work (with goals, time structure, outcomes) the more PWE believers would be satisfied by them. Certainly, the idea that PWE may be seen as an adaptive coping strategy merits further research.

However, the somewhat negative attitudes of PWE believers to the poor and unemployed seem related to their ideas and beliefs about psychopathology. It seems as if PWE beliefs are generally associated with negative beliefs about mental illness, particularly with regard to prognoses. It seems, then, highly paradoxical, if not misleading, that at one and the same time PWE beliefs are adaptive yet are linked to considerable prejudice against the mentally ill. Certainly, the research on the psychopathology of PWE believers as well as their beliefs about mental illness is minimal and weak, hence no firm conclusions can be drawn. It certainly seems as if researchers' instinctive attitudes to the PWE as being either pro or anti in part determine whether they believe it is adaptive or not.

Finally, the relationship between Christian ethics and the PWE was discussed. Depending no doubt on one's ethical position, one could find biblical justification either for or against the PWE. However, more astute theologians have looked more carefully at the PWE and tried to determine which and how much of its thesis can be found in, and supported by, Christian doctrines. In doing so simplistic and equivocal conclusions can be avoided.

Chapter seven

Changes in the work ethic

Work is the refuge of people who have nothing better to do.

Oscar Wilde

It is Enterprise which builds and improves the world's possessions....

If enterprise is afoot, wealth accumulates whatever may be happening to Thrift, and if Enterprise is asleep, Wealth decays, whatever Thrift is doing.

J.M. Keynes

It is necessary to work, if not from inclination at least from despair.

Everything considered, work is less boring than amusing oneself.

C.P. Baudelaire

Work seven days a week and nothing can stop you.

John Moore

Introduction

There has been no shortage of popular speculation about changes in PWE beliefs over time. Indeed it is one of the inevitable consequences of the popularization of an 'explanatory concept' like the PWE that it is debated by journalists, politicians, and lay people. However, what is noteworthy about using the PWE as an explanatory cause of decline, is that it fulfils various psychological functions. Katzell and Yankelovich (1976) found that whereas 79 per cent of managers believed 'The nation's productivity is suffering because the traditional American work ethic has eroded' only 35 per cent of union leaders held this perception. In other words, it is a convenient concept with which to blame (or praise) particular groups in society.

Despite the plethora of speculation about the PWE – most notably its decline – the level of analysis is weak. Indeed it could be argued that blaming the decline of the industrialized west in certain countries in particular (like Great Britain), relative to other countries, on declining PWE beliefs and behaviours is extremely naive. Furthermore, it illustrates nicely the fundamental and ultimate attribution error which occurs when observers overestimate the role of the actor/individuals in the cause of events rather than take full cognizance of the numerous and powerful environmental forces which could be having a dramatic effect on the outcome. To suggest that a country's economic decline is due primarily or exclusively to a change in work beliefs and habits is to naively psychologize a complex economic question.

More importantly perhaps, people who have speculated on changes in the PWE – decline, change, metamorphosis, increase – have not answered some of the more interesting, important, or difficult questions concerning change. For instance:

- If the PWE has begun to decline, *when* did this decline occur? What is the shape of the decline (or incline) curve?
- Had the PWE remained *unchanged* from Luther till this relatively recent decline?
- *Why* did the PWE begin to decline? Should we blame Freudian ideas, Dr Spock, or more nebulous phenomena such as the permissive society?
- *How* has the decline occurred? That is, have some facets of the PWE remained intact (i.e. moral attitude) while others have changed (i.e. leisure attitude) or have they all declined similarly?
- More importantly perhaps, what is the direct, unambiguous, and indisputable *evidence* for the change in these beliefs? And are the beliefs related to behaviour?

These and other interesting questions remain largely unanswered by impressionistic and journalistic speculation on changes in the PWE. Certainly many people, both in Europe and North America, believe that there was a golden past of the PWE, notably in the last half of the last century, and there has been a consistent and lamentable decline. However, historical analysis suggests this simplified 'rosy' view of the past is far from the truth.

Victorian values and the PWE

The PWE concept was conceived of in the Victorian era (usually conceived of by historians as 1815 to 1914) but was about an earlier period in history notably the Reformation. Nevertheless, much has been said about the PWE in the Victorian period in Europe and America, but particularly Great Britain. Indeed a cursory examination of contemporary writings between 1850 and 1890 appears to provide much evidence for the PWE in mid-Victorian times (Golby, 1986). The work of Samuel Smiles, Ford Madox Brown, and William Morris is well known. Consider some of the statements by Samuel Smiles:

'National progress is the sum of individual industry, energy and uprightness, as national decay is of individual idleness, selfishness, and vice'; 'The spirit of self-help as exhibited in the energetic action of individuals, has in all times been a marked failure in the English

196

character, and furnishes the true measure of our power as a nation'.

But historians are agreed that Victorian values and the PWE did not 'cause' the industrial enterprise of the last century:

Nor can the Protestant Reformation be made responsible for *it* (The Industrial Revolution), either directly or via some special 'capitalistic spirit' or other change of economic attitude induced by Protestantism; not even for why it occurred in Britain and not in France. The Reformation occurred more than two centuries before the Industrial Revolution. By no means all areas which converted to Protestantism became pioneers of industrial revolution and – to take an obvious example – the parts of the Netherlands which remained Catholic (Belgium) industrialized before the part which became Protestant (Holland).

(Hobsbawm, 1986, pp. 37–8)

It was argued that the victorious Victorian capitalism and the work ethic had become an accepted way of life and that to strive for wealth, power, and security was sport. Weber (1905) acknowledged no clear relationship between PWE and religious beliefs in his day, yet there is the belief in popular writing that PWE values were strongly related to Victorian values and that all Victorians endorsed PWE values. The British Prime Minister, Margaret Thatcher, said in 1983: 'I was brought up to work jolly hard. We were taught to live within our incomes, that cleanliness is next to Godliness. We were taught self-respect. You were taught tremendous pride in your country. All those are Victorian values' *(The Standard)*.

Victorian values are thought to include the following: chastity, honesty, industry, obedience, patriotism, piety, and thrift. Many of these are clearly related to the PWE. But the question remains, were they actually consensually held and espoused? Walvin (1987) argues that the above Victorian values were only marginally Victorian. For instance, the virtue of saving long predated the nineteenth century. Other virtues like chastity and piety, tended to be the values and ideals of a small vocal minority and willed upon a resistant majority.

As regards attitudes to work, Walvin (1987) argued that urbanization and industrialization in the mid to late nineteenth century led to many important and significant changes:

The patterns and rhythms of work changed substantially in the course of the nineteenth century. As industry, the machine and the clock came to dominate more lives, the earlier work disciplines gave way to those familiar to modern eyes. It was a slow, uneven progress, fought initially by pioneering industrialists keen to discipline their labourers' work habits to the demand of machinery. In time the battle was joined by other important institutions and their spokesmen. Sunday schools and later the compulsory elementary schools placed great emphasis on punctuality and application. Diligence, good time-keeping and good behaviour were rewarded by the gift of books. By the end of the century, institutions of all kinds rewarded a lifetime's activities of their older members by the gift of a watch or clock. Time measured out by the machine, not that dictated by the sun or seasons, had come to impose a different and totally new discipline on the British people. For those with no timepiece of their own, major Victorian buildings were often topped by a clock; while industries had their own system of communal timekeeping, using hooters or a peripatetic 'knocker-up'.

(p. 139)

But hard work, certainly compared to the practices of today, was the lot of nearly all Victorians, particularly those from working-class background. Why, then, asked Walvin (1987), did the Victorians feel such a need to encourage work if it were the lot of so many Victorians anyway?

Firstly, as the advocates of hard work from Josiah Wedgwood to Samuel Smiles; clearly they had a vested interest in their pleas. Secondly, Victorians firmly believed that they had cast the word anew, that their energies had created the wealth of the industrial world, as indeed they had. Furthermore there were enough examples of rags-to-riches to convince people that anyone could improve himself. In an age which believed in progress, it seemed natural to believe that material progress would emerge from hard work. For a small handful of people, the self-made, this had been unquestionably true. No less true, however, was the converse; that for millions of Victorians a lifetime's hard work petered out in the poverty of old age. Hard work on its own could not transmute inadequate wages into the stuff of self-improvement.

There was a further, more complicated dimension to the belief in hard work as the inevitable route to personal and collective salvation. Its proponents were, in essence, wedded to the belief that human behaviour had its roots in personal, not social, explanations. Social problems were thus a result of collective personal weaknesses and flaws and did not derive from failings in society itself. For those Victorians who viewed social problems in this way hard work seemed to offer an antidote to the major ills of individuals, and therefore society. This view of the world was totally at variance with the evidence from the great investigations into poverty in the last twenty years of the century, but it was an article of faith, an assumption about human nature, which could not be readily shaken, still less disproved by statistics.

(p. 142)

With their peculiar individualistic ethic it is not difficult to see why Victorians saw poverty as the inability to manage finance. Also this accounts for why so much advice was available in print on thrift, penny-wise household economies. Similarly it accounts for the Victorian obsession with drunkenness:

> The belief in self-improvement through industry and thrift was so
> ingrained in many propertied Victorians that the continuing plight of the
> many in the midst of a prospering nation merely confirmed their view
> that personal weakness was responsible. There was evidence available
> which seemed at first glance to confirm their judgement. Many
> working-class people were indeed actively improving themselves. The
> money deposited in local penny savings banks came primarily from low
> income groups, often from domestic servants. The Post Office Savings
> Bank was established in 1861 for a similar purpose; by the 1890s it had
> almost six million savers, large numbers of them women and children. By
> the 1870s more than one and a quarter million members paid money into
> friendly societies, which were the acme of prudent, long-term thrift and
> economy. Indeed, at that time they had more members than the trades
> unions. And in the various and flourishing co-operative organisations
> there were clear signs of working-class material self-improvement
> through thrift, economy and self-help. All of these institutions, when
> linked to that profusion of learning facilities rooted in late-century
> working-class communities (which also spanned the century), provided
> ample evidence of a thriving plebeian commitment to the very virtues so
> many of their betters urged upon them. More often than not, however,
> these organisations were created by the upper reaches of the working
> class, the 'aristocrats of labour'. Membership and funds of these bodies
> increased markedly by the late century and their efforts at
> self-improvement were universally admired by all who knew them. Such
> self-help and material improvement served to wean working people away
> from radical politics. But what could be done for those troublesome
> layers of urban life which remained beyond the pale of self-improvement
> and immune to theories of thrift? It was not possible for a man on
> inadequate, or irregular wages to be won over to the idea of thrift as a way
> of life.

(p. 144)

The essence of Walvin's (1987) thesis is this: there are numerous examples of Victorian attempts to encourage PWE values of thrift, hard-work, and sobriety. But these must be seen as responses to contemporary problems and difficulties and not consequences of Victorian achievement. The PWE Victorian values were those of middle-class reformers who encouraged a code of ideal behaviour

> It was thus the problems of working-class urban life rather than its merits
> that gave rise to the propagation of 'Victorian Values'.

(p. 146)

The PWE Victorian values are thus no more than the persistent moral crusade songs of prosperous and concerned Victorians – they were by and large held by the working mass and they were certainly not responsible for Victorian achievement or the establishment of the Greatest Empire upon which the sun never set.

Historians on both sides of the Atlantic have doubted the existence of the PWE in the Victorian era, stressing the idleness, drinking, and leisure pursuits of the workers (Thompson, 1986). However, these beliefs are being reassessed. For instance Stott (1985) examined the reactions of British and Irish working-class immigrants to work patterns in the USA and found they reported considerable evidence of PWE behaviour. They thought the Americans worked faster, more rigorously, and with less leisure and drinking than they were used to: in short the Americans seem to practise the PWE a lot more efficiently than those from Great Britain.

Kelvin and Jarrett (1985), in examining evidence for the PWE in Great Britain, also came to the conclusion. They argue:

> ... anyone who believes that ours is, or ever predominantly was, a society rooted in the Protestant Work Ethic has failed to understand its most essential teaching: for the one thing which the PWE would *not* have tolerated is that productivity should increase the profits, wages and luxuries of some, at the cost of unemployment for others. However, these values and sentiments were never more than those of a minority and of middle-class rather than working-or-upper-class origin. The notion that the generality of English workers were imbued with this Ethic just does not survive examination.
>
> (p. 102)

The argument put forward by Kelvin and Jarrett (1985) is that the PWE was in fact a wealth ethic (see Chapter 8):

> We hope we have shown that the PWE is very largely a myth: that for the vast majority of people work is and always has been, a matter of labouring 'for the necessities of life', which may be a *norm*. But it is not an *ethic*: it is 'expected' on the good statistical ground of its very high incidence, not on the basis of its moral significance. Moral significance does not attach to work as such, but to 'not living off others', the only exception being weakness of body or mind so that one 'cannot work because of one's inadequacy'.
>
> (p. 109)

One reason why Victorian values and the PWE during the nineteenth century have been so frequently involved in popular explanation, is no doubt because it offers an explanation for the relative decline of British economic progress and the industrial spirit. Whilst all historians reject the idea pointing out the crucial role of economic factors, there is some suggestion that certain bourgeois or elitist values changed over the 130-year period from the middle of the last century to the current day. Wiener (1985) has argued that the anti-PWE or at least anti-industrial values reject progress; salesmanship and the rat-race; and favour small over big; community over income; peace-of-mind over rate of growth.

> Over the past century, then, high among the internal checks upon British economic growth has been a pattern of industrial behaviour suspicious of change, reluctant to innovate, energetic only in maintaining the status quo. This pattern of behaviour traces back in large measure to the cultural absorption of the middle classes into a quasi aristocratic elite, which nurtured both the mystic and nostalgic myth of an 'English way of life' and the transfer of interest and energies away from the creation of wealth.
>
> (p. 154)

Possible patterns of change

If it is supposed that the work ethic has changed, a number of possible patterns could occur:

- The PWE never existed, it is a myth that it ever existed in this, or any other century. Either it existed for a small elite for a certain limited period of time, or else is a completely historical myth.
- The PWE is dead, dying, or on the decline – for some this is to be lamented, for others it is to be welcomed.
- Depending on the nature of the job and the biography of the worker, the PWE is on the increase for some and decrease for others – for meaningful, interesting, involving, autonomous jobs, and for people with ambition and enthusiasm the PWE is on the increase whereas for boring, repetitive jobs, and people more interested in an easy life the PWE is on the decline.
- The PWE is alive, well, and even flourishing – this suggests that not only is the PWE not declining it is, as a belief system, actually on the increase.
- The PWE has changed, metamorphosed into a new ethic which is a natural successor of the PWE, and shares some of its original features.

The PWE never existed

For one school of thought, the idea that the PWE ever existed is false. Thus if there is little evidence for it today it does not mean that it declined or changed but rather that it never actually existed in the first place. Some argue that the PWE explanation is romantic and distorted and that the PWE, if it ever existed, became an abstraction increasingly out of place in the new realities of the assembly line. The PWE is then nothing more than theoretical shibboleth, or political invective.

Kelvin (1984, 1985) masters a number of historic quotations from the fifteenth century to the nineteenth century, to refute the basic PWE suggestion that people are motivated by the fact that work is an end in itself. All the quotations lament the idleness of the workers. Yet whereas Kelvin takes this to assume this provides evidence for the fact that the PWE was not widespread, it could be used to provide evidence that the PWE was very widespread, especially among employers who felt confident enough to chastise non-believers.

> There never was a work ethic in the sense that work was treated as a virtuous end in itself....There has always been a very small number of people for whom work has been an end in itself; they are mostly in small religious groups and communities. But for the greater majority, work has always, and for most people, only been a means to an end for making a living, not an end in itself....The history of what the gentry did shows this perfectly well. A member of the gentry would perhaps collect butterflies, or attend to one's estates on a Friday; but one could enjoy oneself and lead a reasonable cultured, civilized water colour-painting life perfectly well, because one had, in fact, the cash to do it with....The issue is really not a work ethic, but a welfare ethic, an ethic that requires one to have enough resources, financial resources, not to be a burden on other people.
>
> (p. 18)

Kelvin (1984) argues that the notion of the PWE deeply embedded in our culture does not survive scrutiny. He admits the probability that small groups followed the ethic but that the vast majority worked, not out of pleasure or sense of moral duty but necessity. Indeed he argues that the concept of the PWE appeals to intellectuals and professionals because they inaccurately extrapolate from their own experience to that of others.

Others have also put forward the PWE-that-never-was hypothesis. Bernstein (1980) argued that although managers may have absorbed the work ethic, the workers never did. Like Kelvin (1985) he provides a great deal of specific historical evidence to support his view that the working class never absorbed the ethic, indeed resisted it. Furthermore it was argued that as a consequence of various historical occurrences such as the rise of 'scientific management', the great depression and the growth of large organizations, the PWE deduced even more. Hence he concludes:

> It is useless to rail against the decline of a work ethic that never had the universal support attributed to it. It is unproductive to compare the contemporary worker with an idealized counterpart of yesteryear, particularly since there is no clear evidence that the passage of time has created a work force that is less motivated than its predecessors. Rather, it is far more useful to ascertain whether the American labour force has largely accepted a new attitude toward work, a meaning that is secular and self-centred.
>
> (p. 25)

However what is not clear from Bernstein's criticism is what previous ethic the workers held, if not the PWE or some form of it.

The PWE is in terminal decline

There have been endless popular as well as academic articles lamenting the causes of economic decline in Britain, America, and other industrialized nations. A number of features characterize these reports: first, they frequently have little or no data or evidence to support propositions either about the (relative) economic decline of a country or the so-called cause; secondly, no attempt is made to classify, order, or prioritize these causes which may be complementary, contradictory, tautological, synonymous, etc.; thirdly, no underlying process or mechanism is proposed to explain, rather than describe, the 'decline' which would allow one to make predictions.

However, these speculations are frequently interesting because they reveal lay, expert, and opinion-leader thinking on the role of the PWE on economic success and decline. For instance, Grant (1982) pinpointed ten causes of employee motivational decline, although he offers no information on whether, in fact, there has been a decline save personal experience and hearsay evidence. The facts were

- Greater instability and diversity of values – unstable goods or the pursuit of leisure and away-from-work activities.
- More guaranteed rewards – this reduces incentive- and performance-based reward systems.
- Inability of rewards to satisfy emergency needs – usual rewards cannot satisfy new needs for 'personal development', 'self actualization', etc.
- Disappearance of the work ethic – fewer individuals believe that hard work is morally good or personally satisfying.
- Reduced costs of failure – penalties for low effort and poor performance are increasing, some of which stimulates motivation.
- Rising income and progressive taxation – taxation policy means that as incomes rise additional increments are perceived as of less and less value and hence less sought after.
- More group production and problem solving – rugged individualism is no longer in demand and people do not perceive such strong links between individual effort and group performance.
- Decreasing employee loyalty – unionization, professional organizations, and greater physical mobility have led to less commitment.
- Less supervisory power – there is less respect for authority as well as influence.
- Shorter time prospectives – because of rapid change and uncertainty, people are now much more present oriented.

Bonani (1978) blamed the slow demise of the Italian PWE or 'work-success ethic' on such things as educational change and the effects of the mass media. In America Calhoun (1980) blames the comparative drop in productivity not on the decline in the PWE but rather the fact that employers don't invest enough money in the training of employees who can't (rather than won't) produce more. Some researchers have however attempted to provide evidence for what they see to be a major decline in the work ethic. Howard and Wilson (1982) compared samples from the 1950s to those of the 1970s and found the latter group had less desire for upward mobility or motivation towards powerful high-status and well-paying positions, and lower expectations. They argue:

> Belief in meritocracy has been upstaged by a psychology of entitlements, so that rewards are no longer reserved for the deserving. In the current value system, such things as a good job, health care, and a secure retirement are considered inalienable rights. As government guarantees of financial subsistence plus two paycheck families mitigate the threat of job loss, traditional penalties for poor performance become impotent. Money is less a symbol of success than a facilitator of one's leisure activities and personal life style. Present sacrifice and hard work as a means to later rewards is now thought to be foolish; immediate gratification and living for today set the style.
>
> (p. 40)

Howard and Wilson (1982) argue that an analysis of popular magazines confirms their impression. They argue that the *cause* of the decline in the PWE began with the post-war, prosperous baby boom generation with its progressive education, stress on materialism, and anti-competitive behaviour. Thus a narcissistic, hedonistic ethic replaced the PWE and they see three possible future scenarios:

> Slowing of the economy and even less pressure to succeed; reindustrialization and the restoration of the PWE; a stress on self-fulfilment rather than self-denial and a quality- rather than a quantity-of-life approach.
>
> It is the third scenario that is thought most likely, but one which is not likely to rekindle the PWE. Calvinism once united virtue, salvation, work and motivation in a productive package, but that package has come undone.
>
> (p. 46)

Along with many speculations as to the decline in the work ethic, there remains evidence from opinion polls done at various times which provides at least modest factual evidence from which conclusions may be drawn. Wood (1981), reporting evidence for the existence of the PWE in America, asked: 'If you had your choice, and money and child care were not a problem, which of the following would you prefer to do: "I wouldn't work, I'd work part-time, I'd work full-time"'. Nearly two-thirds (61 per cent) of men in the representative sample of 1,500 chose to continue with full-time work, even if they no longer had to do so. However, what is unclear is *'why'* people choose to work.

However, in comparing results collected in 1947 with those collected in 1977, fewer people in 1977 (48 per cent) compared to 1947 (60 per cent) preferred the entrepreneurial experience of owning their own business, nearly half in 1977 (44 per cent) preferring employment working for somebody else compared to 24 per cent in 1947. This appears to partly contradict the above finding though it is not necessarily the case that entrepreneurship and the PWE are synonymous. Most interestingly, Wood (1981) reported on data from 2,000 interviews done in eleven countries with young people (18–24) on the major factors involved in vocational success (see Table 7.1).

It is most interesting to note that with few exceptions effort is considered a more important factor than ability. Again this could not be said to indicate completely unequivocal support for the PWE but does seem to indicate that young people believe personal effort and ability to be better predictors of success than factors such as one's social position or luck/fate.

Finally, there have been studies looking at ordinary people's ideas about the causes of the much lamented decline in productivity. The results in Table 7.2 come from a representative sample of 1,000 American top business executives surveyed in 1978.

Note that the second and third most important reasons could easily be taken as evidence for the decline of the PWE. Businessmen may blame the government for a decline in productivity but ordinary working people tend to blame themselves. In another survey almost two-thirds (64 per cent) thought workers were less conscientious and were the major cause of a decline in productivity, while 45 per cent thought it was due to poor management, 42 per cent government interventions, and 23 per cent the lack of investment in capital equipment.

Table 7.1 Factors in becoming successful

Country	Personal effort	Personal ability	Good education	Social position	Luck/ fate	Don't know
	%	%	%	%	%	%
Australia	77	55	39	11	9	2
USA	70	59	43	13	9	1
Japan	68	48	44	5	14	3
United Kingdom	64	65	37	11	17	1
Sweden	61	62	47	9	11	4
France	57	48	19	38	27	1
West Germany	57	61	11	22	31	3
Philippines	56	60	43	20	18	1
Brazil	52	52	30	36	23	1
Switzerland	52	53	35	27	24	1
India	45	37	48	23	38	2

Source: Wood, 1981.

Table 7.2 Opinions about what has caused the slowdown in the rate of growth in productivity during the past ten years

Federal government regulations	70%
Worker attitudes	48%
Welfare, unemployment, and other income security benefits	45%
State government regulations	39%
Central climate for business	38%
Labour union activity	37%
Capital gains taxes	33%
Inadequate plant and equipment investment	31%
Local government regulations	25%
Skill level of workers	22%
Corporate income taxes	21%
Energy cost of availability	20%
Inadequate research and development spending	18%
Personal income taxes	16%
Management attitude	13%

Source: Wood, 1981.

It appears that the major source of evidence used to answer the question about the status of the PWE concerns polls on the commitment to work and job satisfaction. Maccoby and Terzi (1979) reviewed numerous surveys done in America in the mid-1970s on work commitment, all of which showed a consistently strong affirmation of the value of work in three-quarters of the population. However, they do believe that commitment to such things as leisure and the family are growing. However, although general job satisfaction appears to be high, job dissatisfaction appears to be growing partly because people perceive their skills as being underutilized. The most satisfied are white middle-aged, graduate-educated professionals, while the least satisfied tend to be black, under 30 years old on low-income, low-skilled jobs that do not test their abilities. Finally, some specific, within-organizational studies (Harmer, 1979) have been done showing how, in certain instances, PWE beliefs and practices are alive and well.

Status quo in the PWE

Jahoda (1982) does not believe that the 1980s and indeed the latter part of the twentieth century will see a decline in the work ethic compared to earlier historical epochs. She believes that there is little evidence that people have lost the willingness to work which is consistent with the view that employment fulfils certain basic functions. She repudiates the argument that major changes in society such as consumerism, progressive secularization, and the rise of the welfare state have led to the demise of the PWE – a social consensus that work is a moral good. She quotes various sources of empirical evidence to support her view:

- Surveys which show that people want to work, even if it were not an economic necessity.

- Growing incidence of organized industrial action in favour of work such as workers taking over factories and strikes against redundancies.
- Examples in countries like Japan, where employers find it difficult to keep their labour force away during legitimate holidays.
- A very small incidence (about 5 per cent) of those who have made themselves voluntarily unemployed because they are better off not working than working.

  So there remains a doubt about regarding the currently prevailing work ethic as fundamentally changed from that in the thirties....

(p. 38)

In fact, Warr (1983) found that high levels of employment commitment (a crucial facet of the PWE) tend to be maintained even among the unemployed. This position then believes that though there might be some minor changes overall there is little reason to suppose any major change in the PWE. However, this position does not rule out the fact that in the future, when the nature of work is radically different (see Chapter 9), there might not be changes in the PWE.

An increasing work ethic

A great deal of the available evidence, at least from surveys, suggests no decline in the PWE. Yankelovich (1982) quoted various sources of evidence from public opinion polls:

- Eighty-eight per cent of Working Americans feel that work is personally important to them, to work hard and do their best on the job.
- Seventy-eight per cent said they had an inner need to do the very best job regardless of pay.
- Seventy-eight per cent feel people take less pride in their work than they did ten years ago.

In fact, some studies suggest a strong increase in the PWE. Hannah (1982), in a study of coal miners, found a very strong PWE among the 'coal-hungry' miners of America. He believed the causes of the strong PWE and high productivity were the need for certainty in the working day, being satisfied, strong competition between crews and shifts, and the fact that hard work made the time pass much faster.

Furthermore, Ditz (1978) has argued convincingly that higher education in America reflects PWE values – egalitarianism, vocational education, bureaucratization. Presumably, therefore, if these remain or flourish, so will the PWE of those people who experience it. On the other hand, the rise of liberal education with its stress on spontaneous, inner-divided, experimental, anti-institutionalism would seem to threaten the PWE. However, the strength of the old system appears to bode well for the PWE.

But Yankelovich (1982) believes that while people still endorse the PWE, productivity is declining because of the reward system. Most workers have it in their power to deliver adequate (minimum effort) vs excellent (maximum effort) work, and many people could be twice as effective (to work twice as hard) as they are. The reason why they are not is because they do not believe that they will benefit from additional productivity. They argue that there is no reason to increase effort if they don't have to, and they believe that others will be beneficiaries of the effort. The PWE is not in decline but productivity is low paradoxically because of the equity concept held so enthusiastically by PWE supporters.

However, the argument is not that all aspects of the PWE remain as they always were (Yankelovich and Immerwahr, 1984). For instance, they see a reduction in self-denial and self-constraint, an erosion in the symbolic potency of the material rewards of success, and a general disrespect for authority. But the general commitment to work remains strong: nearly three quarters of people surveyed rejected the idea that work is an unpleasant necessity or is morally neutral. In fact Yankelovich and Immerwaher (1984) believe there are good reasons to assume that the PWE is on the increase:

- Education is closely related to the work ethic and as people are getting better educated they are more likely to believe in the PWE.
- An emphasis on self-growth, actualization, and post-materialist values, rather than leading to a decline in the PWE, causes the opposite when people who focus on personal growth see their jobs as an outlet for their own self-expression and development.
- The upgrading of jobs from low-to-high discretionary work, where work conveys a sense of purpose, challenge, and accomplishment.

As jobs become more challenging and more autonomous, and as people become better educated and focus more on personal growth, employees are also likely to see work as having a positive and central place in their lives. They are also much more likely to bring greater demands to their jobs. The degree to which these demands are met will have a great deal to do with whether the work ethic is harnessed and channelled into more productive work.

(p. 66)

However, the argument is that paradoxically while the cultural norms still adhere to many aspects of the PWE the social practices in the work-place, as a function of the reward structure, undermine the strong work-ethic values that people bring to their jobs. Of course, if the gap between what people value and the rewards, incentives, and punishments that they receive undercuts the PWE, this may in time undermine it. Currently, according to Yankelovich and Immerwahr (1984), today's work force brings a remarkably pluralistic set of values to the work-place which puts great strain on the existing, single-value reward system.

Thus they believe the American economy is failing to use one of its most powerful assets – commitment to the PWE – because the work-place discourages it. However, they do offer a solution to this problem of the paradox of an increasing PWE and declining productivity. These steps include placing greater responsibility for the quality of work on the workers themselves; restructuring and providing different incentives; and attempting to change the adversarial relationship between labour and management. In other words, they argue that reinforcing a new work contract is an essential part of putting the PWE into practice.

A change in the PWE

The fact that the PWE is changing is not particularly noteworthy – it has evolved over centuries and adapted to new circumstances and has been challenged, changed, and been revitalized. But what is new is the *rate* and *degree* of change in people's work and private lives. These changes include:

- The average working day has been steadily declining.
- As some jobs have disappeared completely new ones have appeared.
- Many labour-intensive, dangerous, and dirty jobs have been greatly transformed.
- The power relationships between employer and employee have undergone great changes.
- The age of retirement is gradually declining.
- The percentage of working women at all levels is on the increase.
- The education of the work force is rising.

For over fifteen years there has been a lot of popular speculation about the emergence of a new PWE. The idea was that work should provide a means of enhancing the quality of life and hence boredom, routinization, and lack of autonomy should be eliminated.

Gartner and Riesman (1974) equate the PWE and job satisfaction and argue that various groups at all levels have expressed job dissatisfaction. Presumably they would argue that an essential tenet of the PWE is that all and any work is good and its execution satisfying, therefore the presence of dissatisfaction must imply the non-existence of the PWE. The new ethic is one of humanization. But the authors believe the new ethic is the consequence of a shift in the kind of work done (many more service industries), and a new work force (with better educated people, more women, and more minority groups) who bring a new set of consumer-oriented values. Hence one new ethic proposed is that of self-fulfilling, life-quality enhancing, self-actualizing work, rather than any work.

If the PWE is changing it is doing so in a number of ways. For instance, if the essential features of the PWE remain the same, the PWE could be on the *decline* or it could be on the *increase* in the sense either that more people hold the belief or else it is held more passionately or strongly by the same people. Another, more probable way in which the PWE may change relates to changes in the features of the PWE. That is, the focus for basic PWE values like thrift, saving, and work may adapt to new conditions. Consider, for instance, some of these factors:

- *Do-it-yourself*. The spirit of self-help so close to the hearts of Victorian propagandists for the PWE is alive and well in the do-it-yourself movement. There are in Great Britain huge warehouses dedicated to DIY. People believe that it is cheaper and more satisfying to acquire the skills to do home repairs oneself rather than be dependent on experts.
- *Time management*. People are encouraged more and more, both in their work and leisure, to manage their time more effectively and efficiently. They go on courses, buy expensive diary-like record-keeping devices to maximize their free and work time through careful planning.
- *Anti-hedonic asceticism*. Fear of sexually transmitted diseases and the desire to live longer through a healthier life-style has made people less hedonistic and more ascetic. Living on a more frugal diet, avoiding alcohol, and taking regular exercise all seem part of the new PWE.
- *The protestantization of play*. Another form of changing PWE belief is the extent to which play is turned into work; leisure becomes work. In a charming essay on the American approach to rock-climbing Csikszentmihaly (1976) notes how dedicated rock-climbers are not interested in the beauty and solitude of the mountains, but exclusively in their ability to use sophisticated techniques to negotiate formidable rock faces.

> The summit is irrelevant, since the climax of the climb is the most difficult move rather than the highest point. I have seen rock-climbers reach an important summit, sit down to check their gear, eat a bit and be off without a glance at the view. The rock-climber becomes embarrassed if the conversation drifts to a subject outside the strictly technical. Even if he is highly educated, as most are, he would sooner fall off a cliff than comment on natural beauty or his feelings.
>
> (p. 486)

He notes the effects of speculation, the drive to quantification, and the emphasis on equipment in the sport:

> The attitudinal changes we are witnessing in mountaineering reflect in a nutshell many changes taking place in the rest of society. A game activity which until a generation ago was performed leisurely, within a complex logico-meaningful framework of experiences, is now becoming a calculated, precise, expert enterprise within a much narrower framework of experience....The value-system of the culture modifies the rules of the game.
>
> (pp. 487–8)

- *Emphasis on sport.* It is not only in the realm of self-help and do-it-your-self that classic PWE beliefs and values can be seen. Ritzer, Kammeyer, and Yelman (1982) have shown how many of the current norms in *sport*, particularly competitive and professional sport reflect PWE values. Values that are consistently stressed include:
- Sportsmanship – playing hard, but fairly in accordance with the rules
- Competition – a belief in the survival of the fittest
- Success – considered as essential and more important than how one plays the game
- Universalism – competition is open to all irrespective of social and personal characteristics as only ability is judged
- Diligence – one needs perseverance and fortitude to succeed
- Self-discipline – only by considerable self-control can one fully develop one's skills
- Teamwork – co-operation and subordination of self to the team is important in certain instances

There may well be other sports 'virtues', 'ideals', or 'norms' that reflect in whole or part the PWE. But it is probably true to point out that many popular sporting characters in different countries when asked to attribute their success and/or recommend strategies for would-be athletes, nominate classic PWE virtues. It is also probably true that *scientists* expound many PWE beliefs. Judeo-Christian traditions share a faith in activism that is a mastery over the social and physical environment, that is closely in accord with the beliefs of empirical scientists.

Conclusion

This chapter has attempted to systematize various speculations about changes in the PWE and more importantly evaluate the evidence in favour of certain positions. It should be pointed out that seeming contradictory arguments such as the PWE is on the increase vs that it is on the decline may be simultaneously true, because depending on which *historical period* is being discussed; which *group of people* are being referred to; and *how the PWE is measured*, it is quite possible that both positions are true. For instance, the PWE may have been in decline in the 1960s but is now showing a revival; whilst PWE beliefs are de-clining among working-class blue-collar workers they are alive and well in middle-class white-collar workers; and that whilst some manifestations of the PWE are in decline as manifested by greater absenteeism and strikes, work commitment seems higher than ever. However, what few speculators do is specify about whom and when their speculations about the PWE apply.

More importantly and seriously, however, rarely is reliable data forthcom-ing about changes in the PWE. There is now ample evidence that some golden period when PWE beliefs and values permeated a whole society never existed.

Careful historical evidence does not support that position and, if anything, tends to suggest the opposite – so much so that some researchers have actually questioned the existence of the PWE.

Not only is the evidence for change weak, circumstantial, and patchy but the 'theory of or for' changes is often weak. People who lament the decline in the ethic blame television or Freud, but fail to explain how either or both of these factors actually influenced the PWE. Nevertheless people are happy to speculate, frequently in high moral tones, about the decline. It would certainly be interesting to classify optimists and pessimists and see what they had in common in terms of their personal experiences and work views. Blaming personal or national economic decline on the abandoned PWE of the workers definitely sounds like a classic attribution error.

Chapter eight

Alternative ethics

There is nothing as ethical, as the work ethic.

Anon

The world is full of willing people. Some willing to work, the rest willing to let them.

Robert Frost

My father taught me to work; but he did not teach me to love it.

Abraham Lincoln

Hard work never killed anybody, but why take the chance?

Charlie McCarthy

Introduction

Ever since scholars read Weber's thesis about the PWE there have been debates about its existence. The critical analyses have taken a number of forms, some of which were to suggest that the identification of the PWE was false and that there existed another 'ethic' or belief system which motivated behaviour. Whereas some scholars have suggested that Weber was wrong, and that another rather different ethic accounted (albeit partially) for the rise of capitalism (Kelvin and Jarrett, 1985), other researchers have attempted to describe quite different systems sometimes the opposite of the PWE, such as the leisure or welfare ethic (Neulinger, 1978) or those more tangentially related to the PWE such as the romantic ethic (Campbell, 1987), or the narcissistic ethic (Lasch, 1985).

Some of these alternative ethics do not challenge the PWE analysis but suggest that the *Zeitgeist* has changed and that new formulations replace the old. In doing so, some researchers have implicitly accepted that the PWE did exist at some specific historical period within a certain group of people, but that it has waned and has been replaced. For instance, Severinsen (1979) has briefly suggested six alternative ethics: emergent values (of group relationships, relativistic morality, hedonism, group conformity, and present-time orientation); the unique ethic (of the struggle to gain approval for industrial work); earning a living (diversify work and eliminate the distinction between work and leisure); existential ethic (emphasizing life's work rather than working life); self-indulgence; and the striving for personally satisfying work. Most of these alternative systems use the word 'ethic' which may well be misleading. The word ethic usually means a set of moral principles or value judgements. The use of the word then may be inappropriate, because for some of the proposed ethics, which the members of a group, sect, or society have internalized, so that actions based upon it may be regarded as acts of choice, there is little or no moral overtone. That is, the alternative ethics are simply beliefs about personal and social conduct, the pursuit of happiness and personal welfare that may or may not have a moral overtone. Secondly these alternative ethics are rarely formulated into a coherent or consistent manner to make up a *system* of principles and judgements. Rather, they constitute a loose association of beliefs and attitudes.

Unlike the PWE thesis, it is not always considered how these alternative ethics arise in societies or groups; how they are maintained or transmitted from one group or generation to another; how those beliefs 'determine' behaviour or the precise relationship between belief and behaviour. Indeed many of these alternative ethics or belief systems that have been proposed have not considered all or even many of the major questions outlined by Furnham (1988). These include: the development of the beliefs; the relationship between various aspects of them; the function of the beliefs; the stability and consistency of the beliefs; the consequences of the beliefs; the changing or manipulation of these beliefs, etc. Nevertheless, some of the proposed alternative ethics will be described. Where they exist, measures of the ethic will be briefly outlined as will studies aimed at comparing them. Finally some tabulation and comparisons of these beliefs will be proposed.

Other ethics

The wealth ethic

In their scholarly and idiosyncratic analysis of the social psychological effects of unemployment, Kelvin and Jarrett (1985) both dismiss the PWE thesis and propose an alternative. The essence of their criticism is a 'wholly false account of the past' – in fact a myth – whose function is more to inspire the present than explain the past. They suggest that a careful analysis of the English middle classes of the sixteenth and seventeenth centuries does not support the Weberian PWE thesis. They are adamant that the PWE is an explanatory concept of our time, invented to explain the past. 'Ours is also a time in which the media quickly pick up, simplify, and disseminate initially subtle and complex technical concepts. Vague notions of a "work ethic" ... have thus become part of everyday language – and in doing so have themselves created expectations in terms of a work ethic....The diffusion of vague concepts then increases the range of phenomena which are perceived to exemplify them – which in its turn is taken as proof of the validity of the concepts' (p. 121). But Kelvin and Jarrett (1985) are not content to dismiss the PWE as a historically incorrect self-fulfilling prophecy. They suggest that what has been incorrectly historically perceived as the work ethic was in fact the *wealth* ethic.

> When one looks at the situation from the very historical perspective
> which ostensibly gave rise to it, explanations in terms of the Protestant
> Ethic emerge as little more than an invention of twentieth-century social
> science, with unwarranted pretensions to an ancient lineage. The 'ethic'
> which has truly been predominant and pervasive is not a work ethic but,
> for want of a better term, a *wealth* ethic. Wealth is (quite correctly)
> perceived as the basis of economic independence: that is the key issue,
> and has been so for centuries. The 'ethic' is to make or to have sufficient
> wealth not to have to depend on others; work is only one means to that
> end, and certainly not the only one universally most esteemed: not in any
> class. Provided that one has money enough to be independent, there is no
> great moral obligation to work, certainly not in the sense of gainful,
> productive employment.
>
> (Kelvin and Jarrett, 1985, p. 104)

Thus it is maintained that work is normative and not an ethic, and that moral significance does not attach to work, but to not living off others. In other words, not only are Kelvin and Jarrett (1985) disputing the historical, or indeed current, existence of the PWE, they believe that the essence of the PWE is the accumulation of wealth in order to ensure *independence* and, to a lesser extent, freedom and leisure. Work is only one, and presumably a moderately unpleasant or at least effortful, way of accumulating wealth.

For Kelvin and Jarrett (1985) all people gain numerous satisfactions from work, as well as money and things which money enables them to have and to do. The wealth ethic adherent then condemns the unemployed not for being idle, but for being poor:

> In the final analysis, explanations in terms of an ethic rest on the
> distinction between the 'good' and the 'bad': explanations based on
> poverty rest on the distinctions between the 'haves' and the 'have-nots'.
> The 'bad' we are entitled to disapprove of, ostracise, punish; the
> 'have-nots' we know from our most basic ethic we ought to help ... given
> our picture of ourselves as fundamentally moral, it is much more
> congenial to us to attribute our attitudes to the unemployed as
> 'conditioned' by an ethic, than as motivated by meanness. The
> inescapable fact, however, is that the 'have-nots' are dependent for their
> material survival on contributions from others, either in the form of
> private charity or of provision from the public purse: and resentment at
> having to feed, clothe, and shelter the bodies of the unemployed poor has

long aroused far more public passion than has concern for the salvation of souls of the leisured rich.

(p. 105)

This is an interesting thesis, though support for it is limited. Kelvin and Jarrett (1985) do supply some historical evidence in support of their thesis. However, it is quite possible to reinterpret the evidence they supply *in favour* of the PWE. For instance they quote the parliamentary papers of 1884: 'An enormous amount of time is lost, not only by want of punctuality in coming to work in the morning and the beginning again after meals, but still more by the general observation of "It's Monday".... One employer has on Monday only 40 or 50 out of 300 or 400'. Whereas Kelvin and Jarrett (1985) appear to use this as evidence for the fact that the PWE *was not* found among the English working classes during the height of Britain's imperial power, one could equally argue that it *was* evidence of the PWE in that a group of adherents or believers were in fact chastising a group of non-believers. The fact that there is or was a large element of people who did not endorse the PWE ethic, does not invalidate its actual existence!

Equally, however, these criticisms do not invalidate the wealth ethic which may be seen to stress one particular theme in the PWE itself – namely independence. A true wealth ethic would place money in the same place that work holds in the PWE – wealth/money should be pursued for itself and it alone should be seen as a desirable product. Possession of wealth, like virtue, may then be flaunted! Furnham and Rose (1987) attempted to measure the wealth ethic and compare it with the PWE. The eight items that they chose are listed in Table 8.1; the means show the extent to which people endorse them.

Whether these statements tap into the theme of wealth ethic as outlined by Kelvin and Jarrett (1985) is not yet certain; people seem to agree relatively

Table 8.1 Wealth ethic: items from Furnham and Rose, (1987)

	Mean
Provided one has enough money to be independent, there should be no moral obligation to work.	4.36
People work mainly to earn money, and thus work is only a means to an end.	4.96
Money gives one independence and choice.	6.13
Entrepreneurs should enjoy a higher status than the aristocracy with all its wealth (R).	3.53
Many of the problems in our society are caused through some people having too much money (R).	4.04
Nobody in their right mind would go back to work after winning the pools or inheriting a great deal (half a million) of money.	3.77
People should be able to retire as early as they wish provided they can be financially independent.	6.02
One should work to live not live to work.	5.52

(R) = reversed item
Mean from scale 7 = Strongly Agree; 1 = Strongly Disagree

strongly with certain aspects of it. Yet as predicted when the total score from the wealth ethic was correlated with the PWE score, the correlation was very low and non significant ($r = -.09$). They also found that whereas the PWE correlated with numerous other variables such as 'postponement of gratification', 'need for achievement', 'internal locus of control', the wealth ethic did not. Finally they did find some evidence for the fact that the wealth ethic was multi-dimensional. The welfare ethic factor analysis also yielded three factors which accounted for about 60 per cent of the variance. The first factor seems to make *financial independence* as a desirable goal, while the second stresses the idea of *wealth status*; that is, that money inherited, more than made, is respect-worthy. The third bipolar factor concerns *wealth contentment*, suggesting that lack of wealth causes problems, not wealth itself. Clearly more work needs to be done on the wealth ethic.

The welfare ethic

Furnham and Rose (1987) have argued that the rise of the welfare state, particularly in Western Europe, and recent high levels of unemployment in many industrialized countries with the consequent fact that many people have to rely on welfare and social security, has seen the emergence of what may be called the *welfare ethic*. This belief system (rather than an ethic) is based on the idea of a cunning claimant of welfare, who believes that because welfare is so easy to obtain (and to some extent one's right), one should enjoy the good life (without work) by living off payments received from the welfare system. People who do this have become known somewhat pejoratively as 'super-scroungers' (Golding and Middleton, 1983). In other words, the 'laxness, excessive generosity, inefficiency and vulnerability to exploitation of the welfare system' (Golding and Middleton, 1983, p. 109) makes it open to less-than-honest people. There has been quite a lot of research on attitudes towards social security claimants (Furnham, 1983, 1985a) which, in fact, suggests that many people *not on* welfare payments believe those who are, are both idle and dishonest. Although there is considerable research to show that this view is misplaced, there is anecdotal evidence of people who thrive on welfare and expose the *welfare ethic*. In that the welfare ethic tends to despise and avoid work, one may expect it to be negatively correlated with the PWE but positively correlated with the leisure and wealth ethics.

Studies done on the attitudes of the public to welfare both in the United States and Europe show a fairly consistent pattern (see Chapter 6). One very consistent finding is that the public as a whole agree that able bodied people should not receive welfare. For instance 81 per cent of whites and 78 per cent of American blacks agreed that 'There are too many people receiving welfare who should be working' while only 25 per cent of whites and 16 per cent of blacks agreed 'There would be fewer people on welfare if jobs were easier to find' (Kallen and Miller, 1971). These attitudes were shown to be affected by ethnicity, education, and general conservatism.

Similarly, Alston and Dean (1972) reported a 1964 Gallup poll of 3,055 Americans who were asked, 'In your opinion, do you think that too much money, or not enough money, is being spent on welfare and relief programs in your area?' They found sex, age, education, and occupational differences. Males more than females, older (over 40) rather than younger, the better rather than the less educated, and professionals rather than skilled or un-skilled workers believed too much rather than too little was being spent on welfare. The same pattern of differences occurred with the other salient question – 'What proportion of persons do you think are on relief for dishonest reasons – most, some, hardly any, or none?' Males, older people, the better educated, and professionals believed more people were dishonest than fe-males, younger people, the less well educated, and the working class. They concluded that these negative evaluations place a heavy burden on welfare personnel, as they are expected to carry out policies not completely accepted by the general public. These results have been replicated in Great Britain (Furnham, 1983, 1985a).

Deacon (1978) has found extensive evidence for the scrounger hypothesis in the 1920s which he attributed not to the media, but a general decline in living standards which had eroded differentials in after-tax income between the unemployed and those at work, especially the relatively poorly paid. Furn-ham (1985a) has replicated empirical evidence that welfare attitudes are multidimensional. Four basic beliefs appear to exist: the belief that welfare recipients are dishonest and idle; the difficulty and discomfort of people living on social security/welfare; the stigma and shame that is attached to being a welfare claimant, dependent on the state; and the needs of social security pay-ments in the future. Predictably those who endorse the PWE tended to see those on social security/welfare as idle and dishonest, did not believe that it was particularly difficult to exist on social security/welfare; and felt that reci-pients suffered little stigma and shame while being recipients.

However, Taylor-Gooby (1983) has pointed out that whereas people are in favour of some aspects of welfare they are against others. More importantly perhaps, Taylor-Gooby (1983) found evidence for various *values* associated with welfare payments. These include:

- Reduces self-help – the idea that welfare makes people less willing to look after themselves.
- Increases integration – it makes for a more integrated, more caring so-ciety.
- Increases the tax burden – that whether it is good or bad, it intolerably in-creases taxes.
- Reduces the work ethic – it saps the will to work, which presumably is ex-trinsic not intrinsic.
- Reduces the family ethic – it makes people less ready to look after their relatives and children.

- Increases stigma – it makes people who get benefits and services from welfare feel like second class citizens.
- Helps the undeserving – it provides people who do not deserve it with a source of income.
- Increases social justice – by being a more compassionate and equally distributed society it increases social justice.
- Increases indiscriminate allocation – paradoxically it tends to help people who do not need help. These various values were shown to be strong statistical predictors of attitudes to welfare. Interestingly, very few studies have sought to compare those on welfare with those not receiving welfare.

In their extensive and scholarly review of press and public attitudes to welfare, Golding and Middleton (1983) report considerable evidence from numerous countries of what they call the welfare backlash – namely negative attitudes to welfare. They document in considerable detail press exposure of people who abuse the system – in other words, those who believe in, or exploit, the welfare ethic. They detected a number of themes:

- The known cases of welfare abuse are just the tip of the iceberg. It is suggested that it is common knowledge that social security/welfare fraud is extremely widespread.
- That although welfare is a right there is no boundary between the taxpayer and the claimant.
- That the welfare umbrella of the nanny state has extended over too wide a range of clients, at great social, bureaucratic, and administrative cost.
- That many of the recipients of welfare are the undeserving poor or super-scroungers.
- That the social security/welfare system is failing adequately to control its clientele, that it has become too easy to get, and that welfare benefits have become excessively generous, encouraging indolence and insulting the honest worker.

Most researchers in this area are sociologists who are eager to expose errors in public opinion and that excessive 'scrounger-hounding' is unnecessary. It may well be the case that the amount of abuse of the welfare system is grossly over-reported. Nevertheless it would be equally erroneous to believe that it did not exist.

What is being suggested is that there are those who endorse the *welfare* ethic. To what extent they abuse the welfare system is not clear. The essence of this ethic is that state welfare payments are a right, should be increased, and that it is more preferable living on state welfare than working in unpleasant or poorly paid work.

Furnham and Rose (1987) attempted to measure what they called the Welfare ethic (see Table 8.2). However, even within this very short series of eight questions, three distinct themes were detectable. This welfare scale seems to have three factors which accounted for nearly 60 per cent of the variance. The

219

Table 8.2 Welfare ethic: items from Furnham and Rose, (1987)

	Mean
1. Unemployed people should try to get as much money from the state as they can.	3.72
2. People on the dole have more time to relax and enjoy themselves.	3.75
3. Too many people think the unemployed are scroungers.	4.86
4. Unemployed people should have their social security payments tripled.	2.54
5. Social security is a right, not a privilege.	5.20
6. Having a social security system only encourages idleness (R).	4.56
7. If one can get as much money on the dole as being at work, it makes much more sense to remain unemployed.	3.96
8. A country's compassion and humanitarianism can be judged by its social security payments.	3.98

(R) = reversed item
Mean from scale: 7 = Strongly Agree, 1 = Strongly Disagree

first factor appears (items 1, 4, and 6) to have items leading on it which suggests people should attempt to *increase welfare* (payments should go up). The second factor (items 3 and 5) has a moral dimension and appears to relate to *welfare justice*, while the third factor has two items (items 2 and 8) at the heart of this belief system, namely that receiving state hand-outs allows for *welfare relaxation*.

As one may predict, the welfare ethic was significantly negatively associated with the PWE but positively correlated with wealth and leisure. However, an important distinction not made in the above scale refers to the extent to which people wish to exploit and extend welfare payments to themselves and others by legal means, and the extent to which they abuse the system by illegal practices. Furthermore, it may be particularly instructive to look at the differences in attitudes between countries that have relatively high vs low levels of welfare payments.

The leisure ethic

> The morality of work is the morality of slaves, and the modern world has no need of slavery.
>
> Bertrand Russell

Many writers have talked about the new leisure ethic that states that 'to leisure' is by far the greatest virtue, namely to develop one's potential in discretionary time (Neulinger, 1978). Although it is not entirely clear what this new ethic stands for, some empirical work has to be done in this field. Thus Buchholz (1976) attempted to measure what he termed *leisure* ethic, which regards work as a means to personal fulfilment through primarily its provision of the means to pursue leisure activities. According to Buchholz (1976) the leisure ethic is defined thus:

Work has no meaning in itself, but only finds meaning in leisure. Jobs cannot be made meaningful or fulfilling, but work is a human necessity to produce goods and services and enable one to earn the money to buy them. Human fulfilment is found in leisure activities where one has a choice regarding the use of his time, and can find pleasure in pursuing activities of interest to him personally. This is where a person can be creative and involved. Thus the less hours one can spend working and the more leisure time one has available the better.

(p. 1180)

Studies using the leisure ethic have found it to be related to occupational status (high status people endorse it less than low status); age (leisure ethic beliefs decline with age); and nationality (Americans endorse it more than Scots (Dickson and Buchholz, 1977)). The leisure ethic has also been shown to be significantly negatively correlated with general conservative beliefs, the PWE, and measures of job involvement (Furnham, 1984b). Iso-Ahola and Buttimer (1981) examined the work and leisure ethic of nearly 500 American school children from 8th to 12th grade (14–18 years). They found, contrary to expectation, that as the PWE declined, the leisure ethic increased. This, they believe, is due to the fact that older children achieve personal independence and responsibility through leisure rather than work. The leisure ethic, then, may be seen as the positive opposite of the work ethic. People who do not endorse the PWE may or may not endorse the leisure ethic, but it is unlikely that people endorse both the PWE and the leisure ethic. Hence, one may predict a sizeable significant negative correlation between the PWE and the leisure ethic.

One way of understanding what this ethic stands for is to examine some of the questionnaire items used to measure it. Table 8.3 gives the eight items from the Buchholz scale, together with means (7 = Agree, 1 = Disagree) from a British population. This is not the only measure of the leisure ethic, however. Crandall and Slivken (1980) developed a simple 10-item scale that

Table 8.3 Leisure ethic: items from Furnham and Rose, (1987)

	Mean
Increased leisure time is bad for society.	4.75
The less hours one spends working and the more leisure time available, the better.	4.15
Success means having ample time to pursue leisure activities.	4.13
The present trend towards a shorter work week is to be encouraged.	4.61
Leisure time activities are more interesting than work.	4.62
Work takes too much of our time, leaving little time to relax.	4.51
More leisure time is good for people.	4.77
The trend towards more leisure is not a good thing (R).	4.84

(R) means reversed scoring
Mean from scale 7 = Strongly Agree, 1 = Strongly Disagree

people respond to on a 4-point agree–disagree scale: (1) My leisure is my most enjoyable time; (2) I admire a person who knows how to relax; (3) I like to do things on the spur of the moment; (4) I would like to lead a life of complete leisure; (5) Most people spend too much time enjoying themselves today; (6) I don't feel guilty about enjoying myself; (7) People should seek as much leisure as possible in their lives; (8) I'd like to have at least two months vacation a year; (9) Leisure is great; (10) It is good for adults to be playful. Preliminary work on the concurrent and predictive validity of this scale showed it to be a useful measure.

Interestingly these authors speculated on the relationship between work and leisure ethics. They argued that since work and leisure activities appear to compete for a finite amount of time, one might suspect they are negatively correlated. Yet it may be that inherently happy people express both work and leisure satisfaction (a high positive correlation), while unhappy people are equally dissatisfied with work and leisure. They believe the two ethics are unrelated at present but if, as suggested, the PWE is in decline and the leisure ethic on the incline, one would expect the orthogonal relationship to become oblique.

Though there is much speculation about the existence of the leisure ethic, others are concerned with how to ensure its survival. Neulinger (1981) has suggested that leisure is a socio-political issue, and that only through such things as a guaranteed health service, guaranteed income, and guaranteed education could the leisure ethic thrive.

The 'new work ethic'

Rosseel (1986) claims that social critics, personnel workers, management consultants, and academic researchers have identified among the young a new work ethic. This is manifest primarily by the desire of (young) people to contribute in a more personal and autonomous way to the goods and service in society, having anti-bureaucratic attitudes and a disapproval of the traditional PWE based upon financial security, individual achievement, and career-making. Work will be seen as only one way of self-realization among a better educated and critical work force.

However, according to Rosseel (1986) the new work ethic was undermined by the employment crisis of the early 1980s which affected all industrialized countries. However, this crisis made the more educated express the new 'critical' work ethic more clearly, while the less educated resorted more to the old PWE. A look at the 'new' PWE items however leads one to suspect that it is simply a non-work ethic. There follows a list of statements measuring the old and new PWE .

1. Enjoying life is more important than working.
2. I prefer lesser earnings if it affords me more leisure time.*
3. I have no sympathy for people that don't like to work.

4.   People who do not work, just benefit from the efforts of others.
5.   Nowadays youth does not like working as much as the youth in earlier times.
6.   Making a successful career does not attract me.
7.   Poor people are just as happy as the rich.*
8.   Work is the most important thing in life.
9.   Most work in this world is dull and lacks human dignity.*
10. Why work hard, if things are going well without?*
11. There are other ways besides working for making one's living.
12. It is unfair that those who do not work, get as much earnings as those who work.
13. I would be terrified by the idea of working my whole life-time in the same company.*
14. If earning much money means less leisure time, then I say no.*
15. Most jobs are so boring and uninteresting that I feel an aversion to working.*
16. Work remains the only way to be socially useful.
17. Career prospects of good earnings and prestige are anyhow very attractive.
18. Most firms are so bureaucratized that work has lost its pleasant aspects.*
19. I'd like to work but not at the cost of losing my independence and freedom.*
20. In earlier times, hard work was more rewarded than nowadays.
21. Anyone who does not work, has as much right to a normal income as those at work.*
22. A life without working would be fine.*
23. Even if I won the first prize of the Lotto-game, I would continue working.
24. Meaningless work would make me sick.*
25. If I had the chance to live without working, I would certainly take it.

* The New Work Ethic items.

There was evidence of the fact that higher educational levels were associated with the new ethic, and lower levels the old, but most importantly relatively few young people (from the population of nearly 700 Belgian army recruits) endorsed the new ethic.

The new PWE is not work nor leisure correlated but centred on the idea of professionalization. In this society, performance (i.e. work) will be contracted and paid for and the activity one performs is self-defined. That is, people are paid to carry out an activity, not specifically to produce goods or services, but because it is seen as a worthy thing to do. It differs from the old PWE in emphasizing the process rather than the product.

The sports ethic

In a very interesting set of observations Ritzer, Kammeyer, and Yelman (1982) have implied that the norms that govern sport are not dissimilar from those of the PWE. Sport is thought of in many countries as an important and healthy socialization experience for young people, and it is assumed that they learn many important lessons.

Consider the sporting norms which have 'become a conservative force functioning to maintain and reinforce certain of the traditional American values, beliefs and practices while countering others' (Ritzer *et al.*, 1982, p. 18). These include:

- Sportsmanship – this emphasizes adherence to the rules; acceptance of the decisions of game officials and the desire to uphold the regulations governing the sport. Also a vital aspect of sportsmanship is the concept of magnanimity in victory and the gracious acceptance of defeat.
- Competition – social Darwinism is alive and well in the philosophy of sporting enthusiasts. There is consistent legitimization of the idea that competition produces the best players.
- Success – the well known statement by Lombardi: 'Winning isn't the important thing – it's the only thing'. In other words, it is not exclusively the joy of participation but the possibility of winning that makes athletes. Hence the numerous and consistent ways in which achievement is recognized through prizes and awards.
- Universalism – sport is open to all, irrespective of race, class, age, sex, etc., and one is judged entirely and exclusively by the quality of one's athletic performance. In other words people are to be evaluated according to one criteria – their sporting prowess.
- Diligence – the great PWE virtues of perseverance, fortitude, and hard work are to be found in sport. Asceticism pervades American sport with its emphasis on personal sacrifice, long and strenuous preparation, and stamina.
- Self-discipline – it is frequently held that sporting people need to develop the necessary internal locus of control and personal habits that will enable them to achieve their best possible performance. A life of order, self-discipline, and self-control is therefore advocated.
- Teamwork – although not true of all sports, this virtue consists of co-operation and unity and is emphasized greatly in team sports.

However, as it is quite apparent, some of these values are in conflict. Individualism conflicts with team work, self-discipline with that of accepting orders. Nevertheless, the outward portrayal of the sporting ethic which may be seen in lockers and slogans, in post-success sporting speeches, and in sports commentators, is remarkably similar to that of the PWE.

The ethic of 'being'

More than one writer has noted the decline of the PWE in terms of it being replaced with another ethic. This new ethic has been seen to have a number of elements, the most central of which is the rise in value placed upon 'being' as opposed to 'doing' or 'having'. Other related ideas are an increased interest in the present time orientation and a decreased interest in the future.

Though he recognized the theme in many other western and eastern writers, Fromm (1980) has exposed this new ethic of being. The argument is predicated on the assumption that the materialistic way of having has failed. Economic and technical progress which at any rate has remained restricted to richer nations is not conducive to well-being. This ethic is based on two erroneous principles: that the aim of life is to maximize pleasure and happiness; and that egoism, selfishness, and greed lead to harmony and peace. Though rather crudely stated, these two assumptions of the way of having are thought to have the seeds of destruction within them.

Thus one needs a new ethic – that of being. Whereas the having mode is characterized by possessing and owning, for which the dictum is I am equal to what I have and what I consume, the being mode is characterized not by greed, envy, and aggressiveness but love, joy, and ascendancy over our material values. Perhaps because it is difficult to elucidate the concept of having – which is rejected and described in straw-man terms – it is described in detail and it is for the reader to infer that the opposite is desirable.

Fromm (1980) reports a change in the PWE character described as authoritarian, obsessive, and hoarding, to what he calls a marketing character. This character type is based on experiencing oneself as a commodity and one's value as exchange value:

> Success depends largely on how well they get their 'personality' across, how nice a 'package' they are; whether they are 'cheerful', 'sound', 'aggressive', 'reliable', 'ambitious'; furthermore, what their family backgrounds are, what clubs they belong to and whether they know the 'right' people. The type of personality required depends to some degree on the special field in which a person may choose to work. A stockbroker, a salesperson, a secretary, a railroad executive, a college professor or a hotel manager each offer a much different kind of personality that, regardless of their differences, must fulfil one condition: to be in demand. What shapes one's attitude towards oneself is the fact that skill and equipment for performing a given task are not sufficient; one must win in competition with many others in order to have success....But since success depends largely on how one sells one's personality, one experiences oneself as a commodity or, rather, simultaneously as the seller *and* the commodity to be sold. A person is not concerned with his or her life and happiness, but with becoming saleable.

(p. 146)

Fromm (1980) goes on to describe the new type, occasionally loosely disguising his contempt for it, and indeed its connection with the PWE. This new ethic of being is spelt out in a number of points such as:

- Acceptance of the fact that nobody and nothing outside oneself gives meaning to life, but that this radical independence and nothingness can become the condition for the fullest activity devoted to caring and sharing.
- Security, sense of identity, and confidence based on faith in what one *is*, in one's need for relatedness, interest, love, solidarity with the world around one instead of on one's desire to have, to possess, to control the world, and thus become a slave of one's possessions.

This new ethic of being is in accordance with many other religious teachings. It is pantheistic, a-materialist, and humanist. Directly opposed to PWE values on some accounts, it is tangential at others. Certainly there is nothing new in this ethic and it is uncertain how widely it is held.

The narcissistic ethic

Many commentators on contemporary culture have attempted to discern trends and patterns that trace the waxing and waning of movements, ethics, or cults. One recent and influential analysis of American culture has been that of Lasch (1985), which argues that the dominant American culture of competitive individualism has changed into the pursuit of happiness and a narcissistic preoccupation with self.

Central to Lasch's (1985) thesis is the decline of the PWE and what he calls 'changing modes of making it'. In doing so he very succinctly describes the PWE as it underpinned American culture.

> Until recently the Protestant work ethic stood as one of the most important underpinnings of American culture. According to the myth of capitalist enterprise, thrift and industry held the key to material success and spiritual fulfilment. America's reputation as a land of opportunity rested on its claim that the destruction of hereditary obstacles to advancement had created conditions in which social mobility depended on individual initiative alone. The self-made man, archetypical embodiment of the American dream, owed his advancement to habits of industry, sobriety, moderation, self-discipline, and avoidance of debt. He lived for the future, shunning self-indulgence in favour of patient, painstaking accumulation; and as long as the collective prospect looked on the whole so bright, he found in the deferral of gratification not only his principal satisfaction but an abundant source of profits. In an expanding economy, the value of investments could be expected to multiply with time, as the spokesmen for self-help, for all their celebration of work as its own reward, seldom neglected to point out.
>
> (pp. 52–3)

Lasch (1985) argued that PWE values no longer excite enthusiasm or command respect for a variety of reasons: inflation erodes investments/savings; the society is fearfully now- rather than confidently future-oriented; self-preservation has become self-improvement; moral codes have changed. But this change has been graduated over the centuries. For Lasch (1985) the Puritan gave way to the Yankee, who secularized the PWE and stressed self-improvement (instead of socially useful work) that consisted of the cultivation of reason, wisdom, and insight as well as money. Wealth was valued because it allowed for a programme of moral self-improvement and was one of the necessary preconditions of moral and intellectual advancement. The nineteenth century saw the rise of the 'cult of compulsive industry' which was obsessed with the 'art of money-getting', as all values would be expressed or operationalized in money terms. Further, there became more emphasis on competition.

The spirit of self-improvement, according to Lasch (1985), was debased into self-culture – the care and training of the mind and body through reading great books and healthy living. Self-help books taught self-confidence, initiative, and other qualities of success. 'The management of interpersonal relations came to be seen as the essence of self-advancement....Young men were told that they had to sell themselves in order to succeed' (p. 58). The new prophets of positive thinking discarded the moral overtones of Protestantism that were attached to the pursuit of wealth, save that it contributed to the total human good. The pursuit of economic success now accepted the need to exploit and intimidate others and to ostentatiously show the winning image of success.

The new ethic meant that people preferred admiration, envy, and the excitement of celebration, to being respected and esteemed. People were less interested in how people acquired success – defined by riches, fame, and power – than in that they had 'made it'. Success had to be ratified and verified by publicity. The quest for a good public image leads to a confusion of successful completion of the task with rhetoric that is aimed to impress or persuade others. Thus impressions overshadow achievements and the images and symbols of success are more important than the actual achievements.

Emphasis shifts from capitalist production to consumption meant that people had to develop a new pattern of social behaviour. It became important to get on with others; to organize one's life in accordance with the requirements of large organizations; to sell one's own personality; to receive affection and reassurance. The dominant perception was that success depends on the psychological manipulation of one's own and others' positive and negative emotions and social behaviours.

The growth of bureaucracy, the cult of consumption with its immediate gratification, but above all the severance of the sense of historical continuity have transformed the Protestant ethic while carrying the underlying principles of capitalistic society to their logical conclusion.

> The pursuit of self-interest, formerly identified with the rational pursuit of gain and the accumulation of wealth, has become a search for pleasure and psychic survival. Social conditions now approximate the vision of republican society conceived by the Marquis de Sade at the very outset of the republican epoch.
>
> (Lasch, 1985, p. 69)

For Lasch (1985) the cult or ethic of narcissism has a number of quite distinct features:

- *The waning of the sense of historical time.* The idea that things are coming to an end means that people have a very limited time perspective, neither confidently forward nor romantically backward. The narcissist lives only in and for the present.
- *The therapeutic sensibility.* Narcissists seek therapy for personal well-being, health, and psychic security. The rise in the human potential movement and the decline in self-help tradition has made people dependent on experts and organizations to validate self-esteem and develop competence. Therapists are used excessively to help develop composure, meaning, and health.
- *From politics to self-examination.* Political theories, issues, and conflicts have been trivialized. The debate has moved from the veridical nature of political propositions to the personal and autobiographical factors that lead proponents to make such suppositions.
- *Confession and anticonfession.* Writers and others attempt simple self-disclosure, rather than critical reflection, to gain insight into the psycho-historical forces that lead to personal development. But these confessions are paradoxical and do not lead to greater, but lesser, insights into the inner life. People disclose not to provide an objective account of reality, but to seduce others to give attention, acclaim, or sympathy and, by doing so, foster the perpetual, faltering sense of self.
- *The void within.* Without psychological peace, meaning, or commitment, people experience an inner emptiness which they try to avoid by living vicariously through the lives of others, or seeking spiritual masters.
- *The progressive critique of privatism.* Self-absorption with dreams of fame, avoidance of failure, and quests for spiritual panacea means that people define social problems as personal ones. The cult suggests a limited investment in love and friendship, avoidance of dependence, and living for the moment.

Lasch (1985) argues that psychological insights into the narcissistic personality of our time fail to miss the social dimension of this behaviour pattern such as pseudo self-insight, calculating seductiveness, and nervous self-deprecatory humour.

In a study of 250 managers from twelve major companies, Michael

Maccoby describes the new corporate leader, not altogether unsympathetically, as a person who works with people rather than with materials and who seeks not to build an empire or accumulate wealth but to experience 'the exhilaration of running his team and of gaining victories'. He wants to 'be known as a winner, and his deepest fear is to be labelled a loser'. Instead of pitting himself against a material task or a problem demanding solution, he pits himself against others, out of a 'need to be in control'. As a recent textbook for managers puts it, success today means 'not simply getting ahead' but 'getting ahead of others'. The new executive, boyish, playful, and seductive, wants in Maccoby's words 'to maintain an illusion of limitless option'. He has little capacity for 'personal intimacy and social commitment'. He feels little loyalty even to the company for which he works. One executive says he experiences power 'as not being pushed around by the company'. In his upward climb, this man cultivates powerful customers and attempts to use them against his own company. 'You need a very big customer', according to his calculations, 'who is always in trouble and demands changes from the company. That way you automatically have power in the company, and with the customer too. I like to keep my options open.' A professor of management endorses this strategy. 'Overidentification' with the company, in his view, 'produces a corporation with enormous power over the careers and destinies of its true believers'. The bigger the company, the more important he thinks it is for executives 'to manage their careers in terms of their own ... free choices' and 'to maintain the widest set of options possible'.

(Lasch, 1985, pp. 44–5)

This narcissism, or the ethic of self-preservation, appears to many people to be the best way of coping with the tensions, vicissitudes, and anxieties of modern life. The traits associated with this ethic – charm, pseudo-awareness, promiscuous pan-sexuality, hypochondria, protective shallowness, avoidance of dependence, inability to mourn, dread of old age and death – are learnt in the family, reinforced in the society, but are corruptible and changeable. Ultimately the paradox of narcissism is that it is the faith of those without faith; the cult of personal relations for those who are disenchanted with personal relations.

This cynical view of the change of the work ethic into the narcissism ethic is an analysis from a socio-historical view of current America. To what extent it is generally or specifically true is uncertain or, indeed, if it applies to other countries with similar political and economic systems. Perhaps because profundity is always associated with pessimism, Lasch's (1985) analysis has failed to reveal much good about this ethic. While it does seem that some PWE ideals and virtues had negative consequences for the individual and society that held them, so some had positive consequences. It would be surprising if there were no positive characteristics of the narcissistic ethic despite the clearly pejorative nature of the term.

The evolution of the PWE: the romantic ethic

In a scholarly, wide-ranging, and fairly radical essay, Campbell (1987) proposed that a cultural, anti-Puritan force – the romantic ethic – was responsible for the rise of the consumer ethic. He attempted to identify an autonomous, imaginative, pleasure-seeking force – the romantic ethic – which created and justified consumer hedonism at the onset of the Industrial Revolution.

Campbell (1987) found neither economic nor sociological theories sufficiently non-tautological or historically based to account for the consumer revolution. He argued that one should distinguish between traditional and modern hedonism – the former concerned with sensory experience and discrete, standardized pleasures while the latter is envisaged as a potential quality in all experience:

> In order to extract this from life, however, the individual has to substitute illusory for real stimuli; and by creating and manipulating illusions and hence the emotive dimension of consciousness, construct his own pleasurable environment....Hedonism of this kind is seen as providing the answer to the problem of distinctive features of modern consumerism, for it explains how the individual's interest is primarily focused on the meanings and images which can be imputed to a product, something which requires novelty to be present. At the same time, the joys of longing rival those of actual gratification, with disillusionment the necessary concomitant of the purchase and use of goods; characteristics which help to explain the dynamic and disacquiring nature of modern consumer behaviour. Such a model not only makes it possible to understand precisely how a consumer creates (and abandons) 'wants' and why it is that this has become a never ending process, but also directs attention to the character of consumption and voluntaristic, self-directed and creative processes in which cultured ideals are necessarily implicated. It is then argued that not only is modern consumerism to be understood in these terms but that romantic love and the crucial modern phenomena of dynamic fashion should be viewed as dependent upon autonomous, self-illusory hedonism.
>
> (p. 203)

Campbell (1987) attempted to explain the high growth of consumerism in the middle classes, supposedly ascetic, puritanical bearers of the PWE. He argued that after the seventeenth century Calvinist Christianity changed to allow emotional sentimentalism. Concern with aesthetics was inherited from the aristocratic ethic, and taste became a sign of moral and spiritual worth. Taste allowed people to take genuine pleasure in the beautiful and respond with tears to the pitiable. In this romantic movement pleasure becomes the crucial means of recognizing that ideal truth and beauty which imagination reveals and becomes the means by which art encourages moral enlightenment. The romantics assured that people could be morally improved through the provision of cultural products that yielded pleasure and which helped people dream about a more perfect world. Consumerism, a sort of self-illusory hedonism, is

> characterized by a longing to experience in reality those pleasures created and enjoyed in imagination, a longing results in the ceaseless consumption of novelty. Such an outlook, with all its characteristic dissatisfaction with real life and an eagerness for new experience, lies at the heart of much conduct that is most typical of modern life, and underpins such central institutions as fiction and romantic love.... In particular, romantic teachings concerning the good, the true and the beautiful, provide both the legitimization and the motivation necessary for modern consumer behaviour to become prevalent throughout the contemporary industrial world.
>
> (pp. 205–6)

Campbell (1987) attempted to explain some of the difficulties, ironies, and non-sequiturs associated with his thesis. For instance, he argues that consumer hedonism 'drove' romanticism, and not vice versa. This allowed him to escape the trap Weber found himself in, where the original ethic had within it seeds of its own destruction. More importantly because romanticism is an outgrowth of Puritanism the ideals of value of the two are more symbolic than in conflict. For instance, it is argued that delay of gratification and suppression of emotion serve both ethics, even the romantic ethic, because they

> work together to create a rich and powerful imaginative inner life within the individual, the necessary prerequisite for a 'romantic' personality. It seems clear that the overall pattern of child-rearing which has been considered characteristic of the middle classes, with its emphasis upon literacy, privacy, individual responsibility, self-denial, emotional inhibition and intellectual accomplishment is conducive to the 'development of romantic personality traits'.
>
> (p. 222)

It is also suggested that both individuals and society have a compatible 'purito'-romantic personality system when the values of puritan-utilitarianism and romantic sentimentalism occur compatibly, but are conveniently compartmentalized in time and space so allowing both to exist. He quotes evidence as wide-ranging as Victorian sentimentalism and utilitarianism, as well as the life-style of the bourgeois individual that passes from youthful romanticism to adult bureaucracy. It is further suggested that Puritanism is primarily socialized into males and romanticism into females; hence the stress on science for males, arts for females.

For Campbell (1987) the transformation of the PWE has seen not a rejection of the rationality of calculation and experiment, but an incorporation of passion and the creative dream born of longing. It is this strain or tension between dream and reality, pleasure and utility that the dynamism of the West depends.

Such a thesis is attractive for a number of reasons – it appears to explain, in historical and sociological terms, recent anomalies in the PWE thesis; it also seems to overcome some of the over-simplifications or traps that alternative theories have fallen into. It is particularly appealing in its treatment of modern consumerism described as autonomous, imaginative hedonism. However, at least for a psychological analysis, it has some serious shortcomings. Psychologists don't always see creative tension as healthy and desirable, and see individuals spending a great deal of their time attempting to reduce conflict, dissonance, and tension.

Further, the author is as long on historical analysis as he is short on data. Some of the most interesting and unanswered questions include:

- Precisely what is the spirit of modern consumerism?
- Is it manifest in all socioeconomic, national, and ethnic groups to the same extent?
- If romanticism like consumerism is ultimately unsatisfactory, why do people attempt to seek the holy grail of unfulfillable self-enlightenment?
- How are the Puritan and romantic ethic compartmentalized in society?
- Given changes in the economic and sociological forces that changed the PWE, what is the future for the romantic ethic?
- Which aspects of the PWE remain intact (i.e. rationality) and which do not (asceticism)?

Despite the list of unanswered or at least unsubstantiated questions, it is to the credit of Campbell (1987) that he attempted an analysis of the current status of the PWE in terms of the scholarly breadth and vision of Weber himself.

Conclusion

This chapter has examined the belief systems or 'ethics' (and where appropriate how to measure them) said to be alternative to the PWE. Various researchers have pointed out that at any one time there are more than one belief system concerning work. Some of these competing or alternative ethics may be seen as overlapping with, antithetical to, or quite unrelated to the PWE. Despite considerable speculation about competing, declining, or ascending ethics, there is precious little empirical evidence to support this conjecture.

However, some attempts have been made to provide measurement devices and look at the relationship between them. Buchholz (1978a) devised self-report measures of the humanistic belief system, Marxist-related beliefs, the organizational belief system, the leisure ethic, and the work ethic (see Chapter 3). Furthermore he demonstrated the validity of this measure by showing, for instance, that, compared to, say, management and professionals, union officials had lower scores on the work ethic, but higher scores on Marxist-related, organizational and humanistic beliefs. He also found a fairly low commitment to the PWE among all groups and concluded that it had changed in the sense that hard work is valued not for its own sake, but for what it contributes to personal development, while leisure is accepted somewhat positively, but interestingly not as a substitute for the fulfilment that work can provide.

Over half a dozen alternative ethics have been considered in this chapter, but various others have been suggested. Some have talked of a 'discretionary' work ethic. For instance, Foegen (1972) lamented the compulsory retirement of people at 65. He argues that many old people benefit from working and wish to preserve the American ideal of being self-supporting. Of course, no objection is made to people who wish to retire, but equally he believes that people should not be forced to retire. This raises an important question about generational differences in the PWE, as well as the moral position of older workers who have had a life-time of employment to relinquish their jobs for the benefit of younger people in times of high unemployment.

How can one classify or taxonomize the ethics listed in this chapter? Essentially they appear to fall into two categories – those ethics *antithetical* to the PWE like the welfare and leisure ethic and the ethic of being; and those said to be *transformations* or developments of the original PWE like the wealth, narcissistic, and romantic ethic. The former group see a thesis–antithesis (possibly followed by a synthesis) model of ethics, while the latter have more of an evolutionary model.

Three major points need to be made about these 'ethics'. The first is that they do overlap conceptually and empirically, though apart from Furnham and Rose (1987) there are few attempts to do so. This 'list' therefore may be reduced to a more manageable and orthogonal group of really alternative ethics. Secondly the evidence for, and ways of measuring, these different ethics are extremely varied. They have been variously proposed by philosophers, social psychologists, historians, psychoanalysts, each of whom is impressed by, and hence provides very different sorts of evidence to support, their case. Whilst it might be seen as a great strength to have such rich and varied evidence, on the other hand it makes it extremely problematic to evaluate from the point of view of any one approach.

Finally none of the above deals satisfactorily with the demise of the PWE save perhaps Campbell (1987) and to some extent Lasch (1985). That is if it is believed that PWE beliefs declined or changed over time for one reason or another, it behoves the theorist to stipulate how, why, and when (see Chapter 7).

Finally it could be proposed that the original PWE is alive and well and simply adapted to prevailing conditions. For instance four current obsessions seem at the heart of the PWE:

- Self-sufficiency – in the form of do-it-yourself, home computers, working at home.

- Time consciousness – extreme interest in time management, wastage, etc.
- Anti-hedonic asceticism – a renewed stress on celibacy, sobriety, and 'healthy living'.
- Rationality – concern with theological and social rationality and the rejection of metaphysical beliefs.

In this sense it could be argued that along with these proposed alternative ethics, the PWE remains alive and well.

Chapter nine

The future of the work ethic

We have based our social structures on the work ethic and now it would appear that it is to become redundant with millions of other people.

Jenkins and Sherman

Nothing can be more harmful to a youth than to have his soul sodden with pleasure.

Samuel Smiles

Man is made to be in the visible universe an image and likeness of God himself, and he is placed in it in order to subdue the Earth. From the beginning therefore he is called to work.

Pope John Paul II

Without work, all life goes rotten. But when work is soulless, life stifles and dies.

Albert Camus

Introduction

The period since the Second World War has seen numerous very important changes. Countries like Great Britain have shown relative economic decline, while others like Japan, Korea, and Hong Kong have shown spectacular growth. More importantly perhaps, there has been a micro-electronics revolution which has meant sudden and vast changes in the number and type of jobs available. All over the world more and more jobs were being done by machines, and consequently liberation from certain tasks has led to major and significant changes.

These changes have been comparatively sudden and we are in the middle of them. Indeed the pace of change appears to be accelerating rather than declining. Hence it may be particularly difficult to predict the future of the work ethic or work itself. There has been periodic concern about a change in work beliefs and values which are both the cause and consequences of major industrial and organizational changes.

Many writers who speculate on the future of work, and the effect of rapid and extensive technological change on the PWE, have neglected to consider the historical evidence for when this happened previously. That is, with the occurrence of the Industrial Revolution in Europe and North America in the nineteenth century, the nature of work and fabric of society changed substantially. Historians such as Rodgers (1978) and Gilbert (1977) considered the effect of the mass and rapid industrialization in America on the PWE. Rodgers' (1978) thesis is thus:

> Harnessing a restless faith in change to an immense capacity for work, Northern entrepreneurs turned the land into a stupendous manufacturing workshop....But it was an ironic triumph. For in the process, Northerners so radically transformed work that the old moral expectations would no longer hold. Born as much in faith as in self-interest, the industrial revolution in the end left in tatters the network of economics and values that had given it birth.
>
> (xii)

His thesis was that the PWE beliefs rooted in the self-directed labour of the artisan did not translate well into the factories of the Industrial Revolution. Various attempts were made to rekindle the PWE that were mainly unsuccessful, but could be seen up to the last war with the Nazi 'Strength Through Joy' and 'Beauty of the Work Office' campaigns.

Industrialization therefore had a highly paradoxical and contradictory effect on the PWE. The growing industrial economy helped the growth of the PWE among the bourgeois, but the factory system of necessity undercut the PWE ideals. The PWE moralists were slow to see that not all machines, like the locomotive, were liberating but enslaved those who had to tend them. In a society where self-employment was a moral norm, and the servant was a term of abuse, there grew an array of 'operators', 'employees', and 'hands'. Hard work alone could not ensure the 'rags-to-riches' success story because now (at the turn of the century) other virtues like 'pep, charm and personality' were necessary – virtues like energy, aggressiveness, decision-making ability, and self-advertising.

In the 1970s a special report was commissioned by the American Department of Health, Education, and Welfare. It concentrated on the new malaise in which workers saw their work as meaningless, boring, repetitive, and dull. Workers it seemed wanted more autonomy in tackling tasks, greater opportunities to increase skills, rewards directly connected to the intrinsic features of work, and greater participation in all tasks. The cause of the dissatisfaction, manifested by such data as the fact that less than half a large section of white-collar workers would choose similar work again, was essentially three-fold:

- Taylorism and essentially misplaced conceptions of work efficiency, industrial efficiency was confused with social efficiency.
- The dream of 'becoming one's own boss' through hard work was increas-

ingly a myth.
- Increasing size of corporations and bureaucracies minimized independence and maximized predictability.

People did not complain about pay, conditions, or hours of work, rather it was about recognition and autonomy. The processes of secularization, urbanization, and industrialization appear to have threatened the old PWE.

There have been few current, multi-disciplinary, empirical as well as conceptual analyses of the PWE. An exception was an edited volume by Barbash *et al.* (1983) commissioned by the Industrial Relations Research Association of America. A dozen or so papers were divided into two sections: the PWE and the labour market; change in work and the PWE. The papers, mainly by economists, involved a dispassionate look at how longitudinal national, economic data could answer some of the central questions concerning the PWE. Some of the major conclusions from the contemporary analysis are given below:

- *Work has survived and indeed flourishes.* If the demise of the work ethic is a threat to civilization, one would never suspect it from official reports of current labour market trends. Whatever their ambivalence, Americans are clinging to jobs more than ever. Productivity gains, growing affluence, and many levels of educational attainment have not triggered a mass exodus from work, and our society has not decayed from idleness and sloth. Instead, both greater numbers and larger proportions of the population have entered the labour force in recent years, and the tenacious hold of work upon the daily activities of more Americans shows few signs of weakening (Levitan and Johnson, 1983, p. 1).
- *Simplistic analysis suggesting the decline in both the PWE ethic and productivity (and hence their relationship) is misplaced.* The decline of the work day, week, and year is blamed but the increase of second jobs, do-it-yourself, the grey economy, and a large influx of women may have upgraded the average work ethic. Decline in productivity since the 1960s is in fact a statistical mirage which deserves more clinical appraisal. Problems of definition, measurement, and analysis provide insufficient excuse for overlooking the obvious challenge to improve work commitment and productive performance, in a world of intensifying competition in markets. In our enterprise economy, a special responsibility devolves upon private-sector management for promoting needed improvement in individual and organizational performance (Siegel, 1983, p. 28).
- *There is no decline in work commitment. Furthermore it is misleading to believe that absence from work, job turnover, and preferred part time work are associated with weak job commitment, neither are overtime and multiple job-holding quite simply indicative of strong commitment.* Most phenomena associated with weak job commitment are largely unreliable indicators: under average scheduled work time and hours at work have declined very

modestly in recent years. 'If the data show a major cause for concern, it is that the desire for hours of work seem greater than the hours available. Several million men and women of every age – black, Hispanics, and white – want to work full-time but can only obtain part-time jobs. The group is growing in number and as a proportion of all workers. Some encouraging signs appear in the data. One is a small reduction in the weekly hours of married men who, traditionally, have worked very long hours. It may be that the rising employment of wives is aiding husbands to move toward a little better distribution of their time between paid work and household responsibilities. A second encouraging sign is that weekly schedules and leave benefits of production workers are approaching those of office workers. Few are likely to read these changes as evidence of a weak work-ethic among married men or production workers' (Hedges, 1983, p. 38).

- *There is evidence of the work ethic even in the retired.* Because people are getting richer, early retirement may be seen as a different way of using leisure time but there is little evidence that the attitudes of older people towards work are changing at all.
- *The strength of an individual's commitment to the work ethic affects various measures of their success in the labour market, which in turn have feedback effects on PWE beliefs.* '... strength of commitment to the work ethic is an important element in conditioning successful adaptation to the labour market of both younger and older workers of both sexes. But the feedback effects of labour market experience on the work ethic means that the work ethic of individuals is not beyond the reach of public policy measures; it may be nurtured and cultivated by labour market policies that increase the payoffs to individual initiative and effort' (Andrisani and Parnes, 1983, p. 117).
- *Despite difficulties in international comparisons it seems that the PWE in advanced industrial market economies is not on the decline.* 'But, what with the continued, quite strong will to work demonstrated by the evidence, and the possibilities available for adapting traditional forms of work, there is no reason to suppose that our societies are not capable of responding to the challenge of the work ethic' (Clarke, 1983, p. 143).
- *There has been, over time and more particularly recently, managerial reinterpretation of the work ethic based upon a new belief in the worker as a psychological self.* Throughout different periods of history (since the Industrial Revolution) there have been different and distinct perspectives on why people work and each one has attempted to implement their vision of the PWE.
- *The work ethic is changing, but has changed before.* There exists a mix of ethics – the Protestant ethic, the craft ethic, the entrepreneurial ethic, the career ethic, and now the self-development ethic. Hence these related ethics emphasize in turn: hard work and ethical behaviour; self-

sufficiency, independence, and control; bold risk taking; other directed-ness and ambitious marketing, and finally the most modern form of the PWE is the self-fulfilment ethic which wants primarily interesting work with enriching emotional relationships in the work-place.

● *The PWE of the workers has always been different from that of managers.* The PWE of working people has a number of components: man does not have to work, he works to live; since it is people, not work, that are to be served, people should attempt to be most efficient; as leisure is more possible, people should participate more. In fact, the PWE of the workers has strengthened the political and economic life of the country rather than weakening it.

● *Examining alternative forms of work (bartering, volunteer work, exchange of services) which frequently do not rely on the PWE.* '... the absence of regular market work behaviour may not mean alienation from work, but rather a retreat from a particular kind of work and a movement to informal work. We have erred in our discourse on the work ethic because we still lack concepts and measures to identify and quantify the work effort involved in informal work' (Ferman, 1983, p. 220).

These essays were concluded by Barbash *et al.* (1983) who make a number of interesting and important points. First, that changes in post-industrial society (a growing service sector; welfare assistance; rising expectations; multi-national organizations) must have an effect on the PWE which originated in an era of scarcity and deprivation. Secondly, a careful, empirically-based longitudinal inspection of the data concerning employment (productivity, hours of work, part-time work) 'do not show anything which can be interpreted as a lessening of the work commitment' (p. 237). Thirdly, the PWE as originally conceived gave moral purpose to oppressive and unavoidable hard work, but conditions in the late twentieth century have transformed or changed the ethic and the meaning of work. The PWE has been psychologized and reinterpreted qualitatively *not* quantitatively. Finally, most people still prefer working even if it costs them something in terms of time and effort. Threats to the PWE come from:

● An affluent society with rising work expectations.
● Employment in the service sector overtaking that of production.
● An increase in population with a weaker PWE.
● Public attitudes that denigrate menial work.

However, the PWE is thought of as being benign in that it recognizes the necessity *and* benefits of adjustment to work precepts such as commitment, workmanship, and discipline:

The evidence such as it is, suggests that the work ethic precepts are best cultivated not by preaching moralisms and ideology, but by structuring the employment margin so as to create a reciprocity between the work ethic's precepts on the one side, and human management 'a fair day's pay for a fair day's work' on the other. This is not to say that a smidgen of ideology is not helpful at the margin, in imparting a moral cutting edge to the work ethic. But, in the main, unless the work ethic is credibly associated with valued outcomes, a work ethic morality and ideology may be 'counter productive' and generate cynicism or even a sense of betrayal. In our kind of 'value system', the work ethic has to 'pay off' and not necessarily in monetary terms alone, or it has little standing.

(Barbash *et al.*, 1983, p. 259)

Forecasting the present

It is always interesting when speculating on the future of work to examine the success of past prognosticators. Indeed, the whole process of predicting future trends, even based on sound empirical sources, is fraught with danger given that quite unexpected and novel occurrences (inventions, wars, economic crises) with substantial wide-ranging effects upset reasonable, rational forecasts.

A decade ago Kerr and Rosow (1979) edited a book entitled *Work in America: The Decade Ahead* which attempted, from historical and sociological analyses, to understand and predict future trends, which they thought would be a great cultural evolution in the labour force. These projective trends may be favourably compared with what, ten years later, is indeed the case. Predictions and expectations include the following:

- The work ethic in the young (i.e. college students) is not on the decline. Nearly eighty per cent of young people believe 'hard work always pays off'.
- Work is being more equally distributed over the different sex and age groups with more women and migrants and fewer older white men.
- There will be three tiers of wage earners: multiple wage earners, single wage earners, and no wage earners.
- Work attitudes will change because better educated, more knowledgeable, mobile people with better resources will decline bad jobs and search for good ones. People will be more tolerant of non-work life-styles. The PWE will not destroy itself in the following cycle: hard work leads to affluence which in turn leads to new life-styles which diminish the ethic because affluence is comparative, as yesterday's affluence is today's minimum acceptable standard of living. Thus although work attitudes will remain affirmative, people will be more selective about the type of job they seek.
- Reductions in productivity can be explained without reference to the diminution of the PWE. There will be no economic decline because of the unwillingness of the new labour force to work hard.
- There will be an increasing need to provide full and equal opportunity jobs.

- Work organizations will have to adjust to the changing expectations of people looking for good (autonomous, interesting) rather than bad (dirty, routine) jobs.
- Productivity will increase because of new improvements in technology, co-operative labour-management committees, and an improvement in the work environment.

Generally most of the speculations are optimistic about the future of work in the 1980s but do see certain changes in attitudes favouring quality-of-life over quantity; self-fulfilment over success. For Yankelovich (1979) six old values at the work place were changing: women not working; men putting up with bad jobs just for economic security; a negative system based mainly on money and status; loyalty to particular organizations; identity primarily achieved through organizations; work as a paid activity that provided steady full time work.

Old symbols of success are rejected in favour of self-development and enlightenment, which is so difficult to define that it leaves people restless, narcissistic, and self-obsessed. Changes include a recognition of the increasing importance of leisure; the important symbolic importance of a paid job to normality; and the refusal of people to subordinate their personalities and needs to the work role. For Yankelovich (1979) rather than lose the enthusiasm for work – a good paid job – the 1980s will see an increase in the demand for employment. However, the incentives in these new paid jobs will have to be less materialistic and more psychological, more diverse and more equitable. To a large extent this scenario for the 1980s has proved true. Etzioni (1979) too foresaw a 'quality-of-life' society, which was more 'continental' and which focused more on culture and recreation than materialism. Others, too, foresaw the greater stress on intrinsic values rather than the extrinsic values at work. The factors thought to influence work attitudes, and hence the future of work, were:

- Reduced concern over economic insecurity.
- Revised definition of less (less material more psychological).
- More flexible and equal sexual role division of work (increasing work androgyny).
- Belief in the entitlement to the good life.
- Increasing questions about efficiency as a criterion of goodness.
- Less emphasis on growth and more on conservation.
- Increased ecological and environmental concerns.
- A belief that work organizations should contribute to the quality of life.
- Increased concern with the welfare of consumers.
- Greater awareness of issues relating to mental and physical health.
- Greater acceptance of ethnic minorities.
- A group conviction that there is more to life than working.

Katzell (1979) who listed numerous caveats concerning the dangers of forecasting considered changing attitudes to work. He, too, believes the current trend will continue for people to stress intrinsic (meaningfulness and challenge) rather than extrinsic (comfort and security) factors. However, as he notes, aggregated figures could mean dramatic, but compensatory, changes in certain groups. He outlines what he sees to be six broad trends:

● The traditional economic significance of work will be supplemented by a rising concern with its psychological quality and social meaningfulness.
● More workers at all levels will want a stronger voice in decisions affecting their jobs and to be less subject to hierarchical control.
● A shrinking proportion of the work force will be content to have routine, unchallenging jobs.
● More people will think in terms of long-range careers and even multiple careers, not just in terms of immediate jobs.
● The importance of nonwork (family, community, retirement, leisure) will increasingly rival that of work.
● The work force will exhibit a wider diversity of attitudes towards work, portending numerous departures from the foregoing.

Rosow (1979) speculated on the future of a whole range of issues like pay, employee benefits, job security, alternative work schedules, occupational stress, participation, and democracy in the work-place. The speculations were not only detailed, but may have come true. Furthermore, he considered obstacles (economic growth, industry, government) to change in work attitudes. The consequence of technological change was also considered.

It could be argued that reasons why these speculations and predictions were by and large accurate were that they were considered over a ten-year period and largely data based. Some would argue that it is not very difficult to accurately extrapolate from extensive data banks over a period such as this. Furthermore, most of the forecasters came up with similar scenarios and hence they were more than likely all to be right (or wrong). Nevertheless, various fairly dramatic economic and sociological changes have occurred in this period, yet the predictions remain mostly true. This, therefore, may lead one to believe that other (more recent) speculations about the future of work – given that they are as carefully and thoughtfully based – might indeed come true.

The future of work

There have been numerous speculations about the future of work and unemployment. One of the earliest and most influential writers on the Future of Work (and Leisure) was Parker (1972) who distinguished six 'components of life space' that fitted nicely into a two dimensional structure: Work, working/sold/substinence time; work-related time, work obligations; leisure at work; existence time meeting psychological needs; non-work obligations, semi-leisure; leisure; free/spare/uncommitted/discretionary time. He suggested that currently it was possible to distinguish quite clearly between satisfying and unsatisfying work. The former, which of course led to job satisfaction, has six identifiable components:

- The feeling that one is creating something – that one was putting something of oneself into that which one was making.
- Using one's skills – being able to use all one's ingenuity and skill at a task.
- Being able to work whole-heartedly in the sense of not being restricted from full productive effort.
- Using initiative and having responsibility to take decisions, having independent authority.
- Mixing with people whether they are colleagues or clients, inferiors or superiors.
- Working with competent and committed people who know their job and are willing and able to see it through.

Conversely there are certain work characteristics closely associated with unsatisfactory work. These are:

- Doing repetitive work that fails to use the capacities of individuals to the full and never appears to achieve anything.
- Making only a small part of something which is frequently the consequence of increasing specialization.
- Doing apparently useless tasks that produce nothing, like guarding property.
- Feeling a sense of insecurity, possibly due to possible redundancy, or industrial change and development.
- Being too closely supervised by people concerned with the minutest of details.

Naturally whereas satisfying work leads to commitment, unsatisfying work leads to alienation. Given the relationship between work and leisure (discussed in some length in Chapter 5), the future of work and leisure are inextricably combined. For Parker (1972) the future of work and leisure will depend on both personal values and personality and on the social structure of society. Clearly, the PWE is a very important individual difference variable in this regard. He paints two alternative scenarios of the future confrontation of work and leisure:

- The differentiation of work and leisure into different segments. This polarity will be of structure and function and can involve changes in both.
- The integration of work and leisure. 'In this fusion, work may lose its present characteristic feature of constraint and gain the creativity now associated mainly with leisure, while leisure may lose its present characteristic feature of opposition to work and gain the status – now associated mainly with the *product* of work – of a resource worthy of planning to provide the greatest possible human satisfaction.'   (p. 122)

Parker (1972) is able to identify both segmentalist and holistic social policies and is quite clear on favouring the former. However, eleven years later Parker (1983) has updated his text considering such things as the microelectronics revolution. This will probably have a number of very important and wide-ranging implications:

- A continuous and accelerating process of specialization meaning the destruction of some jobs but the development of others.
- Considerable occupational change during a life-time.
- More application of science and technology principles to organizational behaviour.
- A decline in working hours and the simultaneous rise in the level of formal education.
- A shift from manufacturing to service occupations.

Just as this revolution affects work, so it will affect leisure and the relationship between work and leisure.

Paradoxically, Parker (1983) believes that leisure will take on more the character of work in the sense that it will be more central to life, and the culture and economy will be dominated more by leisure values. Equally there will be less distinction between work and leisure as the two will become integrated. As regards changing attitudes, Parker (1983) predicts:

> The work ethic which has been strong for the last two centuries, but now shows signs of weakening, places work at the centre of the meaning and purpose in life with leisure as its servant. A leisure ethic would seek to reverse these priorities and make leisure the central area of meaning, fulfilment and personal identity with work as a means to these ends. Perceptive critics of the work ethic, however, do not want to abolish work – rather, they want to retain and enhance it in creative functions while imbuing it with qualities such as choice and pleasurable activity which are now often associated only with leisure.
>
> (p. 106)

Finally, individual differences in needs and preferences for work and leisure will be recognized.

Parker (1983) reiterates his distinction between segmentalist and holistic viewpoints:

> Segmentalists will want to tackle the problems of work and leisure in relative isolation from each other, on the assumption that differentiation of spheres makes this possible; holists will want to pursue a more difficult and longer-term policy of integration, on the assumption that the interdependence of spheres makes this necessary. At the level of general theories of society there are again implications for this policy. Segmentalists will want to make 'practical' reforms to the existing work and leisure spheres starting with the experiences and immediate

environments of individuals. Holists will insist that more far reaching policies aimed at changes in the social and economic structure as a whole are necessary.

(p. 136)

Handy (1985), in a book entitled *The Future of Work*, noted eight major changes in the pattern of work in post-industrialized countries:

1. A full-employment society was becoming part-employment.
2. Manual skills were being replaced by knowledge as the basis of work.
3. Industry was declining and services growing.
4. Hierarchies and bureaucracies were being replaced by networks and partnerships.
5. One-organization careers are being replaced by job mobility and career change.
6. The 'third stage' of life (post-employment) was becoming more and more important.
7. Sex roles at work and at home are no longer rigid.
8. Work was shifting southwards, inside countries and between countries.

Handy (1985) argues that the world of work in the future will be different and needs to be planned for. He argues that if the trends he has related turn out to be significant, one can expect a number of important changes which include:

- More people than present *not* working for an organization.
- Shorter working lives for many people.
- Fewer mammoth bureaucracies and more tiny businesses.
- More requirements for specialists and professionals in organizations.
- More importance given to the informal, uncounted economy.
- A smaller manufacturing sector, bigger in output.
- A smaller earning population with a bigger dependent population.
- A greatly increased demand for education.
- New forms of social organization to complement the employment organization.

Handy (1985) concentrates not on the market or state economy but the *informal* economy (black, voluntary, and household) and the *information* (as opposed to industrial, services, or agriculture) job sector where most future jobs will lie. Work, he argues, will change: there will be new worlds of work (in the black, mauve, and grey economy), new meanings of work (job, marginal, and gift), and new patterns of work (shorter working week, year, and lives in general). In the new re-organized work dials will replace tools (i.e. machines will do all heavy labour), terminals will replace trains (people will work from home), fees will replace wages (we will be paid for services, not time).

Handy (1985) does not mention the PWE but his note on education for tomorrow has implications for it. He argues for more flexibility, variety,

Table 9.1 The values of HE and SHE

HE	SHE
quantitative values and goals	qualitative values and goals
economic growth	human developments
organizational values and goals	personal and inter-personal values and goals
money values	real needs and aspirations
contractual relationships	mutual exchange relationships
intellectual, rational, detached	intuitive, experiential, empathetic
masculine priorities	feminine priorities
specialization/helplessness	all-round competence
technocracy/dependency	self-reliance
centralizing	local
urban	country-wide
European	planetary
anthropocentric	ecological

Table 9.2 Three possible futures

Business as usual	HE	SHE
Full employment can be restored, and employment will remain the dominant form of work. Other activities (e.g. housework, family care, voluntary work) will continue to have lower status. Sharp distinctions will continue to exist between education for the young, work for adults, and retirement for the old, and between work and leisure.	Full employment will not be restored. All necessary work will be done by a skilled elite of professionals and experts, backed by automation, other capital-intensive technology, and specialist know-how. Others will not work. They will merely consume the goods and services provided by the working minority – including leisure, information, and education services. Society will be split between workers and drones.	Full employment will not be restored. Work will be redefined to include many forms of useful and valued activity in addition to paid employment. Paid and unpaid work will be shared around more equally, e.g. between men and women. Part-time employment will be common. Many different patterns of working will be possible, according to people's circumstances and preferences. Households and neighbourhoods will become recognized workplaces and centres of production. Young and old will have valued work roles. Work and leisure activities will overlap.

choice, and participation in education. He believes that education is an investment, not a cost that can be measured on a number of scales. He argues that education does not only happen in one place (school, university) and that people should be able to choose what and where to learn. He appears to approve of entrepreneurship and enterprise and to rejoice in 'choice and responsibility'. Certainly there is little here that is incompatible with the PWE, which may assume to increase under this system.

It is more important to challenge and to discard our assumptions than to explore all the possible tentacles of the future. We are fixated, both as a nation and as individuals, by the employment organization. Work is defined as employment. Money is distributed through employment. Status and identity stem from employment. We therefore hang on to employment as long as we can; we measure our success in terms of it; we expect great things from it, for the country and for ourselves; and we cannot conceive of a future without it. And yet, ironically, we are very bad at it because there is an individualistic streak in all of us which agrees with Marx that it is alienating to sell ourselves or our time to another.

Break through that constraint and all sorts of things become possible, even if they are hard to visualize before they exist. The employment organization is the avenue of elms referred to at the very start of this book. Cut it down and a new landscape appears, a landscape yet to be designed and replanted. Leave the constraint alone and the scene will gradually decay and wither, ushering in a time of shabby gentility as Britain begins to resemble an old country house which has known better days and for which no one has yet found an alternative use, although the oil well in the backyard continues to provide for its dependants.

It is new imaginings which are needed to start a fresh debate among the 80 percent. If we discard the shibboleth of employment, can we find a new liberty and a new energy without losing compassion and the requisite level of equality? The imaginings of this book may be wrong or unreal, but if they stir up further imaginings to help us to look beyond employment and beyond the status quo, they will have served their purpose.

(Handy, 1985, p. 180)

From the humanist, ecological perspective Robertson (1985) has categorized the future of work into three opposing camps: BAU (business as usual); HE (hyper-expansionist); and SHE (sane, humane, ecological). From these acronyms alone it is quite clear which alternative the author favours. The values of HE and SHE are set out in Table 9.1. He then systematically draws out the implications of these three quite different scenarios for the economy, technology, etc., but also for work (see Table 9.2). He argues, as of course have many others, that industrial and post-industrial forms of work will have to change. It will become more autonomous, self-controlled, and directly related to the needs and purposes of those doing the work.

Robertson (1985) discussed the PWE in some detail. He argued that from the PWE stemmed the basis on which work in late industrial societies is based – the idea that work means employment and that everyone should have a job. He noted that the PWE should, more strictly, be called the job ethic because most people believed they ought to have a job. The true PWE is to be found among the self-employed and those doing often unconventional or craft jobs, that gives meaning to their lives and which brings opportunities for develop-

Table 9.3 Symbols of success

Past symbols of success	Present symbols of success	Future symbols of success
Fame	Unlisted phone number	Free time any time
Being in *Who's Who*	Swiss bank account	Recognition as a creative
Five-figure salary	Connections with celebrities	person
College degree	Deskless office	Oneness of work and play
Splendid home	Second and third home	Regarded less by money
Executive position	Being a vice president	than by respect and
Live-in servants	Being published	affection
New car every year	Frequent world travel	Major societal commitments
		Easy laughter,
		unembarrassed tears
		Philosophical
		independence
		Loving, and in touch with
		self

ment and fulfilment. Whereas both Marxists and Christians see work as central to human life, Robertson (1985) seems to favour the ecological view which stresses participating in the process of rather than subduing or changing nature. Further, this view distinguishes between good and bad work.

According to Robertson, supporters of the HE vision of the future see the work ethic being replaced by the leisure ethic while SHE visionaries believe a new work ethic will be central to the new type of work. The new work ethic, thought to be more powerful than either the job or leisure ethic, will be based on the new, more meaningful 'own work'. The old work ethic based on the values of achievement, money, and time will change as the new ecological values are acquired. The new ethic, like the old one, will be pioneered by nonconforming minorities supporting the SHE communal vision of the future. And like the old work ethic the new one will liberate people, but with the latter ethic it will liberate *all* people enabling them to become more self-reliant.

This optimistic view of the future sees major changes in values. For Robertson there are three eras of success symbols (see Table 9.3). The future will see such things as the feminization of work, completely different criteria used in the valuation of work (qualitative rather than quantitative), and the end of the employment empire. There will be a paradigm shift to the SHE vision of own work with its own specific agenda.

This vision of future work is essentially optimistic, humanist, and sociological. It shares in many ways, which the author recognizes, the vision of the early Protestants – that is the belief that small groups of people with the same beliefs and vision of the role of work, find ways of organizing work for themselves and develop a coherent and explicit philosophy for it.

Theologians, too, have been interested in the future of work. Davis and

Gosling (1985) have suggested that the church has a major responsibility to search for an *ethic for living* which will replace the inherited ethic of *working to make a living*. Cressey (1985) has argued that the PWE is restricted to a very limited number of people; that it is frequently distorted and that it is particularly hard on the unemployed. He argues for a new work ethic but believes this can only be achieved once greater work-force involvement and participation has been achieved. However, he is pessimistic about the development of a new humanized alternative work ethic for a number of reasons:

- Job insecurity has made protectionism the primary issue making more important issues less relevant.
- Recession has led to a strengthening of hierarchical forms of management.
- Workers remain involved in sectional struggles.
- Market criteria are more important than paternalism or welfare.
- Less partnership between management and workers.

Collste (1985) believes that while the possibilities for gratifying material demands have increased as a result of new technology, the opposite has occurred for psychological and social needs. We therefore need a new PWE in the new technological age. The message seems to be that the old PWE is increasingly out of date and that a new one needs to replace it. However, what is not clear is how, or which facets of the PWE were out of date. Indeed, some may argue the precise opposite. What seems to most concern theologians is the competitive, individualistic self-interest of the PWE rather than ambitiousness or the desire to work hard or sublimate passion at work.

Over the last twenty years there have been a host of writers speculating on the future of work. What is perhaps most noticeable about these various attempts to analyse current and future changes, is the relatively little consensus that has been reached. Thus while all researchers expect considerable change some are optimistic, others pessimistic, and some neutral. Some expect only superficial changes, others massive sociological change. For some the beliefs, ethics, and values established over the past 200 years will be altered completely while others see slow, imperceptible and minimal changes.

Hence there are various scenarios, some of which will be considered here. For instance, it has been argued that there is, and will be, little decline in the attachment to work. Littler (1985) has suggested that an inspection of the available evidence suggests the desire to obtain paid work for economic, personal, or social reasons seems to be ingrained in most members of society. He cites as evidence all sorts of studies: Japanese firms recruiting working-class British workers, finding a strongly rooted work-ethic; working women being extraordinarily attached to paid employment regardless of the quality of work experience; men finding that work is an integral part of their daily social relations as men.

At the level of society, there seems to be *more* emphasis, not less, on the work ethic during the 1980s depression, and unemployment still carries the social stigma as during the years of full employment.

(p. 81)

There will always be a need for jobs that demand a degree of knowledge, skill, and fairly lengthy socialization and it seems too difficult to imagine how they will change dramatically.

There is no shortage of recent books, particularly those written by trade unionists and politicians, who seem intensely pessimistic about the future of work. Their scenarios might have slightly different emphases, but all see inevitable and inexorable changes as deeply undesirable. Jenkins and Sherman (1979) in their book *The Collapse of Work* argue that modern societies will be unable to provide enough work for people and that the resultant high underemployment or unemployment will be stabilizing. These analyses are often long on polemic and short on data or analysis, e.g.:

> Work became important in the industrial revolution, a revolution that was heavily dependent on Protestant values. People had to work, otherwise capitalism would have halted at an early stage.

(p. 140)

Various forms of state intervention are suggested, to share jobs and revolutionize attitudes to work and leisure. Williams (1985), too, is gloomy, believing that service jobs cannot and will not replace old production jobs because

> without an efficient competitive manufacturing industry, the demand for the services will decline.

(p. 75)

Moynagh (1985) states the question most clearly:

> No one can be sure exactly what new industries will flourish in the next century as a result of new technologies. What is clear is that these technologies are combining to reveal both undreamed of opportunities and the possibility of an unprecedented destruction of jobs. What people want to know is whether the jobs created by these opportunities will exceed the number destroyed.

(p. 71).

He argues that there are essentially three possibilities

- The return of work – based on Kondratiev cycles some argue that an upturn in the economy will lead to the return of work.
- The collapse of work – the scenario, it is argued, exaggerates the speed of change, the number of jobs lost, and the absence of new work.
- The change of work – these include changes in the number, length, and importance of jobs.

Moynagh (1985) appears agnostic as to which of these various scenarios is most likely to occur. However, he does argue that there will be a definite change in the nature of work which we can both anticipate and plan for. These include changing the meaning of work and believing that work is not the basis of worth.

Moynagh (1985) addresses directly the issue of the PWE. He argues that one of the most enduring aspects of the PWE is that work is a moral duty and that the unemployed feel guilty, which compounds their sense of failure. The author argues rather unconvincingly, with little textual support, that biblical teachings on the PWE are antithetical to the PWE. He argues for a new anti-individualistic, socialist new work scheme of job sharing that essentially sees current levels of unemployment as inevitable.

However, as well as pessimists some, but few, have outlined optimistic scenarios about the future of work. The predominance of pessimistic over optimistic scenarios reflects the fact, no doubt, that pessimism sounds more profound and less naive than optimism. Leadbeater and Lloyd (1987), too, have speculated on the future of work and the PWE:

A new social ethic of work would not, of course, be simply a matter of mass moral conversion. It would require an entirely different view of how the economy works and to what end. A new work ethic that praised sharing or even abstention from work to provide others with opportunities could be based only on people seeing jobs as society's rather than individuals' property. Explanations for unemployment that stress either personal frailty (laziness) or the mysterious working of the world economy would have to be replaced by explanations that stress society's control over, and responsibility for, unemployment. Such a transformation in public thinking about work will take an enormously long time.

(p. 20)

They stress the changes that have occurred in recent times that might affect the PWE: the rise of entrepreneurship, the decline of the trade unions; the decline of industrial manufacturing and the increase in the service industries; the rise of new technology.

In short, there is great uncertainty over where changes in the character of work may lead the advanced societies. There seem to be at least two extremes we could pursue. One is relatively benign public philosophy, which would include a long-term commitment to ensuring greater equality of access to jobs. If the advanced economies have to bear the burden of unemployment, that burden could be more equally shared. It would include too some longer-term commitment to attempting to restore full employment. This benign approach would also entail some measure of income redistribution towards the poor, the unemployed and those in insecure jobs. Their uncertainty offers companies, and the economy as a whole, greater flexibility. This approach would try to ensure that flexibility was not necessarily accompanied by loss of protection. New ways would have to be found to combine flexibility with security through measures of income support and new legal rights. Within the firm the line between management and workers would blur, thanks to new methods of participation and employee involvement backed by a wider spread of capital ownership.

But realism demands that another general public philosophy should be taken much more seriously: a new, divisive one that stems from the way that the character and distribution of work have changed, and will continue to change, the distribution of power in the advanced economies. New social divisions are opening up around work. The rift between the employed and the unemployed is the starkest. But within the world of work there are also new divisions. There is growing evidence that sub-contracting and the use of temporary and part-time workers are erecting a new feudalism. 'Core' workers, the key skilled personnel that a company needs to retain and motivate, are inside the walls, defended both by the firm and by unions or trade associations. 'Peripheral' workers come and go through the gates. The unemployed are on the outside. Admittedly, as we have shown, there is some evidence that firms are adopting a larger social role in the communities in which they operate. There is a greater sense that companies have to assume responsibility for the effects that their actions have beyond the walls. This is most pronounced in the USA and is growing in the United Kingdom. But the extent of this movement should not be overstated. The primary task of coping with the effects of redundancy and unemployment still rests with the state.

(p. 203)

Optimists about the future see the decline of heavy, dirty, tedious manufacturing industry as a benefit rather than a loss. Rather than stressing job losses they believe that people in work in the future will be more flexible, have more free-time, will be richer, better educated, and, indeed, more happy. Optimists don't say whether their new world will be the same for everyone but anticipate the worst jobs being replaced.

Speculations on the future of work are numerous and varied though there do seem some common threats. But along with specific sociological and political speculations about the future of work *per se* there are numerous futurological views of life in general.

British futurologists appear to believe that pessimism is profound, while American futurologists optimistically see the future as having limitless opportunities. There is no shortage of people interested in speculating about the future of work, leisure, employment, etc. Some of these speculations are fairly global, others more specific. On the global level, for instance, Naisbitt (1984) has speculated on ten major trends that he sees as a 'road map to the 21st century'. These include trends from:

- An industrial society to an informational society when the new wealth is knowhow and adaptable generalists.
- 'Forced' technology to high tech/high touch, that is high technology designed with and for the human touch.
- National to world economy and hence the globalization of economies, languages, and greater interdependence.
- Short term to long term planning, investment, and development with strategic vision as well as planning.
- Centralized to decentralized societies with an aggressive bidding from the bottom-up regionalism.
- Institutional to self-help particularly in the areas of health, education, and unemployment.
- Representative to participative democracy in occupational, political, and business spheres.
- Hierarchies to networking in the structure of organizations and communities sharing knowledge.
- North to South meant in terms of America but probably applying to the world in general.
- Either/or to multiple options in terms of nuclear family, options for women, work, leisure.

Naisbitt (1984) is clearly an optimist having the vision of a democratic, egalitarian, and healthy society.

Toffler (1984), a famous futurologist, has also considered the future of work in what he calls the third wave. He sees the new worker as independent, resourceful, flexible, and skilful. He distinguishes between seven types of employment: structural, trade-related, technological, frictional, normal, informational, and natrogenic (policy decisions), the first being most important. He believes the concept of a job is an anachronistic part of the old second way. Current crises at work are part of the inevitable process of restructuring. The tone of vision can best be shown by the following quote:

> In the Second Wave industries, you're getting layoffs and wage cuts, deferred benefits, tighter and tighter pressures on the worker. In Third Wave industries, the talk is all about employee participation in decision-making; about job enlargement and enrichment, instead of fractionalization; about flexi-time instead of rigid hours; about cafeteria-style fringe benefits which give employees a choice, rather than a *fait accompli*; about how to encourage creativity rather than blind obedience.
>
> (p. 33)

These futurological speculations make interesting reading. Almost as interesting are readings of older futurologists predicting the present. Orwell's *1984* did not fortunately come to fruition at least in many of its manifestations. It is of course impossible to determine the veridical nature of these predictions. But what could be done and has not, is to try to gauge how these changes will affect the PWE. This will be considered in due course, after various educative changes are considered.

Education and the future of work

It is, of course, not only vocational guidance counsellors who have been forced to rethink their job in the light of current changes and unemployment. All involved in education have had to consider the relevance, salience, and usefulness of what they teach to young people. Watts (1983) has argued that education functions in a number of ways, overtly or covertly, to prepare young people for employment or unemployment. Education functions to:

- Select people for education in particular skills and avenues of work.
- Socialize people into attitudes appropriate for the world of work.
- Orient people to understand the world of employment, and to prepare for the choices and transitions they will have to make on entering it.
- Prepare specific skills and knowledge which students will be able to apply in a direct way after entering employment.

Given these and presumably other important functions, it remains crucial that educationists prepare pupils for hire outside school. But the question remains – what has the future to hold? Watts (1983) speculated on four quite different scenarios: *Unemployment* would continue to grow; a *leisure*, non-stigmatized class outside unemployment would emerge; *unemployment* would remain but income and status would be distributed more evenly; *work* would change in that there would be greater attachment to self-employment and to forms of work outside the formal economy. Watts (1987) later seems to feel the unemployment scenario most likely as computers and mechanization reduce the need for many jobs. He believes countries are faced with artificially or corporately sustaining full employment (and with it social harmony, economic growth), or the fact that both work and unemployment will become more and more skewed. Watts (1987) appears to favour the idea of destroying the concept of unemployment by offering a basic guaranteed income for all, received as a right with no sense of stigma and guilt and with many other possible advantages.

However, along with this Utopian speculation, Watts (1987) more realistically speculates on the implication for education. He does not see education for leisure as an alternative to education for work but complementary to it. But he does believe educational practices should change to reflect present and future employment opportunities. These include:

- More emphasis on criterion-referenced forms of assessment with explicit definitions of skills and levels of competence in performing them.
- More varied forms of learning to more varied purposes.

- More attempts to educate in enterprise or co-operative principles so as to instil the notion of creating and managing one's own work.
- Affirming the importance of the use of, rather than the mere acquisition of, knowledge.
- More subtle and useful political education.

He offers six major changes within the world of education:

1. *From* education as narrowly preparing for vocational and other 'slots' with little concern for developing a critical awareness — *To* education as a broad preparation for life, including social understanding and awareness and social criticism

2. *From* education as a discrete experience, probably within and end-on to schooling — *To* education as a continuous lifelong process of learning

3. *From* education as based on limited access, involving selection of, rather than choice by, individuals — *To* education as based on open access, widely available in varied forms within which choices can be made

4. *From* education as a determinant of life-chances from an early age, on a basis which largely reproduces existing differentials and inequalities — *To* education as a catalyst for social mobility throughout life

5. *From* education as the prerogative of professionals based within the formal education institutions — *To* education as a task shared by and sometimes led by non-professional educators

6. *From* education as a centralized activity based on 'core curricula' and centrally controlled standards — *To* education as a decentralized activity with curricula which are negotiated and evaluated locally

Watts (1983) also speculated on the present and future of the PWE. He argues that capitalism, Christianity, and communism share a basic preoccupation with the importance of economic values built around an ideology of work. Marx believed that man was distinguished from other animals by his capacity to invent tools and produce the means of subsistence. Hence the need to work was the essence of man's humanity. In capitalist countries work frequently became alienating, hence the stress on the artist and craftsman as being satisfied at their work, as opposed to employment.

All the psychological writers have stressed the importance of early primary and secondary socialization on the development of the PWE (see Chapter 4). Hence education, particularly vocational education, should impact strikingly not only on the future of work but the future of the PWE.

The future of the PWE

There have been various speculations about the future of the PWE in a rapidly changing society. Perhaps the most comprehensive, empirically based, and debated is the thesis of Yankelovich (1981). His argument proceeds thus – there is currently a major irreversible cultural revolution transforming the ethics and rules of life (particularly in America). At the heart of the change is a self-fulfilment contradiction – the *goal* of American life is self-fulfilment (almost the opposite of self-denial) but the *means* and strategies to fulfil those goals are defective. Essentially the cultural homes of increased freedom are antithetical to the economic needs of constraint.

The major problem is that seekers after self-fulfilment believe this is achieved by gratifying all needs and desires, which is described as the Maslow-inspired duty-to-self ethic. This ethic, which has clearly replaced the PWE, is seriously flawed. Yankelovich (1981) has described this new ethic thus:

> It has, to be sure, some benefits to offer the individual, but the core idea is a moral and social absurdity. It gives moral sanction to desires that do not contribute to society's well-being. It contains no principle for synchronizing the requirements of the society with the goals of the individual. It fails to discriminate between socially valuable desires and socially destructive ones, and often works perversely against the real goals of both individuals and society. It provides no principles other than hedonism for interpreting the meaning of the changes and sacrifices we must make to adapt to new economic-political conditions.
>
> (p. 47)

Yankelovich (1981), who argues for the suppression of desires, provides survey evidence for the beliefs and desires of those seeking primarily the ethic of self-fulfilment. Still the great majority hold traditional (PWE compatible) values but more and more they are beginning to question traditional values of sacrifice, self-denial, and hard work. Whereas in the past to achieve self-improvement meant achieving worldly success or material possessions and professional success, now, self-improvement means improvement of the self.

Perhaps the most salient analysis in this thesis is of the declining value of work. Yankelovich (1981) has evidence from surveys done over the past 30 years that fewer and fewer young people believe that 'hard work always pays off'. But there has been little decline in the willingness to work. Indeed over 80 per cent of men, and over 70 per cent of women, said they would go on working for pay even if they didn't have to. In fact the freer attitudes to work may be more adaptive to the new economic realities than the old fashioned unconditional acceptance of authority. What appears to be necessary is a new ethic of commitment to forming closer and deeper personal relationships, and the trading of some instrumental values for sacred or expressive ones. This means redeveloping a spirit of community. Yankelovich (1981) does not see the return of the self-denial ethic, nor the decline in the willingness to work, but a welcome decrease in self-absorption and an increase in this new ethic.

Rose (1985) attempted an assessment of whether the PWE, currently heavily politicized, is being discarded or revived. Three quite different scenarios are spelt out for the future of the PWE:

- General disenculturation – the abandonment of the PWE in post-industrial society as Weber predicted.
- Constrained commitment – the continued commitment to the PWE independent of major social and economic changes.
- Differential reconstruction – depending on their circumstances different and distinct social groups will have altering work values.

He favours the third possibility stressing the fluidity and complexity of work values and some of the influences (e.g. structure of the labour market) on them.

Rose (1985) is quite rightly critical of the studies using largely impressionistic material with little or no attempt to place it in a social, economic, or historical context. Furthermore he attempts to disabuse one of the myths that there was a homogeneous and widely accepted work ethic in pre-capitalist society. The importance of the PWE in the past has been exaggerated: in any case, people cannot be forced by economic peril to 'readapt' values they never had – rather, changes in social and economic structure call for more ingenious ways of organizing and motivating people. He traces four economic periods since the war: the Growth era followed by the Protest era characterized by demands of self-actualization at work as well as hedonism and consumerism; a slowdown period characterized by entitlementalism or the belief that both the top and bottom of society had rights as well as obligations in the work place; and finally Recession, characterized by an obsession with productivity and efficiency. Rose (1985) showed how work beliefs and values change as a function of these historical changes and epochs. More importantly he has stressed that there is never, or very rarely, a widespread adoption of work-related values such as the PWE. The 're-Victorianization' of work values has not, cannot, and will not spread through society. Different groups in society for sociological and economic reasons will hold quite different work values. There is not then either a general rejection (disenculturation) or revival (re-commitment) in the PWE overall, as *both* continually occur in different groups.

Conclusion

This chapter has looked at studies that have attempted to predict the future of the PWE – whether it has revived; is in terminal decline; has changed and adapted to new conditions; or has been adapted by some groups and rejected by others. Historical analysis has shown that popular beliefs about the PWE in the past are both simplified and misleading. More recent sociological analysis has however been more successful in analysing the current state of work values and predicting, in the short term, the future of these values.

It is generally agreed that the future of the PWE is highly dependent on the future of work itself. Relatively recent and highly dramatic changes in the nature of work suggest significant changes in the PWE. However, although there is general agreement about the amount of change that is and will continue to occur, there is no agreement as to precisely how this will affect work. More importantly, few of those happy to speculate about the future of work are as clear about the future of the PWE.

Most of those who have speculated about the future of work have taken a sociological and historical rather than a psychological perspective. To take a psychological perspective on the future of the PWE requires understanding how PWE beliefs are maintained and transferred in individuals and small groups. It has been pointed out by Rose (1985) that to talk of the decline or revival of the PWE is misleading, as work values and beliefs change from group to group. Why then do social and socioeconomic groups differ in their PWE beliefs? This is partly due to their different educational and socializing experiences and partly due to their experience of work. Thus at the same time and in the same region, two groups (based on class, religion, occupation) may show radically different changes in their PWE beliefs.

This is not to suggest therefore that *post-hoc* one may find evidence to support any or all speculations about the future. Rather it is to argue that predictions about the PWE need to consider two related but separate features – first a specific prediction about changes in the PWE in clearly defined and different social groups, and secondly the mechanism or processes whereby those changes occur. The advantage of accurate, analytic predictions is that should one wish to intervene in the inexorable change in PWE beliefs one would know how to do so.

Chapter ten

Conclusion

Energy accomplishes more than genius.

Samuel Smiles

Few tricks of the unsophisticated intellect are more curious than the naive psychology of the business man, who ascribes his achievements to his own unaided efforts, in bland unconsciousness of a social order without whose continuous support and vigilant protection he would be as a lamb bleating in the desert.

R.H. Tawney

If work were a good thing, the rich would have found a way to keep it to themselves.

Haitian proverb

The sum of wisdom is, that the time is never lost that is devoted to work.

Ralph Waldo Emerson

Introduction

The PWE remains a topic of considerable interest to academics and laymen alike. For some the concept is descriptively inaccurate, explanatory tautologous, and scientifically meaningless. As Rose (1985) has noted:

> The term 'Protestant Work Ethic', one begins to suspect, is commonly muttered as a talisman: a phrase to conjure up an image of diligent effort without any sense of historical roots or real meaning.

(p. 41)

Yet for others too it provides a helpful concept through which to understand both the past and present. It has been used as an ideological construct, a potential device, and an explanatory catch phrase. Because the term has been so widely used and abused, much academic research has attempted to ascertain the validity of a number of theses concerning the PWE including the most fundamental – namely its existence.

There have been some interesting recent reviews on values at work partly because of their political and practical importance. Nord *et al.* (1988) argue that much academic and popular writing on the PWE, which reflects the conventional view, is historical, untenable, and misleading. They believe that the PWE is used as a short-hand, self-explanatory concept to attribute economic increase or decline. However, they argue that the conventional view neglects two major points in the PWE:

1. The idea that *all* work is potentially worthy – a content-free view of work. Thus to explain work recalcitrance or innovative job design, both specifically concerned with the content and process of work, is alien to Weber's PWE concept.
2. Social relations implied in PWE beliefs did not discourage sociological relationships that might support collective action and solely encouraged individualism. It has been suggested that PWE values of alienated individualism reduced any possibility of collective action, which was not true.

Nord *et al.* (1988) suggest that these erroneous omissions about PWE beliefs mean that using the PWE as an explanation has induced people to misinterpret the past and present, and, indeed, incorrectly predict the future. For instance, they argue that the enormous economical growth in America from 1850 to 1920 had little to do with the PWE of the working class. The PWE was used by the minority middle class, who may have endorsed it to increase work among the working class and where necessary explain their lack of it. However, they are equally critical of the alternative, 'Marxist' explanations.

They argue that PWE stresses extrinsic, non-secular outcomes (salvation). That is, it does *not* emphasize intrinsic values – i.e. positive outcomes that can be gained through work itself, or secular benefits such as money, power, and prestige. Thus 2×2 classification (locus of benefits as being secular or non-secular X relationship of preferred state and work activity as being intrinsic or extrinsic) leads to the joint classification of odd bed fellows. For instance, Marxists and humanistic organizational theorists both stress intrinsic virtues of work and secular rewards, both diametrically opposed to the PWE.

More interestingly, Nord *et al.* (1988) return to the question of how and why organizational behaviourists have misunderstood the work ethic. Their arguments are essentially threefold:

- Most social scientists are a-historical and born into a PWE culture; industrial psychology was essentially secular and did not consider the benefits of work.
- Working conditions have changed markedly since the last century and hence emphasis has moved from extrinsic problems associated with blue-collar labour to intrinsic problems associated with white-collar labour.
- The PWE was psychologized into a personal need.

They note:

> In sum, what the neo-conventional view and the psychological work ethic
> appear to share with the Protestant ethic is a result more of process than
> of substance. Both the traditional and the psychological work ethic are
> the creations of middle-class workers. Both seem to ignore the concrete
> experience of work advanced by the alternative view. Both seem oriented
> to reducing conflict at the organizational level without considering causes
> that may be at a more sociological level.
>
> (p. 58)

They believe that the study of work values like the PWE may have been handicapped by:

- The personal bias of researchers and practitioners.
- Over generalizing the complexity and variety of activities that constitute
  work.
- Construct deficiency, in the sense that academic concepts are
  insufficiently rich or salient to encompass the observable phenomena.

They argue for work values being seen as historically and geographically con-
structed and hence changeable; for an examination of the realities of work for
the working class; for an examination of work beliefs as well as values; and for
an examination of the wider determinants of these values.

While the recent critique of thinking on the PWE by Nord *et al.* (1988) is to
be welcomed, it too has its dangers. It is all very well to accuse organizational
psychologists of unconscious ideology while simultaneously supposing that
one is entirely objective. Secondly, it is too easy to find straw men to knock
down to prove one's point. Thirdly, seeking historical evidence cannot always
enlighten issues. Whilst it is no doubt true that PWE beliefs have been used
naively, incorrectly, even maliciously, to 'explain' macro- or microeconomic
forces, few academics have ever argued that PWE beliefs as made explicit by
Weber or recent social scientists (for they are not always the same) are responsible for these actions. To argue that a psychological level of explanation
should be replaced by a sociological or historical type of explanation is to miss
the point. Psychologists, by definition, approach the problem in a particular
way which is shaped not only by the epistemological tradition of their discipline, but also their personal work values (which indeed may have partly accounted for why they are psychologists). To point out that their work on the
PWE is biased and insufficient is no doubt fair, but to suggest that it makes
strong fundamental claims for PWE values being all-explanatory is misleading. Nord *et al.* (1988) noted:

> Our quarrel with the neo-conventional writers is their tendency to treat
> work values as psychological phenomena only while often ignoring major
> historical, sociological, philosophical and economic processes.
>
> (p. 69)

To accuse PWE researchers of unconscious ideology or false consciousness is however to commit the same sin; namely that individuals within the same society, and economic and historical period, hold different beliefs and values which relate to their actual working processes.

Can PWE beliefs predict economic development?

It is the dream of some psychologists to be able to identify and measure an individual difference variable (i.e. PWE beliefs) which if measured in small or large populations is able to predict micro- or even macroeconomic variables. Is it possible that PWE beliefs could be used to predict a country's or region's economic development? First, there are numerous practical problems to be considered if such a task is to be undertaken:

- Which measures of PWE beliefs to use?
- Who to sample?
- Which economic variables should be considered?
- Which intervening or moderating variables should be taken into consideration?
- What actual relationship (linear, curvilinear, etc.) should one predict?

For instance, one measure of the PWE may have more predictive validity than another; some influential groups' PWE scores may be related to economic variables whereas the beliefs of other groups are not predictive; some economic variables like saving, gambling, or investing are predictable from PWE scores while others, like the growth of the money supply, are not; PWE scores are moderated by class, age, and sex such that when these variables are 'partialled out' no remaining influence is noticeable; and finally to expect a simple linear relationship between (multi-dimensional) PWE beliefs and (any) economic variables is surely naive.

Despite these formidable empirical problems it may indeed be possible to investigate the relationship between PWE in a group, region, and country at some specified point in time and relate it to some economic variables. Indeed McClelland's work outlined in Chapters 2 and 6 was an attempt to do just that. But can PWE beliefs predict economic behaviour? There are indeed a number of reasons why it is unlikely that PWE beliefs predict economic development:

- As Weber pointed out, it is necessary that certain industrial, bureaucratic, or formal structures are in place that support entrepreneurial work. Without various economic, legal, and commercial practices, the individual enterprise of individuals may not flower. Taxation systems, accounting principles, and legal constraints may help or hinder PWE beliefs and practices. Thus in some countries or regions, moderate to low PWE beliefs may be greatly facilitated by legal and economic systems that lead to economic development, while in other regions or countries high PWE beliefs on the part of individuals are thwarted by inappropriate or absent systems.

- It seems that PWE beliefs decline after significant developments have been reached. Thus after the 'economic miracle' in Germany observers report that her young people now openly and explicitly reject the PWE of their parents which *may* have played a part in the recovery. One therefore needs a historical appreciation and base rate measures of the PWE to establish its effect on the economy. Furthermore one needs to look at the factors that influence economic variables – i.e. growth may be greater in developing countries for historic reasons that have nothing to do with its citizens' work beliefs or behaviours.
- Usually PWE beliefs are held by minorities in most cultures. Therefore the size, power, and influence of these minorities are as important as the absolute level of beliefs that they hold. For instance, it has been observed in various central European countries like Hungary or Yugoslavia, that the reason for substantial differences in the economic development and personal wealth of certain groups is due to their propensity for work and their beliefs in the PWE. However, ethnic and geographic reasons appear to prevent those people from having an influence over the country as a whole.
- Inherent in traditional PWE beliefs is strong risk aversion and conservatism. Most wealth creators and entrepreneurs have at certain stages of their life to take risks which may be deeply antithetical to the PWE. In this sense it may be argued that PWE beliefs predict poor economic development because if a group has not the courage to venture certain changes they will inevitably fall behind in beneficial developments. On the other hand, if people with enterprise are not carefully supported by those with strong PWE beliefs their courage and foresight may not be realized.
- It has been argued that PWE beliefs are multi-dimensional. Hence two people or groups may attain equal scores by scoring similarly high and low on *different* dimensions, but because the scores are summated they appear equivalent. It may also be that some of these PWE dimensions are related to economic variables and others not. Indeed it is possible that, of those that do predict economic development, some are positive and others negative. Therefore by obtaining only a gross, single, average score the differences between different factors are ignored and their predictability is significantly reduced.
- The sort of people from whom PWE beliefs are obtained tend to be unrepresentative, being educated and articulate. There is frequently a bias in data gathering because the people interviewed have to be literate, insightful, and helpful.

However, although it is unlikely that psychological variables *alone* can account for or predict economic variables, it is possible that they do account for some unique variance. McClelland's (1961) pioneering work was perhaps too optimistic, but laid down the idea and model for psychological as well as sociological, historical, and economic variables actually having a direct effect on economic development, albeit small.

The work ethic among young people

One way of anticipating both the future of work and the future of the work ethic is to look at the PWE beliefs of young people. Various researchers have attempted to do precisely this. For instance, Schab (1978) looked at PWE beliefs of gifted, black, American adolescents and concluded that

> the general opinions and attitudes of these students as they looked to the future were pretty much in keeping with the so-called Protestant work ethic under which our society wants them to be.

(p. 299)

However, Harris and Stokes (1978) found evidence that certain groups of black youth have lower PWE beliefs than whites, paradoxically because they (the blacks) have higher self-esteem as a function of being able to fulfil lesser ambitions.

But studies from numerous countries appear to show that young people remain optimistic, highly motivated, and work oriented. In Belgium Rosseel (1986) found young people were instrumental and pragmatic in their choice of school topic and that those young people who manifest an enterprising attitude, self-confidence, and optimism about the future develop an orientation of individualistic careerism. Similarly, in Australia in a study of nearly 1,000 young workers, Williams (1983) found a strong adherence to the PWE. Measured by commitment to work, she argued that the PWE was stronger than ever because it provided ideological support for a system which still requires labour discipline. And, no doubt, until that changes, PWE beliefs are likely to remain high. Another feature of young people's attitude to the PWE is their attitudes to new technology. There have been a number of studies looking at beliefs about new technology within organizations, comparing management and labour views (Mueller *et al.*, 1986) but there have been various studies using children and adolescents.

Breakwell *et al.* (1985) looked at the attitudes to new technology of over 500 undergraduates. They found various factors in the attitudinal scale, the most important of which were labelled general benefits (the idea that new technology will have primarily positive benefits), the acceptance of the inevitability of the new technology (which should therefore be mastered), and anti-industrial values (negative attitudes towards industry). Attitude scores on these factors were correlated with a shortened PWE scale (Cronbach's alpha of .70) and a short conservation scale (Cronbach's alpha .67). Interestingly, PWE beliefs were positively correlated with beliefs both about the general benefits and acceptance/inevitability of new technology, and negatively correlated with anti-industrial values.

Breakwell and Fife-Schaw (1987) believe that young people's attitudes to new technology are largely pragmatic rather than evaluative and are strongly related to psychological factors, as well as educational and familial background. In a study of school-children's motivation to new technology, they found greater motivation was associated with higher self-esteem, better well-being, and stronger PWE. It is possibly because of the fact the PWE places a greater value upon work and success that provides the major motive for the pro-technology orientation. However, because these attitudes and beliefs are confounded with and mediated by a whole range of other variables, Breakwell and Fife-Schaw (1987) attempted to find which of a range of psychographic and demographic variables best predicted levels of motivation to new technology in young people. The PWE comes first, self-esteem second, year of school third, father's job fourth, with sex trailing behind and accounting for only a small, additional, barely significant portion of the variability in motivation.

> Given the findings, it might be worthwhile reiterating why PWE and self-esteem might be expected to produce high motivation. PWE provides the motive for wishing mastery of new technology by emphasising the importance of work, particularly that highly valued by mass society. With the current emphasis upon technology, PWE should be channelled into the motivation towards work with it. Self-esteem provides the psychological basis for believing oneself capable of acquiring skills deemed difficult to gain and of considerable value. Hence, self-esteem should and does engender motivation. This is the rationalisation for the assumed direction of causality, with PWE and self-esteem as sources of motivation.
>
> (p. 23)

These results suggest that young people's PWE beliefs are highly adaptive in the modern world. Indeed, having low PWE beliefs seems to be associated with low self-esteem, poor well-being, and reactionary views. All the more important, then, that adolescents are inculcated with PWE beliefs and values.

Increasing the work ethic

With all the popular speculation about the decline of the PWE, some commentators have turned their attention to rejuvenating the PWE. Yankelovich and Immerwahr (1984) argued that with the emergence of new jobs, new technologies and values in America, PWE values are threatened. They believe that in order to enhance the PWE managers need to develop performance incentives, set high standards, flatten hierarchies, and found job motivators. Rather simplistically and without any empirical support they offer the ten commandments to change the PWE (see Table 10.1). These recommendations may well be effective. But they remain specific to the work-place. It has been pointed out in Chapter 2 that most of the various facets of the PWE, such as internal locus of control and need for achievement, are shaped early in life. Presumably by the time a person begins work, his or her early primary and secondary socialization has shaped his or her PWE beliefs and behaviours. Experiences at work may modify these beliefs within a certain range but are unlikely to

Table 10.1 Dos and don'ts for supporting the work ethic

Do tie remuneration directly to performance that enhances the efficiency and effectiveness of the enterprise.

Do give public and tangible recognition to people whose effort and quality of results exceed the average satisfactory job performance.

Do accept wholeheartedly the principle that employees should share directly and significantly in overall productivity gains.

Do encourage jobholders to participate with management in defining recognizable goals and standards against which individual performance can be judged.

Do give special attention to the difficulties that middle managers face in supporting and enforcing programmes to reconstruct the workplace.

Don't permit situations to develop where the interests of employees run counter to the well-being of the firm – e.g., by introducing new technology in a way that threatens employees' job security or overtime.

Don't attempt to improve standards of quality unless you are prepared to accept the full costs – e.g., discarding substandard products, paying more for better components, or transferring or dismissing people who cannot do quality work.

Don't permit a significant gap to develop between management rhetoric and the actual reward system.

Don't pretend that programmes designed to increase productivity are really intended to enhance job satisfaction and the dignity of work.

Don't support special privileges for managers that serve to enhance the status of managers by widening the gap between them and those who actually do the work.

Source: Yankelovich and Immerwahr, 1984.

radically change a non-PWE believer into a strong endorser or vice versa. Indeed from the work on the PWE and vocational choice (see Chapter 5) it is likely that people choose and avoid certain jobs on the basis that PWE values are manifest there.

Hence to ensure an overall increase (or decrease) in the PWE intervention is required much earlier. Apart from the powerful early experiences of family life, primary and secondary school experiences in particular are fundamentally important in shaping PWE beliefs. It is here that attitudes to leisure, money, time, and success (see Chapter 2) are established. And it is here that achievement motivation, postponement of gratification, and inner locus of control beliefs are rewarded. It is of course difficult, and some would argue highly undesirable, to attempt any mass indoctrination of PWE beliefs and values through state-controlled education. Indeed, in that state control is unlikely to foster, but rather punish, individualism, it is possible that it would not succeed. Nevertheless, on an individual basis or working in a small and contained milieu, it may be possible to train and maintain and, where necessary, increase PWE values, beliefs, behaviours, and attitudes.

Post-industrial values

Many have seen the PWE beliefs and behaviours as a response to industrialism not a cause of it. Horne (1986) in a study of the values of industrialism notes:

> Modern industrial states could not survive without a 'labour force' of human bodies trained in logistical conformity (to play their part in the great transport systems of the cities), in punctuality (to arrive at work on time), and, when they are at work, in talents such as performing set, rostered tasks, obedience and marginal adaptability (learning new instructions). Among the potent symbols of industrial societies are the queue, the roster, the factory whistle. Schooling can be seen as a training for 'life' in that it drills us in punctuality and queuing; in working within a timetable at set tasks for set periods; in neatness, cleanliness and obedience; in skills in learning new techniques; in working when we are tired and bored; in learning to work within the rules of an institution and to accept its hierarchical structure. Given this, perhaps it is not so much the factory whistle that is a symbol of an industrial society, but the school bell.
>
> (p. 82)

Horne (1986) has argued that both capitalist and communist countries of east and west are dominated by the values of industrialism which, however, are being challenged partly because many countries have deindustrialized. He argues that in the industrial societies the privileged do not justify their importance by displays of frivolity, or enjoyment, but hard work.

But people have recently talked about a post-industrial era. If PWE beliefs are a response to industrialism, how will they survive in a post-industrial era? It has been argued that most developed countries are in a post-industrial phase and that the young, educated, urban people in them manifest 'post-materialist' values. They aim at a new type of society (democratic participation, self-management, rights for the minorities, protection of nature) and have frequent recourse to new types of extra-parliamentary action (Inglehart, 1971). The new pattern which encompasses the social, economic, and political spheres is distinguished by the priority given to such values as freedom, participation, quality of life, and self-expression. Post- materialists put low priority on material rewards and the idea that economic progress is the major solution for the well-being of both individuals and the society at large is no longer accepted. Thus material rewards, careerism, and socioeconomic mobility are not pursued.

An EEC report on the perception of poverty in Europe found beliefs about poverty clearly related to materialist values. It showed that, in all the EEC countries, materialists blamed the individual more than society for poverty, whereas post-materialists did the precise opposite. However, Yuchtman-Yaar (1987) is sceptical about the existence and distribution of these values, partly because of the cultural contradictions in post-industrialism. He believes that people want both material *and* non-material rewards and hence embrace the spirit of industrialism *and* post-industrialism. In a six-nation study looking at attitudes to economic growth, work commitment and goals, and reactions to technology, he found the economic orientation of all nationals were generally compatible with the credo of industrialism. Curiously, the Japanese seemed to endorse post-industrial values most clearly. Certainly those that endorse post-industrial values can remain a significant, disenchanted minority, who are not coherent in their values. That is they appear not to be consistently 'post-industrial' in their beliefs. Is the PWE threatened by post-materialist values? The answer appears to be no.

Psychology and the PWE

Since the late 1960s there have been more and more psychological studies on the PWE. This can be seen by tracing the citations of the papers reporting on PWE measures. But some psychologists remain sceptical as to the explanatory power of the PWE concept. For instance Lea *et al.* (1987) wrote:

> There have been numerous attempts to produce psychometric tests which would measure the extent to which individuals hold the work ethic. Such a measure would make it possible to determine how the ethic relates to work behaviour....But in our view, the whole concept of the work ethic will not stand up to inspection as a direct cause of individuals' work behaviour....We have already seen there are many powerful motivations for working, and we see no need to add this speculative morality to them. There may be some kind of 'employment ethic'; that is, if someone is prepared to pay for an activity, that activity itself, or the person who performs it, is socially 'valid'. But this too seems doubtful; the evidence, if anything, favours an opposite process.
>
> (pp. 154–5)

Unfortunately Lea *et al.* (1987) provide no evidence for their rejection of the PWE. But their position does indicate the response of a number of psychologists.

Psychologists have tended to treat the PWE as a belief system – a set of values and attitudes (and attendant behaviours) concerning work and related issues such as money. It has been suggested that these PWE beliefs are learnt at various periods of life and hence may be changed. More importantly it is suggested that these beliefs are 'related to' behaviour. There are two points here that are the focus of a considerable debate in psychology. The first concerns the relationship between attitudes and behaviour, and the second, whether personality or individual difference systems predict social behaviour. A vast empirical literature stretching back 50 years and concerning both of these topics, has attempted to explain why the relationship between the two variables attitudes and behaviour; personality and behaviour is so low. For many people it is intuitively true, even tautologous, that attitudes are closely related to behaviour or that personality types (be they extraverts, scrooges, entrepreneurs, or whatever) predict or dictate social behaviour. And yet the literature suggests neither is true.

There are many reasons why there is no simple clear correspondence (or correlation) between attitudes and behaviour:

- The level of specificity at which attitudes and behaviours are defined. If one uses a short general PWE measure that looks at general attitudes to work and hopes to use this to predict a very specific, work-related behaviour (absenteeism, punctuality, productivity) it may not be surprising that such a general measure of attitude does not fare well in predicting such a specific behaviour.
- The question of single vs multiple acts. Often PWE researchers have selected a single, simple work-related behaviour to test their predictions. For any single act, there may be a variety of factors that influence the behaviour; over a wide range, however, the general attitude may exert a more powerful influence.
- All behaviour is complex and multi-determined. Many factors, attitudinal, personality, etc., determine social behaviour including work-related behaviour. In short, one-shot measures of behaviour may not give us much information about the strength of the attitude–behaviour relationship.
- Specific, temporary situational factors may also influence behaviour. When situational pressures are strong, people of widely differing attitudes may act in a similar way, and vice versa.

Thus it may be misleading to suggest that because PWE beliefs have only a weak relationship to social behaviour, the PWE concept is wrong, unnecessary, or unrelated to behaviour.

The second issue has been called the person-situation debate and is related to the above. It is concerned primarily with the stability of personality over time, the consistency of behaviour over situations, and the extent to which personality/individual difference variables predict behaviour. Once again there are a variety of methodological reasons why studies have shown that personality variables do only moderately well (i.e. account for 10–20 per cent of the variance) in predicting behaviour. But the current consensus on the debate seems to be that individual differences are both stable over time and highly salient in predicting social behaviour.

As an independent (or for that matter dependent) variable in psychology the PWE has a comparatively short history. The concept of extraversion, for instance, has been examined empirically since the discipline of psychology was first established, while related concepts like authoritarianism have been investigated for almost half a century. The future of the PWE as a psychological variable will no doubt follow a fairly predictable pattern with various components:

- There will be increased concern on the dimensional structure of the PWE concept which will lead to the development of multi-dimensional measures and theoretical speculation on the relationship between the dimensions. It may in fact be argued by some that the concept is so diffuse and multifaceted that it is redundant, and that we should concentrate on the component parts as we have done in the past; others will argue that the concept does have value and provides a valuable conceptual tool for understanding behaviour.
- The usefulness of the PWE as a predictor of social and work-related behaviour will increase as the psychometric work increases. Indeed this will revive the debate started by McClelland (1961) on the extent to which psychological variables can predict micro- and macroeconomic behaviour. Most of the psychological work is expected to be small-scale experimental work, but it is possible that some large-scale survey and archival data will be done that adds spice to the debate.
- The PWE will also become a dependent variable worthy of investigation. That is, there will be work on the effect of early childhood, work-specific or event-related experiences on the PWE. Just as much of the work on authoritarianism was concerned with how people came to hold such beliefs and attitudes, so researchers will be interested, no doubt for pragmatic reasons associated with trying to change them, in how PWE values arise.

Conclusion

This book has been concerned with a psychological perspective on the PWE. It has attempted to 'translate' the original socio-theological concept into psychological terms which may be interpreted at the level of the individual. This is not to suggest that this particular approach is the only valid one or that economic, sociological, or theological analyses are invalid. It is, however, true, that apart from McClelland's (1961) impressive and scholarly attempt to offer a psychological perspective on economic growth, few psychologists have speculated on how individual difference variables relate to micro or macro socioeconomic changes. McClelland (1961) ended his book thus:

> So we end on a practical note: a plan for accelerating economic growth through mobilizing more effectively the high *n* Achievement resources of a developed country to select and work directly with the scarcer high *n* Achievement resources in undeveloped countries particularly in small and medium scale businesses located in provincial areas and organized in 'productive complexes' to save on scarce capital and manpower resources. While the plan may have defects, it has at least three merits: it suggests an

alternative to current aid programs that may be more effective in starting
an undeveloped economy on the path to sustained growth; it provides a
method of testing in the hard school of reality the theoretical
superstructure from which it derived; and last but not least, it
demonstrates how focusing on psychological objectives and manpower
resources can alter thinking about what means are most likely to be
effective in producing social change. For in the end, it is men, and in
particular their deepest concerns, that shape history.

(p. 437)

He argued that psychologists have

developed tools for finding out what a generation wants, better than it
knows itself, and *before* it has had a chance of showing by its actions what
it was after.

(p. 437)

Unfortunately, thirty years later it seems McClelland's dream remains unfulfilled, at least with respect to the psychologist's role in predicting and shaping economic growth. The reasons are manifold: the measurement of need for
achievement remains problematic (indeed one of the most difficult in the
whole of personality theory); the concept of need for achievement has not
'fired' social scientists; replicative and extensional work to that of McClelland
has proved only modestly helpful; and finally, it is doubtful how need for
achievement relates to the numerous and powerful other sociological and
economic variables that determine economic growth and decline.

Although much more modest in scope this book has attempted to do for
the PWE what McClelland did for *n* Ach. McClelland (1961) 'psychologized'
and restricted the PWE to *n* Ach to which it is clearly related (see Chapter 2).
This book sought to do likewise but rather than change, albeit subtly, the concept, it tries to remain faithful, in so far as possible, to the original PWE idea
and the voluminous concomitant literature. An attempt was made to trace on
an individual level the origin, maintenance, and consequences of PWE beliefs;
to look at the components of PWE beliefs and behaviours; how the PWE is
measured; how PWE beliefs relate to work and non-work behaviours; alternative and competing belief systems; and many of the speculations about the future of work and the work ethic. Unlike McClelland (1961) it is not suggested
that PWE beliefs alone account for, or can predict, macroeconomic change.
There are too many other factors in this necessarily complicated equation. But
equally, it is argued that these beliefs cannot and should not be ignored. Just
as it is unwise for psychologists to ignore sociological and economic variables
in predicting behaviour, so it is unwise for sociological thinkers to ignore psychological variables.

Appendix

The 'book' itself

Weber's original work is divided into five sections with an introduction. The first part is entitled 'The Problem' and has three sections, while the second is called 'The Practical Ethics of the Ascetic Branches of Protestantism' and has two chapters. There are extensive footnotes, almost as long as the book itself. The various sections of the book will be briefly reviewed.

The introduction

This begins with the exposition that 'Only in the West does science exist at a stage of development which we recognize today as valid.' He claims that the rational, systematic, and specialized pursuit of science with trained and technically specialized officials, organized into political and social groups, are exclusive to the West. Capitalism, too, in its present form is exclusive to the West.

> And the same is true of the most fateful force in our modern life, capitalism. The impulse to acquisition, pursuit of gain, of money, of the greatest possible amount of money, has in itself nothing to do with capitalism. This impulse exists and has excited among waiters, physicians, coachmen, artists, prostitutes, dishonest officials, soldiers, nobles, crusaders, gamblers and beggars. One may say that it has been common to all sorts and conditions of men at all times and in all countries of the earth, wherever the objective possibility of it is or has been given. It should be taught in the kindergarten of cultural history that this naive idea of capitalism must be given up once and for all. Unlimited greed for gain is not in the least identical with capitalism, and is still less its spirit. Capitalism *may* even be identical with the restraint, or at least a rational tempering, of this irrational impulse. But capitalism is identical with the pursuit of profit, and forever *renewed* profit, by means of continuous, rational, capitalistic enterprise. For it must be so: in a wholly capitalistic

order and society, an individual capitalist enterprise which did not take advantage of its opportunities for profit-making would be doomed to extinction.

(p. 17)

Weber also attempted to define certain concepts such as capitalism, which he said was the rational and calculated expectation of profit by the utilization of opportunities for exchange. He noted that although capitalistic enterprise and entrepreneurs have existed in other times and places, it is only in the West (Occident) that it developed into a particular type, form, extent, and direction. The new exclusive capitalism is the rational organization of (formally free) labour. This occurred because business was separated from the household and rational bookkeeping was introduced. 'Exact calculation – the basis of everything else – is only possible on a basis of free labour' (p. 22).

For Weber, the problem worthy of analysis and explanation is the origin of the specified and particular *sober, bourgeois, capitalism with its rational organization of free labour.* What particular Western features served to promote rational capitalism? Weber argued that the rational structures of law and administration added to which the rational ethics of ascetic Protestantism causally accounted for the spirit of modern capitalism.

Chapter I: Religious affiliation and social stratification

Statistics (from Europe) indicated that business leaders and owners of capital were overwhelmingly Protestant. He did admit that this Protestant superiority may be partly explained in terms of historical circumstances in which religious affiliation is not the cause but the consequence of economic conditions. But Weber provided numerous counter examples and argued the principal explanation must be sought in the permanent intrinsic character of Protestants, not only in their temporary external historico-political inheritance.

One possible explanation is the *other-worldliness* of Catholicism with its asceticism of high ideals and great indifferences to things of this world, vs the alleged *this-worldliness* of Protestants and their materialistic joy of living. However, he argues that this thesis is simply not borne out by the facts of his time or those of the past. In fact, most zealous forms of pietism (e.g. St Francis of Asissi) arose from families dedicated to Mammon, while many great capitalistic entrepreneurs (e.g. Cecil Rhodes) came from clergymen's families. Some other explanation is therefore required.

Chapter II: The spirit of capitalism

In order to define exactly what it is he was trying to explain, Weber quoted extensively from Benjamin Ferdinand who in 1736 wrote *Necessary Hints to those that would be Rich* frequently also quoted by the American President Benjamin Franklin. Weber wrote:

Thus, if we try to determine the object, the analysis and historical explanation of which we are attempting, it cannot be in the form of a conceptual definition, but at least in the beginning only a provisional description of what is here meant by the spirit of capitalism. Such a description is, however, indispensable in order clearly to understand the object of the investigation. For this purpose we turn to a document of that spirit which contains what we are looking for in almost classical purity, and at the same time has the advantage of being free from all direct relationship to religion, being thus, for our purposes, free of preconceptions.

'Remember, that *time* is money. He that can earn ten shillings a day by his labour, and goes abroad, or sits idle, one half of that day, though he spends but sixpence during his diversion or idleness, ought not to reckon *that* the only expense; he has really spent, or rather thrown away, five shillings besides.'

'Remember, that *credit* is money. If a man lets his money lie in my hands after it is due, he gives me the interest, or so much as I can make of it during that time. This amounts to a considerable sum where a man has good and large credit, and makes good use of it.'

'Remember, that money is of the prolific, generating nature. Money can beget money, and its offspring can beget more, and so on. Five shillings turned is six, turned again it is seven and threepence, and so on, till it becomes a hundred pounds. The more there is of it, the more it produces every turning, so that the profits rise quicker and quicker. He that kills a breeding-sow, destroys all her offspring to the thousandth generation. He that murders a crown, destroys all that it might have produced, even scores of pounds.'

'Remember this saying, *The good paymaster is lord of another man's purse*. He that is known to pay punctually and exactly to the time he promises, may at any time, and on any occasion, raise all the money his friends can spare. This is sometimes of great use. After industry and frugality, nothing contributes more to the raising of a young man in the world than punctuality and justice in all his dealing; therefore never keep borrowed money an hour beyond the time you promised, lest a disappointment shut up your friend's purse for ever.'

'The most trifling actions that affect a man's credit are to be regarded. The sound of your hammer at five in the morning, or eight at night, heard by a creditor, makes him easy six months longer; but if he sees you at a billiard-table or hears your voice at a tavern, when you should be at work, he sends for his money the next day; demands it, before he can receive it, in a lump.'

'It shows, besides, that you are mindful of what you owe; it makes you appear a careful as well as an honest man, and that still increases your credit.'

'Beware of thinking all your own that you possess, and of living accordingly. It is a mistake that many people who have credit fall into. To prevent this, keep an exact account for some time both of your expenses and your income. If you take the pains at first to mention particulars, it will have this good effect: you will discover how wonderfully small, trifling expenses mount up to large sums, and will discern what might have been, and may for the future be saved, without occasioning any great inconvenience.'

'For six pounds a year you may have the use of a hundred pounds, provided you are a man of known prudence and honesty.'

'He that spends a groat a day idly, spend idly above six pounds a year, which is the price for the use of one hundred pounds.'

'He that wastes idly a groat's worth of his time per day, one day with another, wastes the privilege of using one hundred pounds each day.'

'He that idly loses five shillings' worth of time, loses five shillings, and might as prudently throw five shillings into the sea.'

'He that loses five shillings, not only loses that sum, but all the advantage that might be made by turning it in dealing, which by the time that a young man becomes old, will amount to a considerable sum of money.'

(pp. 47-50)

This is the essence of the PWE because the ideal of this philosophy of avarice appears to be an honest man of recognized credit and the increase of capital, which is one's duty, is an end in itself. The moralism in the work ethic can also be clearly seen in Franklin's utilitarianism, which stressed the virtues of honesty, industry, and frugality.

The ultimate aim of the ethic, the accumulation of more and more wealth in conjunction with a strict asceticism, appears at first sight to be irrational. Thus economic acquisition is the end, not the means, to satisfaction. This ethic was not an opportunistic and unscrupulous pursuit of selfish interests to one's own in-group (dealing among brothers), though to foreigners – the out-group – it did not apply.

However, the introduction of the ethic was not easy and early capitalists had to struggle against traditional views and early Luddites.

The question of the motive forces in the expansion of modern capitalism is not in the first instance a question of the origin of the capital sums which were first available for capitalistic uses, but, above all, of the development of the spirit of capitalism.Where it appears and is able to work itself out, it produces its own capital and monetary supplies as the means to its ends, but the reverse is not true. Its entry on the scene was not generally peaceful. A flood of mistrust, sometimes of hatred, above all of moral indignation, regularly opposed itself to the first innovator. Often – I know of several cases of the sort – regular legends of mysterious shady spots in his previous life have been produced. It is very easy not to recognize that only an unusually strong character could save an entrepreneur of this new type from the loss of his temperate self-control and from both moral and economic shipwreck. Furthermore, along with clarity of vision and ability to act, it is only by virtue of very definite and highly developed ethical qualities that it has been possible for him to command the absolutely indispensable confidence of his customers and workmen. Nothing else could have given him the strength to overcome the innumerable obstacles, above all the infinitely more intensive work which is demanded of the modern entrepreneur. But these are ethical qualities of quite a different sort from those adapted to the traditionalism of the past.

And, as a rule, it has been neither dare-devil and unscrupulous speculators, economic adventurers such as we meet at all periods of economic history, nor simply great financiers who have carried through this change, outwardly so inconspicuous, but nevertheless so decisive for the penetration of economic life with the new spirit. On the contrary, they were men who had grown up in the hard school of life, calculating and daring at the same time, above all temperate and reliable, shrewd and completely devoted to their business, with strictly bourgeois opinions and principles.

(pp. 68-9)

The erstwhile leisurely way of life of the business bourgeoisie came to an end and gave way to a new frugality because the desire was not to consume but to earn. Believers in the PWE tended to be diffident rather than hostile to the Church, which appeared to them to draw people away from labour in this world to thoughts of paradise.

The true PWE believer did not seek power and recognition, rather he/she avoided ostentation, unnecessary expenditure, conscious enjoyment of power, and outward signs of social recognition. The PWE believer modestly gets nothing out of his or her wealth except the irrational sense of having done his or her job well. It is this belief that no doubt seemed to pre-capitalistic man so incomprehensible and mysterious, so unworldly and contemptible. The question remains as to why and how people develop the idea of calling to the PWE.

Chapter III: Luther's conception of the calling

According to the PWE, one's calling to a way of life acceptable by God was not a monastic asceticism, but solely through the fulfilment of the obligations imposed upon the individual by his position in the world. One's calling, whatever it is, is morally neutral and thus every legitimate calling has exactly the same worth in the sight of God.

Luther cannot be accused of developing the spirit of capitalism, but his conception of calling was very susceptible to quite different interpretations.

What his views did do, according to Weber, was increase the moral emphasis on, and religious sanction of, organized worldly labour. Salvation may be obtained in any form of life and the individual should remain once and for all in the station and calling in which God had placed him. The calling for Luther was something man had to accept as divine ordinance and to which he had to adapt himself. Thus, worldly duties were no longer subordinate to ascetic ones and obedience to authority and the status quo was emphasized. Luther, Calvin, Zwingli, and other Protestants' views cannot be seen as promoting the PWE. However, their religious views did provide the ethical ideal upon which the PWE is based.

Chapter IV: The religious foundation of worldly asceticism

Weber argued that there were four principal groups of ascetic Protestant – Calvinists, Pietists, Methodists, and Baptists – often called Puritans. Furthermore, he argued that although they had different dogmatic foundations they shared similar ethical maxims. His interest, theoretically, was to see how the influence of those psychological sanctions, while originating in religious beliefs and practices, gave direction to practical everyday behaviour and influenced individual behavioural norms.

Calvinism

In the writings of the Calvinists, Weber found evidence for some of the cornerstones of the PWE: the idea of their being a small elect (doctrine of predestination); the idea that all work in the world was for God's glory alone and was good; that God helps them who help themselves in the sense that people create their own salvation; a distrust of the Catholic sacramental system.

> The rationalization of the world, the elimination of magic as a means to salvation, the Catholics had not carried nearly so far as the Puritans (and before them the Jews) had done. To the Catholic the absolution of his Church was a compensation for his own imperfection. The priest was a magician who performed the miracle of transubstantiation, and who held the key to eternal life in his hand. One could turn to him in grief and penitence. He dispensed atonement, hope of grace, certainty of forgiveness, and thereby granted release from that tremendous tension to which the Calvinist was doomed by an inexorable fate, admitting of no mitigation. For him such friendly and human comforts did not exist. He could not hope to atone for hours of weakness or of thoughtlessness by increased good will at other times, as the Catholic or even the Lutherans could. The God of Calvinism demanded of his believers not single good works, but a life of good work combined into a unified system. There was no place for the very human Catholic cycle of sin, repentance, atonement, release, followed by renewed sin. Nor was there any balance of merit for a

life as a whole which could be adjusted by temporal punishment or the Churches' means of grace.

The moral conduct of the average man was thus deprived of its planless and unsystematic character and subjected to a consistent method for conduct as a whole. It is no accident that the name of Methodists stuck to the participants in the last great revival of Puritan ideas in the eighteenth century just as the term Precisians, which has the same meaning, was applied to their spiritual ancestors in the seventeenth century.

(p. 117)

The idea of the predestination of the elect, whose evidence of God's grace one could see in this world, meant one could equally recognize and detect the eternally damned. Weber wrote: 'This consciousness of divine grace of the elect and holy was accompanied by an attitude toward the sin of one's neighbour, not of sympathetic understanding based on consciousness of one's own weakness, but of hatred and contempt for him as an enemy of God bearing the signs of eternal damnation' (p. 122).

Pietism

Pietists, on the continent of Europe, were also interested in the doctrine of predestination and the doctrine of proof which could not be proved by theological learning, hence the lack of need for theologians. Weber pointed out that the distinctive character of Pietism was its intensified emotional nature which stressed strict, temperate, methodically controlled, supervised, ascetic conduct. Pietists established an aristocracy of the elect resting on God's special grace, which could only be effective under certain unique and peculiar circumstances, especially repentance. The virtues of Pietism were more those of the faithful official, clerk, labourer, and domestic worker, while Calvinism was more closely related to hard legalism and active enterprise of bourgeois, capitalist entrepreneurs.

Methodism

Mainly found in the Anglo-Saxon world, Methodism was the combination of the emotional and ascetic but indifferent or even hostile to Calvinistic asceticism. Emotional ecstasies often took place publicly and were the basis of a belief in the undeserved possession of divine grace. Wesley's doctrine of sanctification stated that one could be reborn by virtue of divine grace working in one, and hence be free of sin. This led to a serene confidence as opposed to the sullen worry of the Calvinists. But good works alone did not suffice, except as the means of knowing one's state of grace.

In the end only the concept of regeneration, an emotional certainty of salvation as the immediate result of faith, was definitely maintained as the indispensable foundation of grace; and with it sanctification, resulting in (at least virtual) freedom from the power of sin, as the consequent proof of grace. The significance of external means of grace, especially the sacraments, was correspondingly diminished. In any case, the general awakening which followed Methodism everywhere, for example in New England, meant a victory for the doctrine of grace and election.

(p. 142)

Baptists

The Baptists, Mennonites, and Quakers, though there were many differences between them, were similar in that they were a sect – a community of personal believers – not a Church. Only adults who personally gained their own faith were baptized. Being reborn meant taking spiritual possession of God's gift of salvation and those alone are the chosen brethren of Christ. Baptists repudiated all idolatry of the flesh, carried out the most radical devaluation of all sacraments as a means to salvation, and accomplished an extreme religious rationalization of the world. Unchallengeable signs of the true rebirth included a sincere repudiation of the world as well as unconditional submission to God as speaking through the conscience. Predestination was rejected, but believers prayed silently for the spirit to descend, the purpose of which was to overcome everything impulsive and irrational, the passions, and subjective interests of the natural man. Hence, the adoption of a quiet, moderate conscientious character of everyday conduct. Baptists were non-political, refused to bear arms, take oaths, and were antagonistic to the aristocratic way of life. On the other hand, the intensity of interests in economic enterprise was considerably increased.

Thus, the conception of a state of religious grace common to all denominations had the status of marking off the possessor from worldly matters. This state could not be attained by magical sacraments, confession, or good works, but a specific type of conduct unmistakably different from the way of life of the natural man. This rationalization of conduct in this world for the sake of the next was a direct consequence of the concept of calling.

Chapter V: Asceticism and the spirit of capitalism

The PWE was not against wealth and possessions as such, but the temptations and idleness that they may encourage. Time wasting through socializing, idle talking, luxury, and excessive sleep was the first and deadliest of sins. Inactive contemplation is not only valueless but directly reprehensible.

Secondly, there is the important principle of hard, continuous, bodily, or mental labour. Unwillingness to work is itself a clear symptom of the lack of grace. Wealth does not exempt one from the unconditional command to work. It was a person's religious duty to work in the occupation, however great or humble, which God had assigned and, therefore, the world had to be accepted as it was. Specialization or division of labour led to the development of skill and hence a quantitative and qualitative increase in productivity, which in turn serves the greatest number of people.

Combining several callings or, indeed, changing one's calling is not objected to if it is more pleasing to God, being measured primarily in moral terms, in other words in terms of the importance of the goods produced in it for the community. In practice the most important criterion is found in private profitableness.

For if that God, whose hand the Puritan sees in all the occurrences of life, shows one of His elect a chance of profit, he must do it with a purpose. Hence the faithful Christian must follow the call by taking advantage of the opportunity. 'If God show you a way in which you may lawfully get more than in another way (without wrong to your soul or to any other), if you refuse this, and choose the less gainful way, you cross one of the ends of your calling, and you refuse to be God's steward, and to accept His gifts and use them for Him when He requireth it; you may labour to be rich for God, though not for the flesh and sin.'

Wealth is thus bad ethically only in so far as it is a temptation to idleness and sinful enjoyment of life, and its acquisition is bad only when it is with the purpose of later living merrily and without care. But as a performance of duty in a calling it is not only morally permissible, but actually enjoined. The parable of the servant who was rejected because he did not increase the talent which was entrusted to him seemed to say so directly. To wish to be poor was, it was often argued, the same as wishing to be unhealthy; it is objectionable as a glorification of works and derogatory to the glory of God. Especially begging, on the part of one able to work, is not only the sin of slothfulness, but a violation of the duty of brotherly love according to the Apostle's own word.

(pp. 162–3)

The Old Testament, not without ambiguity, was frequently used to give a powerful impetus to the spirit of self-righteousness and sober legality. Puritan asceticism preached against the spontaneous enjoyment of life and all it had to offer, such as the enjoyment of sports. Sport was condemned because it is purely a means of enjoyment, an awakening of pride, raw instincts, and irrational gambling instincts.

Puritan, solemn, narrow-minded contempt of culture did not mean they were philistines. Indeed, they were well educated men of science. But they were against scholarship and superstitious, magical, spontaneous religious art or festivals. Being against idle talk, superfluities, and vain ostentation served to condemn many artistic tendencies such as the theatre. Some cultural goods could be enjoyed ascetically, but they imposed responsibility on the owner, whose duty it was to collect and increase them solely for the glory of God.

Puritans approved of the rational uses of wealth but were against covetousness. When the idea of limitation of consumption was united with acquisitive activity, the result was the accumulation of capital through the ascetic compulsion to save. Weber quoted Wesley, who wrote:

> I fear, wherever riches have increased, the essence of religion has decreased in the same proportion. Therefore I do not see how it is possible, in the nature of things, for any revival of true religion to continue long. For religion must necessarily produce both industry and frugality, and these cannot but produce riches. But as riches increase, so will pride, anger and love of the world in all its branches. How then is it possible that Methodism, that is, a religion of the heart, though it flourishes now as a green bay tree, should continue in this state? For the Methodists in every place grow diligent and frugal; consequently they increase in goods. Hence they proportionately increase in pride, in anger, in the desire of the flesh, the desire of the eyes, and the pride of life. So, although the form of religion remains, the spirit is swiftly vanishing away. Is there no way to prevent this – this continual decay of pure religion? We ought not to prevent people from being diligent and frugal; *we must exhort all Christians to gain all they can, and to save all they can; that is, in effect, to grow rich.*

Finally, the PWE allowed for the unequal distribution of the goals of this world, which was seen as a special dispensation of God. After all, faithful labour even at low wages, on the part of those to whom life offers no other opportunity, is pleasing to God.

Weber ends the essay by speculating about the future, but it is worth quoting the final paragraph, if nothing else, to see the caution in his work.

> Here we have only attempted to trace the fact and the direction of its influence to their motives in one, though a very important, point. But it would also further be necessary to investigate how Protestant Asceticism was in turn influenced in its development and character by the totality of social conditions, especially economic. The modern man is in general, even with the best will, unable to give religious ideas a significance for culture and national character which they deserve. But it is, of course, not my aim to substitute for a one-sided materialistic an equally one-sided spiritualistic causal interpretation of culture and of history. Each is equally possible, but each, if it does not serve as the preparation, but as the conclusion of an investigation, accomplishes equally little in the interest of historical truth.

(p. 183)

References

Abraham, G. (1983) 'The Protestant ethic and the spirit of utilitarianism – the case of EST', *Theory and Society 12*: 739–73.

Abrams, M. (1985) 'Demographic correlates of values', in M. Abrams, D. Gerard, and N. Timms (eds), *Values and Social Changes in Britain*, London: Macmillan, pp. 21–49.

Abrams, M., Gerard, D., and Timms, N. (1985) *Values and Social Changes in Britain*, London: Macmillan.

Adorno, T., Frenkel-Brunswick, E., Levinson, D., and Sanford, N. (1950) *The Authoritarian Personality*, New York: Harper.

Aho, J. (1979) 'The Protestant ethic and the spirit of violence', *Journal of Political and Military Sociology 7*: 103–19.

Albee, G. (1977) 'The Protestant ethic, sex and psychotherapy', *American Psychologist 61*: 150–61.

Albee, G. (1978) 'Sex vs capitalism: the paradox of the Protestant Ethic', *Wharton Magazine 1*: 28–34.

Aldag, R. and Brief, A. (1975) 'Some correlates of work values', *Journal of Applied Psychology 60*: 757–60.

Allen, V. (1970) *Psychological Factors in Poverty*, Chicago: Markham.

Alston, J. and Dean, K. (1972) 'Socioeconomic factors associated with attitudes towards welfare recipients and the cause of poverty', *Social Service Review 46*: 13–23.

Alwin, D. (1986) 'Religion and parental child-rearing orientations: evidence of a Catholic–Protestant convergence', *American Journal of Sociology 92*: 412–40.

Andrisani, P. and Nestle, G. (1976) 'Internal–external control as contributor to and outcome of work experience', *Journal of Applied Psychology 61*: 156–63.

Andrisani, P. and Parnes, H. (1983) 'Commitment to the work ethic and success in the labour market', in J. Barbash, R. Lampman, S. Levitan, and G. Tyler (eds), *The Work Ethic: A Critical Analysis*, Madison: IRRA, pp. 101–20.

Anthony, P. (1984) *The Ideology of Work*, London: Tavistock.

Armenakis, A., Field, H., Holley, W., Bedenan, A., and Ledbetter, B. (1977) 'Human resource considerations in textile work redesign', *Human Relations 30*: 1147–56.

Atieh, J., Brief, A., and Vollrath, D. (1987) 'The Protestant work ethic – conservatism paradox: beliefs and values in work and life', *Personality and Individual Differences 8*: 577–80.

Atkinson, J. (ed.) (1958) *Motives in Fantasy, Action and Society*, Princeton, N.J.: Van Nostrand.

Atkinson, J. (1964) *An Introduction to Motivation*, Princeton, N.J.: Van Nostrand.

Ball-Rokeach, S., Rokeach, M., and Grube, J. (1984) 'The great American values test',

Psychology Today, November, 34–41.

Barbash, J., Lampman, R., Levitan, S., and Tyler, G. (eds) (1983) *The Work Ethic: a critical analysis*, Madison: IRRA.

Barclay, W. (1972) *Ethics in a Permissive Society*, London: Fontana.

Beard, J. and Ragheb, M. (1979) 'Measuring leisure satisfaction', *Journal of Leisure Research 12*: 20–33.

Beit-Hallahmi, B. (1979) 'Personal and social components of the Protestant ethic', *Journal of Social Psychology 109*: 263–7.

Bellah, R. (1963) 'Reflection on the Protestant ethic analogy in Asia', *Journal of Social Issues 19*: 52–60.

Berglas, S. (1986) *The Success Syndrome: Hitting Bottom When You Reach the Top*, London: Plenum.

Bernstein, P. (1980) 'The work ethic that never was', *Wharton Magazine 4*: 19–25.

Blood, M. (1969) 'Work values and job satisfaction', *Journal of Applied Psychology 53*: 456–9.

Bluen, S. and Barling, J. (1983) 'Work values in white South African males', *Journal of Cross-Cultural Psychology 14*: 329–35.

Bonani, G. (1978) 'The slow demise of the work ethic', *International Development Review 20*: 57–60.

Bothin, R. (1977) 'An investigation of the relationship of the Protestant Ethic values to success in accounting courses', *Accounting Review 52*: 479–84.

Bouma, G. (1973) 'Beyond Lenski: a critical review of recent "Protestant Ethic" research', *Journal for the Scientific Study of Religion 14*: 141–55.

Breakwell, G., Fife-Schaw, C., Lee, T., and Spencer, J. (1985) 'Attitudes to new technology in relation to social beliefs and group memberships', *Current Psychological Research and Reviews 5*: 34–47.

Breakwell, G. and Fife-Schaw, C. (1987) 'Young people's attitudes to new technology: source and structure', in J. Lewko (ed.), *Children and Work*, California: Jossey-Bass.

Bruhn, J. (1982) 'The ecological crisis and the work ethic', *International Journal of Environmental Studies 3*: 43–7.

Buchholz, R. (1976) 'Measurement of beliefs', *Human Relations 29*: 1177–88.

Buchholz, R. (1977) 'The belief structure of managers relative to work concepts measured by a factor analytic model', *Personnel Psychology 30*: 567–87.

Buchholz, R. (1978a) 'An empirical study of contemporary beliefs about work in American society', *Journal of Applied Psychology 63*: 219–27.

Buchholz, R. (1978b) 'The work ethic reconsidered', *Industrial and Labor Relations Review 31*: 450–9.

Buchholz, R. (1983) 'The Protestant Ethic as an ideological justification of capitalism', *Journal of Business Ethics 2*: 51–60.

Burger, J. (1985) 'Desire for control and achievement related behaviours', *Journal of Personality and Social Psychology 48*: 1520–33.

Calhoun, R. (1980) 'The new work ethic', *Training and Development Journal 5*: 127–30.

Cameron, C. and Elusorr, S. (1986) *Thank God it's Monday: Strategies for Increasing Job Satisfaction*, London: Ebury.

Campbell, C. (1987) *The Romantic Ethic and the Spirit of Modern Consumerism*, Oxford: Blackwell.

Carlson, P. (1982) '"Updating" individualism and the work ethic: corporate logic in the classroom', *Curriculum Inquiry 12*: 125–59.

Chebat, J-C. and Filiatrault, P. (1986) 'Locus of control and attitudes toward the economic crisis', *Journal of Psychology 126*: 559–61.

Cherrington, D. (1980) *The Work Ethic: Working Values and Values that Work*, New York: AMACOM.

Chi, S. and Houseknecht, S. (1984) 'Protestant fundamentalism and marital success',

Sociology and Social Research 69: 351–75.

Chusmir, L. and Hood, J. (1986) 'Relationship between type A behaviour pattern and motivational needs', *Psychological Reports 58*: 783–94.

Chusmir, L. and Koberg, C. (1988) 'Religion and attitudes toward work. A new look at an old question', *Journal of Organizational Behaviour 9*: 251–62.

Clark, C., Worthington, E., and Danser, D. (1988) 'The transmission of religious beliefs and practices from parents to first born early adolescent sons', *Journal of Marriage and the Family 50*: 463–72.

Clarke, O. (1983) 'The work ethic: an international perspective', in J. Barbash, R. Lampman, S. Levitan, and G. Tyler (eds), *The Work Ethic: A Critical Analysis*, Madison: IRRA, pp. 121–49.

Cohen, J. (1985) 'Protestant ethic and status-attainment', *Sociological Analysis 46*: 49–58.

Collste, G. (1985) 'Towards a normative work ethic', in H. Davis and D. Gosling (eds), *Will the Future Work?* Geneva: WCC.

Cook, J., Hepworth, S., Wall, T., and Warr, P. (1981) *The Experience of Work*, London: Academic Press.

Corson, D. (ed.) (1988) *Education for Work: Background to Policy and Curriculum*, Palmerston North: Dunmore Press.

Costa, P., McCrae, R., and Holland, J. (1984) 'Personality and vocational interests in an adult sample', *Journal of Applied Psychology 69*: 390–400.

Crandall, R. and Slivken, K. (1980) 'Leisure attitudes and their measurement', in S. Iso-Ahola (ed.), *Social Psychological Perspectives on Leisure and Recreation*, Springfield, Illinois: C.C. Thomas, pp. 261–84.

Cressey, P. (1985) 'Work ideologies: prospects for participation', in H. Davis and D. Gosling (eds), *Will the Future Work?* Geneva: WCC.

Csikszentmihaly, M. (1976) 'The Americanization of rock-climbing', in J. Bruner, A. Jolly, and K. Sylva (eds), *Play: Its Role in Development and Evolution*, New York: Basic Books.

Cuzzort, R. (1969) *Humanity and Modern Sociological Thought*, London: Holt, Rinehart and Winston.

Dapkus, M. (1985) 'A thematic analysis of the experience of time', *Journal of Personality and Social Psychology 49*: 408–19.

Davidson, C. and Gaitz, C. (1974) '"Are the poor different?" A comparison of work behaviour and attitudes among the urban poor and non poor', *Social Problems 22*: 229–45.

Davis, H. and Gosling, D. (1985) *Will the Future Work? Values for Emerging Patterns of Work and Employment*, Geneva: World Council of Churches.

Davis, K. and Taylor, T. (1979) *Kids and Cash: Solving a Parent's Dilemma*, La Jolla: Oak Tree.

Davis, W. (1985) *The Rich: A Study of the Species*, Tiptree: Arrow.

Deacon, A. (1978) 'The scrounging controversy: public attitudes towards the unemployed in contemporary Britain', *Social and Economic Administration 12*: 120–35.

Deal, T. and Kennedy, A. (1982) *Corporate Cultures: The Rites and Rituals of Corporate Life*, New York: Addison-Wesley.

Debutts, T. (1975) 'The work ethic is alive and well', *Personnel 52*: 22–31.

de Charms, R. and Moeller, G. (1962) 'Values expressed in American children's readers: 1800–1950', *Journal of Abnormal and Social Psychology 64*: 136–42.

de Vries, K.M. (1980) *Organizational Paradoxes*, London: Tavistock.

Dickson, J. and Buchholz, R. (1977) 'Differences in beliefs about work between managers and blue-collar workers', *Journal of Management Studies 16*: 235–51.

Dickson, J. and Buchholz, R. (1979) 'Management and beliefs about work in Scotland

and the USA', *Journal of Management Studies 14*: 80–101.

Dickson, T. and McLachlan, H. (1983) 'Scottish capitalism and Weber's Protestant Ethic thesis', *Sociology 17*: 560–8.

Ditz, G. (1978) 'The Protestant ethic and higher education in America', *Oxford Review of Education 4*: 161–71.

Ditz, G. (1980) 'The Protestant ethic and the market economy', *Kyklos 33*: 623–57.

Dorst, G., Leon, J., and Philbrick, J. (1978) 'American college students' Protestant ethic: a smallest space analysis', *Social Behaviour and Personality 6*: 187–90.

Eisenberger, R. and Shank, D. (1985) 'Personal work ethic and effort training affect cheating', *Journal of Personality and Social Psychology 49*: 520–8.

Eisenstadt, S. (1963) 'The need for achievement', *Economic Development and Cultural Change 11*: 420–31.

Elizur, D. (1984) 'Facet of work values: a structual analysis of work outcomes', *Journal of Applied Psychology 69*: 379–89.

Elizur, D. (1986) 'Achievement motive and sport performance', *International Review of Applied Psychology 35*: 209–24.

Elizur, D. (1987) 'Work and nonwork relations: a facet analysis', *Journal of General Psychology 114*: 47–55.

England, G. and Misumi, J. (1986) 'Work centrality in Japan and the United States', *Journal of Cross-Cultural Psychology 17*: 399–410.

Erwee, R. and Pottas, C. (1982) 'Locus of control and achievement motivation of managers', *Psychologia Africana 21*: 79–102.

Etzioni, A. (1979) 'Work in the American future: reindustrialization or quality of life', in C. Kerr, and J. Rosow (eds), *Work in America: The Decade Ahead*, New York: Van Nostrand, pp. 27–34.

Fagin, L. and Little, M. (1984) *The Forsaken Families*, Harmondsworth: Penguin.

Farnsworth, T. (1987) *Test Your Executive Skills*, London: Ebury Press.

Feagin, J. (1972) 'Poverty: We still believe that God helps them who help themselves', *Psychology Today 6*: 101–29.

Feather, N. (1975) *Values in Education and Society*, New York: Free Press.

Feather, N. (1978) 'Family resemblances in conservation: are daughters more similar to parents than sons?' *Journal of Personality 46*: 260–78.

Feather, N. (1979) 'Value correlates of conservatism', *Journal of Personality and Social Psychology 37*: 1617–30.

Feather, N. (1982) 'Unemployment and its psychological correlates: a study of depressive symptoms, self-esteem, protestant-ethic values, attributional style and apathy', *Australian Journal of Psychology 34*: 309–23.

Feather, N. (1983a) 'Some correlates of attributional style: depressive symptoms, self-esteem and Protestant ethic values', *Personality and Social Psychology Bulletin 9*: 125–35.

Feather, N. (1983b) 'Observers' reactions to allocations in relation to input of allocator, type of distribution, and Protestant ethic values', *Australian Journal of Psychology 35*: 61–70.

Feather, N. (1984) 'Protestant ethic, conservatism, and values', *Journal of Personality and Social Psychology 46*: 1132–41.

Feather, N. (1985) 'Attitudes, values and attributions: explanations of unemployment', *Journal of Personality and Social Psychology 48*: 876–89.

Feather, N. and Bond, M. (1983) 'Time structure and purposeful activity among employed and unemployed university graduates', *Journal of Occupational Psychology 56*: 241–54.

Feather, N. and O'Brien, G. (1986a) 'A longitudinal study of the effects of employment and unemployment on school-leavers', *Journal of Occupational Psychology 59*: 121–44.

Feather, N. and O'Brien, G. (1986b) 'A longitudinal analysis of the effects of different patterns of employment and unemployment on school-leavers', *British Journal of Psychology* 77: 459–79.

Feather, N. and O'Brien, G. (1987) 'Looking for employment: an expectancy – valence analysis of job seeking behaviour among young people', *British Journal of Psychology* 78 : 251–72.

Feather, N. and O'Driscoll, M. (1980) 'Observers' reactions to an equal or equitable allocator in relation to allocator input, causal attributions, and value importance', *European Journal of Psychology 10*: 107–29.

Ferenczi, S. (1926) *Further Contributions to the Theory and Techniques of Psycho-Analysis*, London: Kröpf.

Ferman, L. (1983) 'The work ethic in the world of informal work', in J. Barbash, R. Lampman, S. Levitan, and G. Tyler (eds), *The Work Ethic: A Critical Analysis*, Madison: IRRA, pp. 211–29.

Fillenbaum, G. and Maddox, G. (1974) 'Work after retirement: an investigation into some psychologically relevant variables', *The Gerontologist 8*: 418–24.

Filley, A. and Aldag, R. (1978) 'Characteristics and measurement of an organizational typology', *Academy of Management Journal 21*: 578–91.

Fineman, S. (1977) 'The achievement motive construct and its measurement: where are we now?' *British Journal of Psychology 68*: 1–22.

Fineman, S. (ed.) (1987) *Unemployment: Personal and Social Consequences*, London: Tavistock.

Flannery, R. (1984) 'The work ethic as moderator variable of life stress: preliminary enquiry', *Psychological Report 55*: 361–2.

Foegen, J. (1972) 'Toward a discretionary work ethic', *Labor Law Journal 25*: 12–17.

Fogarty, M. (1985) 'British attitudes to work', in M. Abrams, D. Gerard, and N. Timms, *Values and Social Changes in Britain*, London: Macmillan, pp. 173–200.

Folger, R. and Greenberg, J. (1985) 'Procedural justice: an interpretive analysis of personal systems', *Research in Personnel and Human Resources Management 3*: 141–83.

Forman, N. (1987) *Mind Over Money: Curing Your Financial Headaches with Money Sanity*, New York: Doubleday.

Frantz, R. (1980) 'The effect of early labour market experience upon internal-external locus of control among male workers', *Journal of Youth and Adolescence 9*: 202–10.

Fraser, J. (1962) *Industrial Psychology*, Oxford: Pergamon.

Freud, S. (1908) *Character and Anal Eroticism*, London: Hogarth.

Freud, S. (1962) *Civilization and its Discontents*, New York: Norton.

Frey, R. (1984a) 'Does *n*-Achievement cause economic development? A cross-lagged panel analysis of the McClelland thesis', *Journal of Social Psychology 122*: 67–70.

Frey, R. (1984b) 'Need for achievement, entrepreneurship, and economic growth: a critique of the McClelland thesis', *Social Science Journal 4*: 125–34.

Fromm, E. (1980) *To Have or to Be?* London: Abacus.

Fryer, D. (1986) 'Employment deprivation and personal agency during unemployment', *Social Behaviour 1*: 3–23.

Fryer, D. and Payne, R. (1984) 'Proactive behaviour in unemployment: findings and implications', *Leisure Studies 3*: 273–95.

Fuller, R. and Rice, B. (1966) *Christianity and the Affluent Society*, London: Hodder and Stoughton.

Funder, D., Block, J., and Block, J. (1983) 'Delay of gratification: some longitudinal personality correlates', *Journal of Personality and Social Psychology 44*: 1198–1213.

Furnham, A. (1982) 'The Protestant work ethic and attitudes towards unemployment', *Journal of Occupational Psychology 55*: 277–85.

Furnham, A. (1983) 'Attitudes towards the unemployed receiving social security benefits', *Human Relations 36*: 135–50.

Furnham, A. (1984a) 'Work values and beliefs in Britain', *Journal of Occupational Behaviour 5*: 281–91.

Furnham, A. (1984b) 'The Protestant work ethic, voting behaviour and attitudes to the trade unions', *Political Studies 32*: 420–36.

Furnham, A. (1984c) 'Many sides of the coin: the psychology of money usage', *Personality and Individual Differences 5*: 501–9.

Furnham, A. (1984d) 'Determinants of attitudes toward taxation in Britain', *Human Relations 37*: 535–46.

Furnham, A. (1984e) 'The Protestant work ethic: a review of the psychological literature', *European Journal of Social Psychology 14*: 87–104.

Furnham, A. (1985a) 'The determinants of attitudes towards social security benefits', *British Journal of Social Psychology 24*: 19–27.

Furnham, A. (1985b) 'A short measure of economic beliefs', *Personality and Individual Differences 6*: 123–6.

Furnham, A. (1986a) 'Economic locus of control', *Human Relations 39*: 29–43.

Furnham, A. (1986b) 'Response bias, social desirability and dissimulation', *Personality and Individual Differences 7*: 385–400.

Furnham, A. (1987a) 'Work related beliefs and human values', *Personality and Individual Differences 8*: 627–37.

Furnham, A. (1987b) 'Predicting protestant work ethic beliefs', *European Journal of Personality 1*: 93–106.

Furnham, A. (1988) *Lay Theories: Everyday Understanding of Problems in the Social Sciences*, Oxford: Pergamon.

Furnham, A. (1989a) 'The Protestant work ethic and A type behaviour', Unpublished paper.

Furnham, A. (1989b) *The Protestant Ethic in Twelve Cultures*, manuscript submitted for publication.

Furnham, A. (1990) 'A content, correlational and factor analytic study of seven measures of the Protestant Work Ethic', *Human Relations*, in press.

Furnham, A. and Bland, C. (1983) 'The protestant work ethic and conservatism', *Personality and Individual Differences 4*: 205–6.

Furnham, A. and Koritsas, E. (1989) 'The Protestant work ethic and vocational preference', *Journal of Organizational Behaviour*, in press.

Furnham, A. and Muhuideen, C. (1984) 'The protestant work ethic in Britain and Malaysia', *Journal of Social Psychology 122*: 157–61.

Furnham, A. and Procter, E. (1989) 'Belief in a just world: a review', *British Journal of Social Psychology*, in press.

Furnham, A. and Quilley, R. (1989) 'The Protestant work ethic and the prisoner's dilemma game', *British Journal of Social Psychology 28*: 79–87.

Furnham, A. and Rose, M. (1987) 'Alternative ethics: the relationship between the wealth, work and leisure ethic', *Human Relations 40*: 561–74.

Furnham, A. and Schaeffer, R. (1984) 'Person-environment fit, job satisfaction and mental health', *Journal of Occupational Psychology 57*: 295–307.

Furnham, A. and Thomas, P. (1984a) 'Pocket money: a study in economic education', *British Journal of Developmental Psychology 2*: 205–12.

Furnham, A. and Thomas, P. (1984b) 'Adult's perceptions of the economic socialization of children', *Journal of Adolescence 7*: 217–31.

Ganster, D. (1980) 'Individual differences and task design: a laboratory experiment', *Organizational Behaviour and Human Performance 26*: 131–48.

Ganster, D. (1981) 'Protestant ethic and performance: a re-examination', *Psychological Reports 48*: 335–8.

Garratt, S. (1985) *Manage Your Time*, London: Collins.

Gartner, A. and Riesman, F. (1974) 'Is there a new work ethic', *American Journal of Orthopsychiatry 44*: 563–7.

Giddens, A. (1972) *Politics and Sociology in the Thought of Max Weber*, London: Macmillan.

Gilbert, L. (1973) 'The changing work ethic and rehabilitation', *Journal of Rehabilitation 34*: 14–17.

Gilbert, J. (1977) *Work Without Salvation: America's Intellectuals and Industrial Alienation, 1880–1910*, Baltimore: Johns Hopkins University.

Goitein, B. and Rotenberg, M. (1977) 'Protestantism and respective labeling: a cross-cultural study in person perception', *Human Relations 30*: 487–97.

Golby, J. (1986) *Culture and Society in Britain: 1850–1890*, Oxford: Oxford University Press.

Goldberg, H. and Lewis, R. (1978) *Money Madness: The Psychology of Saving, Spending, Loving and Hating Money*, London: Springwood Books.

Golding, P. and Middleton, S. (1983) *Images of Welfare*, Oxford: Martin Robertson.

Goldsmith, W. and Clutterbuck, D. (1985) *The Winning Streak*, Harmondsworth: Penguin.

Goldstein, B. and Eichhorn, R. (1961) 'The changing Protestant ethic: rural patterns in health, work and leisure', *American Sociological Review 26*: 557–65.

Gonsalves, S. and Bernard, G. (1983) 'The relationship between the Protestant ethic and social class for Afro-Caribbeans and Afro-Americans', *Psychological Reports 53*: 645–6.

Gonsalves, S. and Bernard, G. (1985) 'The relationship between parental social class and endorsement of items on the Protestant ethic and conservatism scales', *Psychological Reports 57*: 919–22.

Goodin, R. (1986) 'Self-reliance versus the welfare state', *Journal of Social Policy 14*: 25–47.

Goodwin, L. (1973) 'Middle-class misperceptions of the high life aspirations and strong work ethic held by the welfare poor', *American Journal of Orthopsychiatry 43*: 554–64.

Grant, P. (1982) 'Why employee motivation has declined in America', *Personnel Journal 39*: 905–9.

Gray, D. (1986) *The Entrepreneur's Complete Self-Assessment Guide*, Worcester: Billing and Sons.

Greeley, A. (1964) 'The Protestant ethic: time for a moratorium', *Sociological Analysis 25*: 20–33.

Green, A. (1973) *Sociology: An Analysis of Life in Modern Society*, New York: McGraw-Hill.

Green, R. (ed.) (1965) *Protestantism and Capitalism: The Weber Thesis and Its Critics*, Boston: D.C. Heath.

Greenberg, J. (1977) 'The Protestant work ethic and reactions to negative performance evaluations on a laboratory task', *Journal of Applied Psychology 62*: 682–90.

Greenberg, J. (1978a) 'Protestant ethic endorsement and attitudes toward commuting to work among mass transit riders', *Journal of Applied Psychology 63*: 755–8.

Greenberg, J. (1978b) 'Equity, equality, and the protestant ethic: allocating rewards following fair and unfair competition', *Journal of Experimental Social Psychology 14*: 217–26.

Greenberg, J. (1979) 'Protestant ethic endorsement and the fairness of equity inputs', *Journal of Research in Personality 13*: 81–90.

Grieco, A. and Lichstein, K. (1981) 'Self reinforcement and the work ethic', *International Journal of Addictions 16*: 1095–1110.

Hafsi, M. (1987) 'The effect of religious involvement on work centrality', *Psychologia*

30: 258–66.

Hall, R. (1986) *Dimensions of Work*, New York: Sage.

Hammar, T. and Vardi, Y. (1981) 'Locus of control and career self-management among non-supervisory employees in industrial settings', *Journal of Vocational Behaviour 18*: 13–29.

Hammond, P. and Williams, K. (1976) 'Protestant ethic thesis: social psychological assessment', *Social Forces 54*: 579–89.

Hampden-Turner, C. (1981) *Maps of the Mind*, Over Wallop: Mitchell Beazley.

Handy, C. (1985) *The Future of Work*, Worcester: Billing & Sons.

Hannah, R. (1982) 'The work ethic of coal miners', *Personnel Journal 10*: 746–8.

Harding, S., Phillips, D., and Fogarty, M. (1986) *Contrasting Values in Western Europe*, London: Macmillan.

Harmer, D. (1979) 'The work ethic is alive, well, and living in Cleveland', in W. Hoffman and T. Wyly (eds), *The Work Ethic in Business*, Cambridge, Mass.: O, G & H Publishers.

Harpaz, I. (1985) 'Meaning of working profiles of various occupational groups', *Journal of Vocational Behaviour 26*: 25–40.

Harpaz, I. (1986) 'The factorial structure of the meaning of working', *Human Relations 39*: 595–614.

Harris, A. and Stokes, R. (1978) 'Race, self-evaluation and the Protestant ethic', *Social Problems 26*: 71–85.

Heaven, P. (1980) 'The Protestant ethic scale in South Africa', *Psychological Reports 47*: 618.

Heaven, P. (1989) 'Structure and personality correlates of the Protestant work ethic', *Personality and Individual Differences*, in press.

Heckhausen, H., Schmalt, H-D., and Schneider, K. (1985) *Achievement Motivation in Perspective*, Orlando, Florida: Academic Press, Inc.

Hedges, J. (1983) 'Job commitment', in J. Barbash, R. Lampman, S. Levitan, and G. Tyler (eds), *The Work Ethic: A Critical Analysis*, Madison: IRRA, pp. 43–60.

Ho, R. (1984) *Adherence to Protestant Work Ethic Values and Helping Judgements Towards the Unemployed*, Unpublished Paper.

Ho, R. and Lloyd, J. (1984) 'Development of an Australian work ethic scale', *Australian Psychology 19*: 321–32.

Hobsbawm, E. (1986) *Industry and Empire*, Harmondsworth: Penguin.

Hodgkinson, H. (1969) *Education, Interaction and Social Change*, Englewood Cliffs: Prentice-Hall.

Hoffman, W. and Wyly, T. (eds) (1981) *The Work Ethic in Business*, Cambridge, Mass.: Oelgeschlager, Gunn, and Hain.

Hofstede, G. (1984) *Culture's Consequences*, New York: Sage.

Holland, J. (1973) *Making Vocational Choices: A Theory of Careers*, Englewood Cliffs: Prentice-Hall.

Hooker, K. and Ventis, D. (1984) 'Work ethic, daily activities and retirement satisfaction', *Journal of Gerontology 39*: 478–84.

Horne, D. (1986) *The Public Culture: The Triumph of Industrialism*, London: Pluto.

Howard, A. and Wilson, J. (1982) 'Leadership in a declining work ethic', *California Management Review 24*: 33–46.

Howard, A., Shudo, K., and Umeshima, M. (1983) 'Motivation and values among Japanese and American managers', *Personnel Psychology 36*: 883–98.

Hudson, W. (1961) 'The Weber thesis re-examined', *Church History 30*: 88–99.

Hulin, C. and Blood, M. (1968) 'Job enlargement, individual differences and worker responses', *Psychological Bulletin 69*: 41–55.

Inglehart, R. (1971) 'The silent revolution in Europe: intergenerational change in the industrial societies', *American Political Science Review 65*: 991–1017.

Iso-Ahola, S. (1976) 'On the theoretical link between personality and leisure', *Psychological Reports 39*: 3–10.

Iso-Ahola, S. and Buttimer, K. (1981) 'The emergence of work and leisure ethic from early adolescence to early adulthood', *Journal of Leisure Research 13*: 282–8.

Iso-Ahola, S. and Buttimer, K. (1982) 'On the measurement of work and leisure ethics and resultant intercorrelations', *Educational and Psychological Measurement 42*: 429–35.

Jackson, J. and Harkins, S. (1985) 'Equity in effort: an explanation of the social loafing effect', *Journal of Personality and Social Psychology 49*: 1199–1206.

Jackson, P., Stafford, E., Banks, M., and Warr, P. (1983) 'Unemployment and psychological distress in young people: the moderating role of employment commitment', *Journal of Applied Psychology 68*: 525–35.

Jahoda, M. (1979) 'The impact of unemployment in the 1930s and the 1970s', *Bulletin of the British Psychological Society 32*: 309–14.

Jahoda, M. (1982) *Employment and Unemployment: A Social-Psychological Analysis*, Cambridge: Cambridge University Press.

Jazarek, J. (1978) 'The work ethic: What are we measuring?' *Industrial Relations 33*: 666–79.

Jenkins, C. and Sherman, B. (1979) *The Collapse of Work*, London: Methuen.

Joe, V. (1974) 'Personality correlates of conservatism', *Journal of Social Psychology 93*: 309–10.

Joe, V., Jones, R., and Miller, P. (1981) 'Value pattern of a conservative', *Personality and Individual Differences 2*: 25–30.

Jonassen, C. (1948) 'The Protestant ethic and the spirit of capitalism in Norway', *American Sociological Review 16*: 676–88.

Johnson, B. (1962) 'Ascetic protestantism and political preference', *Public Opinion Quarterly 26*: 35–46.

Johnson, V. (1976) 'Contemporary influences on sexual response: 1. The work ethic', *Journal of School Health 66*: 211–15.

Johnson, V. and Masters, W. (1972) 'Contemporary influences on sexual response: 1. The work ethic', *Journal of School Health 44*: 211–15.

Kabanoff, B. (1980) 'Work and non work: a review of models, methods, and findings', *Psychological Bulletin 88*: 60–77.

Kabanoff, B. and O'Brien, G. (1980) 'Work and leisure: a task attributes analysis', *Journal of Applied Psychology 65*: 595–609.

Kabanoff, B. and O'Brien, G. (1982) 'Relationships between work and leisure attributes across occupational and sex groups in Australia', *Australian Journal of Psychology 34*: 165–82.

Kahn, R. (1981) *Work and Health*, New York: Wiley.

Kallen, D. and Miller, D. (1971) 'Public attitudes towards welfare', *Social Work 2*: 83–90.

Kanter, R. (1983) *The Change Masters: Corporate Entrepreneurs at Work*, London: Counter-point.

Katzell, R. (1979) 'Changing attitudes to work', in C. Kerr and J. Rosow (eds), *Work in America: The Decade Ahead*, New York: Van Nostrand, pp. 35–7.

Katzell, R. and Yankelovich, D. (1976) *Work, Productivity and Job Satisfaction*, New York: Psychological Corporation.

Kay, W. (1986) *Tycoons: Where They Came From and How They Made It*, London: Pan.

Kelly, J. (1983) *Leisure Identities and Interactions*, London: George Allen & Unwin.

Kelvin, P. (1984) 'The historical dimension of social psychology: the case of unemployment', in H. Tajfel (ed.), *The Social Dimension*, Cambridge: Cambridge University Press, pp. 405–22.

Kelvin, P. (1985) 'Work and the work ethic', in B. Whelan (ed.), *Life Without Work*, Dublin: Mental Health Association.

Kelvin, P. and Jarrett, J. (1985) *Unemployment: Its Social Psychological Effects*, Cambridge: Cambridge University Press.

Kennedy, R. (1962) 'The Protestant ethic and the parsis', *American Journal of Psychology 41*: 11–20.

Kerr, C. and Rosow, J. (eds) (1979) *Work in America: The Decade Ahead*, New York: Van Nostrand.

Kidron, A. (1978) 'Work values and organizational commitment', *Academy of Management Journal 21*: 239–47.

Kim, H. (1977) 'The relationship of Protestant ethic beliefs and values of achievement', *Journal for the Scientific Study of Religion 16*: 255–62.

Kohn, M. and Schooler, C. (1973) 'Occupational experience and psychological functioning: an assessment of reciprocal effects', *American Sociological Review 38*: 97–118.

Kramer, Y. (1977) 'Work compulsion – a psychoanalytic study', *Psychological Quarterly 46*: 361–71.

Kramer, Y. and Harpaz, J. (1982) 'Leisure patterns among retired workers: spillover or compensating trends?' *Journal of Vocational Behaviour 21*: 183–95.

Kubota, A. (1983) 'Japan: social structure and work ethic', *Asia Pacific Community 20*: 35–65.

Lakein, A. (1974) *How to Get Control of Your Time and Your Life*, New York: Signet Books.

Lasch, C. (1985) *The Culture of Narcissism*, Glasgow: Collins.

Lavoie, R. (1986) 'Toward developing a philosophy of education: a re-examination of competition, fairness and the work ethic', *Journal of Learning Disabilities 19*: 62–3.

Lawler, E. (1971) *Pay and Organizational Effectiveness: A Psychological Review*, New York: McGraw-Hill.

Lay, C. (1986) 'At last, my research article on procrastination', *Journal of Research in Personality 20*: 474–95.

Lea, S. and Webley, P. (1981) *Théorie psychologique de la monnaie*, Paper given at the Economic Psychology Conference, Paris.

Lea, S., Tarpy, R., and Webley, P. (1987) *The Individual in the Economy: A Survey of Economic Psychology*, Cambridge: Cambridge University Press.

Leadbeater, C. and Lloyd, J. (1987) *In Search of Work*, Harmondsworth: Penguin.

Lenski, G. (1961) *The Religious Factor: Study of Religion's Impact on Politics, Economics, and Family Life*, New York: Doubleday.

Lenski, G. (1971) 'The religious factor in Detroit, revisited', *American Sociological Review 36*: 48–50.

Lerner, M. (1973) *The Social Psychology of Justice and Reactions to Victims*, Canada Council Grant.

Lerner, M. (1980) *The Belief in A Just World: A Fundamental delusion*, New York: Plenum Press.

Lerner, M. and Miller, D. (1978) 'Just world research and the attribution process: looking back and ahead', *Psychological Bulletin 85*: 1030–50.

Leung, K. and Lind, E. (1986) 'Procedural justice and culture. Effects of culture, gender, and investigator status on procedural preferences', *Journal of Personality and Social Psychology 50*: 1134–40.

Levenson, H. (1973) 'Perceived parental antecedents of internal, powerful others, and chance locus of control orientations', *Development of Psychology 9*: 268–74.

Levitan, S. and Johnson, C. (1983) 'The survival of work', in J. Barbash, R. Lampman, S. Levitan, and G. Tyler (eds), *The Work Ethic: A Critical Analysis*, Madison: IRRA, pp. 1–25.

Lied, T. and Pritchard, R. (1976) 'Relationships between personality variables and components of the expectancy-valence model', *Journal of Applied Psychology 61*: 463–7.

Littler, C. (ed.) (1985) *The Experience of Work*, Aldershot: Gower.

Lucas, M., Wilson, K., and Hart, E. (1986) *How to Survive 9 to 5*, London: Methuen.

Lynn, R., Hampson, S., and Magee, M. (1984) 'Home background, intelligence, personality and education as predicators of unemployment in young people', *Personality and Individual Differences 5*: 549–57.

Ma, L-C. (1986) 'The Protestant ethic among Taiwanese college students', *Journal of Psychology 120*: 219–24.

Ma, L. and Smith, K. (1985) 'Individual and social correlates of the just world belief: a study of Taiwanese college students', *Psychological Reports 57*: 35–8.

Maccoby, M. and Terzi, R. (1979) 'What happened to the work ethic?' in W. Hoffman and T. Wyly (eds), *The Work Ethic in Business*, Cambridge, Mass.: O, G & H Publishers.

MacDonald, A. (1971) 'Correlates of the ethics of personal conscience and the ethics of social responsibility', *Journal of Consulting and Clinical Psychology 37*: 443.

MacDonald, A. (1972) 'More on the Protestant ethic', *Journal of Consulting and Clinical Psychology 39*: 116–22.

Machlowitz, M. (1980) *Workaholics*, New York: Mentor.

Mann, M. (1986) 'Work and the work ethic', in R. Jowell, S. Witherspoon, and L. Brook, *British Social Attitudes: The 1986 report*, Aldershot: Gower, pp. 17–36.

Mars, G. (1984) *Cheats at Work: An Anthropology of Workplace Crime*, London: Unwin.

Marshall, G. (1980) *Presbyteries and Profits: Calvinism and the Development of Capitalism in Scotland, 1560–1707*, Oxford: Clarendon Press.

Marshall, G. (1982) *In Search of the Spirit of Capitalism*, London: Hutchinson.

Marshall, H. and Magruder, L. (1960) 'Relations between parent money education practices and children's knowledge and use of money', *Child Development 31*: 253–84.

Marx, K. (1844) *Economic and Philosophic Manuscripts of 1844*, Moscow: Progress Publishers.

Mayer, A. and Sharp, H. (1962) 'Religious preference and worldly success', *American Sociological Review 27*: 220–7.

McClelland, D. (1961) *The Achieving Society*, New York: Free Press.

McClelland, D. (1971) *Assessing Human Motivations*, New Jersey: General Learning Press.

McClelland, D., Atkinson, J., Clark, R., and Lowell, E. (1953) *The Achievement Motive*, New York: Appleton-Century-Crofts.

McClintock, C., Kramer, R., and Keil, L. (1982) 'Equity and social exchange in human relationships', in L. Berkowitz (ed.), *Advances in Experimental Social Psychology*, Vol. 17, New York: Academic Press, pp. 184–226.

McGoldrick, A. (1973) *Early Retirement: A New Leisure Opportunity?* Polytechnic of Central London: Unpublished Paper.

McGrath, J. and Kelly, J. (1986) *Time and Human Interaction: Toward a Social Psychology of Time*, New York: Guildford Press.

Merrens, M. and Garrett, J. (1975) 'The Protestant ethic scale as a predictor of repetitive work performance', *Journal of Applied Psychology 60*: 125–7.

Merton, R. (1957) *Social Theory and Social Structure*, New York: Free Press.

Miller, L. and Weiss, R. (1982) 'The work–leisure relationship: evidence for the compensatory hypothesis', *Human Relations 35*: 763–71.

Mirels, H. and Garrett, J. (1971) 'The Protestant ethic as a personality variable', *Journal of Consulting and Clinical Psychology 36*: 40–4.

Mischel, W. (1981) *Introduction to Personality*, New York: Holt, Rinehart and Winston.

Morgan, J. (1966) 'The achievement motive and economic behaviour', in J.W. Alkinson, and N.T. Feather (eds), *A Theory of Achievement Motivation*, New York: Wiley, pp. 205–30.

Morse, N. and Weiss, R. (1955) 'The function and meaning of work and the job', *American Sociological Review 20*: 191–8.

M.O.W. International Research Team (1987) *The Meaning of Working*, London: Academic Press.

Moynagh, M. (1985) *Making Unemployment Work*, Reading: Lion.

Mueller, W., Clegg, C., Wall, T., Kemp, N., and Davies, R. (1986) 'Pluralist beliefs about new technology within a manufacturing organization', *New Technology, Work and Employment 1*: 127–38.

Munroe, R. and Munroe, R. (1986) 'Weber's Protestant ethic revisited: an African case', *Journal of Psychology 120*: 447–56.

Murray, H. (1938) *Exploration in Personality*, New York: Oxford University Press.

Naisbitt, J. (1984) *Megatrends: Ten New Directions Transforming Our Lives*, New York: Warner.

Neff, W. (1965) 'Psychoanalytic conceptions of the meaning of work', *Psychiatry 28*: 324–34.

Neff, W. (1977) *Work and Human Behavior*, Chicago: Aldine Publishing Co.

Nelson, B. (1973) 'Weber's Protestant ethic: its origins, wanderings, and foreseeable future', in C. Glock and P. Hamond (eds), *Beyond the Classics*, New York: Harper & Row.

Neulinger, J. (1978) *The Psychology of Leisure*, Springfield: C.C. Thomas.

Neulinger, J. (1981) *To Leisure: An Introduction*, Boston: Allyn & Baron.

Newson, J. and Newson, E. (1976) *Seven Years Old in the Home Environment*, London: George Allen & Unwin.

Nichols, T. (1986) *The British Worker Question: A New Look at Workers and Productivity in Manufacturing*, London: Routledge.

Nord, W., Brief, A., Atieh, J., and Doherty, E. (1988) 'Work values and the conduct of organizational behaviour', in B. Staw and L. Cummings (eds), *Research in Organizational Behaviour*, Vol. 10, London: JAI Press.

Oates, W. (1971) *Confessions of a Workaholic: The Facts About Work Addiction*, New York: World Publishing Company.

O'Brien, G. (1986) *Psychology of Work and Unemployment*, Chichester: Wiley.

O'Brien, G. and Kabanoff, B. (1979) 'Comparison of unemployed and employed workers on work values, locus of control and health variables', *Australian Psychologist 14*: 143–54.

O'Leary, J. (1973) 'Skole and Plato's work ethic', *Journal of Leisure Research 5*: 49–55.

Pacey, A. (1983) *The Culture of Technology*, Oxford: Blackwell.

Parker, S. (1972) *The Future of Work and Leisure*, London: Granada.

Parker, S. (1983) *Leisure and Work*, London: George Allen.

Peraino, I. and Willerman, L. (1983) 'Personality correlates of occupational states according to Holland types', *Journal of Vocational Behaviour 22*: 268–77.

Peters, L. and Rudolf, C. (1980) 'Protestant work ethic beliefs and job scope at three organizational levels', *Journal of Occupational Behaviour 1*: 241–51.

Peters, T. and Waterman, R. (1982) *In Search of Excellence*, New York: Harper & Row.

Philbrick, J. (1976) 'The Protestant ethic in East Africa', *Psychologia Africana 16*: 173–5.

Poetler, L. and Stewart, H. (1975) 'Fundamental values, the work ethic and spirituality are basic for the therapeutic program at Anneewakee', *Adolescence 38*: 247–53.

Portes, A. (1976) 'On the sociology of national development theories and issues', *American Journal of Sociology 82*: 68–74.

Preston, R. (1987) *The Future of Christian Ethics*, London: SCM.

Price, V. (1982) *Type A Behaviour Pattern: A Model for Research and Practice*, London: Academic Press.

Pryor, R. (1982) 'Values, preferences, needs, work ethics, and orientations to work: toward a conceptual and empirical integration', *Journal of Vocational Behaviour 20*: 40–52.

Ragheb, M. (1980) 'Social psychology and leisure behaviour: a frame of reference and implications for research', in S. Iso-Ahola (ed.), *Social Psychological Perspectives on Leisure and Recreation*, Springfield, Illinois: C.C. Thomas, pp. 38–61.

Ragheb, M. and Beard, J. (1980) 'Leisure satisfaction: concept, theory, and measurement', in S. Iso-Ahola (ed.), *Social Psychological Perspectives on Leisure and Recreation*, Springfield, Illinois: C.C. Thomas, pp. 329–58.

Rasinski, K. (1987) 'What's fair is fair – or is it? Value differences underlying public views about social justice', *Journal of Personality and Social Psychology 53*: 201–11.

Ray, J. (1970) 'Christianism...The Protestant ethic among unbelievers', *Journal of Christian Education 13*: 169–76.

Ray, J. (1982) 'The Protestant ethic in Australia', *Journal of Social Psychology 116*: 127–38.

Ray, J. and Najman, J. (1985) 'The generalizability of deferment of gratification', *Journal of Social Psychology 126*: 117–19.

Ray, J. and Singh, S. (1980) 'Effects of individual differences on productivity among farmers in India', *Journal of Social Psychology 112*: 11–17.

Razzell, P. (1977) 'The Protestant ethic and the spirit of capitalism: a natural scientific critique', *British Journal of Sociology 28*: 17–37.

Reid, I. (1977) *Social Class Differences in Britain*, London: Open Books.

Rhodes, S. (1983) 'Age-related differences in work attitudes and behaviour: a review and conceptual analysis', *Psychological Bulletin 93*: 328–67.

Richards, V. (ed.) (1983) *Why Work? Arguments for the Leisure Society*, London: Freedom Press.

Rim, Y. (1977) 'Significance of work and personality', *Journal of Occupational Psychology 50*: 135–8.

Rischin, M. (1965) *The American Gospel of Success*, Chicago: Quadrangle Books.

Ritzer, G., Kammeyer, C., and Yelman, N. (1982) *Sociology: Experiencing a Changing Society*, Boston: Allyn & Bacon.

Robertson, J. (1985) *Future Work: Jobs, Self-Employment and Leisure After the Industrial Age*, Aldershot: Gower.

Rodgers, D. (1978) *The Work Ethic in Industrial America 1850–1920*, Chicago: University of Chicago Press.

Rohrlich, J. (1980) *Work and Love: The Crucial Balance*, New York: Summit Books.

Rojek, D. (1973) 'The Protestant ethic and political preference', *Social Forces 52*: 168–77.

Rokeach, M. (1973) *The Nature of Human Values*, New York: Free Press.

Rose, M. (1985a) *Re-working the Work Ethic*, London: Batsford.

Rose, M. (1985b) *Industrial Behaviour: Theoretical Development Since Taylor*, Harmondsworth: Penguin.

Rosow, J. (1979) 'Quality-of-work-life issues for the 1980s', in C. Kerr and J. Rosow (eds), *Work in America: The Decade Ahead*, New York: Van Nostrand, pp. 157–203.

Rosseel, E. (1985) 'Work ethic and orientation to work of the young generation: the impact of educational level', *Social Indicators Research 17*: 171–87.

Rosseel, E. (1986) 'The impact of changes in work ethics upon organization life', in G.

Debus, and H-W. Schroiff (eds), *The Psychology of Work and Organization*, Amsterdam: North Holland.

Rotenberg, M. (1975) 'The Protestant ethic against the spirit of psychiatry: the other side of Weber's thesis', *British Journal of Sociology 26*: 52–65.

Rotenberg, M. (1978) *Damnation and Deviance: The Protestant Ethic and the Spirit of Failure*, New York: Free Press.

Rubin, Z. and Peplau, L. (1973) 'Belief in a just world and reactions to another's lot', *Journal of Social Issues 21*: 73–93.

Rubin, Z. and Peplau, L. (1975) 'Who believes in a just world?' *Journal of Social Issues 31*: 65–90.

Salaman, G. (1986) *Working*, Chichester: Ellis Horwood.

Sales, L. and Strauss, G. (1966) *Human Behaviour in Organization*, London: Prentice-Hall.

Sampson, A. (1981) *The Changing Anatomy of Britain*, London: Book Club Associates.

Schab, F. (1976) 'The work ethic among black secondary students in the south', *Journal of Negro Education*, pp. 339–41.

Schab, F. (1978) 'Work ethic of gifted black adolescence', *Journal of Youth and Adolescence 7*: 295–9.

Scott, D. (1970) *The Psychology of Work*, London: Duckworth.

Segalman, R. (1968) 'The Protestant ethic and social welfare', *Journal of Social Issues 24*: 125–41.

Severinsen, K. (1979) 'Should career education be founded in the Protestant ethic?' *Personnel and Guidance Journal 14*: 111–14.

Shaffer, G. (1987) 'Patterns of work and nonwork satisfaction', *Journal of Applied Psychology 72*: 115–24.

Shamir, B. (1983) 'Some antecedents of work–nonwork conflicts', *Journal of Vocational Behaviour 23*: 98–111.

Shamir, B. (1985) 'Unemployment and "free-time" – the role of Protestant work ethic and work involvement', *Leisure Studies 4*: 333–45.

Shamir, B. (1986) 'Protestant work ethic, work involvement and the psychological impact of unemployment', *Journal of Occupational Behaviour 7*: 25–38.

Shamir, B. (1987) *The Stability of the Protestant Work Ethic and Work Involvement*, Unpublished paper.

Shepherdson, K. (1984) 'The meaning of work and employment: psychological research and psychologists' values', *Australian Psychology 19*: 311–20.

Sherman, B. (1986) *Working at Leisure*, London: Methuen.

Shimmin, S. (1966) 'Concepts of work', *Occupational Psychology 40*: 195–201.

Siegel, I. (1983) 'Work ethic and productivity', in J. Barbash, R. Lampson, S. Levitan, and G. Tyler (eds), *The Work Ethic: A Critical Analysis*, Madison: IRRA, pp. 27–42.

Smith, K. and Green, D. (1984) 'Individual correlates of the belief in a just world', *Psychological Reports 54*: 435–8.

Spector, P. (1982) 'Behaviour in organizations as a function of employees' locus of control', *Psychological Bulletin 91*: 482–97.

Spence, J. (1985) 'Achievement American style: the rewards and costs of individualism', *American Psychologist 40*: 1285–95.

Sprinzak, E. (1972) 'Weber's thesis as an historical explanation', *History and Theory 11*: 43–65.

Stacey, B. (1982) 'Economic socialization in the pre-adult years', *British Journal of Social Psychology 21*: 159–73.

Staines, G. (1980) 'Spillover versus compensation: a review of the literature on the relationship between work and non work', *Human Relations 33*: 111–29.

Stake, J. (1983) 'Factors in reward distribution: allocator motive, gender, and Protestant ethic endorsement', *Journal of Personality and Social Psychology 44*:

410–18.

Steiner, D. and Truxillo, D. (1987) 'Another look at the job satisfaction–life satisfaction relationship: a test of the disaggregation hypothesis', *Journal of Occupational Behaviour 8*: 71–7.

Stephens, R., Metze, L., and Craig, J. (1975) 'The Protestant ethic effect in a multichoice environment', *Bulletin of the Psychonomic Society 6*: 137–9.

Stokes, R. (1975) Report quoted in Ritzer, G., Kammeyer, C., and Yelman, N. *Sociology: Experiencing a Changing Society*, Boston: Allyn & Bacon.

Stone, E. (1975) 'Job scope, job satisfaction and the Protestant ethic: a study of enlisted men in the US navy', *Journal of Vocational Behaviour 7*: 215–34.

Stone, E. (1976) 'The moderating effect of work related values on the job scope – job satisfaction relationship', *Organizational Behaviour and Human Performance 15*: 147–67.

Stones, C. (1988) 'The Protestant work ethic and apartheid', *Youth and Society 19*: 435–40.

Stott, R. (1985) 'British immigrants and the American "work ethic" in the mid-nineteenth century', *Labour History 26*: 86–102.

Tang, T. (1985) 'Effects of the Protestant work ethic and effort performance feedback on intrinsic motivation', in W. Hamel (ed.), *Human Resources Management and Organizational Behaviour*, New York: Maximilian Press, pp. 350–4.

Tang, T. (1986) 'Effects of type A personality and task labels (work vs leisure) on task preference', *Journal of Leisure Research 18*: 1–11.

Tang, T. and Baumeister, R. (1984) 'Effects of personal values, perceived surveillance and task preference: the ideology of turning play into work', *Journal of Applied Psychology 69*: 99–105.

Tawney, R. (1963) *Religion and the Rise of Capitalism*, Harmondsworth: Penguin.

Taylor-Gooby, P. (1983) 'Legitimation deficit, public opinion, and the welfare state', *Sociology 17*: 165–84.

Terkel, S. (1975) *Working*, Harmondsworth: Penguin.

Thompson, K. (1986) *Beliefs and Ideology*, London: Tavistock.

Thompson, P. (1982) *The Nature of Work*, London: Macmillan.

Toffler, A. (1984) *Previews and Premises*, London: Pan.

Tziner, A. and Elizur, D. (1985) 'Achievement motive: a reconceptualization and new instrument', *Journal of Occupation Behaviour 6*: 209–28.

Vandewiele, M. and Philbrick, J. (1986) 'The Protestant ethic in West Africa', *Psychological Reports 58*: 946.

Venkatapathy, R. (1983) 'Biographical characteristics of the first and second generation entrepreneurs', *Journal of Small Enterprise: Development, Management and Extension 10*: 15–24.

Venkatapathy, R. (1984) 'Holland personality model among entrepreneurs', *Personality Study and Group Behaviour 4*: 86–93.

Venkatapathy, R. and Subramanian, S. (1984) 'Aberration among industrial entrepreneurs and industrial workers', *Psychological Reports 55*: 774.

Wagstaff, G. (1983) 'Attitudes to poverty, the Protestant ethic, and political affiliation: a preliminary investigation', *Social Behaviour and Personality 11*: 45–7.

Walvin, J. (1987) *Victorian Values*, London: André Deutsch.

Wanous, J. (1974) 'Individual differences and reactions to job characteristics', *Journal of Applied Psychology 59*: 616–22.

Warr, P. (1983) 'Job loss, unemployment and psychological well-being', in E. van de Vliert and V. Allen (eds), *Role Transitions*, New York: Plenum.

Warr, P. (1987) *Work, Unemployment and Mental Health*, Oxford: Clarendon Press.

Waters, L., Bathis, N., and Waters, C. (1975) 'Protestant ethic attitudes among college students', *Educational and Psychological Measurement 35*: 447–50.

Watts, A. (1983) *Education, Unemployment and the Future of Work*, Milton Keynes: Open University Press.

Watts, A. (1987) 'Beyond unemployment? Schools and the future of work', *British Journal of Educational Studies 35*: 3–18.

Weber, M. (1905) 'Die protestantische Ethik und der "Geist" des Kapitalismus', *Archiv für Sozialwissenschaft und Sozialpolitik 20*: 1–54.

Weisz, J., Rothbaum, F., and Blackburn, T. (1984) 'Standing out and standing in: the psychology of control in America and Japan', *American Psychologist 39*: 955–69.

Wernimont, P. and Fitzpatrick, S. (1972) 'The meaning of money', *Journal of Applied Psychology 56*: 218–26.

Wessman, A. (1973) 'Personality and the subjective experience of time', *Journal of Personality Assessment 37*: 103–14.

Wiener, M. (1985) *English Culture and the Decline of the Industrial Spirit 1850–1980*, Harmondsworth: Penguin.

Wiener, Y., Muczyk, J., and Gable, M. (1987) 'Relationship between work commitments and experience of personal well-being', *Psychological Reports 60*: 459–66.

Wijting, J., Arnold, C., and Conrad, K. (1978) 'Generational differences in work values between parents and children and between boys and girls across grade levels 6, 9, 10 and 12', *Journal of Vocational Behaviour 12*: 245–60.

Wilensky, H. (1960) 'Work, careers and social integration', *International Social Science Journal 12*: 543–60.

Williams, C. (1983) 'The "work ethic", non-work and leisure in an age of automation', *Australian and New Zealand Journal of Sociology 19*: 216–37.

Williams, R. (1970) *Sociology*, New York: McGraw-Hill.

Williams, R., Morea, P., and Ives, J. (1975) 'The significance of work: an empirical study', *Journal of Occupational Psychology 48*: 45–51.

Williams, S. (1985) *A Job To Live*, Harmondsworth: Penguin.

Williamson, J. (1974) 'Beliefs about the motivation of the poor and attitudes towards poverty policy', *Social Problems 18*: 634–49.

Wilson, G. (ed.) (1973) *The Psychology of Conservatism*, New York: Academic Press.

Wilson, J. (1980) 'Sociology of leisure', *Annual Review of Sociology 6*: 21–40.

Winfield, I. (1984) *People in Business*, London: Heinemann.

Winterbottom, M. (1958) 'The relation of need for achievement to learning experiences in independence and mastery', in J. Atkinson (ed.), *Motives in Fantasy, Action and Society*, Princeton: N. Van Nostrand, pp. 453–78.

Winters, R. (1972) 'Another view of the American work ethic', *Vocational Guidance Quarterly 4*: 31–4.

Wiseman, T. (1974) *The Money Motive*, London: Hodder & Stoughton.

Wolf, F. and Savickas, M. (1985) 'Time perspective and causal attributions for achievement', *Journal of Educational Psychology 77*: 471–80.

Wollack, S., Goodale, J., Wyting, J., and Smith, P. (1971) 'Development of survey of work values', *Journal of Applied Psychology 55*: 331–8.

Wood, L. (1979) 'Changing attitudes and the work ethic', in W. Hoffman and T. Wyly (eds), *The Work Ethic in Business*, Cambridge, Mass.: O, G & H Publishers.

Wood, S. (ed.) (1981) *The Degradation of Work*, London: Hutchinson.

Wortman, M. (1987) 'Entrepreneurship: an integrating typology and evaluation of the empirical research in the field', *Journal of Management 13*: 259–79.

Yamanchi, K. and Templer, D. (1982) 'The development of the money attitude scale', *Journal of Personality Assessment 46*: 522–8.

Yankelovich, D. (1979) 'Work, values, and the new breed', in C. Kerr and J. Rosow (eds), *Work in America: The Decade Ahead*, New York: Van Nostrand, pp. 3–26.

Yankelovich, D. (1981) 'New rules in American life: searching for self-fulfilment in a world turned upside down', *Psychology Today*, April, 35–91.

Yankelovich, D. (1982a) *New Rules: Searching for Self-Fulfilment in a World Turned Upside Down*, New York: Bantam Books.

Yankelovich, D. (1982b) 'The work ethic is underemployed', *Psychology Today*, May, 5–8.

Yankelovich, D. and Immerwahr, J. (1984) 'Putting the work ethic to work', *Society*, January, 58–76.

Young, R. (1984) 'Vocational choice and values in adolescent women', *Sex Roles 10*: 485–92.

Yuchtman-Yaar, E. (1987) 'Economic culture in post-industrial society: orientation towards growth, work and technology', *International Society 2*: 77–101.

Index